CRITICAL ISSUES
IN
RESTORATIVE JUSTICE

Howard Zehr
and
Barb Toews

editors

Monsey, New York
Criminal Justice Press

and

Cullompton, Devon, UK
Willan Publishing

2004

ISBN: 1-881798-51-8.

Cover design by Laurey Lebenson.

CONTENTS

continued...

Contents

Part III. Government and Systems

Part V. Indigenous and Religious Traditions

Part VI. Social Justice

Preface.
Opening The Dialogue

In a mere quarter-century, restorative justice has grown from a few scattered experimental projects into a social movement, and then into an identifiable field of practice and study.

Moving out from its origins within the criminal justice arena, restorative justice is being applied in schools, in homes, and in the workplace. Restorative justice approaches and concepts are being used to address issues on the micro level — among individuals, within communities — but, as illustrated by South Africa's Truth and Reconciliation Commission, are also being applied to the macro level. Restorative justice programs are being operated and promoted by individuals and by community-based organizations, but also by government bodies. Some advocates are arguing that restorative justice has implications for our social and economic systems, but also for the way we live our personal lives. With a few exceptions, evaluations of restorative processes and outcomes have been remarkably positive.

The trickle has turned into a river in a remarkably short time.

So if restorative justice has been so successful, so widely embraced, why a book that raises hard issues about the field?

WHY THIS BOOK?

We, the creators and editors of this book, are long-term advocates and practitioners of restorative justice. It goes without saying that we believe it has great potential for doing good for individuals, for communities, for society; otherwise, we would not have devoted so much of our lives to it.

But we also are convinced that all efforts to do good, no matter how well intended, tend to go astray. Every social intervention has unintended consequences. In addition to their intended and apparent purposes, every social phenomenon also has latent, unintended functions. All efforts at change are destined to be co-opted, at least to some extent, and to be diverted from their intended paths. All reforms at some point need to be reformed. We see no inherent reason why the history of restorative justice will be different.

The lessons of the modern prison, born just over two centuries ago as an alternative to corporal and capital punishment, weigh heavily on us. Quakers and others who advocated the first modern prisons did so with the best of motives but created a monster. Indeed, good intentions went astray so quickly that the first prison reform organization — the Pennsylvania Prison Society, for which editor Barb Toews works — was started only a few years after the penitentiary was born. And already in a 1987 report on British mediation and "reparation" programs, researchers warned that co-optation might be under way within the restorative justice movement (Davis et al., 1987).

As the history of prisons suggests, reform movements tend to get sidetracked and diverted from their intended purposes. But there is a second lesson from the birth of prisons. Research into the social circumstances of early prison advocates has revealed that some of the Quaker promoters of penitentiaries had themselves been imprisoned for conscience's sake (Cromwell, 1986). Because they were men of substance, they were not treated as badly as they would have been otherwise. Because they were men of reflection, they found their incarceration to be a time for contemplation. Consequently, they advocated prison as a place to reflect on the Bible and become penitent. Unfortunately, what was liberating to them became oppressive to others. So a second lesson is this: What seems good for me may not necessarily be good for others. We must be cautious about imposing our realities on others. We must recognize that who we are, what we believe, how we construct realities is shaped by our biographies: our histories, our gender, our ethnicity, our nationality.

As we contemplate the restorative justice movement, we see three possible threats to its "soul." First, restorative justice could lose its soul. It may be so co-opted and diverted from its core, or it may have such serious unintended consequences, that the integrity of the field as a whole becomes seriously compromised. It could end up serving purposes quite different from those intended. Second, it may retain its soul, its integrity, but be so marginalized as to be ineffective. This could happen, for example, if restorative approaches are relegated to so-called minor problems without impacting the overall system. Third, restorative justice's "soul" may be inherently flawed. Perhaps, as some authors in the following chapters suggest, it is too individualized or astructural, ignoring or even perpetuating social problems. Perhaps, as others suggest, there are serious cultural and gender biases in the field as currently articulated and practiced.

We who advocate restorative justice are therefore also obligated to have our eyes wide open, to listen to our critics, to balance our visions against realities. Indeed, we must be both advocates and critics. We must practice two fundamental values of restorative justice: respect, and humility. We must respect those who differ as well as those who agree, those who are critics as well as those who support what we do. And we must have the humility to recognize the limits of what we know and to incorporate other realities along with our own.

ABOUT THIS BOOK

To this end, then, we have invited the authors to contribute their perspectives to what we hope will be an ongoing and expanding dialogue on critical issues that confront the field of restorative justice. In doing this, we have used the following definition of "critical issues":

> *Critical issues* are questions, forces or directions that affect the integrity or overall direction of the field — including gaps in theory or practice and ways that restorative justice is in danger of going astray or failing to live up to its promise. The term "critical" suggests that these issues are crucial to the field, but also implies a critical stance toward the field.

For our purposes, we have differentiated between critical issues and "frontier issues." We define "frontier issues" as follows:

> *Frontier issues* are issues that have to do with "new" applications of restorative justice — the extension of restorative justice into fields where it has not been applied, or has not been sufficiently considered. Examples include post-conflict situations, severe violence, pardons and parole.

While these "frontier issues" may overlap with critical issues, the latter are not the subject of this book.

We began this project by developing an outline of critical questions (see Appendix). These questions were refined through participation in a series of "palavers" or "*hui*" (a Maori word): dialogues between practitioners, policymakers and academics in the United Kingdom, South Africa, New Zealand, the United States and Canada. Included in this dialogue was a "Listening Project" conducted by a group of restorative justice and victim advocates to listen to the ideas and concerns of victims and victim service providers in various areas of the United States (Mika et al., 2003).

We then invited an international group of writers to each contribute a chapter responding to a question, or set of questions, that we gave them from this outline. These writers reflect a wide geographical scope: continental Europe, the United Kingdom, New Zealand, South Africa, Canada, Australia and the United States. They include practitioners as well as academics, both from within and outside the field of restorative justice. We asked each contributor to outline the issues involved, then to give his or her "take" on the problem and possible solutions. We asked them to keep in mind that many of the readers — indeed, perhaps the most important ones — would be practitioners and students. We gave them strict word limits and asked them to limit their citations to only the essentials.

Obviously, not all the questions that could be asked were asked, and not all the issues that could be explored under each chapter heading or question have been addressed. However, we believe that this collection lays the groundwork for what we hope will be an ongoing, open-ended dialogue.

The following chapters are divided into six main parts or sections: principles and concepts; stakeholder issues; governments and systems; practice and practitioners; indigenous and religious traditions; and social justice. Obviously these distinctions are somewhat arbitrary and overlap is inevitable. Concerns that restorative justice may reflect an unconscious Euro-centric worldview are raised, for example, by Val Napoleon in Part I (principles) and also by Morris Jenkins in Part IV (practice). Such overlap is useful, reminding us that the topical divisions are somewhat arbitrary and that the concerns cut across the field.

Each section is provided with a short introduction describing the scope or importance of the topic and suggesting ways that the reader might engage with the issues raised.

We begin, then, with the theory and principles of restorative justice.

REFERENCES

Cromwell, P.F. (1986). "The Holy Experiment: An Examination of the Influence of the Society of Friends upon the Development and Evolution of American Correctional Philosophy." Unpublished doctoral dissertation, School of Criminology, Florida State University.

Davis, G., J. Boucherat and D. Watson (1987). *A Preliminary Study of Victim/Offender Mediation and Reparation Schemes in England and Wales.* (Research and Planning Unit Paper 42.) London, UK: Home Office.

Mika, H., M. Achilles, E. Halbert, L.S. Amstutz and H. Zehr (2002). *Taking Victims and their Advocates Seriously: A Listening Project.* Akron, PA: Mennonite Central Committee.

About The Authors

Mary Achilles is the Governor's Victim Advocate for the Commonwealth of Pennsylvania. Appointed by the governor and confirmed by the legislature in 1995, she is the first to hold such a statewide position in Pennsylvania and in the U.S. Under her leadership, the Office of the Victim Advocate has gained national recognition for its pioneering work for victims. This includes the Mediation Program for Victims of Violent Crime established under her leadership.

Lorraine Stutzman Amstutz is Director of the Mennonite Central Committee US Office on Crime and Justice. She has provided technical assistance, training and consulting for numerous communities throughout the U.S. and has worked in the victim offender field since 1984 when she began working in Elkhart, Indiana, the site of the first Victim Offender Reconciliation Program in the U.S. She is co-author (with Howard Zehr) of *Victim Offender Conferencing in PA's Juvenile Justice System*. For seven years Lorraine served on the international Victim Offender Mediation Association (VOMA) Board. She received her B.S. in Social Work from Eastern Mennonite University in Harrisonburg, VA (where she was awarded the Distinguished Service Award for 2002), and her Master's in Social Work from Marywood University, Scranton, Pennsylvania.

Mike Batley obtained his B.A. in social work in 1985. After working as a social worker for several years, he served as a probation officer, then a probation manager, in Pretoria, South Africa. In 2001, he co-founded the Restorative Justice Centre in Pretoria and currently serves as its executive director. He also is a member of the steering committee of the Restorative Justice Initiative, a network of non-government organizations implementing restorative justice.

Gordon Bazemore is Professor of Criminology and Criminal Justice and Director of the Community Justice Institute at Florida Atlantic University. An active researcher and trainer in restorative justice, his publications appear in many journals. He has completed two books, *Restorative Juvenile Justice: Repairing the Harm of Youth Crime* (co-edited with Lode

Walgrave) and *Restorative and Community Justice: Cultivating Common Ground for Victims, Communities and Offenders* (co-edited with Mara Schiff), and is currently completing a national study of restorative justice conferencing in the U.S and an evaluation of Vermont's restorative justice programs for juveniles.

Dee Bell is the Administrator of the Community Justice Institute at Florida Atlantic University, which includes restorative justice within its training agenda. Prior to this she worked for 28 years in community corrections in Georgia and Florida. She received her education at Clemson and Emory Universities. She has completed numerous evaluations and has authored and co-authored a number of articles and curricula.

Helen Bowen has been a youth advocate (appointed under the Children, Young Persons and Their Families Act 1989) in New Zealand since 1989, and in this role has attended many restorative justice conferences for youth and adult offenders. She has been a trainer and an ongoing supervisor of facilitators for the government-sponsored restorative justice court-referred pilot project in 2001. She co-authored the *New Zealand Restorative Justice Practice Manual* (with Jim Boyack) and *Restorative Justice: Contemporary Themes and Practice* (with Jim Consedine).

Jim Boyack is a New Zealand criminal lawyer, a youth advocate (appointed under the Children, Young Persons and Their Families Act 1989) and a long-time advocate for restorative justice processes in the criminal law context. He is a trustee of the Restorative Justice Trust and co-author of the *New Zealand Restorative Justice Practice Manual* (with Helen Bowen). He has written frequently on the topic of restorative justice and, together with Helen Bowen, was chosen by the Department for Courts to train facilitators taking part in the four-year government restorative justice pilot project.

Carolyn Boyes-Watson is Associate Professor of Sociology and founding director of the Center for Restorative Justice at Suffolk University. She has published in the fields of restorative justice, juvenile justice, and criminal justice policy; a recent book is *Crime and Justice: A Casebook Approach*. She currently serves as President of the board for Massachusetts Correctional Legal Services, the prisoners' legal advocacy organization for the state of Massachusetts.

Chris Cunneen is Associate Professor and Director of the Institute of Criminology at the University of Sydney Law School, Australia. He has worked with a number of Australian Royal Commissions and Inquiries and the federal Human Rights and Equal Opportunity Commission. He is also Chairperson of the Juvenile Justice Advisory Council. He has published widely in the area of juvenile justice, policing, and indigenous issues. His books include *Juvenile Justice, Youth and Crime in Australia*; *Conflict, Politics and Crime*; and *Indigenous People and the Law in Australia.*

Dave Dyck has been working and studying in restorative justice and conflict resolution for more than 15 years. He worked with Mediation Services of Winnipeg from 1991-97 and continues to train and work with their volunteers. He conducts a variety of training and consulting programs in restorative justice and conflict resolution throughout North America, and also teaches at both the University of Prince Edward Island and Eastern Mennonite University's Summer Peacebuilding Institute. He holds a Master of Arts degree in Conflict Transformation from Eastern Mennonite University and a Diploma in Mediation Skills.

Carsten Erbe is a former Project Coordinator/Research Associate with the Community Justice Institute at Florida Atlantic University, and in this capacity has worked on several national restorative justice studies. Prior to this he worked in the Yukon Territory with the Royal Canadian Mounted Police (RCMP) and a community-based mediation group in a circle peacekeeping process. His masters degree is in Cross-Cultural Studies from Queensland University of Technology in Australia. For this degree he evaluated a small Aborigine community's attempt to implement restorative justice practices amongst their people. He currently lives in Canada.

Cheryl Frank obtained a Bachelor of Social Science degree in 1992 at the University of Natal, South Africa, and an MBA at the Graduate School of Business, University of Cape Town. She worked for four years at NICRO, a non-government organization working with ex-offenders, and then joined the Institute of Criminology at the University of Cape Town as Senior Researcher in Juvenile Justice. She is currently the Director of the Criminal Justice Initiative at the Open Society Foundation of South Africa, and specializes in crime prevention.

Dave Gustafson is Co-Director and founding director of Fraser Region Community Justice Initiatives Association in Langley, British Columbia. CJI specializes in training, program development, conferencing and victim offender mediation across the spectrum from minor school conflicts to the most serious offenses. He is Adjunct Professor in the School of Criminology at Simon Fraser University and also maintains a small psychotherapeutic private practice specializing in trauma recovery. He is currently a doctoral candidate at the Katholic University of Leuven, Belgium, where his dissertation will focus on the clinical implications of facilitated encounter between trauma survivors and those responsible for the harms.

Matt Hakiaha is a New Zealand Parole Board Member. He is a former youth justice coordinator and more recently has served as a facilitator for the adult conferencing pilot project in New Zealand. He is also a trustee with Te Whanau o Waipareira Trust, the largest Urban Maori Organisation in New Zealand, and is Chairperson for Te Runanga o te Kareti Paipera o Aotearoa (Maori Advisory Council for the Bible College of New Zealand).

Susan Herman is Executive Director of the National Center for Victims of Crime in Washington, DC. She has also served as the Director of Community Services at the Enterprise Foundation, as Director of the Domestic Violence Division of Victim Services (now Safe Horizon) in New York City, as Special Counsel to the Commissioner of the New York City Police Department, and as Director of Mediation Services at the Institute for Mediation and Conflict Resolution. She has previously served as an attorney at the NOW Legal Defense and Education Fund and as an instructor at New York University's School of Law and its Wagner Graduate School of Public Service. She is a graduate of the Antioch School of Law.

Russ Immarigeon, MSW, is editor of *Women, Girls & Criminal Justice, Offender Programs Report*, and *VOMA Connections*, the newsletter of the Victim-Offender Mediation Association. He contributes regularly to national newsletters on crime victims, community corrections, probation and correctional management. With Shadd Maruna, he co-edited *After Crime and Punishment*, a volume of original articles on crime desistance and offender reintegration. He was recently elected to a term as Town Justice in Hillsdale, New York.

Vernon E. Jantzi, Professor of Sociology at Eastern Mennonite University, has been involved in international development practice, research and teaching for many years. Within the past five years he has given special attention to the relationship between restorative justice and civil society. He helped found Eastern Mennonite University's graduate Conflict Transformation Program and served as director from 1996 through 2002. He has lived and worked in a number of Latin American countries and New Zealand, and has been involved in numerous short-term projects in Africa and South Asia. Professor Jantzi holds a doctorate in the sociology of development from Cornell University.

Morris Jenkins received his JD from Stetson University College of Law and his Ph.D. from Northeastern University. He has been involved with many community-based organizations, and has taught and trained students and practitioners at every level, including elementary school and law and graduate students, in law-related education (LRE), conflict resolution, and mediation. In addition, he has provided multicultural/diversity training to many police departments, probation departments and corrections staff. A current research interest is the effectiveness of Eurocentric, enculturated, multicultural and Afrocentric programs that deal with at-risk youth in the Black community, as well as the cultural foundations of gang and non-gang youth.

Gerry Johnstone is Professor of Law at the University of Hull, United Kingdom. His recent books include *Restorative Justice: Ideas, Values, Debates* and *A Restorative Justice Reader: Texts, Sources, Context.* He is currently co-editing an international handbook of restorative justice.

Jackie Katounas is an ex-offender who, after 138 criminal convictions and 12 years' imprisonment, turned her life around after an encounter with a victim from one of her crimes. She is a founding member of Hawkes Bay Restorative Justice Inc. in New Zealand, and went on to successfully pilot the first restorative justice program in a New Zealand prison. She is now the Restorative Justice Project Manager for Prison Fellowship New Zealand and is taking restorative justice programs into other jails throughout the country.

Chris Marshall teaches New Testament at the Tyndale Graduate School of Theology in New Zealand and is a facilitator and trustee of the Waitakere Restorative Justice Community Group in West Auckland. His publications include *Beyond Retribution: A New Testament Vision for Crime, Justice and Punishment.* He received his Ph.D. from the University of London.

Guy Masters is currently Referral Order Coordinator for Wandsworth Youth Offending Team in London, United Kingdom, working with young offenders, victims and community volunteers. He has been involved in the restorative justice field since 1993 as a practitioner, researcher and consultant, and has written widely on practice. His key area of interest is the mainstreaming of effective restorative practice.

Gabrielle Maxwell is a psychologist and criminologist working as an Associate of the Crime and Justice Research Centre at Victoria University of Wellington, New Zealand. In recent years, much of her research has focused on restorative justice and the New Zealand youth justice system in particular. Her most recent book (co-edited with Allison Morris) is *Restorative Justice for Juveniles: Conferencing, Mediation and Circles.* She has just completed a major study, "Achieving Effective Outcomes in Youth Justice in New Zealand." Other recent work has focused on family violence, crime prevention and children's rights.

Paul McCold is a research criminologist and the Director of Research for the International Institute for Restorative Practices in Bethlehem, Pennsylvania, USA. Paul received his Ph.D. from the University of Albany and for 10 years was a Research Scientist with the New York State Division for Youth. He has taught at Old Dominion and Temple Universities and was principal investigator on the Bethlehem Restorative Policing Experiment. He has been actively involved with the UN Alliance of NGOs on Crime Prevention and Criminal Justice (NY) since 1995. He is the author of numerous articles on restorative justice and family group conferencing, as well as the *Restorative Justice Handbook* and *Restorative Justice: An Annotated Bibliography.*

Allison Morris was, until 2001, Professor of Criminology at Victoria University of Wellington, and has many publications in the restorative justice field. She is now a freelance researcher and is involved in an evaluation of restorative justice conferences for adult offenders.

Val Napoleon is of Cree-Saulteaux-Dunne Zah heritage and is also an adopted member of the Gitanyow (Gitxsan) House of Luuxhon, Ganeda (Frog) clan. She worked as a community activist and consultant in northwestern British Columbia, Canada, for over 25 years, and she has served on a number of provincial, regional, and local boards. She received her LL.B. from the University of Victoria in 2001, articled with the Victoria law firm Arvay Finlay, and was called to the bar in 2002. She is currently completing an interdisciplinary Ph.D. (law and history) at the University of Victoria.

George Pavlich is Professor in the Department of Sociology and an Associate Dean in the Faculty of Graduate Studies and Research at the University of Alberta, Edmonton, Canada. His journal articles have dealt with critical criminological theory, restorative justice, governmental research, social theory, and socio-legal studies. He is the author of *Justice Fragmented: Mediating Community Disputes Under Postmodern Conditions*; and *Critique and Radical Discourses on Crime*; co-editor of *Rethinking Law, Society and Governance* (with G. Wickham); and co-editor of *Sociology for the Asking* (with M. Hird; forthcoming). He is currently working on book analyzing the paradoxes of restorative justice governance.

Bonnie Price Lofton is Director of Development for the Conflict Transformation Program at Eastern Mennonite University. She formerly worked as a reporter for the Montreal Gazette and several other newspapers, and as a writer/editor for the University of Virginia and for private publishers. She has a master's degree in Conflict Transformation at EMU.

Barbara Raye is Executive Director of the Center for Policy, Planning and Performance, a nonprofit consulting and training organization working with organizations committed to social justice. She is also Executive Administrator for the Victim Offender Mediation Association (VOMA). Among other assignments, she has served as Director of Victim Services for the Minnesota Department of Corrections and has established shelters for battered women and their children, a violent partner program and a family reintegration program. She helped form the Indiana Coalition Against Domestic Violence and was an early member of the National Coalition Against Domestic Violence. She received her

MBA from the University of St. Thomas, St. Paul, Minnesota, and is a frequent trainer and consultant in restorative justice and related areas.

Susan Sharpe, Ph.D., is best known as the author of *Restorative Justice: A Vision for Healing and Change*. Formerly of Edmonton, Alberta, she now lives in Seattle, Washington, while continuing to work on restorative justice projects in Canada. She received her Ph.D. from the University of Denver in Colorado.

Ann Skelton obtained her LLB degree in 1985 and was admitted as an Advocate of the High Court of South Africa in 1988. She was employed by Lawyers for Human Rights for 11 years and has been at the forefront of efforts to bring about changes to the system for children charged with crimes in South Africa for many years. In 1997 she was appointed by the South African Minister of Justice to lead a project of the South African Law Commission to develop a comprehensive new statute regarding children accused of crimes. From 1999 to 2003 she was the national coordinator of the Child Justice Project, a UN technical assistance project based in the Department of Justice in Pretoria. She has recently joined the Centre for Child Law at the University of Pretoria, where she is the coordinator of a Children's Litigation Project.

Dr. Heather Strang is a criminologist and Director of the Centre for Restorative Justice at the Australian National University. Since 1995 she has been involved in studies investigating the effectiveness of restorative justice as an alternative, or in addition, to normal criminal justice processing of offenders. She has particularly focused on the emotional harm experienced by victims and the potential for emotional restoration offered by restorative justice. This has recently resulted in a book, *Repair or Revenge: Victims and Restorative Justice*. She is currently co-directing a series of experiments in the United Kingdom to test the impact of restorative justice on serious adult violent and property offenders and their victims.

Larry Tifft and Dennis Sullivan have been collaborating on writing and activist projects about justice since they first taught together at the University of Illinois-Chicago in 1972. In 1980, their *The Struggle To Be Human: Crime, Criminology, and Anarchism* was published in the Orkney Islands, the first pacifist-anarchist treatise to appear on crime, punishment, and justice. This was followed by Dennis's *The Mask of Love: Corrections in America; Toward a Mutual Aid Alternative* and Larry's *Battering of*

Women: The Failure of Intervention and the Case for Prevention, and Dennis's *The Punishment of Crime in Colonial New York: The Dutch Experience in Albany During the Seventeenth Century.* They are authors of the recent *Restorative Justice: Healing the Foundations of Our Everyday Lives.* Dennis and Larry also founded and currently serve as editors of the *Contemporary Justice Review.* They were also instrumental in establishing the Justice Studies Association, an association of scholars, practitioners, and activists committed to restorative and social justice. Larry teaches at Central Michigan University and Dennis is an Adjunct Professor of Criminal Justice at the University at Albany.

Barb Toews has worked in the restorative justice field since 1992, when she began working in Fresno, California at the Victim Offender Reconciliation Program of the Central Valley. Following this experience, she was the founding director of the Lancaster Area Victim Offender Reconciliation Program in Lancaster, Pennsylvania. Currently working with the Pennsylvania Prison Society, Barb explores the application of restorative justice in prison and facilitates programs that provide restorative opportunities for incarcerated men and women. She also facilitates educational forums and skills training in restorative justice and victim offender mediation in Pennsylvania and around the U.S. She has written or co-written a number of articles in the area of restorative justice. Barb holds a masters degree in Conflict Transformation from Eastern Mennonite University.

Lode Walgrave is emeritus professor in Criminology at the Katholieke Universiteit Leuven, Belgium, where he is director of the Research Group of Youth Criminology. He has been founding member and the first coordinator of the International Network for Research on Restorative Justice for Juveniles. In recent years, he has published many articles and book chapters on restorative justice, especially on its normative aspects. Among the books he has edited recently is *Restorative Justice and the Law.*

Annie Warner Roberts is Outreach Director at the Center for Restorative Justice and Peacemaking, University of Minnesota, School of Social Work, providing technical assistance and consulting. She is also a practitioner, mediating/facilitating minor to serious and violent criminal justice cases. She is current Co-chair of the Board of Directors of the Victim Offender Mediation Association (VOMA). Additionally, she is a practitioner trainer, both nationally and internationally, for the National Restorative Justice Training Institute, the Victim Offender Mediation Association (VOMA), the National Institute of Corrections (NIC) and Balanced and Restorative Justice (BARJ).

Wonshé served as midwife to numerous rural and urban communities throughout the U.S. for more than 13 years. During that time, she founded and directed the Traditional Midwifery and Womancraft School, offering community-based education and apprenticeship to aspiring midwives. Throughout these years she researched historical midwifery practices, violence in contemporary birthing practices, and non-violent alternatives. She received her BA in Expressive Arts for Conflict Transformation at Hollins University (Virginia) and is currently completing her Master in Conflict Transformation, with a concentration in restorative justice at Eastern Mennonite University in Virginia.

Howard Zehr is Professor of Restorative Justice and Co-Director of the graduate Conflict Transformation Program, Eastern Mennonite University, Virginia. He directed the first Victim Offender Reconciliation Program in the U.S. and for 17 years served as Director of the Mennonite Central Committee U.S. Office on Crime and Justice. He has lectured, trained and consulted in many countries, and in 2003 was the first recipient of Prison Fellowship International's Restorative Justice Prize. His publications include *Changing Lenses: A New Focus for Crime and Justice; Doing Life: Reflections of Men and Women Serving Life Sentences,* and *Transcending: Reflections of Crime Victims.* He is editor of the series *The Little Books of Justice and Peacebuilding,* and has authored or co-authored several in the series. He received his Ph.D. from Rutgers University.

PART I.
PRINCIPLES AND CONCEPTS OF RESTORATIVE JUSTICE

What Is Restorative Justice?

Most of us have asked this question at some point, whether it was upon first hearing about the concept or after many years of practice. As simple as the question seems, the answer, or *answers,* are profound and varied. The definitions we use are based on a number of factors: our personal life experiences, our culture and worldviews, the audience to whom we are speaking, our experiences as practitioners or academics, our understandings of victimization and offending, our experiences with a particular application, to name a few.

This diversity of definitions and understandings contributes to richness in the restorative justice field, but it is also a source of confusion and even conflict. Relationships between practitioners, and even stakeholders, can be either strengthened or weakened based on their definitions. Practice, and our perceptions of one another's practice, is equally influenced. The diversity sometimes contributes to divisions among practitioners and theorists into camps of like-minded individuals. Holding tightly to these definitional differences, the differing camps often find it difficult to bridge the divide and to engage in dialogue with others. Equally damaging, these divisions may minimize the important contributions the different perspectives bring to the overall field.

Principles and concepts provide the overarching frameworks for our work in restorative justice and even, as some suggest, our daily lives. Moreover, our ability to engage with each other on principles and concepts enhances our ability to practice with integrity. As a result, it is crucial that we give this topic substantial and careful thought. These first four chapters offer a start to this dialogue.

We are not necessarily suggesting the elimination of the confusion or the creation of an all-encompassing definition to be used by all. Indeed, the diversity may bring a dynamic vitality to the field. We are, however, suggesting that the confusion and conflict merits exploration around questions such as these:

- What problems — and possibilities — emerge from the lack of a standard definition and how are they playing themselves out in the real world?

- Do we need consensus on the principles and concepts? If so, what are the possibilities for reaching one?

- How do we hold ourselves accountable to the principles that we espouse and ensure that they are fully realized in our practice?

This conversation will certainly raise a host of other issues. For instance, in North America the field is only beginning to really explore Native-American and African-American cultural worldviews, these groups' experiences with criminal justice, and the implications of these experiences and worldviews for restorative justice. As this exploration grows, we who are European Americans may be faced with hard questions about our willingness to fully include Native Americans, African Americans, and other minority groups in the definitional discussion. Similarly, a serious consideration of conceptual issues may force us to reconsider our evaluation methods, to name factors that contribute to co-optation and to explore benchmarks to ensure that we are doing good practice and resisting forces that compromise the work. All this may challenge us as practitioners and theorists to reconsider our own assumptions and understandings about restorative justice — an uncomfortable task for many people.

The authors represented in this opening section raise many of these issues. Gerry Johnstone examines the various ways that restorative justice is viewed and articulated, and notes some of the tensions that arise from these differences. Susan Sharpe asks how inclusive our definitions should be, arguing that we have done better at defining "restorative" than "justice"; she goes on to propose a social contract theory of restorative justice. Val Napoleon, writing from the perspective of an aboriginal community member, asks challenging questions about the assumptions that underlie our ideas about restorative justice. Finally, Lode Walgrave examines the tensions and affinities between retribution and restorative justice, concluding that restoration is "reversed, constructive retributivism."

We invite you to consider what you believe are the core principles and concepts of restorative justice. As you read this section, and the rest of the book, challenge yourself to explore the strengths, weaknesses and implications of your definition. One thing is certain: your definition and underlying assumptions will definitely affect how you respond to the questions posed to the authors throughout this book.

Chapter 1.
How, And In What Terms, Should Restorative Justice Be Conceived?

by

Gerry Johnstone

What is restorative justice? One way of addressing this question is to find out what those promoting "restorative justice" are trying to make happen. However, different proponents have different ideas about this. Most advocates of restorative justice are primarily concerned to devise and promote an innovative way of dealing with crime, delinquency and perhaps bullying. However, some leading advocates are much more ambitious. For example, Dennis Sullivan and Larry Tifft maintain that pursuing restorative justice involves committing ourselves to the creation of "patterns of social interaction that foster human dignity, mutual respect and equal well-being" (see their chapter in this volume). And, for John Braithwaite:

> [R]estorative justice is not simply a way of reforming the criminal justice system, it is a way of transforming the entire legal system, our family lives, our conduct in the workplace, our practice of politics. Its vision is of a holistic change in the way we do justice in the world (2003:1).

So, should we first try to determine what reforms to the criminal justice system are being promoted under the rubric of restorative justice? Or should we start by trying to find out about the personal, social and political transformations the more ambitious proponents of restorative justice are after? I suggest that, initially, we should focus upon what distinguishes restorative justice from other ways of dealing with crime. If we find out first what restorative justice campaigners are trying to bring about in this more limited sphere, we probably stand a better chance of subsequently grasping what they have in mind when they advocate "a holistic change in the way we do justice in the world." However, even in this narrower area, there are some quite different ways of thinking about what distinguishes restorative justice from more established ways of dealing with crime.

A SENTENCING ALTERNATIVE?

Many proponents of restorative justice envisage it as a sentencing alternative. When sentencing somebody found guilty of a criminal offence, sentencers have to select one or more types of sentence from the range legally available. In contemporary Western societies, this typically includes fines, probation orders, community service orders, imprisonment and, in some jurisdictions, death. Restorative justice proponents might be understood as wanting to add a new option to this list and to encourage sentencers to use it in appropriate cases. They hope that, as the benefits of restorative justice become clear, it will increasingly become the routine type of sentence for the majority of offences. So, what distinguishes restorative sentences from other types of sentence?

First, the offender may be required to take part in a meeting with the victim (or a victim representative) and, perhaps, other people affected fairly directly by the crime, such as members of the victim's and even the offender's own family. In such meetings, offenders are required to listen respectfully while those harmed by their behaviour describe how they have been affected by it. Offenders are also expected to answer any questions their victims may have. Hence, restorative sentences are distinctive in that they may require offenders to meet face-to-face with those affected by their behaviour, and to engage in constructive, respectful dialogue with them.

Second, the offender may be expected to apologize and undertake a reparative task. Hence, restorative sentences differ from other sentences in which offenders are expected to "pay for" their crimes by undergoing pain. In restorative justice, offenders make amends for their crime through positive acts intended to benefit their victim(s).

Third, the precise way in which the offender will make amends is determined, not by professional sentencers, but by the victims and offenders and other participants in the restorative "conference." The aim is to have all parties agree upon what should be done about the matter.

Restorative justice, then, has affinities to informal community-based processes of mediation, in which lay mediators attempt to produce agreement among parties to a conflict without being closely bound by prescribed legal solutions. In particular, there is scope for people to formulate ways of repairing harm that make sense to them. The only apparent constraint is that what is agreed upon must not violate any party's human rights, and that any "restorative actions" the offender agrees to undertake should not, to the extent that they might be construed as punitive, go above upper limits which the courts or legislatures have deemed appropriate for the type of crime committed.

Variations

There are some variations on this concept of restorative justice as a sentencing alternative. Some campaigners envisage restorative justice being introduced as something to which people who informally admit involvement in a criminal offence to the police or other enforcement agency might be diverted, instead of being prosecuted and tried. For instance, restorative justice might take the place of police cautions for offences considered too serious for a simple police caution. Another variation is that processes designed to deliver restorative justice can be established, not as formal sentences, but as optional extras for those who wish to use them. For example, offenders serving prison sentences — or even awaiting execution (Umbreit and Vos, 2000) — might be invited to participate in a restorative process as a way of putting things right before their sentence is completed.

A NEW MODEL OF CRIMINAL JUSTICE?

The above account of restorative sentences, while perhaps useful as a starting point, is too limited to serve as an adequate description of restorative justice. It fails to capture the broader goals of the international campaign for restorative justice. Many of those campaigning for restorative justice are not content simply to bring about a major reform in sentencing policy and practice. Rather, their aim is to transform the assumptions that underlie the entire practice of criminal justice in contemporary society. In particular, they propose a new pattern of thinking about "crime" and "justice."

A New Understanding Of "Crime"

Conventionally, crime tends to be regarded as an "exceptional" type of behaviour, qualitatively distinct from "ordinary" acts of harmful wrongdoing. Indeed, despite centuries of secularization, there is still a tendency in public discourse to represent crime as a violation of some divine order imposed upon people "from above." Hence, it is widely assumed that crime cannot be made up for *simply* by apologizing to the individuals or groups actually harmed or wronged, repairing the damage inflicted, and promising to avoid further offences. Instead, it tends to be taken for granted that crimes can only be fully expiated by undergoing "purgatorial suffering" (Gorringe, 1996).

One of the things about this conventional understanding of crime that troubles proponents of restorative justice is that it excludes the victim's perspective. Crime is viewed as a blameworthy transgression of some fundamental — perhaps divinely-inspired — law, rather than looked at from the victim's perspective, i.e., as a traumatic, dehumanizing attack upon their person. Hence, the widely acknowledged neglect of victims by contemporary criminal justice is seen as closely bound up with the way crime itself is conventionally defined and understood (Strang, 2002).

Another troubling feature is the way the conventional understanding creates "artificial borders around crime" (Kennedy, 1990:1). This discourages society from focusing upon and addressing the conflicts, social problems and social disparities beyond those borders that may have contributed to the criminal event and which need to be dealt with in any adequate social response. It also discourages people from thinking that the methods frequently advocated and sometimes used to handle harmful behavior not defined as crime — especially methods involving repentance and restitution on the one side and a combination of reprobation and social support on the other — might be appropriate for dealing with crime (Hulsman, 1986).

So, restorative justice proponents want us to understand crime as behavior that:

- troubles us, less because it violates some cosmic order, but because it causes tangible harm to real people and relationships;

- can only be properly understood if viewed as having its roots in broader and deeper social conflicts, problems and disparities; and,

- necessitates a social response, but not necessarily one that differs qualitatively from the way we informally and legally respond to non-criminalized harmful behavior.

A New Understanding Of "Justice"

Conventional and restorative thinking about criminal justice share the assumption that crime arouses anger and resentment — or at least creates a sense of injustice — in its victims and in members of the society in which it occurs. They further agree that, in the name of justice, something must be done to satisfy such anger and resentment and to restore a sense of justice. However, proponents of restorative justice urge us to think differently about what that something is.

A conventional assumption is that those found guilty of crime must suffer in return. In order to avoid overreaction and cycles of tit-for-tat violence, this suffering must be imposed by the state and must be governed by principles of proportionality and legality. That is to say, what is required is state-delivered retributive punishment.

Proponents of restorative justice question whether state punishment is either *sufficient* or *necessary* to meet people's needs for justice. They argue that although people often demand punishment, this is because punishment is the only method available to obtain criminal justice. Yet, it is maintained, state punishment of offenders creates only a short-lived sense that justice has been done. It fails to provide crime victims with a rich and enduring experience of justice because it fails to meet their needs. Victims, it is argued, have needs for: a process where their views count, information, participation in their cases, respect, and material and emotional reparation (Strang, 2002). For these needs to be met, something other than state punishment is required; perhaps a family group conference (in which all stakeholders affected by the crime meet in a circle to discuss how they have been affected and to come to some agreement on what should be done to put things right), followed by reparative action to meet people's needs. Hence, (restorative) justice is done, not when something negative is done to the offender, but when something positive is done to meet the needs of people harmed by crime.

Moreover, many proponents of restorative justice claim to have found that, once the needs of victims and communities are met through such a process, demands for punishment tend to subside. Hence, punishment of offenders may not be as necessary as is conventionally assumed for people affected by crime to experience justice. Restorative processes resulting in restorative dispositions might suffice and will certainly provide a richer experience of justice than that provided by state punishment.

One impediment to our grasping such a conception of justice may be the deeply ingrained idea that what is required to do justice is dictated by natural and universally applicable moral principles. State punishment has become so familiar to us that we fail to realize that it is a *social convention* and that it is only in the past several centuries that people of Western societies have adopted it (Zehr, 1990:97). Hence, proponents of restorative justice argue that to grasp the case for restorative justice we need to understand that it was the norm in the past and that many societies and communities have functioned very well without state punishment (Johnstone, 2002:ch. 2). We will find it difficult to fully appreciate the case for restorative justice unless we engage with accounts of its use in historical societies and in contemporary indigenous communities.

TENSIONS AT THE HEART OF RESTORATIVE JUSTICE

It is worthwhile discussing briefly an apparent tension within this restorative understanding of justice. This tension has been identified explicitly by Braithwaite and Strang (2001:1-2), who seem to suggest that there is not one but two conceptions of restorative justice: "Restorative justice is conceived in the literature in two different ways. One is a process conception, the other a values conception." Braithwaite and Strang's position seems to be that the restorative justice movement is after *two quite different things*:

    (1) A change in the *process* by which we deal with offending: in contrast to conventional criminal justice processes, which exclude and hence disempower stakeholders affected by a crime, restorative justice processes include and empower all stakeholders; and,

(2) A shift in the *values* that undergird criminal justice interventions: instead of being guided by vindictiveness and the desire for vengeance, restorative justice is motivated by the desire for healing and reconciliation.

The Nature Of This Tension

Braithwaite and Strang have identified a significant tension at the heart of restorative justice. However, in my view, they misrepresent this by describing it as a tension between processes and values. The problem with drawing the distinction in these terms is that a particular process can itself be deemed desirable, not because of any substantive consequences likely to result from it, but because *it is in line with certain value-commitments*. This can be illustrated by reference to arguments about the role of victims in the criminal justice process.

A central theme in the literature advocating restorative justice is that victims should have an active role in criminal proceedings (Strang, 2002; Johnstone, 2002:ch. 4). What is the *rationale* for this proposal?

One possible set of reasons is that victim participation might have a number of beneficial consequences. For instance, it might benefit victims: when victims participate in the criminal justice process they are more likely to recover from the trauma of victimization. Victim participation might also benefit the criminal justice system, since it increases the chance that victims will cooperate with the system's goals by reporting offences, giving evidence, etc. And, victim participation might benefit society, since offenders — especially young offenders — are more likely to see the point in refraining from crime when they directly encounter the sufferings of a flesh-and-blood victim, than when they encounter only professionals enforcing an abstract legal code.

An important empirical question is whether victim participation does, in fact, have such consequences. However, an even more important question to ask is whether the possibility of obtaining such consequences is the main justification for victim participation. In this context, it is interesting to ask what would happen if new research results were produced demonstrating that such beneficial consequences were in fact unlikely to result from victim participation in criminal justice proceedings or could be achieved without such participation. Suppose, further, that this research confirmed some of the suspicions of those who have tended to regard "the idea that a victim should have an active role in criminal proceedings...with alarm and distaste" (Strang, 2002:5). Would the proposal for victim participation then be withdrawn?

My guess is that arguments for victim participation in criminal justice would still be heard, regardless of empirical findings. This is because there is another rationale for this proposal which, although rarely articulated carefully, is in fact probably the more important. This is that victims are considered to have a *right* to participate in their case. If victims are the owners of their conflicts — as restorative justice proponents, drawing upon Christie (1977), frequently remind us — then there is a strong case for affording them *the rights of ownership*, even if there are no obvious desirable consequences of doing so and, indeed, even if there are some undesirable consequences. The rights of victims to participate in criminal proceedings should only be denied them where the exercise of their rights results in the infringement of equally or more important rights of others — in which case one has a complex policy decision to make.

Once we grasp this point, we realize that the tension alluded to by Braithwaite and Strang is not actually between a process conception and a values conception. Rather, *the tension is between two competing value-commitments*: (i) to a process in which victims and other stakeholders can participate meaningfully in criminal justice proceedings; and (ii) to case *dispositions* which are designed to further restorative rather than punitive goals.

The Sources Of The Tension

Why, then, does this tension arise? It arises because *many* people — victims and community members — are likely to favor punishment over restorative dispositions even when presented with the option of the latter. Therefore, if one includes in criminal justice processes victims and other stakeholders, one will inevitably include and empower many people who will opt for punishment. While proponents of restorative justice can hope that the process will lead to many people seeing the merits of a restorative rather than punitive disposition, there can be no guarantee that the majority of people will be so persuaded. Indeed, to imagine this will occur in many cases seems wishful thinking (Daly, 2002). Hence, it may be necessary (at least for the foreseeable future) to choose whether to prioritize:

(1) the goal of devolving deliberation and decision making about criminal cases to victims and stakeholders; or

(2) the goal of marginalizing punishment and replacing it with restorative dispositions to criminal cases.

CORRECTIONAL ALTERNATIVE OR LIFE ETHOS?

So far, I have discussed restorative justice as it applies to sentencing reform and to our understanding of what crime is and what it means to do *criminal* justice? However, as indicated at the outset, some chief advocates of restorative justice suggest that it is applicable beyond the world of criminal justice. For some, restorative justice consists of a set of tenets that enable us to identify and reduce injustices, currently unrecognized as such, in socio-economic arrangements, other institutional settings such as schools and workplaces, family life, and intimate relationships (see Sullivan and Tifft's chapter).

A question that needs to be addressed is how this larger ambition relates, if at all, to the smaller (but nevertheless immense) ambition of reforming the criminal justice system. Can those who are interested in criminal justice reform, even if they are sympathetic to positions such as that of Sullivan and Tifft, nevertheless leave the task of "healing our everyday lives" to others, on the grounds that it is hopelessly ambitious, a distraction, or beyond their professional remit? Some clearly think so. But, as will be seen, for a number of reasons, Sullivan and Tifft reject such an approach.

Perhaps the most important reason for rejecting a narrow focus upon criminal justice is that — as labeling theorists and critical criminologists have long made clear — defining certain behavior as "criminal" and other behavior as lawful is itself an exercise of power. The criminal law is frequently used, not to prevent patently harmful behavior, but rather to prohibit behavior which those with social power find tiresome or distasteful. By the same token, social power is often used to prevent criminal labels and sanctions being applied to behavior that seems — by many accounts — to be patently harmful to the majority of citizens. By trying to sidestep this issue in order to focus narrowly on criminal justice reform, the restorative justice movement leaves itself open to the charge that it is working within and therefore helping to sustain an ideological definition of the problems facing modern societies.

It is an act of power to direct social resources and people's minds towards waging battle against "crime," as officially defined, as opposed to preventing and remedying the distress, poverty and inequality that frequently arises from "lawful" social policies and practices. A serious charge against the movement for restorative justice is that instead of questioning this power-based act of defining and prioritizing social problems, it restricts itself to the question of how the battle against crime should be waged. We might well agree that it is better that, in the battle against crime, it is both more ethical and more effective to deploy restorative justice rather than retributive justice. Yet, to the extent that the movement for restorative justice has so far (with the exception of writers such as Sullivan and Tifft and Braithwaite) put the spotlight on crime, as officially-defined, and deflected it from other forms of social harm, it is open to the charge that it is itself acting inconsistently with the principles of restorative justice (at least as conceived by the likes of Sullivan and Tifft).

A CONTESTED CONCEPT

How should restorative justice be conceived? Some readers may be perturbed to find that I have not offered a straight answer to this question. What I have tried to show is that, while it can be useful to start by thinking about restorative justice as a new type of criminal justice sentence, we fail to grasp what restorative justice is about (and fail to evaluate it adequately) unless we treat it as a profound challenge to the assumptions dominant in public discourse about crime and justice. Further, we need to take very seriously the arguments of those who think that criminal justice reform is just one goal, and perhaps not even the central one, for a movement which should aim to create a just community. Restorative justice is, to this extent, usefully understood as a contested concept.

Address correspondence to: Gerry Johnstone, Law School, University of Hull, Hull HU6 7RX, UK. E-mail: <J.G.Johnstone@hull.ac.uk>.

REFERENCES

Braithwaite, J. (2003). "Principles of Restorative Justice." In: A. von Hirsch, J. Roberts, A. Bottoms, J. Roach and M. Schiff (eds.), *Restorative Justice and Criminal Justice: Competing or Reconcilable Paradigms*. Oxford: Hart.

—— and H. Strang (2001). "Introduction: Restorative Justice and Civil Society." In: H. Strang and J. Braithwaite (eds.), *Restorative Justice and Civil Society*. Cambridge, UK: Cambridge University Press.

Christie, N. (1977). "Conflicts as Property." *British Journal of Criminology* 17(1):1-15.

Daly, K. (2002). "Restorative Justice: The True Story." *Punishment and Society* 4(1):55-79.

Gorringe, T. (1996). *God's Just Vengeance*. Cambridge, UK: Cambridge University Press.

Hulsman, L. (1986). "Critical Criminology and the Concept of Crime." *Contemporary Crises* 10(1):63-80.

Johnstone, G. (2002). *Restorative Justice: Ideas, Values, Debates*. Cullompton, Devon, UK: Willan Publishing.

Kennedy, L. (1990). *On the Borders of Crime: Conflict Management and Criminology*. New York, NY and London, UK: Longman.

Strang, H. (2002). *Repair or Revenge: Victims and Restorative Justice*. Oxford, UK: Clarendon Press.

Umbreit, M. and B. Vos (2000). "Homicide Survivors Meet the Offender Prior to Execution: Restorative Justice through Dialogue." *Homicide Studies* 4(1):63-87.

Zehr, H. (1990). *Changing Lenses: A New Focus for Crime and Justice*. Scottdale, PA: Herald Press.

Chapter 2.
How Large Should The Restorative Justice "Tent" Be?

by

Susan Sharpe

INTRODUCTION

Restorative justice has grown dramatically in the past 15 years, developing in many directions at once. Its best-known forms — victim-offender mediation, circles, and conferencing — are being continually refined, both as a result of experience and also in order to respond better to participants' needs. A label such as "mediation," "conferencing," or "circles" is no longer enough to clarify what a restorative justice program does.

On the whole, these are positive signs. Restorative justice is still a young field, and this much diversity reflects exploration, refinement, and responsiveness to local circumstances. It enriches the field and infuses energy into the exploration of good practice.

Still, many people would like more consensus on what restorative justice is and what kinds of practice it includes — that is, how wide a range of activity should be included under the term "restorative justice." One reason is that the rapid growth of restorative justice has led to increased confusion. People inside the field sometimes wonder how much their work has in common with other work also known as restorative justice. People outside the field naturally assume — often incorrectly — that what they have heard about one program is also true of others. Advocacy groups, for example, sometimes block restorative justice initiatives because of concerns that might be well founded in some programs but unfounded in others.

Another reason many people would like more consensus is their concern over credibility. Some of this concern comes from people outside the field. Those who refer cases to restorative justice programs are learning more about the risks as well as the benefits of restorative justice, and want to ensure that programs they refer to are doing responsible work. Government officials responsible for the administration of justice need to ensure that restorative justice done in conjunction with criminal cases does not violate legal rights or otherwise put participants at risk. Some of the concern about credibility comes from restorative justice practitioners who are uncomfortable having their work carry the same name as, and sometimes be confused with, work they do not endorse.

In the first half of this chapter I will briefly highlight several areas where it appears that consensus has emerged among restorative justice theorists and practitioners, and then will point to some of the areas where opinion remains divided. In the second half of the chapter I will present a theory that may help us think in new ways about how large to make the restorative justice tent.

What We Can Agree On...

We are far from reaching agreement on what restorative justice is and how much variety it can accommodate without losing its identity or its integrity. But we do have substantial agreement on several key perspectives.

The Need For Basic Definition

Many theorists strongly caution against establishing firm definitions of restorative justice or setting standards for its practice, for fear of closing off innovation or responsiveness to local needs. At the same time, many agree that we do need to define restorative justice clearly enough to distinguish it from retribution and rehabilitation (Weitekamp, 1999:75), from other kinds of alternative justice processes (Rudin, 2003:11), and from strikingly bad practice (Braithwaite, 2002a:565).

Key Restorative Justice Values

There is wide agreement that restorative justice is fundamentally characterized by certain kinds of values. These values are expressed in many different ways and at different levels of specificity (see, for example, Sawatsky, 2003; Van Ness, 2002; Braithwaite, 2002b; Moore and McDonald, 2000). While articulated differently, the values ascribed to restorative justice tend to cluster around concepts like inclusion, democracy, responsibility, reparation, safety, healing, and reintegration.

Howard Zehr distills these values into one core concept. He says, "If I had to put restorative justice into one word, I would choose respect.... The value of respect underlies restorative justice principles and must guide and shape their application" (2002:36).

A Restorative Justice Continuum

Daniel Van Ness says, "Restorative justice reflects values, and is not limited to particular programme elements, which means that it is possible to reflect those values fully or partially. When they are partially expressed, there will be some restorative impact, but not a fully restorative outcome" (2002:131). Thus, restorative justice lies on a continuum such that a given process, or its outcome, might be fully, partly, or not at all restorative.

Recognizing that restorative justice lies on a continuum gives us flexibility. We can agree on how the two ends of the continuum differ, while acknowledging that a given process could combine elements of both (such as when a judge's sentence reflects the decisions reached through a restorative process). Recognizing this continuum also gives us time to continue experimenting, evaluating, and reflecting on the middle ground as we learn how far we can move away from the ideal of restorative justice without compromising its integrity.

Needing Further Reflection...

Research is gradually giving us more information about the effectiveness of various kinds of restorative justice practice, but there is growing tension over differences that may not be resolvable through research. James Dignan calls some of these "fault-lines...that delineate significantly different strands of restorative justice thinking" (2002:171).

Purist Or Maximalist?

One such fault-line has to do with how inclusive we want to be in defining restorative justice: do we want to be "purist" or "maximalist" in deciding what the tent should cover?

Paul McCold argues for what he calls a purist model, that is, "a holistic approach to restorative justice because it focuses equally on the needs of victims, offenders, and communities, and it seeks to meet those needs simultaneously" (2000:401).

There is no question that this holistic definition reflects restorative justice; this lies at the ideal end of the restorative justice continuum. The question is whether it reflects all of restorative justice, or whether the term restorative justice covers a wider range.

Two other scholars, Gordon Bazemore and Lode Walgrave, both argue that we unnecessarily limit the potential of restorative justice by holding to a purist definition. Walgrave explains this view when he says, "Restorative justice rhetoric is too often kept within some kind of a 'national park' for good people and peacemakers... But the major part of life happens outside and includes non-pure elements which often threaten to overrule nature completely" (2000:416).

Bazemore and Walgrave therefore recommend a maximalist definition, so that restorative justice might reach as many people as possible, even if the circumstances are not ideal. In their view, restorative justice is "every action that is primarily oriented toward doing justice by repairing the harm that has been caused by a crime" (1999:48). This means, they say (introducing the tent metaphor that frames this chapter), "We also include under the restorative justice tent, for example, a wide variety of services provided for victims, whether or not an offender is involved or even known to the system or the community" (1999:48).

The question of whether to be purist or maximalist draws spirited discussion because of its implications for how restorative justice is practiced — i.e., what is required or allowed under the restorative justice tent.

Practice Issues

Many questions follow from the purist/maximalist distinction. For example,

- Who must be involved in a restorative process? Must the victim agree to take part? The offender? Do community members always have a role? Can surrogates take the place of key parties?

- Must an offender's participation always be fully voluntary? Is there any role for coercion?

- Is there a role for punishment, to express a community's disapproval of certain behavior?

- Is there a role for overt reintegrative shaming?[1]

- How does it help or hinder a restorative process to help the parties prepare beforehand?

- What does the facilitator's role include and exclude?

- Who should decide how the offender makes amends? Must it be the people most affected by the incident? Can it be community volunteers? Can justice officials order restorative actions?

This is not an exhaustive list, but these are some of the things currently at issue among restorative justice theorists and practitioners. Some of these questions have the potential to be quite divisive, moving us further away from consensus instead of toward it.

Whether or not we ever come to full agreement on these issues, it is important to grapple with them because our choices can shape how restorative justice evolves and thus what it is able to accomplish. The goal is not to standardize restorative justice practice, but to explore thorny issues in light of theory and experience, deepening our understandings and refining our practice.

So how do we decide how to answer such questions? Restorative values give us a reasonably stable point of reference. But even when we agree on what those values are, there is room to disagree on how they are best expressed. By themselves, values do not tell us how much diversity restorative justice can accommodate without being compromised.

It may be that we need an additional point of reference. As Bazemore and Walgrave remind us, "Restorative justice is not only about restoration; it is also about 'justice' broadly defined" (1999:53).

We have done a good job of answering, "What makes something restorative?" It is equally important to ask, "What makes it justice?"

A SOCIAL CONTRACT THEORY OF RESTORATIVE JUSTICE

I have seen little in the restorative justice literature regarding the nature of justice. Many discussions do refer to justice, but usually in passing or in order to provide context, rather than in relation to its role in restorative justice.[2] This is understandable. Justice is such a familiar concept that it makes sense to take this as a given and call attention to the seemingly new restorative approach. But to fully understand what is happening when restorative justice "works" — and therefore to know what is essential and what is optional in how we practice it — we need to be sure we understand the justice dimension of restorative justice as well as the restorative dimension.

The remainder of this chapter looks at one well established perspective on justice, and proposes an explanation of the underlying mechanism at work in restorative justice. There is not room in this chapter to thoroughly argue this theory, but I'll sketch its highlights in order to suggest another way of thinking about what belongs under the restorative justice tent.

Conceptions Of Justice

In Western culture we have come to think of justice as an intervention to punish and correct wrongdoing. But justice has meant something quite different in other cultures and throughout much of human history (e.g., Van Ness and Strong, 2002; Ury, 2000; Weitekamp, 1999; Zehr, 1990). In many societies "justice" has been understood as a state of balance — a system of social cooperation that supports and encourages peaceful coexistence. This ancient concept of justice still resonates for us, even through our Western reliance on an institutional justice system.

Political philosopher John Rawls posits a comprehensive theory he calls "justice as fairness." Rawls's theory is a political conception of justice specific to modern democratic society (2001:14,7). I suggest that it can also be applied to the maintenance of justice within such a society, helping to explain how and why restorative justice works as it does.

For Rawls, justice as fairness is based on a fair system of social cooperation, in which:

- people regulate their behavior on the basis of widely accepted rules, which are

- seen as being fair and reciprocal, applying to and benefiting everyone in the society equally, and which

- give each person equal opportunity to act for the sake of their own good (2001:6).

In other words, we create and maintain justice through social cooperation, which is carried out through social contracts. These "contracts" are the agreements we have (often unconscious, usually unspoken, though sometimes codified in laws or other rules) about how we will behave in relation to each other and what kinds of behavior we can expect from each other. These behavioral expectations are contractual (rather than imposed) to the extent that they are reciprocal, and fair to the extent that they give each party equal freedom of opportunity. Such contracts form a system of social cooperation insofar as the parties voluntarily honor them out of respect for each other.[3]

All of us abide by many social contracts at once. What signals the presence of a social contract (at least as perceived by the person upset by a particular behavior) is that violating it provokes a sense of indignation or outrage: "That's not fair!"

If justice lies in a fair system of social cooperation, then it is not an idealized state so much as a fluid and personal experience, one that increases and decreases as we interact and as our circumstances change. There is justice between us as long as, and to the extent that, our interactions allow each of us equal opportunity to seek what is important to our own good. When one of us has more such freedom than the other, there is injustice between us. Thus someone might work every day in an environment that functions like a "just society," but live in painful injustice while at home with their family. Or vice versa.

Injustice

Some injustices are small, easily corrected, and quickly forgotten; others create serious and sometimes lasting harm. They can result from accident or intent. Some are unforeseen; some are expressly forbidden. When we say that crime is fundamentally a violation of relationship, we are pointing to the violation of social contracts.

Injustice debilitates to the extent that it suspends a functional social contract, limiting a person's quality of life and the ability to get his or her needs met. That is why we want to see wrongs righted. We want to restore at least the degree of freedom in place up to the time of the violation.

Maximizing Justice

If justice lies in social cooperation that helps each of us pursue our own good, then it is in our own best interest to make our interactions as fair and as mutually supportive as possible. This might involve three things at various times (and in various relationships):

- Maintaining justice — that is, abiding by our social contracts, immediately correcting injustices, and being mindful of fairness in all our interactions;

- Fostering justice — encouraging, assisting, or motivating people to uphold their social contracts (such as by bringing victim impact panels into prisons, or by teaching children responsibility and empathy); and,

- Restoring justice — addressing the harms involved in an injustice and (re)establishing social contracts that feel fair to both parties.

Restoring Justice

From this perspective, restorative justice can be viewed as a forum in which the people affected by the violation of a social contract can consider and decide together how to restore justice between them. Justice can be restored by:

- Reinstating the social contract that was violated (e.g., putting the incident behind them and carrying on as they did before the injustice occurred);

- Renegotiating the social contract: setting new terms for potential interactions (e.g., "If we pass each other on the sidewalk, we'll both say hello"); or,

- Terminating the contract they had and setting terms to limit (or prohibit) future interaction (such as expelling a student or banishing someone from the community).

Depending on the circumstances, any of these options — reinstating, revising, or terminating the violated contract — might be the best way for given parties, under given circumstances, to have the maximum safety and freedom (which may not always be equal freedom) to seek their own good.

In order to make an informed decision about whether to reinstate, renegotiate, or terminate a social contract that was violated, each of the affected parties needs certain things — things we recognize as being central to restorative justice.

Someone who has been harmed needs:

- *Acknowledgement*:
    o that the contract was in place and that the behavior violated it — that is, an apology;
    o that violating the contract was wrong — that is, a credible showing of remorse.

- *Information* about:
    o how and why the violation occurred;
    o factors affecting the probability that the other party would abide by a renewed or renegotiated contract (e.g., addictions or peer pressure might lower the probability, while family support might raise it).

A person responsible for causing harm needs:

- *An opportunity* to ask for, or to consider, recontracting;

- *Information* about the consequences of the violation:
    o for the other party: what harms occurred and what needs have resulted;
    o for themselves: what trust, opportunities, or support have been withdrawn or jeopardized because of the violation.

Both (or all) parties need:[4]

- *Full expression* (including the emotional and spiritual dimensions) of what the social contract has meant in each party's life and the implications of its violation — both to express this for themselves and to hear it from the other;

- *Exploration* of what might be necessary in order for
    - the responsible party to fulfill the obligations created by the violation;
    - both parties to feel confident that a renewed or revised contract would be honored (e.g., improved job performance might demonstrate responsibility).

- *Information* about what the other party might want or expect in a reinstated or revised contract (e.g., "I'd like to come by and help out with your yard work").

- *Clarification* of the terms they will abide by in moving forward, so that each knows what is expected and what is permissible.

Implications For Restorative Justice Practice

In order for justice to be restored, it seems essential that:

- The parties to the contract[5] decide for themselves (with input from any supporters they include or consult) how to restore justice between them to the extent possible.

- The parties communicate with each other about the incident and its consequences, in order to make an informed decision about how to restore justice between them. Face-to-face dialogue allows the richest exchange of information and helps each party gauge the sincerity of the other's intentions about recontracting, but these needs might also be met through indirect communication such as correspondence or video recordings.

Justice is more likely to be restored when:

- The parties prepare for meeting (or otherwise communicate with) each other, thus increasing the likelihood that they will get and give all the information they need from each other.

- The parties' communication is marked by mutual respect, which can help increase each party's confidence that the other would respect a new social contract between them.

Viewing restorative justice as a vehicle for determining how to restore (or establish) just social contracts may suggest additional answers to the questions posed earlier in this chapter, but there is not room to address them here. I'll close with a final suggestion for how we might understand restorative justice.

Seeing restorative practices as helping people (re)gain justice through their social contracts suggests that restorative justice lies on two continua, not one. One continuum reflects the degree of fairness in the parties' new (or renewed) social contract. The other continuum reflects the degree of mutuality informing that contract: the degree of respect, empathy, personal accountability, and commitment each of them brings to the new (or renewed) social contract. The combination of the two — the degree to which they come away with equality of opportunity to seek their own good, and the degree to which they mutually and voluntarily commit to that outcome — is the degree to which justice is restored.

CONCLUSION

As indicated at the start of this chapter, there is a growing need for consensus on what restorative justice is and where its boundaries might lie. To this point, however, we have agreed only on more basic perspectives, including the need for definition, the nature of restorative justice values, and the idea that restorative justice lies on a continuum. There are many more areas of disagreement, both regarding how inclusive to be in defining restorative justice and regarding specific aspects of practice. To date, what we have been calling "restorativeness" has given us a useful bridge between differing perspectives, but it has not clarified which of those perspectives are most theoretically sound. In hopes of speaking to that gap, I have suggested that what occurs between parties during a restorative justice process is fundamentally the renegotiation of social contracts, based on information gained and judgments made during the discussion of harmful behavior and its consequences. I hope this suggestion will stimulate new ways of approaching the complex issues involved in this work, including what belongs under the restorative justice tent.

Address correspondence to: Susan Sharpe, 4700 Latona Avenue NE, Seattle Washington 98105. E-mail: <susanlsharpe@earthlink.net>.

FOR FURTHER READING

Crawford, A. and T. Newburn (2003). "Implementing Restorative Justice Initiatives." In: A. Crawford and T. Newburn (eds.), *Youth Offending and Restorative Justice: Implementing Reform in Youth Justice*. Cullompton, Devon, UK and Portland, OR: Willan Publishing.

Eliaerts, C. and E. Dumortier (2002). "Restorative Justice for Children: In Need of Procedural Safeguards and Standards." In: G.M. Weitekamp and H. Kerner (eds.), *Restorative Justice: Theoretical Foundations*. Cullomptom, Devon, UK and Portland, OR: Willan Publishing.

Johnstone, G. (2002). "Central Themes and Critical Issues." In: G. Johnstone (ed.), *Restorative Justice: Ideas, Values, Debates*. Cullompton, Devon, UK and Portland, OR: Willan Publishing.

Van Ness, D.W. (2002). "Creating Restorative Systems." In: L. Walgrave (ed.), *Restorative Justice and the Law*. Cullompton, Devon, UK and Portland, OR: Willan Publishing.

Zehr, H. (2002). *The Little Book of Restorative Justice*. Intercourse, PA: Good Books.

REFERENCES

Bazemore, G. and L. Walgrave (1999). "Restorative Juvenile Justice: In Search of Fundamentals and an Outline for Systemic Reform." In: G. Bazemore and L. Walgrave (eds.), *Restorative Juvenile Justice: Repairing the Harm of Youth Crime*. Monsey, NY: Criminal Justice Press.

Braithwaite, J. (2002a). "Setting Standards for Restorative Justice." *British Journal of Criminology* 42:563-577.

—— (2002b). "In Search of Restorative Jurisprudence." In: L. Walgrave (ed.), *Restorative Justice and the Law*. Cullompton, Devon, UK and Portland, OR: Willan Publishing.

—— (1989). *Crime, Shame and Reintegration*. Cambridge, UK: Cambridge University Press.

—— and D. Roche (2001). "Responsibility and Restorative Justice." In: G. Bazemore and M. Schiff (eds.), *Restorative Community Justice: Repairing Harm and Transforming Communities*. Cincinnati, OH: Anderson Publishing.

Dignan, J. (2002). "Restorative Justice and the Law: The Case for an Integrated, Systemic Approach." In: L. Walgrave (ed.), *Restorative Justice and the Law*. Cullompton, Devon, UK and Portland, OR: Willan Publishing.

Fattah, E.A. (2002). "From Philosophical Abstraction to Restorative Action, From Senseless Retribution to Meaningful Restitution: Just Deserts and Restorative Justice Revisited." In: G.M. Weitekamp and H. Kerner (eds.), *Restorative Justice: Theoretical Foundations*. Cullompton, Devon, UK and Portland, OR: Willan Publishing.

Mannozzi, G. (2002). "From the 'Sword' to Dialogue: Towards a 'Dialectic' Basis for Penal Mediation." In: G.M. Weitekamp and H. Kerner (eds.), *Restorative Justice: Theoretical Foundations*. Cullompton, Devon, UK and Portland, OR: Willan Publishing.

Maxwell, G. and A. Morris (2002). "The Role of Shame, Guilt and Remorse in Restorative Justice Processes for Young People." In: G.M. Weitekamp and H. Kerner (eds.), *Restorative Justice: Theoretical Foundations*. Cullompton, Devon, UK and Portland, OR: Willan Publishing.

McCold, P. (2000). "Toward a Holistic Vision of Restorative Juvenile Justice: A Reply to the Maximalist Model." *Contemporary Justice Review* 3(4):357-414.

Moore, D.B. and J.M. McDonald (2000). *Transforming Conflict: In Workplaces and Other Communities*. Sydney, AUS: Transformative Justice Australia.

Rawls, J. (2001). *Justice as Fairness: A Restatement*. Cambridge, MA: The Belknap Press of Harvard University Press.

Rudin, J. (2003). "Pushing Back: A Response to the Drive for the Standardization of Restorative Justice Programs in Canada." Paper presented at the 6th International Conference on Restorative Justice, Vancouver, B.C., June 1-4.

Sawatsky, J. (2003). "Restorative Values: Where Means and Ends Converge." Paper presented at the 6th International Conference on Restorative Justice, Vancouver, B.C., June 1-4.

Ury, W.L. (2000). *The Third Side: Why We Fight and How We Can Stop.* (Published in 1999 as *Getting to Peace: Transforming Conflict at Home, at Work, and in the World.*) New York: Penguin.

Van Ness, D.W. (2002). "Creating Restorative Systems." In: L. Walgrave (ed.), *Restorative Justice and the Law.* Cullompton, Devon, UK and Portland, OR: Willan Publishing.

—— and K.H. Strong (2002). *Restoring Justice* (2nd ed.). Cincinnati, OH: Anderson.

Walgrave, L. (2000). "How Pure Can a Maximalist Approach to Restorative Justice Remain? Or Can a Purist Model of Restorative Justice Become Maximalist?" *Contemporary Justice Review* 3(4):415-432.

Weitekamp, E.G.M. (1999). "The History of Restorative Justice." In: G. Bazemore and L. Walgrave (eds.), *Restorative Juvenile Justice: Repairing the Harm of Youth Crime.* Monsey, NY: Criminal Justice Press.

Zehr, H. (2002). *The Little Book of Restorative Justice.* Intercourse, PA: Good Books.

—— (1990). *Changing Lenses.* Scottsdale, PA: Herald Press.

NOTES

1. John Braithwaite, who introduced this term, says "Reintegrative shaming means that expressions of community disapproval, which may range from mild rebuke to degradation ceremonies (serious denunciations), are followed by gestures of reacceptance into the community of law-abiding citizens" (1989:55). While Braithwaite emphasizes the centrality of reintegration in this concept (e.g., Braithwaite and Roche, 2001:74), other scholars have raised concerns about any intentional use of shaming. For discussion of this issue, see Maxwell and Morris (2002).

2. There are substantive discussions of justice in the restorative justice literature, but their purpose usually is to provide context for other issues. For example, Zehr (1990) and Van Ness and Strong (2002) trace the history of Western justice as distinct from restorative justice, (Mannozzi, 2002) looks at the iconography associated with justice in prelude to a discussion of victim-offender mediation, and Fattah (2002) discusses restorative justice in relation to other models and paradigms of justice.

3. It is important to clarify that:

a. I am not using "social contract" at the macro level of political philosophy, or in the sense of making a bargain, but as an implicit agreement about how we will treat each other and what we can expect from each other under certain circumstances.

b. Social contracts are upheld voluntarily. They may be disliked or resented, but they are in place as long as (and only as long as) people choose to behave on the basis of what is expected of them (as opposed to following rules).

c. We often behave according to social contracts that
- are not spelled out or even consciously recognized, and
- are not necessarily fair to everyone who accepts and honors them.

d. The parties to a given social contract may assume it to contain different terms (a difference that is the source of much conflict).

4. The community (such as the neighborhood, extended family, school, business community, or state) may have a role in deciding how justice is restored, given that others also count on the contract that was violated. The community also has an interest in seeing that the primary parties' decision about how to restore justice does not violate community-wide social contracts in place.

5. Some social contracts have both a personal and a community dimension. If I break into your home, I have broken my contract with you (one that each of us has with every other member of the community) to respect your property. In addition, I have broken my contract with the whole community to respect others' property, thus forfeiting my right to their trust as well as yours. I have also broken your contract with the whole community (in that you trusted me and everyone else to uphold that contract), thus undermining your ability to trust anyone in the community. To restore justice as far as possible, you and I must not only decide whether to renew, renegotiate, or terminate the social contract linking you and me; each of us also needs to regain functional social contracts with the rest of the community.

Chapter 3.
By Whom, And By What Processes, Is Restorative Justice Defined, And What Bias Might This Introduce?

by

Val Napoleon

INTRODUCTION

A Reflection

I watched him emerge from the shadows and move toward me. Hesitantly. His shoulders hunched. Moving ever so lightly on his feet, skulking-like, apologizing with his whole body — apologizing for being, for living, for breathing, for existing. I recognized these hopeless messages because I'd seen them before in times of other troubles. I'd sometimes read the same messages on the bodies of other family members, homeless people and others living in terrible and harsh circumstances: "Don't look at me. Don't see me. I'm not really here. I'm so sorry. Sorry. Sorry." Pain squeezed my heart, constricted my throat, and leaked from my eyes.

I had persuaded my younger brother to let me pick him up after a botched bank robbery. I took him first to a criminal-law lawyer, then to the police station. He'd been out of prison for one month. This is part of a long, complicated story that causes me to continually think about justice, punishment, and rehabilitation. It also causes me to think about love, hope, and enduring human spirits. Indeed, the inadvertent lessons my brother teaches me are invariably the most painful and difficult, and the most important for me to learn. In this chapter, I will share some of them.

Guide To This Chapter

Until its proponents have made profound shift in thinking, restorative justice will remain trapped within Western rational thought, constrained by unexamined assumptions. We must challenge our assumptions about human nature and our relationships, and contextualize restorative justice politically, socially, and economically in the larger world. Only then can restorative justice become a force for positive social change.

My overarching concern is about definitions of restorative justice. Who decides what it is, and what are the consequences of these definitions? In this chapter, I explore three main themes as they affect the tangle of issues in restorative justice and its definition: human nature, harmony, and relationships. My basic contention is that if we view human beings as essentially individualistic and in need of coercive social control to suppress an innate warlike and competitive nature, then we will relate to one another, structure our institutions, and define justice — and restorative justice — accordingly. By the same token, if we understand ourselves to be fundamentally cooperative beings, we will see and treat each other, both individually and collectively, according to that model. Finally, I recommend that we maintain a dual perspective on restorative justice that includes seeing the personal within the political and the individual within the collective.

Having said this, I caution against simply ascribing certain human behaviours to an inherent human nature (essentialism). I also caution against romanticizing human beings, cultures, or communities, because this will short-circuit the necessary critical and creative thought required to create positive social change through restorative justice. For example, romanticization puts pressure on aboriginal people to fulfil unrealistic expectations, to be less fallible, and to make fewer mistakes than non-aboriginals (Barron, 2002:232). Both essentialism and romanticism can cause us to gloss over and perpetuate power imbalances, oppression, and structural problems (Nader and Ou, 1998:15). We know that we are capable of doing terrible harms to one another and capable of great love, compassion, intelligence, and sacrifice. Our thinking must straddle this great range of positive and negative human potential. We must engage in an exercise of conscious cognitive dissonance. Coming to terms with human complexity and contradictions is one of the greatest challenges we face in doing the work of restorative justice.

CHALLENGING ASSUMPTIONS

How a society defines and implements something called "justice" determines whether it will rely more on punishment or on reconciliation in attempting to restore order and prevent renewed disorder. Though societies vary greatly in their tendency toward disorder, the very nature of human beings...is internally conflicted...: a tension exists between one's social needs for bonding and shared meaning and one's need for autonomy. Hence, no real society ever permanently solves the ongoing potential for social conflict, but some are much better than others at managing it without overly restricting individual behaviour (Clark, 2002:340; footnote omitted).

Human Nature

Scientist and writer Mary Clark presents a wise and comprehensive challenge to commonly held Western assumptions about human nature that may be fruitfully incorporated into the restorative justice discourse. How human beings "see" reality and what we comprehend is always constructed. The Western model of reality profoundly affects both our understanding of nature and the way that we treat the earth. Its increasing global dominance is leading to dangerous and pathological consequences for human beings. Clark (2002:3) writes: "All human thought, all our knowledge, ultimately is grounded in certain 'givens' — certain inescapable beliefs and assumptions. On them we construct our model of reality or 'truth' that allows us to function with confidence, more or less automatically."

Like the movement of billiard balls, human beings in the Western model of reality act in isolation, independently colliding and rebounding. It is a model of the cause-and-effect linear interactions of individualistic worldviews in which the self is discrete and separate from the whole. While Western science has recently moved on to less deterministic theories, such as quantum mechanics and chaos, most westerners still see their daily world as the billiard-ball model. This has given rise to theories that human beings are rationalist and self-centred, inwardly driven to compete in a world of scarcity. According to Clark (2002:8), "[the Western] view of human society demands that people compete (for jobs, status) to survive; it also expects they will try to be free riders (go on welfare), or cheat (lie, steal); and so it protects itself by threats of severe punishment (homeless, punitive fines, harsh jail sentences) for those who don't 'measure up.'"

The consequent Western emphasis on individual rights and individual guilt and the endless drive for more "social efficiency," measured only by economic criteria, is intensifying our feelings of alienation, insecurity, powerlessness, and meaninglessness. For aboriginal peoples, these experiences are compounded by colonialism (Proulx, 2003; Jackson, 1992; Coker, 1999; McGillivray and Comaskey, 1999). "Yet given our assumptions about human nature as selfish, individualistic, and materially motivated, we do not see these stresses as stemming from social problems, but from the inability of individuals to conform" (Clark, 2002:16).

However, there is as an alternative to the billiard-ball model that is both preferable and necessary — the gestalt of a net. The net is a metaphor for interconnected and interacting entities, whether they are human bodies, economic or social systems, or ecosystems. Each entity contains interdependent parts that interact reciprocally and are all necessary for the survival of the whole. There are no discrete billiard balls. The validity of the net metaphor is supported by several biological arguments deriving from the extended period of helplessness of the human infant and human physiology and behaviour (Clark, 2002:8-9, 43).

Clark's main thesis is that there is a human nature, and it comprises three propensities that frame all our social behaviour: bonding (belonging), autonomy, and meaning. She uses the term "propensities" because while they are powerful innate tendencies, they can be satisfied by a variety of behavioural responses. These propensities are linked to and reflected in emotion, language, culture, and identity. From this perspective, the negative side of human nature does not derive from some genetic selfishness or warlike characteristic, but rather from our need to belong to a meaningful society. In other words, most human violence and mayhem results from clashes between meaning systems including those conflicts between groups whose identities are threatened (Clark, 2002:58-60).

I think it is fair to say that the billiard-ball model underpins the Western legal system, and despite the proliferation of rhetoric, it is arguable that it also underpins at least some aboriginal restorative justice initiatives (Miller, 2000; Tauri, n.d.).

In my experience with aboriginal communities,[1] the challenge of restorative justice for aboriginal peoples is not created simply by a clash between aboriginal and non-aboriginal cultures — not that this is a simple matter (LeBaron, 2002, 2003). Rather, within aboriginal communities there are often fundamental clashes that have been generated by colonialism and neo-colonialism. Often these internal conflicts involve spirituality/religion, identity, and a range of social, political, economic, and legal issues. Given this, there is no one aboriginal understanding of human nature that can inform restorative justice. Rather, ongoing, in-depth discussions about beliefs, identity, human nature, and conflict management are necessary in both aboriginal (and non-aboriginal) communities if restorative justice initiatives are to create a more positive and inclusive future.

Harmony

What is harmony? When is harmony a mutually beneficial goal? When is harmony a justification for exerting power and maintaining power imbalances? What causes disharmony? How do our assumptions about harmony shape the restorative justice initiatives that we create? I have concerns about restorative justice, particularly in aboriginal communities, that have to do with the potential for coercive social control in the name of harmony.

My first apprehension arises from the pervasive insistence in restorative justice programs that offenders "accept" personal responsibility for their crime and resultant injuries to others. I agree that offenders bear personal responsibility for their decisions and actions. However, I think there is a parallel collective, societal responsibility that must also be accepted and expressed in the work of restorative justice. In other words, do we believe that crime is simply a matter of personal failing? How are societal problems such as structural power imbalances, oppression, exploitation, and colonialism part of the crime?

Our beliefs about crime determine our focus and the kind of restorative justice initiatives we create. The underclass does not exist without the "overclass"; they are two sides of the same coin. An exclusive focus on the individual offender in our demands for personal accountability, in isolation from the larger political context, is arguably another form of individualistic social control in the name of harmony. A similarly oppressive dynamic exists when victims are compelled to forgive, forget, or participate in oppressive processes in the name of harmony. If we are to create restorative justice initiatives that are forces for positive social change, we must take a broader, collective, and political approach to understanding crime, rather than solely poking at wayward, individual billiard balls.

My second apprehension arises when the ideology of harmony is applied collectively and coercively. According to anthropologist Laura Nader, a hierarchy of values hides in idealized contemporary legal notions, so that harmony is valued over conflict or confrontation:

> Conciliation, harmony, and resolution have such different uses and consequences as to merit different labels. Harmony that leads to autonomy is different from harmony that leads to control or oppression or pacification; conciliation may lead to conflict as well as to peace; and resolution may lead to injustice as well as justice (Nader, 1990:320-21).

For aboriginal people, there are at least two sides to harmony ideology.

On one hand, claiming that an internal, social harmony already exists is a way of promoting self-determination in that it discourages state intrusion into their internal affairs. Some aboriginal communities "have responded [to state impositions] by a conscious rejection of mainstream values and practices in reaction to the mainstream, thereby distorting their own legacy by emphasizing harmony and de-emphasizing problems" (Miller, 2000:5). In these situations, harmony is used to describe aboriginal societies idealistically, especially in matters of justice and social services. Government easily buys into the simplistic descriptions of aboriginal harmony because of wishful thinking, romanticism, and/or ignorance, or to meet its own agenda (Nader and Ou, 1998:14-16).

On the other hand, the promise of harmony may serve as another colonial tool to pacify resistance against the state in indigenous and civil rights movements, and in environmental conflicts. Take, for example, the British practice of indirect rule in Kenya, Tanzania, and Uganda:

> [T]he principle of indirect rule [is defined] as that "of adapting for the purposes of local government the institutions [e.g., native courts] which the native peoples have evolved for themselves, so that they may develop in a constitutional manner from their own past, guided and restrained by the traditions and sanctions which they have inherited (moulded or modified as they may be on the advice of British Officers) and by the general advice and control of those officers" (Morris and Read, 1972:1).

It is arguable that indirect rule of aboriginal people was and is employed in Canada through the Indian Act (R.S.C. 1985, c. I-5) and various financial arrangements between aboriginal communities and the state. Whether internally or externally imposed, coercive harmony ideology is destructive to aboriginal communities because it masks abuses of power and suppresses critical discourse through the language of "primordiality" and sacredness (Miller, 2000:204; McGillivray and Comaskey, 1999:52).

Harmony ideology is also destructive to mainstream society. Laura Nader is quoted as saying, "I think America's been flattened. We've been flattened by what I describe as 'harmony ideology' — you mustn't be contentious, you mustn't raise issues; and by fear — fear of the loss of jobs, fear that you won't be able to afford what your parents were able to afford, and so forth" (California Alumni Association, 2000).

It is important to articulate our expectations of harmony and our understanding of conflict. It is also critical to examine the consequences of our demands for harmony in terms of whose voices are privileged or silenced and, most importantly, how the harmony will actually benefit the aboriginal community. How can we accept and express our collective responsibility for our communities and the larger world in our restorative justice work?

Relationships

The third theme I set out to explore is the assumptions we hold about human relationships. Previously, I suggested that if restorative justice is to become a vehicle for positive social change, we must fundamentally shift our thinking about human nature and harmony. This shift in thinking must necessarily include examining how we create relationships, the kind of relationships we create, and what we expect from our relationships. To explore our relationships means that we must look at our concepts of the self and the other in our relationships.

Anthropologist Michael Asch (1997:8) argues that there are two approaches to thinking about the self and the other: the self and the "oppositional other," and the self and the "relational other." The common goals and behavior of the self in "oppositional other" relationships are to seek freedom to act politically without reference to the other, or to struggle for freedom against the other. In contrast, the common goals and behaviour of the self in "relational other" relationships are to act autonomously and with free will with reference to the other, and to understand the other as someone with whom the self has a responsibility to form a relationship (Asch, 1997:8, 17).

Our position in relation to the other will determine both how we work with the other and the solutions we imagine (i.e., separate or shared worlds). Anthropologist Harvey Feit (in press) cautions that members of the dominant society should be sensitive to approaches to relationships when dealing cross-culturally with aboriginal peoples. I also think that, in cross-cultural situations, it is important to keep in mind that colonization has had deeply pervasive and damaging effects on aboriginal cultures, including how we relate to one another.

While I do not suggest that it is possible, or desirable, to attempt the exclusive adoption of the relational approach in an oppositional-other world, I do think we must be conscious of how we position ourselves in relation to others. Insofar as restorative justice is concerned, it is critical that we be purposely self-reflective about how we think of persons who commit crimes, are victims of crimes, or are members of offenders' and victims' families. This thinking needs to extend to how we think about our communities, community factions, and broader societal relationships. Who is the "them"? Who is the "us"? How are we related? How can we practically incorporate a more relational approach into our restorative justice work?

Learning To See Double

Finally, all of us must learn to see double. We must cultivate a dual perspective on our worlds, so that we view individuals within the political context surrounding them. What surrounds my brother and his children? What surrounded his family? It's not just about trying to "fix him" so that he is a "better human being," but about creating a better world to which he can belong and in which he can find meaning. The following table is a useful illustration of the macro and micro aspects of a dual perspective.

Table 1: Dual Perspective (Lundeberg, 2003:13)

Issues	Personal/Individual Perspective (Micro Justice — Billiard Ball Reality)	Political/Contextual Perspective (Macro Justice — Inter-connected Net Reality)
Responsibility	Individualization: Concerned with individual acts and personal responsibility.	Structuralism: Concerned with collective responsibility and structural issues of power and imbalance.
Matters in dispute	Depoliticization: Focuses on specific incidents and behaviours of crime and injury. Adopts a narrow frame of reference relating to the individuals involved.	Politicization: Focuses on social conditions that surround the individual. Adopts a wide frame of reference that includes the community and society.
Remedy	Decontextualization: Adopts an ahistoric perspective and treats people as juridical equals. Focuses on the treatment of individuals as equals and on the restoration of human rights.	Contextualization: Adopts a structural perspective that considers the substantive political, social, and economic inequalities of class. Focuses on building relationships between people and groups of people.

In Clark's billiard-ball model, the criminal justice universe is filled with lazy, self-centred, and individualistic human beings who are an economic and social burden to hard-working taxpayers. From this perspective, someone like my brother is a complete failure who must be dealt with punitively so that he shapes up, gets a job, takes "personal responsibility" for himself, and is "accountable" to society for crimes he has committed. In this constructed reality, there is no need to examine why my brother is so damaged and there is no acceptance of any collective responsibility for him.

From the metaphor of the net, I know that my brother did not make himself this way. While he certainly bears a degree of personal responsibility for his actions, that responsibility ends where the larger societal forces and structural imbalances buffet his life and limit his power. He is an aboriginal man with little education or community support. There is a collective societal responsibility for my brother and his children. He does the best he can and needs help to survive with dignity and a sense of worth.

The collective responsibility includes supporting my brother to meet his human needs so that he belongs somewhere, develops a measure of independence and autonomy, and is able to develop and rely on his own "meaning-making" capacity (LeBaron, 2002:87). But it is not enough to address only my brother's individual needs. Larger questions and challenges must be developed to combat the impacts of colonialism, including the dislocation of aboriginal people from community and land.

CLOSING REFLECTIONS

At the end of the day, we are fundamentally unable to manage conflict in our society. All too often, the result is crime. Restorative justice work needs to be situated against the broader goal of creating positive social change. This does not mean that the everyday, practical work in which we are engaged must stop while we develop a political consciousness. Rather, our work must be conducted in the light of a vision toward what is possible for our communities and society. And we must learn to see double — the individual and the collective, and the personal and the political.

How does any of this relate to my brother's current incarceration? From a billiard-ball perspective, our lives are simply the sum of the decisions we make. But when I think back to the days of our adolescent panhandling, shoplifting, heavy drinking, and general disruptive behaviour, I see that the only difference between my brother's experience and my own was that he was caught and I wasn't. Listen! There is an audible snick as the balls collide on the billiard table — he went one way and I went another. We were living in a billiard-ball universe.

However, from the perspective of the net, the broader context is that my siblings and I were born into the oppression created by colonization. Like many aboriginal persons, we lived a marginalized existence with the attendant alcoholism, drug addiction, violence, mental illness, racism, foster homes, and poverty. From this vantage point, I can see that in and of itself, poverty doesn't create crime; it is the powerlessness and alienation that is soul crushing.

Since there was no net, my brother's and my circumstances were formed by chance. Consequently, he began a cycle of serving time as a child and I escaped. He has done some terrible things and he is damaged. Decades later, I am a lawyer and he is incarcerated. Listen! Snick. What if there had been a net there for him? Snick. What if I had been the one caught?

Address correspondence to: Val Napoleon, LL.B., Interdisciplinary Graduate Student (Law & History), University Of Victoria, 3005 Baynes Road, Victoria, BC V8N 1Y4. E-mail: <muskwah@shaw.ca>.

REFERENCES

Asch, M. (1997). "Self-Determination of Indigenous Peoples and the Global-ization of Human Rights Discourse: The Canadian Example." Paper presented at the CONGLASS III [1997 Anthropology Conference], New York: New York University.

Atkinson, B. (2002). "VAC-RCMP Transition Needs Analysis: Report & Recommendations Based on Findings from Interviews & Discussion Groups Conducted in 'E' Division & Pacific Region September, 2002 — December, 2002." Prepared for Veterans Affairs Canada, Vancouver.

Barron, J. (2002). "Romancing the 'Other' in Aboriginal Support Work." In: J. Bird, L. Land and M. MacAdam (eds.), *Nation to Nation: Aboriginal Sovereignty and the Future of Canada*. Toronto, CAN: Public Justice Resource Centre.

California Alumni Association at UC Berkeley (2000). "Q and A: A Conversation with Laura Nader." *California Monthly*, Berkeley.

Clark, M.E. (2002). *In Search of Human Nature*. London, UK: Routledge.

Coker, D. (1999). "Enhancing Autonomy for Battered Women: Lessons From Navajo Peacemaking." *UCLA Law Review* 47(1):1.

Feit, H. (in press). "James Bay Crees' Life Projects and Politics: Histories of Place, Animal Partners and Enduring Relationships." In: M. Blaser, H.A. Feit and G. McCrae (eds.), *In the Way of Development: Indigenous Peoples' Life Projects* (tentative title). London, UK: Zed Books.

Indian Act R.S.C. 1985, c. 1-5.

Jackson, M. (1992). "In Search of the Pathways to Justice: Alternative Dispute Resolution in Aboriginal Communities." *UBC Law Review* 26(Special Issue):147.

LeBaron, M. (2003). *Bridging Cultural Conflicts: A New Approach for a Changing World*. San Francisco, CA: Jossey-Bass.

——— (2002). *Bridging Troubled Waters: Conflict Resolution From the Heart*. San Francisco, CA: Jossey-Bass.

Lundeberg, I.R. (2003). "Sociology of Law and Human Rights." Paper presented at Aging Societies, New Sociology, the 6th ESA Conference, Murcia, Spain.

McGillivray, A. and B. Comaskey (1999). *Black Eyes All of the Time: Intimate Violence, Aboriginal Women, and the Justice System*. Toronto, CAN: University of Toronto Press.

Miller, B.J. (2000). *The Problem of Justice: Tradition and Law in the Coast Salish World*. Lincoln, NE: University of Nebraska Press.

Morris, H.F. and J.S. Read (1972). *Indirect Rule and the Search for Justice: Essays in East African Legal History*. Oxford, UK: Clarendon Press.

Nader, L. (1990). *Harmony Ideology: Justice and Control in a Mountain Zapotec Village*. Stanford, CA: Stanford University Press.

——— and J. Ou (1998). "Idealization and Power: Legality and Tradition in Native American Law." *Oklahoma City University Law Review* 23(1&2):13-42.

Proulx, C. (2003). *Reclaiming Aboriginal Justice, Identity, and Community*. Saskatoon, CAN.: Purich Publishing.

Sutherland, J. (2002). "Colonialism, Crime, and Dispute Resolution: A Critical Analysis of Canada's Aboriginal Justice Strategy." Winning essay, Boskey Dispute Resolution Essay Competition, Association of Conflict Resolution, Washington, DC. (Available online at www.acresolution.org/research.)

Tauri, J.M. (n.d.) "Family Group Conferencing: The Myth of Indigenous Empowerment in New Zealand." Saskatoon, CAN: Native Law Centre. (Available online at www.usask.ca/nativelaw/publications [undated, accessed 2003.])

NOTES

1. I am from northeastern British Columbia and am of Cree, Saulteaux and Dunneza heritage. I am also an adopted member of the Gitanyow (Gitxsan) House of Luxhon, Ganeda (Frog) clan.

Chapter 4.
Has Restorative Justice Appropriately Responded To Retribution Theory And Impulses?

by

Lode Walgrave

No society can survive without rules and enforcement of these rules. If a transgression happens, a response is needed to mark the wrongfulness of the transgression and the determination to keep the rules respected.

For many centuries, the mainstream response to crime in the Western world has been punishment by public authorities. In recent decades, restorative justice has been advanced as an alternative to traditional criminal justice, which is criticized for being socially destructive (Zehr, 1990/95; Bazemore and Walgrave, 1999; McCold, 2000; Braithwaite, 2002a).

Recent literature, however, has challenged this opposition. This chapter explores the relation between restoration and retribution. After clarifying the differences between restoration and punishment, we will explore retribution as a major philosophical justification for criminal punishment, and keep only one argument for punishment as being viable: possible censuring of wrongful behavior. Restoration will then be presented as a more effective and more ethical way of censuring behavior. Finally, a comparison of the essentials of both retribution and restoration leads to the conclusion that restoration can be seen as kind of reversed retribution.

PUNISHMENT AND RESTORATION

Some influential authors consider the difference between punishment and restoration exaggerated. Daly argues, for example, that restorative justice unavoidably contains punitive aspects, and that it therefore "should embrace the concept of punishment as the main activity of the state's response to crime" (Daly, 2000:34). According to Duff (2002), the retributive response to crime is indispensable, but it should be combined with the social constructiveness of restorative approaches: "Restorative justice processes are not alternatives to punitive 'pain delivery': they are themselves ways of trying to induce the appropriate kind of pain" (Duff, 2002:97).

Much depends on how punishment is defined. If you consider as punishment every painful obligation that follows, then of course, most initiatives in view of reparation can certainly be called punishments. The direct confrontation with the victim and the disapproval of the offender's beloved ones is painful for the offender; the execution of the mediation agreement or of an imposed community service can be a demanding and unpleasant deprivation of liberty. However, I do not consider these as punishments, for the reasons below (Walgrave, 2003).

Intention

The intentionality in the punishment or "pain delivery" (Christie, 1981) is a critical element. "Punishing someone consists of visiting a deprivation (hard treatment) on him, because he supposedly has committed a wrong,..."[1] (von Hirsch, 1993:9). Three elements are distinguished: hard treatment, the link with the wrong committed before, and also the intention of inflicting the pain. There is a crucial difference between obligations that are inevitably painful, like paying taxes or compensation, and obligations that are imposed with the purpose of imposing pain, like paying a fine (Fatic, 1995:197).

What matters here is the intention of the punisher, not the experience of the one who is punished (Wright, 2003). It is the punisher who considers an action to be wrong and who wants the wrongdoer to suffer for it. Even if a juvenile sees the punishment first of all as a prestigious event for his reputation in his peer group, it will remain a punishment. Conversely, even if he feels the obligation to repair the harm to be hard and calls it a punishment, it actually is no punishment if the intention of the judge was not to make the juvenile suffer, but rather to request from him a reasonable contribution to reparation.

Nevertheless, the hardship of a restorative obligation should be taken into account. Requiring a deprived juvenile who stole and crashed a Jaguar to pay back the full amount of the car would condemn him to a lifetime of repaying and poverty. Even if there is no intention to inflict pain, there must be an awareness of the painful effects. The boy will have to contribute to restoration. It will transcend the material repayment, which will be reduced to a small amount, in view of the boy's financial, mental and social capacities, and his future. The remaining material damage to the victim should be repaid by the insurance or by a Victims' Fund.

Knowing that something will hurt, and taking the hardship into account, is not the same as intentionally inflicting hurt. Pain in restorative justice is only a reason to possibly reduce the obligation, never to augment it. In retributive punishment, on the contrary, the painfulness is the principal yardstick, and its amount may be increased or decreased in order to achieve proportionality in punishment.

Means Versus Goals

Punishment is a means. Restoration is a goal. Punishment can be used to enforce any legal and political system, in the most truly democratic societies as well as the most dictatorial regimes. It is an act of power to express disapproval, possibly to enforce compliance, but it is neutral about the value system it enforces. Restoration, on the contrary, is a potential outcome. The reparation in view includes the victims' losses, and the larger social consequences. This is not morally neutral, but an expression of restoration's orientation to the quality of social life.

Punishment is not the most appropriate way to achieve restoration. On the contrary, empirical research clearly shows that the fixation on pain infliction is very counterproductive for whatever goal is sought (Sherman, 1993, 2003), and especially for achieving possible restoration. The procedure to determine punishment often interferes with the attention to the harm and suffering caused; the threat of punishment makes genuine communication about harm and reparation impossible; and the penalty itself seriously hampers the offender's effort to repair and compensate.

Communication

The most important function of criminal justice is to express social disapproval. The focus on punishment in criminal justice, however, interferes with effective and constructive communication. The sentence may communicate a clear disapproval to the public at large, but it fails to communicate adequately to the other key actors in the crime — the victim and the offender. Good communication needs adequate settings. This is not the case in court, where confrontation prevails over communication, in front of the judge who will at the end decide upon the kind and degree of hard treatment. The offender does not listen to the moralizing message but tries to get away with as lenient a punishment as possible. He does not hear the invitation, but experiences the threat (Wright, 2003).

Understanding the traditional courts' poor communicative potentials, Duff advances another approach to punishment, based on communication through mediation (Duff, 2001): "criminal mediation" would be intended to provoke in the offender a kind of repentance, which is intentionally meant to be a burden. However, mediation is here not seen in its restorative context, but is considered a technique to make the offender suffer morally. It is this sustained centrality of inflicting pain that remains the obstacle for true communication: the offender will be less open for the messages and the victim risks being misused in a process focused on the offender.

RETRIBUTION

Justifications for punishments in penal law can be divided into consequentionalist (utilitarian) or retributivist (essentialist) arguments. According to consequentionalist arguments, the evil of punishment is needed to achieve a greater social good: social order and peace. It is believed that punishment teaches the public at large about the social wrongfulness of certain behavior, or that possible offenders would be deterred by the threat of punishment. In addition, the individual offender could be reformed, or at least incapacitated during a period of incarceration. However, empirical research clearly shows that these ambitions are not fulfilled (Braithwaite, 1999; Sherman, 2003). On the contrary, there is an increasing awareness that relying on punishment for dealing with crime leads to more imprisonment, more human and financial costs, weaker ethics and less public safety (Skolnick, 1995; Tonry, 1995).

Several versions of retributivism exist, but they all basically go back to the Kantian principle that punishing the wrongdoing is a "categorical imperative": it is inherent in morality that wrongdoing must be responded to by imposing hard treatment on the wrongdoer. Because of the wrongdoing, the offender intrinsically deserves to be punished. In fact, the offender has the right to be punished in order to be considered as a morally responsible person. Contrary to consequentionalism, retributivism does not primarily ask questions about possible effects of punishment. The amount of pain to be inflicted depends on the amount of illegitimate advantage or the degree of blameworthiness of the crime (von Hirsch, 1993). By referring solely to the crime already committed, retributivists base sentencing on retrospective considerations, and find in the past the guidelines for assuring proportionality.

The necessity of censure is easy to accept. No community can survive without norms, and they must be enforced. Clear denunciation of norm transgression is a minimum requirement of a justice response.

The question is, however, whether this censure is possible only through intentional infliction of pain. Most ethical systems consider deliberately and coercively imposing suffering on another person as unethical and socially destructive. Why does that not apply to punishment? What arguments do retributivists advance to maintain that punitive pain infliction is an exception in the general rejection of pain infliction?

A Human Need

It is often argued that punishing the evil is a deep human need, to overcome our "resentment"[2] (Moore, 1995/1987), or to express our adherence to the good.

It is doubtful whether anger against wrongdoing is inspired primarily by attachment to the good. Maybe, in fact, the "evil" is not an abstract moral category opposed to another category, the "good." Maybe the sources of both are pragmatic or experiential. In that case, evil is what threatens me, or already has hurt me in my human dignity, my social and material territory, my physical integrity.[3] Anger, then, would be a self-interested emotion in victimized or threatened humans that can provoke actions of revenge. This is, however, no reason for anger to ground the well-reflected, rational, systemic punishment, organized by the state. Civilization is a process of trying to control spontaneous violence, and to make the violence a monopoly of the state (Elias, 1994). Maybe the next step in civilization is to reduce state violence itself by not taking for granted pain infliction after a crime.

There are also empirical reasons to be skeptical about the punishment-as-general-human-need position. Historical studies show that reparation was originally more a concern after norm transgression than paying back through pain infliction (Weitekamp, 1999). Also, systematic surveys of public preferences for ways of responding to crime undoubtedly conclude that making good what was done wrong is preferred over punishing (Sessar, 1999).

An Ethical Obligation

Retributive arguments are basically grounded on ethical foundations: it is a moral imperative that norm transgressions result in punishment. Surprisingly, retributivism hardly questions the ethical value of the normative system itself, the system that punishment is supposed to enforce (Fatic, 1995). Instead, most retributivists seem to equate the legal order with the moral order.

But this equation is not at all evident. Why, for example, is penal law predominantly geared to public order, to individual security and property, and not to social peace, solidarity, and social and economic equity? As mentioned above, punishments can be used in any regime, to enforce any legal rule, including the most immoral ones. Leaving the statutory use of pain infliction open to all these possibilities is a dangerous game, as daily practice overwhelmingly demonstrates.

Proportionality

Because retribution focuses on wrongfulness committed in the past, it provides a manageable yardstick for determining proportionality in the degree of pain delivery (von Hirsch, 1993). For some, this proportionality issue is one of the main reasons for skepticism about restorative justice. With its future-oriented focus on repairing needs and harms, restorative justice would not offer satisfying grounds for proportionality (von Hirsch, 1998).

It is true that the response to crime must be kept within just and reasonable limits. That is why controllable measurements must be available to check the use of power and deprivation of liberty. However, the way proportionality is constructed in punishment is itself highly problematic (Wright, 2003). Moreover, there is no reason to suppose that only punitive retributivism can provide retrospective yardsticks for the intervention. For example, instead of linking the wrongfulness of a behavior to the degree of pain inflicted, the seriousness of harm caused might be related to the intensity of reparative effort required (Walgrave and Geudens, 1996). Deliberative processes might be more appropriate to assess a reasonable and just balance than is traditional criminal justice (Braithwaite, 2002b).

Censure remains the only valid argument for retributivism. Good societies guarantee "dominion" to their citizens, which means that rights and freedoms are assured and taken seriously (Braithwaite and Pettit, 1990). Only when citizens trust in their fellow citizens and in their authorities can democracies really work (Putnam, 1993). But is censure possible only through pain infliction?

CENSURE AND PUNISHMENT

Do we need to punish to express blame? No — and this is true even for punitive retributivists. Von Hirsch (1993:14) accepts that "a condemnatory response to injurious conduct...can be expressed either in a purely...symbolic mode; or else ...." He chooses the punitive way only because of its possible "prudential," or preventative impact.

Von Hirsch's reason for punishment thus is prevention through deterrence, not censure. Empirical research shows that deterrence does not work as universally as is suggested in the theory. If proportionality can be modeled without punishing, the relation between censure and punishment drops off.

In daily life, in families and in schools, disapproval is routinely expressed without punishment. Morally authoritative persons without any power to punish are more effective in influencing moral thinking and behavior than is punishment.

After a crime has occurred, the restorative settings and processes are more appropriate for communicating moral disapproval and provoking repentance than are traditional punitive procedures and sanctions. Without intentional pain infliction, victim-offender mediation or family group conferences, for example, intensely disapprove of the act through those who care for the offender and for whom the offender cares. Most offenders are open to communication if they themselves experience respect and understanding (Bazemore and O'Brien, 2002). They can feel empathy for the suffering of their victims (Harris, 2001) and by that emotionally understand the sense of the norm. Restorative processes position the harm and suffering centrally, presenting victimization as the focal concern, and that provides huge communicative potentials.

Thus, while censuring is needed, punishment is not the only way to do it. Moreover, punishment causes serious social ethical problems that are not resolved by penal theories. In fact, the centrality of punishment as the mainstream response to crime is in itself ethically doubtful. That is why the possible ways of expressing blame without punishment must thoroughly be explored.

Censure, Restoration And Social Ethics

Restorative justice could point the way to a form of censure that is predominantly constructive. Restorative justice is primarily oriented towards repairing as much as possible all harm, suffering and social unrest that have been caused by a crime. The most appropriate ways of achieving this goal are informal deliberative processes that include all parties with a stake in the aftermath of the crime. If deliberative processes cannot be achieved, possible coercive judicial sanctions should as much as possible serve reparative goals.[4] The application of restorative principles goes well beyond crime: these principles are being applied in conflict resolution in neighborhoods, schools, families, and even in international peacemaking and peacekeeping (Braithwaite, 2002a).

The social-ethical foundations of restorative justice are clearly different from those in penal justice. The former approach values the pursuit of a social life in which the collectivity would draw its strength not from top-down rules enforced by threat, coercion, and fear, but from bottom-up motivation based on trust, participation, and support. Elsewhere I have tried to show that such a view promotes social-ethical guidelines or virtues like respect, solidarity, and active responsibility, and that these guidelines are better achieved through restorative justice than through the traditional criminal justice approach (Walgrave, 2002a, 2003). Restorative justice thus escapes the ethical criticism made of punishment because it does not intentionally inflict pain.

Empirical research leads to optimism about the feasibility of restorative justice (e.g., Braithwaite, 1999; McCold, 2003; Kurki, 2003). Victims, offenders, and their communities do come together and do reach constructive agreements, which are carried out reasonably well. Involved parties generally express higher degrees of satisfaction than they do with traditional approaches, and reoffending risks are mostly lower, and certainly not higher. Variations in outcomes depend on several variables, but even the most serious crimes can be dealt with restoratively. There are no indications that social life and public security are adversely affected by restorative practices, and the public appears to support their implementation.

Many ethical and instrumental reasons thus exist for further exploring the potentials of restorative justice to ground a fully-fledged system, as an alternative to traditional penal justice. But does restorative justice also fulfill the functions of retributivism?

RESTORATION AS REVERSED RETRIBUTION?

In retribution, (1) the blameworthiness of the unlawful behavior is clearly expressed, (2) the responsibility of the offender is indicated, and (3) the imbalance is supposed to be repaired by paying back to the offender the suffering he caused by his offence. *Retribuere*, in Latin, literally means to pay back.

Restorative justice clearly articulates the limits of social tolerance because disapproval of the wrong is expressed in the restorative processes. Restorative justice thus provides the essentials of censuring. What distinguishes restorative censuring from punitive censuring is that the reasons for the disapproval are rooted in social relations. The wrongfulness disapproved is directly related to the harm to another person and to social life. Restorative censuring does not refer to an abstract ethical or legal rule, but to the obligation to respect quality of social life.

As in punitive retributivism, restorative justice refers to the responsibility of the offender. In responsibility, the offender is considered as a moral agent by linking the person to his acts and its consequences. Punitive retributivism is based on a passive concept of responsibility: the offender is confronted with his/her responsibility by others, and must submit to the consequences imposed by the criminal justice system. Restorative justice refers to a concept of active responsibility: the offender must take active responsibility by contributing actively to repairing the negative consequences of the offence (Braithwaite and Roche, 2001). Whereas passive responsibility is retrospective only, active responsibility is both retrospective and prospective.

In addition, the "paying back" idea is present in restorative justice, and maybe even in a more genuine form than in punitive retributivism. In punitive retributivism, the balance (whatever this balance may be) is restored by paying back to the offender the suffering and harm he has caused. It is supposed that things are then evened out: both suffer equally much. The problem is, however, that "...balancing the harm done by the offender with further harm inflicted on the offender...only adds to the total amount of harm in the world" (Wright, 1992:525). The amount of suffering is doubled, but equally spread.

In restorative justice, the offender's "paying-back" role in punitive retributivism is reversed from a passive to an active role: he must himself pay back by repairing as much as possible the harm and suffering caused. Instead of restoring the balance by doubling the total amount of suffering, it is now restored by taking suffering away. Retribution in its genuine meaning is achieved, in a constructive way. This reversed, restorative retributivism also may include a kind of proportionality that, however, refers not to "just desert," but to "just due." The question now is what can reasonably be expected from the offender to "pay back" for the losses he has caused.

CONCLUSION

Surprisingly, perhaps, restoration and retribution appear to have much in common (Zehr, 2002): clear censure of unacceptable behavior, an appeal to responsibility, a trial to restore a balance. Further exploration of this holds great promises. Finding commonalities also helps to point to fundamental differences. In my view, "restorativists" should come to grips with the necessity of using coercive power when deliberative processes appear to be impossible. The phobia of many of them against considering it not only obscures commonalities with retributivists, but also makes it difficult to explore the essential difference: the assumption that intentional pain infliction is indispensable to censuring wrongful behavior. That is, in my view, a principle that restorative justice cannot encompass.

Address correspondence to: Lode Walgrave, Professor of Criminology, Katholieke Universiteit Leuven (Belgium), Hooverplein 10 B-3000 Leuven, Belgium. E-mail: <Lode.walgrave@law.kuleuven.ac.be>.

REFERENCES

Bazemore, G. and S. O'Brien (2002). "The Quest for a Restorative Model of Rehabilitation: Theory-for-Practice and Practice-for-Theory." In: L. Walgrave (ed.), *Restorative Justice and the Law*. Cullompton, Devon, UK: Willan Publishing.

—— and L. Walgrave (1999). "Restorative Juvenile Justice. In Search of Fundamentals and an Outline for Systemic Reform." In: G. Bazemore and L. Walgrave (eds.), *Restorative Juvenile Justice. Restoring the Harm of Youth Crime*. Monsey, NY: Criminal Justice Press.

Braithwaite, J. (2002a). *Restorative Justice and Responsive Regulation*. Oxford, UK: Oxford University Press.

—— (2002b). "In Search of Restorative Jurisprudence." In: L. Walgrave (ed.), *Restorative Justice and the Law*. Cullompton, Devon, UK: Willan Publishing.

—— (1999). "Restorative Justice: Assessing Optimistic and Pessimistic Accounts." In: M. Tonry (ed.), *Crime and Justice: A Review of Research*. Chicago, IL: University of Chicago Press.

—— and D. Roche (2001). "Responsibility and Restorative Justice." In: G. Bazemore and M. Schiff (eds.), *Restorative Community Justice: Repairing Harm and Transforming Communities*. Cincinnati, OH: Anderson.

—— and Ph. Pettit (1990). *Not Just Desert. A Republican Theory of Criminal Justice*. Oxford, UK: Clarendon.

Christie, N. (1981). *Limits to Pain*. London, UK: Martinson.

Daly, K. (2000). "Revisiting the Relationship between Retributive and Restorative Justice." In: H. Strang and J. Braithwaite (eds.), *Restorative Justice: Philosophy to Practice*. Dartmouth, UK: Ashgate.

Debuyst, C. (1990). "Pour Introduire une Histoire de la Criminologie: Les Problématique du Départ." *Déviance et Société* 14(4):347-376.

Dignan, J. (2002). "Restorative Justice and the Law: The Case for an Integrated, Systemic Approach." In: L. Walgrave (ed.), *Restorative Justice and the Law*. Cullompton, Devon, UK: Willan Publishing.

Duff, A. (2002). "Restorative Punishment and Punitive Restoration." In: L. Walgrave (ed.), *Restorative Justice and the Law*. Cullompton, Devon, UK: Willan Publishing.

—— (2001). *Punishment, Communication and Community*. Oxford, UK: Oxford University Press.

Eglash, A. (1979). "Beyond Retribution: Creative Restitution." In: J. Hudson and B. Galaway (eds.), *Restitution in Criminal Justice*. Lexington, MA: Heath and Company.

Elias, N. (1994). *The Civilisation Process*. Oxford, UK: Blackwell.

Fatic, A. (1995). *Punishment and Restorative Crime-Handling*. Aldershot, UK: Avebury.

Harris, N. (2001). "Shaming and Shame: Regulating Drink-Driving." In: E. Ahmed, N. Harris, J. Braithwaite and V. Braithwaite (eds.), *Shame Management through Reintegration*. Cambridge, UK: Cambridge University Press.

Kurki, L. (2003). "Evaluating Restorative Justice Practices." In: A. von Hirsch, J. Roberts, A. Bottoms, K. Roach and M. Schiff (eds.), *Restorative Justice and Criminal Justice. Competing or Reconcilable Paradigms?* Oxford: Hart.

McCold, P. (2003). "A Survey of Assessment Research on Mediation and Conferencing." In: L. Walgrave (ed.), *Repositioning Restorative Justice*. Cullompton, Devon, UK: Willan Publishing.

—— (2000). "Towards a Holistic Vision of Restorative Juvenile Justice: A Reply to the Maximalist Model." *Contemporary Justice Review* 3(4):357-414.

Moore, M. (1995). "The Moral Worth of Retribution." In: J. Murphy (ed.), *Punishment and Rehabilitation*. Belmont, CA: Wadsworth Publishing. (Reprinted from F. Schoeman [ed.], [1987], *Responsibility, Character and Emotions*. Cambridge University Press.)

Putnam, R. (1993). *Making Democracy Work: Civic Traditions in Modern Italy*. Princeton, NJ: Princeton University Press.

Sessar, K. (1999). "Punitive Attitudes of the Public: Reality and Myth." In: G. Bazemore and L. Walgrave (eds.), *Restorative Juvenile Justice: Repairing the Harm of Youth Crime*. Monsey, NY: Criminal Justice Press.

Sherman, L. (2003). "Reason for Emotion: Reinventing Justice with Theories, Innovations and Research. The American Society of Criminology 2002 Presidential Address." *Criminology* 41(1):1-37.

—— (1993). "Defiance, Deterrence and Irrelevance: A Theory of the Criminal Sanction." *Journal of Research in Crime and Delinquency* 30:445-473.

Skolnick, J. (1995). "What Not To Do about Crime. The American Society of Criminology 1994 Presidential Address." *Criminology* 33(10):1-15.

Tonry, M. (1995). *Malign Neglect: Race, Crime and Punishment in America*. New York, NY: Oxford University Press.

Van Ness, D. and K. Heetderks Strong (2002). *Restoring Justice* (2nd ed.). Cincinnati, OH: Anderson.

von Hirsch, A. (1998). "Penal Theories." In: M. Tonry (ed.), *The Handbook of Crime and Punishment*. New York/Oxford: Oxford University Press.

—— (1993). *Censure and Sanctions*. Oxford, UK: Clarendon.

—— J. Roberts, A. Bottoms, K. Roach and M. Schiff (eds.) (2003). *Restorative Justice and Criminal Justice: Competing or Reconcilable Paradigms?* Oxford, UK: Hart.

Walgrave, L. (2003). "Imposing Restoration Instead of Inflicting Pain: Reflections on the Judicial Reaction to Crime." In: A. von Hirsch, J. Roberts, A.E. Bottoms, K. Roach and M. Schiff (eds.), *Restorative Justice and Criminal Justice: Competing or Reconcilable Paradigms?* Oxford, UK: Hart.

—— (2002a). "From Community to Dominion: In Search of Social Values for Restorative Justice." In: E. Weitekamp and H-J. Kerner (eds.), *Restorative Justice: Theoretical Foundations*. Cullompton, Devon, UK: Willan Publishing.

—— (2002b). "Restorative Justice and the Law: Socio-Ethical and Juridical Foundations for a Systemic Approach." In: L. Walgrave (ed.), *Restorative Justice and the Law*. Cullompton, Devon, UK: Willan Publishing.

—— and H. Geudens (1996). "The Restorative Proportionality of Community Service for Juveniles." *European Journal of Crime, Criminal Law and Criminal Justice* 4(4):361-380.

Weitekamp, E. (1999). "History of Restorative Justice." In: G. Bazemore and L. Walgrave (eds.), *Restorative Juvenile Justice. Repairing the Harm of Youth Crime*. Monsey, NY: Criminal Justice Press.

Wright, M. (1992). "Victim-Offender Mediation as a Step Toward a Restorative System of Justice." In: H. Messmer and H.U. Otto (eds.), *Restorative Justice on Trial*. Dordrecht/Boston: Kluwer Academic Publishers.

Wright, M. (2003). "Is it Time to Question the Concept of Punishment?" In: L. Walgrave (ed.), *Repositioning Restorative Justice*. Cullompton, Devon, UK: Willan Publishing.

Zehr, H. (2002). "Journey to Belonging." In: E. Weitekamp and H-J. Kerner (eds.), *Restorative Justice: Theoretical Foundations*. Cullompton, Devon, UK: Willan Publishing.

—— (1990/95). *Changing Lenses: A New Focus for Crime and Justice*. Scottsdale, Pa: Herald Press.

NOTES

1. Contrary to von Hirsch, I do not add disapprobation as another characteristic. Punishment is often administered routinely, and experienced as a "prize" to be paid, without any moral reflection at all.

2. Moore uses this word to refer to the enduring indignation or anger that a crime may provoke.

3. "Le crime ne blesse les sentiments que d'une façon secondaire et dérivée; primitivement, ce sont les intérêts qu'il lèse." ("Crime hurts feelings only in a secondary and a derived way; originally it is the interests that it hurts.") (Maxwel, 1914, cited in Debuyst, 1990:357.)

4. It is a point of debate whether coercion can be included in restorative justice. I do believe that, while deliberative processes are the most appropriate for achieving restorative goals, (judicial) sanctions in view of reparation should complete the restorative approach, if the deliberative processes cannot take place (Bazemore and Walgrave, 1999; Dignan, 2002; Walgrave, 2003).

PART II.
STAKEHOLDER ISSUES

Who Are The "Players," And How Do We Involve Them?

The criminal justice system is captured in the image of lady justice balancing her scales. Blindfolded under the pretense of fairness, she is frequently unable to see the experiences of those impacted by crime. Restorative justice removes this blindfold, exposing the people — victims, offenders and community — to full view.

Restorative justice advocates have created their own images to represent the philosophy. Many use the image of a triangle, with each point representing a stakeholder individual or group of individuals.[1] Others have created artistic expressions such as a patchwork "quilt" stamped with handprints. Still others imagine a "do no harm room" furnished with, among other things, comfortable chairs arranged in a circle. These more human images suggest that the core of restorative justice focuses on people.

People — victims, offenders and communities — do indeed make up the heart of restorative justice. Concerned with their experiences and needs, the philosophy invites each stakeholder to sit at the head of the justice table. While at that table, they have the opportunity to talk about their experiences with the crime, the depth and nature of their pain, and their needs in order to be able to move through their experiences and to seek ways in which to continue on their life's journey. All such "stakeholders," whether sitting alone at the table or joined by the others, sit in the head chair.

The authors who follow in this section share ideas and concerns about the roles, responsibilities and possibilities that exist for victims, offenders and communities within the philosophy and practice of restorative justice. Mary Achilles begins the victim exploration by suggesting that restorative justice challenges victim advocates to respond to victim needs in a new way. Susan Herman critiques restorative justice and suggests a "parallel justice" system to meet victims' needs, especially those needs that have nothing to do with the offender. Lorraine Stutzman Amstutz invites us to improve how restorative justice practitioners understand and work with victim service providers. Heather Strang argues that restorative justice, by providing the opportunity for face-to-face encounters, creates necessary space for such feelings as anger and outrage and the powerful impact these emotions can have on the offender.

Barb Toews and Jackie Katounas turn to offender issues and suggest that there are significant gaps in the philosophy and its current practice from this perspective; they challenge practitioners to understand restorative justice from an offender's point of view. Gordon Bazemore and Dee Bell explore how restorative justice and rehabilitation can work together. Allison Morris and Gabrielle Maxwell take a critical look at how shame is currently being understood and used in practice, warning that its use is a risky venture. Russ Immarigeon closes this section by challenging the field for its inattention to the role of restorative justice as an alternative to incarceration.

Paul McCold and George Pavlich offer their perspectives on the role of community in the philosophy. McCold considers the definition of both the "micro-" and "macro-"communities, and outlines roles for each community in response to crime. Pavlich offers a critique of "community" and suggests the notion of "hospitality" as way to approach the community's role in restorative justice.

These authors raise many issues but do not exhaust all the questions under consideration for stakeholders. Questions such as these merit careful consideration:

- How open are we to what stakeholders have to tell us about their experiences and needs? To what extent are we determining stakeholder needs for them or allowing stakeholders to tell us their needs?

- Are we involving stakeholders in programs, practices and theory-building in the manner and to the degree that they are requesting or requiring?

- To what degree do the experiences of some stakeholders take priority over, co-opt or influence the needs of other stakeholders? Who decides this? What are the implications for this?

- What are the impressions and perceptions of restorative justice among various stakeholder groups and their advocates?

- Can or should efforts to promote healing and provide symbolic reparation fully take the place of punishment, retribution or prisons?

- How can we find an appropriate division between community and individual concerns and interests?

While these questions are relevant to all stakeholders, there are in addition a host of specific questions that pertain to each individual group of stakeholders. Whether broad or specific, however, all these questions challenge us to listen. Through listening we can begin to understand the issues — including the nuances — important to victims, offenders and communities. We may also be challenged to identify the biases and misperceptions that we bring with us to restorative justice practice. Ultimately, we may be afforded a new vision of what is true and necessary for justice.

NOTES

1. The term "stakeholder," widely used in restorative justice, is somewhat unfortunate in its origins. It derives, apparently, from European settlers of North America driving a stake into the ground to claim land — land that was originally held by aboriginal or First Nation peoples. Perhaps the field should be challenged to find an alternative term.

Chapter 5.
Can Restorative Justice Live Up To Its Promise To Victims?

by

Mary Achilles

Several years ago, Howard Zehr and I co-authored an article (2001) on the promises and challenges of restorative justice for crime victims. In our discussion, we emphasized a variety of issues and dangers. We raised concerns, for example, about the offender-oriented nature of many restorative justice programs and practitioners, and warned about the dangers of the field being co-opted away from a genuine concern about victims. We questioned whether the growing focus on the community as stakeholder might cause victims to be sidelined.

While those concerns remain legitimate, I am now inclined to take a more expanded view about whether restorative justice can or is living up to the promise that it makes to victims. More importantly, I have reached a conclusion about the nature of my role as a victim advocate in advancing the concept of restorative justice.

As I see it, the promise of restorative justice is the elevation of victims to the position of stakeholders in a justice process that starts immediately from the point of the harm. They are no longer relegated to the sidelines, dependent on someone else to let them in. For a victim advocate such as myself who has spent most of her professional career working with crime victims, this is a dream worth chasing! However, it has become clear to me that we are a long way from seeing a fully restorative system. The journey toward a society that accepts its obligations toward both the victim and the offender will be a long one and is not unlike the journey of a victim to build a new life in the aftermath of his or her victimization.

In order to deliver on the promise that restorative justice makes to crime victims, we all must change the way we respond to victims. I suggest that we use the framework and principles of restorative justice outlined by Zehr and Mika (Zehr, 2002:64-69) to ensure that our response is holistic. These start from three premises: (1) Crime is fundamentally a violation of people and interpersonal relationships, (2) violations create obligations and liabilities, and (3) justice should seek to heal and put right wrongs. Zehr and Mika then elaborate the implications of these premises.

In considering restorative justice for victims, we need to focus on both individual victims and on the victim rights and services community as a whole. These principles offer a framework with which to explore how to change our responses to each of them.

CHANGING OUR RESPONSE TO INDIVIDUAL VICTIMS

In order to change our response to victims, we need to focus on making a difference in the justice experience for our individual clients. Since understanding and accepting restorative justice principles, my work with crime victims has been a new, different and exciting experience. Years ago, I was shocked by my internal response when a victim, who had been seriously assaulted, presented me with my first request to meet with an offender. I had a thousand thoughts about why she should not do it and why she was mistaken in making this request. Even though she could clearly articulate her reason for meeting, her journey in working through the issues that arose in the aftermath of the crime, and her readiness for this encounter, I had great difficulty dealing with my own reactions so that I could assist her properly. She was making a request that did not fit into my framework of what her needs were or should be. I began to wonder how many other victims had tried to ask me for this service, or some other type of service, about which I did not, could not or would not hear them.

Our ability to see, hear and experience victims in our work makes a difference in how we respond to them. If we truly want to respond to them in a restorative way, we need to be completely open to what it is they may need as they define their needs. We cannot limit their selections for services to only those available choices that fit our prescribed menu.

Listening to victims requires that we understand the framework and assumptions we bring to this work. I have found that my judgment came from the framework I had built through the eyes of the justice system. The more I exposed myself to other views, particularly to the principles of restorative justice, the better able I was to change my perspective from judgment to curiosity. While I was able to hear victims before, this curiosity expanded my current capacity to do so. Now, when hearing requests from victims, I am able to hear those requests within a framework of curiosity and respond with an attitude of "How can I assist you in making that happen? Tell me more of why you need that."

For instance, when a victim expresses interest in finding the stolen property that was not recovered by the police, I no longer say, as I had said for years, "That stuff is long gone." Instead, I think differently about my response and ask how I can help her to find it.

This kind of curiosity is an interesting concept, simple yet easily elusive. The above victim of theft, still heartbroken and distraught several years after the crime, continued to talk to people, including my program staff, about finding the victrola that was stolen. Eventually we had a unique idea — how about we ask the offender?! Although we were not about to find out specifics, we were able to obtain information on the general location and the type of store to which the victrola had been sold. Finding this information helpful, the victim was able to make some attempts to locate the property. In the end, the victim never located the victrola, but she was more empowered and more satisfied knowing that she had done everything that she could to try to find this treasured item.

This exchange of judgment for curiosity has been foundational to the work that we do everyday in the Office of the Victim Advocate in Pennsylvania. We are statutorily required to provide notice to victims of inmate releases and to petition the Board of Probation and Parole to deny parole or set conditions of parole. But this framework helps us to listen to victims and design our program accordingly. We now feel obligated to provide some element of education and information on how the system works. This includes our representation of their position to the board, but knowing that at some point 90% of the inmates in the state correctional system will be released to the street, we also help victims to assess what they need to prepare for this eventuality. These two services, representing their positions and predicting and preparing for inmates' eventual release, are equally important services. One without the other seems less than acceptable to us now.

The question remains: Can restorative justice deliver on its promise to those victims who say things that we do not want to hear? For instance:

- Can we truly live with the results of what victims want?

- Are we able to stand with them while they are on this long and circuitous journey?

- Can we make room for victims in a restorative process when they are screaming out in pain or when they are vengeful, angry and full of rage?

- Can we make room for victims when they are not interested in what happens to the offender or, if they are interested in what happens, their interest does not fit with what some of us would refer to as a restorative response?

The answers to these questions remain to be seen.

Little by little, case by case we learn what victims and offenders want. These are the situations that both broaden my vision and provide greater clarity about restorative justice. Through our Office of the Victim Advocate Mediation Program for Victims of Violent Crime, I have learned that no one victim enters this mediation/facilitated dialogue process for the same reasons as another victim. I have experienced my ability to care for and advocate for the offender in this process without losing my sense of dedication to crime victims. I value and respect our volunteer facilitators, despite the great differences among them in their reasons for volunteering and the differing frameworks they bring. I have witnessed how the program is restorative to a significant degree even though that does not necessarily mean that everyone is happy with each other in the end. I would venture to say that mediation/facilitated dialogue is a stepping-stone to the next level of their lifelong journeys.

I have not yet seen a system or a program model that is fully restorative. I have only seen those that are restorative to varying degrees. Within the Office of the Victim Advocate, I run a few programs that, to varying degrees, are restorative in that they offer victims a variety of service options that did not exist previously in Pennsylvania. However, not all victims choose the option of speaking to inmates or even caring about them. Are they bad? The victims at the national level who are touting restorative justice are exceptional in their ability to turn their experience into advocacy and action. Not all victims take this road. Are victims expected to educate themselves about and understand the need for the community to be responsive to the offender also? I think not. However, I am concerned that there is an underlying assumption that they are expected to do so. The victim's journey is so long and circuitous that there is a question of whether restorative justice can wait for the victim to be ready to identify all his or her needs, including those that never surface until much later in the recovery process.

It often appears that mediation/facilitated dialogue has become synonymous with the term restorative justice. Even though I know this not to be true, I rarely see any program calling itself restorative that does not have these engagements between victims and their offenders as a fundamental part of the program. In these cases, the impression that one gets is that a victim who does not want to participate in such a program is less worthy of justice. Many people advocating for restorative justice will highlight this engagement as something that a restorative program offers that the current system of justice does not offer. This same restorative program, however, does not offer other options for victims that might be currently available in the existing system. These include issues of statutory and constitutionally guaranteed rights to notice, to input and overall participation, protection and the validation that occurs from the system when an offender is identified, processed and sanctioned within a known range of sanctions.

I am also frustrated when I hear restorative justice advocates describe a restorative system by contrasting it to the current justice system that they call retributive. Typically it is a presentation of what the current system does not offer victims and what a better role the restorative system grants to victims. Unfortunately, however, there is no completely restorative system in the United States to point to. Also, there is no recognition that there are good things for victims in the current system. This last point seems to have gotten lost on many proponents of restorative justice. I so often felt that I am being asked to throw the baby out with the bath water.

A victim's guaranteed right, either by statute or constitution, within the current system is not something that would be easy for victims to give up. How can we be sure that we will not have to fight for inclusion in a restorative system the same way we have needed to do in our current system? Issues like incarceration or protection of the victim from the offender are clearly defined in our current system of justice, but they seem quite fuzzy in the theory of restorative justice. Victims might be willing to trade reduced offender jail time in exchange for having other needs, such as restitution, met. But in a domestic violence situation, for example, would a restorative system place a priority on offender incarceration over rehabilitation so that the victim can have some emotional space to pull her life together?

Since most presentations on restorative justice use mediation/facilitated dialogue as the best example of restorative justice, I am compelled to ask, "Would I want to trade off the protections of the current system for an opportunity to meet with the offender?" There is, as I have learned first hand, a great need to offer such encounters to victims and offenders. What this opportunity presents to these parties is unique and not currently routinely offered in the current system. I would be the first to say to my colleagues that we as victim service providers must work to ensure that these services are available in all communities for all victims. However, addressing the basic needs of victims for safety and security, ventilation and validation, preparation and prediction and information and education requires more than an opportunity to meet with your offender. I would now say that mediation/facilitated dialogue is a need but it is not necessarily at the top of the list of needs.

Victims may have needs related to meeting with their offender, but that does not mean that they should be required to do so or even that the system should be designed to suggest that they do so. The issue of obligations that are created by the offender toward the victim as a result of the crime is a challenging issue in terms of program design. Is the victim required to participate in an encounter to provide an opportunity for the offender to make amends? Sometimes the greatest need of an individual victim may be to keep distance between them and their offender. Can a restorative justice system accommodate this? Can it value and respect this request? Sometimes the only way to pay on our obligations is to give back to someone else other than the one that we have harmed. Sometimes the obligation may be best met simply becoming a productive citizen. This is an under-explored concept in restorative justice.

CHANGING OUR RESPONSE TO THE VICTIM SERVICE COMMUNITY

In order to change our response to the victim services community, we need to be willing to learn from each other. Once I recognized, understood and accepted the concept and principles of restorative justice, I became a better advocate for victims and for victim service providers. My ability to hear them better made me better able to assist them. Equally important, I found that the very work I had been doing, no matter how minimal by my standards, was restorative. Restorative justice starts with a holistic community response to crime victims. While I initially thought that restorative justice advocates were forcing me to get on a train that was already out of the station, I realized that, in fact, I was on the train.

Those of us in the victim services community need a variety of things from restorative justice advocates, and even the community as a whole. For instance, we need:

- Discussion about the services and protections that victims need from all aspects of the community in the aftermath of crime.

- Language that is similar to that of the victim service community so we know that there is an understanding of the crisis and trauma of victimization and the experiences of victims.

- Receptivity when we talk about our collective experiences and knowledge of picking up the human carnage in the aftermath of crime.

- Recognition that the majority of victim needs are not related to the offender or anything that he or she can do.

- Awareness that the community as a whole has a great responsibility toward the victim.

- Understanding that the fundamental message in all responses and services to victims is that they are valued. This means recognizing their experiences, validating their worth and providing the short- and long-term care that they require.

- Acknowledgement that the victim is not responsible for rehabilitating the offender nor is the victim required to actively care about the offender in any way.

There are also things that those of us in the victim services community can do. We can recognize that restorative justice, in whatever form is presented, may in fact offer some new and different options for our clients. This may mean that, even though we may view a program to be for offenders, it may have something to offer a victim. We can collectively, as an advocacy and service community, replace our judgment with curiosity.

We should challenge ourselves to think about the nexus that is created between the victim and offender during the commission of a crime. From this nexus, specific needs may arise for the victim that can only be addressed by the offender. We cannot deny that this may require engagement between them, be it direct, indirect or through a third party. We need not be afraid if a man wants to meet with his wife's killer or, as mentioned earlier, a victim needs to have someone ask the offender about the location of stolen property. We must, then, recognize the need to talk about this with victims, and offer these opportunities for engagement as part of basic services to crime victims. They may not need them within the first 24 hours after the crime, but these options need to be available in every community for all victims who may choose this service.

Victim services can make a contribution by helping people within the system to view victims differently. Often the views of actors within the system are shared by the loudest and harshest voices. If system actors are viewing all victims as vengeful and punishment-driven, then it is our responsibility to show them how victims truly experience crime and to help them understand that victims want different things from the system depending on who they are and their particular needs.

In my view, the services that victim service programs currently provide are restorative. Crisis hotlines, medical and legal accompaniment, free counseling services, assistance with crime victim compensation and other financial recovery programs — all these are restorative services. These are services that must be provided before we can think about justice as it relates to the offender. Justice for victims would include the availability of these services in all communities, and at an adequate level.

All of the various communities that are drawn to restorative justice need to be more understanding and respectful of each other if we are to deliver on its promise to victims. We need to acknowledge that we each have something to offer victims and to understand where in the order of priorities our services fall. In our commitment to empowering crime victims, we must be open to all that they may need and to all of the components of the community that may have something to offer them, including the offender. Perhaps we need to stop defining ourselves as belonging to different camps and start seeing ourselves as parts of a whole. We all have a part — the parts just may not yet be connected.

Address correspondence to: Mary Achilles, Victim Advocate, Office of the Victim Advocate, 1101 South Front Street, Suite 5200, Harrisburg, PA 17104.

REFERENCES

Achilles, M. and H. Zehr (2001). "Restorative Justice for Crime Victims: The Promise, The Challenge." In: G. Bazemore, G. Schiff and M. Schiff (eds.), *Restorative Community Justice: Repairing Harm and Transforming Communities.* Cincinnati, OH: Anderson.

Zehr, H. (2002). *The Little Book of Restorative Justice.* Intercourse, PA: Good Books.

Chapter 6.
Is Restorative Justice Possible Without A Parallel System for Victims?

by

Susan Herman

Many victims of crime feel ignored, excluded, and profoundly disrespected by the criminal justice system. The opportunities to participate are narrowly defined and few. Victims' emotional, physical, and financial needs are rarely fully addressed, if addressed at all. And, for those who seek it, the traditional criminal justice system provides no meaningful interaction with offenders. As a result, notwithstanding the many reforms and legal protections created on behalf of crime victims during the last 30 years, victims frequently still feel alienated by and unsatisfied with their experiences of our justice system.

Proponents of restorative justice have argued that this alternative response to crime has the potential to address victims' needs. Restorative justice promotes healing and strengthens the social bonds which serve as the foundation of our communities. Empathy, mutual understanding, restitution and accountability are guideposts of restorative justice. A high priority is placed on maintaining or restoring individual dignity. Crime is not depersonalized, as it is in our criminal justice system. Rather, crime is viewed as an experience between individuals, in the midst of a community. All three parties — victims, offenders, and communities — have the opportunity to acknowledge how the crime has harmed each, and all three attempt to rebuild social ties and recreate healthy and productive relationships.

This essay examines whether restorative justice, so defined, provides a sufficient framework for addressing victims' needs. After reaching the conclusion that restorative justice, although quite valuable in many respects, still falls short in critical ways, the essay outlines a proposal that attempts to address these gaps. The discussion which follows is a proposal for parallel justice, a framework developed by the National Center for Victims of Crime for two separate responses to crime, one focused on the offender, the other focused on the victim.

A CRITIQUE FROM THE VICTIM'S PERSPECTIVE

From a victim's point of view, restorative justice offers a number of important improvements over the traditional criminal justice process. Victims are given an opportunity to tell their story and to be heard. Restorative justice views victims as stakeholders in the process, not just witnesses who provide evidence. Restorative justice provides opportunities for discussions about how to resolve the underlying problems that gave rise to the crime as well as problems created by the crime. Through a dialogue with the offender, victims are often able to answer many of their questions about the circumstances of and motivation for the crime. For many victims, when an offender offers an apology or shows remorse, the experience can be very meaningful. Victims often feel isolated in the aftermath of crime; restorative justice can help them reconnect with other members of their community. Yet, notwithstanding these positive attributes, restorative justice still fails to meet critical needs of crime victims in at least four respects.

Restorative Justice Can Serve Only A Small Number Of Victims

Most victims do not participate in any formal process to resolve the issues surrounding their victimization. There are many reasons for this. The victim may not report the crime to the police, the police may not find the offender, the offender may not be arrested, the prosecutor may not pursue the case, or the case may never make it to trial. To the extent that restorative justice models depend upon an arrest, an official complaint, or a criminal justice disposition to trigger the restorative justice process, only a small percentage of victims will be able to take advantage of their benefits.

Even those restorative justice programs that do not operate within the criminal justice system typically still require the active participation of an offender, and that offender is required to admit some culpability. Consequently, the number of these cases eligible for restorative justice interventions is also limited. For those few victims with identified offenders who acknowledge some responsibility for the harms they have caused, restorative justice may present a far more appealing option than the traditional criminal justice system. Unfortunately, however, only a small percentage of crime victims have that option.

Restorative Justice Processes Are Offender-Centered

Even though they are often referred to as victim-centered, restorative justice programs are still very offender-oriented: the process is limited to those cases with an offender who admits culpability and wants to participate, and the remedies are limited to what the offender and, secondarily, the community can provide.

A more victim-oriented response to crime would ask, what do victims need to repair the harm caused by crime — in other words, to be "restored" as much as possible. If the process and the remedies were more victim-oriented, our justice response would begin whenever a crime occurs and would attend to the needs of all victims. Restorative justice processes currently can occur with or without the victim as long as the victim's perspective is represented by someone. A more satisfying justice process would also take place with or without offenders and address the needs of all victims.

Restorative Justice Does Not Address Many Critical Needs Of Victims

While restorative justice programs can promote healing, repairing the harm experienced by victims is often far more complicated than apologies, restitution and relationship-building. Some victims move on with their lives fairly easily, but many suffer continuing trauma without the services and support they need. Victims often suffer lowered academic performance, decreased work productivity, and severe loss of confidence. Mental illness, drug and alcohol abuse, and suicide are far more common among crime victims than the general public. Addressing these needs can require long-term sophisticated counseling, assistance with safety planning, or relocation. Any number of social services may be required to rebuild a life — emergency day care for the parent who needs to get a job to handle new crime-related expenses, substance abuse treatment for the traumatized victim who has turned to drugs, an escort service for the victim now too afraid to leave home or go to the store alone, employment counseling or training for the victim who no longer can perform his or her old job, or even something as simple as new locks or windows for his or her home.

Many, if not most, of these needs cannot be met by individual offenders or other stakeholders who participate in restorative justice because there is only so much they can do. And sometimes, the restoration victims seek has very little to do with an ongoing relationship with an offender or a community. The restoration of victims should not be limited to the resources that an offender and a community of stakeholders bring to the table.

Restorative Justice Provides No Active Role For The Government In Rebuilding Victims' Lives

From a victim's perspective, one of the reasons the traditional criminal justice system is inadequate is that it does not have authority to call upon the full range of resources necessary to meet the many needs of victims. Many restorative justice practitioners, in a commendable effort to humanize the justice system and reinforce interpersonal relationships, have chosen to keep the state in the background, or not involve the government at all. Only the state, however, has the authority to marshal the full range of resources necessary to address victims' potentially long-term, complicated problems. The day care, the employment counseling, the substance abuse treatment, or the long-range housing needs of victims usually cannot be adequately addressed by offenders and communities alone. When a crime occurs, society as a whole should be asked to help victims rebuild their lives.

Furthermore, a governmental role in responding to all crime victims would convey an important message — one not heard in either the traditional criminal justice system or restorative justice programs. The government can speak on behalf of society at large when it acknowledges that what happened to a victim is wrong. This could be a powerful and enormously beneficial statement for victims because it would not only validate their experiences, it would elevate it to a public concern. While restorative justice can provide important opportunities for offenders and communities to acknowledge the harm caused to a victim, this interaction is qualitatively different from a statement by the government on behalf of society at large. The traditional criminal justice system does not fulfill this societal obligation to victims. Neither does restorative justice.

PARALLEL JUSTICE: A NEW FRAMEWORK FOR PROVIDING JUSTICE

Parallel justice envisions a very different response to crime. It addresses many of the limitations of our traditional criminal justice and restorative justice paradigms and draws upon the strengths of each. Parallel justice provides two separate paths to justice — one for victims and one for offenders.

For every reported crime, our society spends enormous resources responding to the incident and trying to apprehend and prosecute the offender. In the parallel justice framework, there would always be a second, *parallel,* set of victim-oriented responses — a focused effort to help ensure the victim's safety, to help the victim recover from the trauma of crime, and to provide resources to help the victim rebuild his or her life.

When offenders are brought to the bar of justice they are held accountable by the state for harms they caused. There is a societal response to the offender that says, "You violated the law and we will hold you accountable, punish you if it is appropriate, isolate you if needed, and offer you services to help reintegrate you back into the community." Society responds to offenders through our government. Less formal restorative processes often complement this response and reinforce individual and community-level relationships. The governmental response to offenders, however, from law enforcement and prosecutors to courts and corrections officials, serves as a foundation for providing justice to offenders and communities harmed by crime. This criminal justice system response reinforces the public nature of crime and the larger concerns and obligations of society at large.

The individuals who have been harmed — the victims of crime — have no comparable experience of a societal response to them. A parallel societal response to victims would be as multifaceted as our societal response to offenders. It would require reorienting and expanding the goals of our criminal justice agencies, as well as developing new government and social service functions.

There are some guiding principles for implementing parallel justice:

First, when a crime is reported, the safety of the victim should be a high priority for police and other criminal justice agencies.

Perhaps our most fundamental imperative for all crime victims is to provide for their safety. Studies have shown that victims of almost any kind of crime are more likely to be victimized again. It is in everyone's interest that reasonable steps be taken to prevent repeat victimization. Therefore, when law enforcement responds to a crime, a primary goal — in addition to collecting evidence and apprehending the offender — should be to reduce the chance that the victim will be victimized again. Every victim deserves a safety plan, and victim advocates should be involved at every step along the way, supporting victims, bringing their expertise into the safety planning process.

The obligation to provide safety for victims, however, should extend beyond law enforcement. For example, when judges set bail conditions, one of their goals should be to keep victims safe. When prosecutors enter into plea agreements, one of their goals should be victim safety. When corrections agencies release prisoners back into the community, and parole agencies supervise them, one of their goals should be victim safety.

Second, every victim of crime should be offered immediate support, compensation for losses, and practical assistance.

Victim compensation should be expanded to cover all victims of crime, both violent and non-violent crime, as well as more categories of losses. Last year, the U.S. Congress appropriated nearly $20 billion for law enforcement and corrections. By contrast, the federal government devotes roughly $550 million each year for victim compensation and support services — money that comes solely from offender fines and penalties. Under parallel justice, compensating victims for their losses would be a responsibility shared by offenders and society at large. Restorative justice programs should continue to promote the payment of restitution by offenders, but we should also use tax revenue to meet victims' needs.

Third, all crime victims should have an opportunity to explain what happened to them, the impact the crime had on their lives, and what resources they need to get back on track.

A key component of parallel justice is a public forum separate from the criminal justice system, which would offer victims an opportunity to explain what happened to them and what they need. Under a system of parallel justice, our society would say to all victims, regardless of whether their offender was ever identified or prosecuted in a criminal court, "What happened to you is wrong and we will help you." Honoring this separate social obligation to acknowledge the harm experienced by victims and actively help them rebuild their lives should be a critical part of providing a just response to crime. It's therapeutic in and of itself to know that society at large (represented by our government) cares enough to take the time to listen. These forums would also provide an opportunity for our society to hear victims' accounts of crime. We need to understand victims' experiences to be able to address crime — to prevent it and to respond to it. We also need to hear victims explain the impact of crime to be able to help them with the most appropriate and effective services and resources.

At a more fundamental level, these forums would reinforce bonds between individual victims and society at large. Just as interpersonal relationships are harmed by crime, a victim's trust and confidence in our social compact are weakened. Parallel justice forums could be profoundly restorative.

Fourth, case managers should coordinate all available resources to meet victims' needs.

Parallel justice forums would provide a mechanism to coordinate the implementation of a comprehensive victim-oriented service plan. For instance, the woman who has been mugged, now too afraid to leave her home to buy food or go to work, might be seeking counseling or transportation. The teller who was held up and can no longer face going to work in a bank might want training to learn how to earn a living a new way. The elderly victim of a telemarketing scam who lost his entire life savings and can't earn it back might want emergency financial assistance or a no-interest loan. The battered woman who wants desperately to leave her violent home may need a job, day care, and new housing. The young victim of sexual assault, incest, or child abuse, who has begun to use drugs to numb the pain, may seek drug treatment.

Case managers should have the authority to ensure that, wherever possible, victims seeking resources and services provided by the government would have priority access to them. And the resources available to victims should not be limited to those provided by the government. While restorative justice involves those immediately affected by the crime, parallel justice would widen the circles of support beyond the neighborhood and other pre-existing interpersonal networks. Consider the roles of block associations, civic groups, faith-based institutions, schools, and businesses. Case managers could draw upon a wide range of resources to help victims of crime rebuild their lives.

The term parallel justice does two things. First, it underscores the need to create a separate path to justice for victims — apart from the criminal justice system, but relating to it. Second, it highlights the contemporaneous nature of these processes. Society must provide justice for both victims and offenders, and much of the work can take place at the same time, with options for connections or interactions between the two processes. Visualize a ladder: two paths to justice that are connected by rungs — opportunities to interact. In many respects restorative justice programs are rungs on this ladder. Parallel justice and restorative justice both have components that focus on accountability and the harm created by crime. Both provide roles for offenders and communities in repairing the harm experienced by victims.

But, parallel justice is distinctive in several ways. It can serve all victims of crime and it marshals a wider range of resources to address victims' safety, and their immediate and long-term needs. In addition, beyond the restorative justice roles for offenders and communities, in a system of parallel justice, there is also a role for society at large, represented by the state, in repairing the harm. Along with families, neighbors, and offenders, society as a whole would be asked to play a role in acknowledging the harm and helping victims of crime rebuild their lives. Although restorative justice offers many benefits to victims, our society owes victims much more. Every crime has a victim and every victim needs our help.

REFERENCES AND SUGGESTED READING

A. Readings On Developing A System Of Justice For Victims

Campbell, R. (2000). *There Are No Victimless Crimes: Community Impact Panels at the Midtown Community Court.* New York: Center for Court Innovation.

van Dijk, J.J.M. (1996). "Crime and Victim Surveys." In: C. Sumner et al. (eds.), *International Victimology: Selected Papers from the 8th International Symposium.* Canberra: Australian Institute of Criminology.

White, R. (2003). "Communities, Conference and Restorative Social Justice." *Criminal Justice* 3(2):139-160.

B. Readings On The Cost And Consequences Of Victimization

Herman, J.L. (1992). *Trauma and Recovery.* New York: Basic Books.

Miller, T.R., M.A. Cohen and B. Wiersema (1996). *Victim Costs and Consequences: A New Look.* Washington, DC: U.S. National Institute of Justice.

National Center for Injury Prevention and Control (2003). *Costs of Intimate Partner Violence Against Women in the United States.* Atlanta, GA: Centers for Disease Control and Prevention.

Sampson, R.J. (1995). "The Community." In: J.Q. Wilson and J. Petersilia (eds.), *Crime.* San Francisco, CA: Institute for Contemporary Studies Press.

Shaffer, J.N. and R.B. Ruback (2002). *Violent Victimization as a Risk Factor for Violent Offending Among Juveniles.* Washington, DC: U.S. Department of Justice, Office of Juvenile Justice and Delinquency Prevention.

Chapter 7.
What Is The Relationship Between Victim Service Organizations And Restorative Justice?

by

Lorraine Stutzman Amstutz

The phone call I received about a year ago from the director of a victim offender mediation program did not surprise me. As a matter of fact, I assume I will get more of these calls as practitioners in the field practice the fundamental principles of restorative justice, which include the importance of collaborating with key stakeholders in the community. These stakeholders, of course, include victim service providers. The director, however, was adamant that he had indeed tried to meet with the director of the victim service agency in his community and had been given the "cold shoulder" and subsequent meetings had not panned out. What should he do?

Relationships between victim service organizations and restorative justice have been tenuous at best. Dialogue between the two groups is increasing, but current discussions often focus on "us and them." Victim groups often feel left out by restorative justice advocates who talk about victim, offender and community needs without involving victim groups in the planning of community initiatives.

Victim Services' Concerns

The extent of the chasm has been evidenced through a project "specifically designed to confront the significant deficiencies of restorative justice practice pertaining to victim participation and impacts for victims, their advocates and victim services generally" (Mika et al., 2002:3).

This project was conducted by a number of people within the restorative justice and victim service field, culminating in a *Listening Project Report.*

Teams representing victim and restorative justice advocates traveled to seven states in 1999-2000 (Florida, Missouri, Ohio, Texas, Vermont, Washington and Wisconsin) to listen to victims and their advocates talk about their impressions of restorative justice, especially as they related to victims' needs and victims' experiences of justice. Following that listening and documentation of experiences, questions and concerns, a structured dialogue was held that included listening team members and site representatives as well as other victims, advocates and restorative justice practitioners. The group spent two days together listening and discussing preliminary findings of the study, identifying areas of agreement and concern regarding restorative justice, and looking at recommendations for ways restorative justice can respond to the findings. How restorative justice advocates respond to those recommendations will determine whether victim groups believe the promises offered by restorative justice.

Two comments from the listening report exemplify the ambivalence with which restorative justice is viewed by victim advocates:

> "There are people in my field (victim services) who when they hear the term 'restorative justice' they think of a very offender-based system that is not informed by knowledge of victim issues. And that is a lot of the fear about restorative justice."

> "I think this is one of the best tools we have had to get offenders to be accountable and to take a good hard look at themselves and their lives, and how crime affects their families, affects the victim and the community...this is the important part of what restorative justice has to be."

On one hand, restorative justice is viewed as providing a more balanced view of crime because it reflects crime as an event that affects many people. It goes beyond the "State vs. Jane Doe" rhetoric that often leaves victims, offenders and communities feeling alienated. Restorative justice encourages direct involvement of those harmed by crime and provides needed change to the current system, as well as opportunities to focus on the harm rather than just focusing on the law breaking.

On the other hand, restorative justice is often viewed as working hand-in-hand with, and therefore reflecting, a justice system that seems more responsive to offender needs rather than victim needs.

> Restorative justice may be offender initiated, and may be oriented to an offender time line. Such needs and practices may not be compatible with victim needs, however. Where offenders are provided with help to change their lives, but victims are not provided help to deal with their trauma, victims feel betrayed by the offender orientation of restorative justice (Mika et al., 2002:5).

An additional challenge raised by victim groups is the lack of an agreed-upon definition not only for the term itself but also the meanings that become attached to restorative justice. As one victim stated:

> "Sometimes I have a little trouble with just the term 'restorative justice.' It is almost offensive if you or the community thinks that they are going to restore me to where I was before my son was murdered. I hope people do not think that is what it is supposed to be."

For many within the victim community, the term restorative justice is synonymous with one specific program, victim offender mediation, in which victims and offenders are provided the opportunity to meet face-to-face. With that narrow perception, it obviously appears to the victim community that restorative justice is limited to those victims where an offender has been arrested, convicted and has agreed to participate. It thus eliminates victims for whom no offender has been caught or when a face-to-face meeting is not appropriate or possible because of offender or system issues. This is a challenge those in the restorative justice community must take seriously.

An encouraging note from those participating in the listening project was the agreement that "the dialogue between restorative justice adherents and the victim community has just begun, and its continuation is vital. And without question, restorative justice must remain vigilant and mindful of its duty to attempt to repair relationships that have been damaged with the victim community" (Mika et al., 2002:15)

Restorative justice advocates must continue to take responsibility for ongoing dialogue in order to gain, regain or maintain credibility with the victim service community. The listening project outlines a number of action steps to keep us moving in that direction. Those action steps include:

- Continue to engage the victim community and establish ongoing dialogue in all states, including initiatives to conduct local "listening" with the victim community.

- Reexamine existing restorative justice programming, including the nature of victim participation and consultation, and effectiveness of programs relative to victim needs.

- Mandate training for restorative justice practitioners in victim-sensitivity, including education on victim trauma. Training (as well as other forms of technical intervention and assistance) should provide a springboard for collaboration with the victim community and should include meaningful sponsorship by the local victim community, including planning and delivery roles.

- Work in partnership with the victim community, not in competition, to advocate for the requisite justice resources to respond to victim needs.

Many of the recommendations listed in the report can be implemented within the broader restorative justice community as well as on local levels. Within Pennsylvania, relationships between restorative justice practitioners and victim service advocates, though developed slowly and with some difficulty, are increasingly positive. An important dimension of this relationship-building has happened through conversations with Mary Achilles, the governor-appointed Victim Advocate for the Commonwealth of Pennsylvania. Discussions began by exploring ways to encourage and support dialogue and collaboration between victim offender programs and victim service organizations. Talking about issues without becoming defensive was an initial challenge. An agreement to be honest, open and respectful about the perceptions of one another's work meant not being offended by what one hears from the other.

Contrasting Perceptions

Based on what we learned through these dialogues, Mary and I began to explore the perceptions that victim service agencies and victim offender mediation programs have of one another. Because we come from the two separate fields — victim services and restorative justice — we were in a position to identify some of these perceptions and suggest strategies for bridging the chasm between the two fields. In a series of workshops and articles (e.g., Achilles and Amstutz, 2003), we tried to represent the perceptions and concerns of the two camps.

Speaking for victim service providers Mary wrote:

> We need to recognize that acknowledging the humanness of the offender and working with programs that view the offender as a client is a new and challenging task for many of our colleagues. We need to recognize that the movement that developed these opportunities for victims was someone else's movement. We also need to acknowledge that victims are asking to meet with the person who caused the harm and that a mechanism for this dialogue to happen should be available in the community. Also, shall we dare say that this should be considered as an element of basic services available in a community for victims? Therefore, we need to work closely with victim offender mediation programs. We need to spend time understanding the work they do and continue to ask questions even if we do not like the answers so that we can build mutual respect.

From the perspective of victim offender mediation providers I wrote:

> As mediation programs we need to recognize that we are viewed by victim services as being offender-driven rather than by our own perception of being an advocate for both victims and offender needs. We need to recognize that victim service providers have worked closely with victims in our cases from the initial trauma and bring a broader understanding of the victims' needs of which we are unaware. We need to recognize that to begin victim offender programs without victim service providers at the table is not only insensitive to victim issues but is antithetical to the practice of restorative justice within our communities. We need to continue to building bridges to cross the information gap between victim offender programs and victim service programs in order to provide those services which best meet the needs of victims, offenders and communities.

We then identified some of the misperceptions that have been discussed since this conversation in 1998:

Victim Service Perceptions	Mediation Program Perceptions
Mediation programs are single-focused, delivering only one service to victims.	Victim service programs are single-focused, concerned solely with victim rather than community needs.
Mediation programs view their services as everything victims need — all encompassing — "making things right."	Victim service programs view their services, exclusive of mediation of course, as everything victims need.
Victim issues are not central to the program since mediation programs are also concerned about offenders.	Opportunities for victims are limited to the services provided by victim service programs who "own" the victim
Mediation programs are offender-driven — they seek "the beautiful thing" where everyone loves and forgives each other.	Victim services programs are victim-driven at the expense of the offender, and without regard for offender or community needs.
Mediation programs are really about restoration for offenders rather than meeting other needs.	Victim services is about punishing the offender rather than meeting other needs.
Mediation programs tend to be aligned with liberal and religiously-oriented organizations.	Victim service programs are law enforcement tools that can be racist and discriminatory.
Mediation programs are interested in victim involvement only to the extent that it benefits offenders.	Victim services programs are not interested in any program that also works with offenders, even if there are victim benefits.

Given those general perceptions of one another, the following are strategies victim service programs and victim offender/restorative justice programs can utilize as they seek to work collaboratively:

Strategies for Working with Victim Service Agencies	Strategies for Working with Victim Offender Programs
Familiarize yourself with the crisis and trauma of victimization.	Familiarize yourself with victim offender mediation/conferencing.
Identify mediation as a potential service to victims.	Recognize that this is an additional service available to victims who choose it.
Contact local victim service programs and ask to meet with them to familiarize yourself with their services.	Contact the local victim offender program and ask to meet with them to familiarize yourself with their services.
Be committed to entering into a relationship with victim service organizations for the long haul.	Work with the victim offender program to identify issues of common concern and common ground.
Volunteer to go through their training.	Volunteer to go through their training.
Invite local victim programs to be represented on your boards and committees.	Invite victim offender programs to participate in your program's activities.
Invite victim programs to present part of your volunteer training on victim issues.	Recognize that as victim service providers, you are focused primarily on victims while they view themselves as multifocused.
Recognize the perceptions they may have of you and that you will need to prove to them that you have the best interests of victims at heart.	Recognize that their mission and philosophical view are different (not better or worse) than your agency's.
Participate in local and state victim rights/service networks.	Invite victim/offender programs to participate in local and state victim service coalitions.
Talk, talk, talk — and listen.	Talk, talk, talk — and listen.

Suggestions For Restorative Justice

For restorative justice advocates working with victim services, there are also a few "do's and don'ts" to keep in mind. It is critical to keep in mind that some of the words we use (e.g., forgiveness, reconciliation, mediation) can be particularly problematic for victims and for their advocates. Restorative justice advocates, particularly those with working with victim offender programs, need to talk about needs addressed through a face-to-face meeting without assuming that these are all the needs of victims. Also, victims should never feel this is a negotiated, settlement-driven process, that assumes that all parties all equal. This is one reason term "mediation" is often problematic.

The issue of forgiveness is often a problematic one. While a restorative justice process may provide opportunities for healing, the course of that journey must be decided by victims in their time. The same is true for forgiveness. A clear danger for practitioners is to think of the road to reconstruction as a linear path leading to a specific destination, one that should include forgiveness in order to reconstruct their lives. Forgiveness cannot be prescribed and cannot be forced. It is often seen by victims as something abstract rather than concrete, and as a burden being placed upon them.

Restorative justice needs to respond to, and understand, the comprehensive, traumatic effects of crime on a victim. Practitioners need to be trained to recognize these signs and the needs that are generated by trauma, and to be clear about how restorative processes such as conferences can and cannot address these needs.

May we continue to work collaboratively rather than coercively as we seek to find ways to ensure that the dialogue includes all those who need to be at the table. Talking through issues together, however difficult, reminds us that we are indeed in this work together.

Address correspondence to: Lorraine Stutzman Amstutz, Mennonite Central Committee, 21 S. 12th Street, P.O. Box 500, Akron, PA 17501. E-mail: <LSA@mcc.org>.

REFERENCES

Achilles, M. and L. Stutzman Amstutz (Winter, 2003). "Victim Services and Victim Offender Mediation Programs: Can They Work Together?" *Conciliation Quarterly* (Mennonite Central Committee, Akron, PA) 22(1):6-8.

Mika, H., M. Achilles, E. Halbert., L. Stutzman Amstutz and H. Zehr (2002). "Taking Victims and Their Advocates Seriously: A Listening Project." Akron, PA: Mennonite Central Committee.

Chapter 8.
Is Restorative Justice Imposing Its Agenda On Victims?

by

Heather Strang

The question to which I am responding contains some implicit assumptions about the meaning of restorative justice and about the role of crime victims within it. Some may read the question as suggesting that restorative justice is primarily for the benefit of offenders, and perhaps communities. It may further suggest that the apparently inappropriate, yet commonly felt, feelings of anger and outrage experienced by victims should disqualify them from participating in a restorative process. I will argue in this chapter that to be effective, restorative justice needs to recognize the legitimate emotions of those who have been harmed by the offenders' actions, provide a means for the expression of these emotions, and create a forum in which the harm caused can be repaired to the satisfaction of those who have directly experienced the harm. I will suggest that for restorative justice to be truly restorative, victims are central to the process, and that if they are central to the process then the question may no longer have meaning.

WHAT IS THE RESTORATIVE JUSTICE AGENDA?

Howard Zehr (2002) has written that when crime is seen through a restorative justice "lens" it becomes a violation of people and of interpersonal relationships, that these violations create obligations and that the central obligation is to put right the wrongs. He summarizes the restorative justice process as a means by which we address victims' harms and needs, hold offenders accountable to put right those harms, and involve victims, offenders and communities in this process. If we agree with this view of restorative justice, then we will most likely see victims as central to any restorative justice agenda.

WHAT IS IMPORTANT TO VICTIMS?

Assertions are frequently made about what victims want. Victims are assumed to be vengeful in their feelings toward their offenders and to want material restitution for their victimization above anything else. But when we take the time actually to ask victims what they want from the justice system and what would allow them to recover from the harm they have experienced, the answers we get are different from those that many victim advocates, lawyers and politicians assume.

It is only in the past 20 years, since the rise of the victim movement worldwide, that research has focused on finding out what victims want. Evidence from at least three continents (see for example, Shapland et al., 1985; Mawby and Gill, 1987; Waller, 1989; Strang, 2002) reveals that when victims are asked, they say they want:

- a less formal process where their views count,

- participation in their case,

- more information about both the processing and outcome of their case,

- respectful and fair treatment,

- material restoration,

- and most importantly of all, emotional restoration, including an apology.

It is plain that the court-based criminal justice system is remarkably unsuited for delivering almost all of these benefits to victims. Victims turn out to be the most unimportant of all the players in formal criminal justice processing. The state assumes the role of the injured party and leaves victims with no part to play beyond that of witnesses. So, little wonder that no provision is made for addressing any of these needs within the formal court system. The injustice of this state of play is self-evident to every victim caught up in the court system, and the lack of a legitimate role comes as a shock to almost all of them. Certainly there is little opportunity for victims to put out their side of the story or to participate in a meaningful way in the manner in which their case is dealt. Because their role is so meager, little attention is given to keeping them informed of progress in their case. Even when legislative amendments require that victims be kept informed, let-out clauses such as "as far as possible" or "whenever feasible" have meant that the police, the prosecution and the courts frequently fail to give victims the information they need. As a result, most victims feel that, at the end of their encounter with the various branches of the criminal justice system, they have not been taken seriously, that no one has responsibility for representing their voice and that no one is interested in repairing the harm they have suffered. As Doreen McBarnett (1988:300) observed: "The state is not just the arbiter in a trial between victims and offender; the state is the victim... If victims feel that nobody cares about their suffering, it is in part because institutionally nobody does."

HOW CAN "JUSTICE" BE DELIVERED TO VICTIMS THROUGH RESTORATIVE JUSTICE?

Let us now consider how restorative justice may be able to remedy the shortcomings of the formal justice system for victims:

- *A less formal process where their views count?* The structure and values of a restorative justice event provide the forum that victims are likely to find most congenial and comfortable for expressing their views and where they can engage in a process that views their contribution as essential.

- *Participation in their case?* Victims are asked to participate in restorative justice because their role is intrinsic to the event. Offenders will pay attention only to those whom they have directly harmed and who have legitimacy to express their feelings; they are not impressed by those who say they speak on their behalf. Thus, not only can victims participate directly, they should be encouraged to do so to generate the emotional power upon which the "success" of restorative justice depends.

- *More information about both the processing and outcome of their case?* The structure of restorative justice events empowers victims to take an active role in the disposition of their case, if they wish to do so.

Victims are never *required* to take this role. But when it is made possible for them, victims have greater opportunity to know about the state of play in their case than the court alternative allows.

- *Respectful and fair treatment?* Ample evidence has emerged in recent years about the capacity of restorative justice to provide the fairness that victims seek (see, for example, Umbreit et al., 1994; McCold and Wachtel, 1998; Strang, 2002). In general, when victims are asked about the way they were treated in their restorative justice experience their approval ratings are in excess of 85%.

- *Material restoration?* When asked about the importance of receiving material reparation from their offenders, many victims indicate that it is mainly important as a gesture of an offender's acceptance of responsibility for the harm. Material or financial amends are, of course, frequently made as part of restorative justice agreements reached between victims and offenders (and offenders tend to comply more often than when similar arrangements are made in the courtroom). Interestingly, Braithwaite (1999) has observed that evaluating the effectiveness of restorative justice to deliver material reparation may be problematic — "some victims will prefer mercy to insisting on getting their money back; indeed it may be that act of grace which gives them a spiritual restoration that is critical for them" (p. 20). Indeed, Shapland et al. (1985) found that victims had completely different ideas from the courts about the amount and kind of compensation they felt they ought to receive. In general, they wanted to get it directly from their offender rather than from any state-organized compensation scheme, and were prepared to accept a good deal less if it came from the offender rather than the state.

- *Emotional restoration, including an apology?* Victims studies over the past decade repeatedly show that what victims want most is not material reparation but instead symbolic reparation, primarily an apology and a sincere expression of remorse (see generally Strang, 2002). Clearly, the opportunity to come face-to-face with one's offender enhances the likelihood that an offender will offer an apology. This is the reverse of the courtroom setting, where the likelihood of an apology is almost zero, no matter how remorseful the offender may feel or how much s/he would like to communicate that remorse. This profound need for emotional restoration has partly to do with a need for vindication — an acknowledgement of the injustice they have suffered. It is also partly a desire in many victims to forgive, not for the sake of their offenders but for their own sakes. With forgiveness, they can put down the burden of anger, vengeance and shame that are all part of the harm they have endured.

VICTIMS' EMOTIONS AND THE DESIRE FOR PUNISHMENT

How do victims who have suffered substantial emotional harm react when first invited to a restorative justice encounter with their offenders? They usually either embrace the prospect of being able to tell the offender directly how they feel about the crime and its perpetrator or they experience considerable fear and anxiety. Others will say that they don't wish to reopen the experience because it would be too painful and because they have "got over the offense." Though more often than not, when victims are encouraged to talk more about this, great swaths of unfinished emotional business are revealed. But whether they wish to meet their offender or not, it is an unusual victim who can say that he or she has reached closure about their offender. It remains true that retributive emotions in these circumstances are frequently the norm and that the more harmful the experience the more retributive victims can be expected to feel. As Kathy Daly (2000:45) has argued: "In short, one cannot begin a restorative justice process by announcing 'let's reconcile,' 'let's negotiate' or 'let's reintegrate.'" We could suggest that any victim who does not harbor these feelings is unlikely to bring the emotional power to a restorative justice event necessary for offenders to understand for what they need to take responsibility.

The Reintegrative Shaming Experiments (RISE) in Australia suggest evidence that emotional power is necessary for successful restorative justice events (Sherman et al., 1999; Strang, 2002). Victims of property crime perpetrated by juvenile offenders rarely expressed strong emotions in their restorative justice conferences, but usually declared themselves satisfied with the conference process. The offenders in these cases were little affected by the conference experience and went on to reoffend at least at the same rate as the control group whose cases were dealt with in court. By contrast, victims of violent crime perpetrated by offenders aged up to 29 years usually brought considerable emotional power to their conferences and tended either to be very satisfied or rather unsatisfied with their conferences (depending almost always on the degree of remorse shown by their offenders). Their offenders were much affected by what transpired in their conferences: they went on to reoffend at a rate almost 40% less than the control group who went to court in the usual way. Moreover, after their cases were processed in court or by a conference, the violent crime victims were asked whether they would harm their offenders if they had the chance. Only 9% of those whose cases went to restorative justice agreed that they would harm the offender, compared with almost half of those whose cases went to court (Strang, 2002). These victims, for whom the emotional consequences of crime are usually greatest, evidently harbor considerable amounts of hostility and anger towards their offenders that is not always discharged by the normal court process.

For all the reasons listed above, many victims feel immensely dissatisfied with the way they are treated by the formal justice system. The anger, anxiety and fear they feel as a result of the crime (Strang, 2002) need to be addressed, not dismissed. Experience shows that angry, anxious, fearful victims who make a decision to take part in restorative justice are able to express their feelings directly to their offenders with a legitimacy that no one else can bring. Restorative justice encounters by their nature are often emotional events, and the greater the harm the greater the emotion. Of course, the facilitator ensures that the meeting proceeds within the bounds of civility while permitting the expression of wounded feelings as far as possible. Offenders sometimes quail under the barrage of angry words uttered by their victims. Tears on both sides are common. For most offenders it is their first opportunity to hear and understand the harm their actions have caused: the rules of the courtroom ensure that these emotions are never expressed in that forum, and admitted offenders who plead guilty may never catch sight of those they have grievously harmed.

The usual consequence of a restorative justice encounter is that offenders begin to experience feelings of empathy towards their victims, which in turn engenders remorse. It is now, after sincere expressions of remorse and apologies have been offered, that a desire for punishment and retribution, even of restitution, usually gives way to concerns about how to stop the offender from reoffending. This is both for the offender's sake and, more especially, for the sake of other future victims: victims care immensely that others will not have to endure what they have experienced.

It seems that this expression of feelings by victims is essential for the experience of empathy by offenders towards their victims. It may be that empathy is the "engine" that drives remorse on the offender's part and the discharge of retributive feelings on the victim's part. It is evident that the "symbolic transaction" (Retzinger and Scheff, 1996) that takes place when a victim recognizes that the offender truly understands and takes responsibility results in a change that often renders retributive emotions largely irrelevant.

Retributive emotions may turn out to be both commonplace and necessary for victims to experience in order to provide the emotional power needed for a successful restorative justice event. Instead of wishing that victims were not so "bad" and that they arrive with emotions of forgiveness, it is more helpful to recognize the purpose of the event from the victim's perspective: namely, to meet their needs, as they tell us, after their experience of victimization. I suggest that part of the essence of restorative justice is to provide the opportunity for victims to express their feelings of anger, fear and outrage, within the bounds of civility set by the facilitator, and their desire for the offender to be hurt as much as they have been hurt. The meeting allows the dynamic between the harmed victim and the harming offender to address the pain caused by the crime. I also suggest that it is not the essence of restorative justice to require victims to rid themselves of their retributive feelings prior to their encounter with their offenders.

PUNITIVE RESTORATIVE JUSTICE OUTCOMES

Restorative justice advocates sometimes argue that we must choose between restoration and retribution, and that there is no room for punishment in any truly restorative outcome. The RISE study certainly suggests evidence that restorative justice has the capacity to greatly reduce feelings of retribution among victims. Furthermore, the RISE study reveals (Strang et al., 1999) that the most frequently discussed justice principle was not punishment or even repaying affected victims and communities, but rather the prevention of future offending.

Nevertheless, punishment remains part of common understandings of a just response to crime, along with stopping wrongdoers from doing it again, keeping them away from the community, teaching them a lesson and finding out ways they can help themselves (Daly, 2000). In RISE there were conferences in which the emotional power had gone out of the meeting and a great deal had been worked through and settled — anger and shame, apologies, forgiveness, plans for the offender to change his/her way — when someone would say: "But what about some punishment?" It seemed that this call for punishment was quite different from the call made by frustrated and furious victims reacting to their perceived inadequacies and exclusion in a courtroom process. In the restorative setting punishment takes on a character described by Duff (2002:90) as "the kind of moral reparation...needed to give an apology for wrongdoing a suitably forceful expression."

For most victims it is satisfying to be able to express feelings about the offence directly to the offender and to explain fully its consequences. It is even more satisfying to see that the offender properly understands, sincerely apologizes for the offence and pledges actions to ensure s/he will never behave this way again. But it seems for most people — not only victims but others closely connected to the crime too — there needs to be more: that restoration to the *status quo ante* is not enough. They usually desire as well some form of censure by the community, a recognition of the wrong as a wrong which is owed to the victim. They also need the offender to undertake a course of action that signals remorse and underlines the sincerity of the apology. This might include writing letters, contributing time or money to a charity, performing a service for the victim or someone else of the victim's choosing, agreeing to take part in rehabilitation or education activities. The participants, both the principals and those present to support them, seem to agree that such tasks represent a moral rightness that reinforces the verbal undertakings made and accepted. It may even be the case that victims can only be truly generous and forgiving after a process in which punishment as a form of censure has been accepted. It is at this point, to return to Kathy Daly's point, that victims truly can say "let's reconcile," "let's negotiate" and "let's reintegrate."

"GOOD" AND "BAD" VICTIMS

How do practitioners react to "bad" and "good" victims? Probably most often by dreading and discouraging the one and encouraging and welcoming the other. Certainly some victims have merciless and punitive attitudes which remain unaltered by anything an offender does or says. For these victims and offenders it is imperative to have ways in which to limit the severity of any restorative justice outcome, even one to which an offender agrees, to the level that would prevail in the courtroom. But for the vast majority of victims, I suggest that their "badness" from the practitioners' viewpoint is primarily a function of the emotional harm they have suffered. "Good" victims may not have suffered nearly so seriously and, if their needs are not so great, may not reap the potential benefits of a restorative justice encounter. "Bad" victims usually are in greatest need of the kind of solace that a contrite offender can give them. They will also be the victims most likely to provide the emotional power necessary for a successful meeting.

CONCLUSION

This chapter has addressed the role of victims in restorative justice and considered whether the principles implicit in restorative justice are being imposed on victims. I have suggested that if we are in accord with Howard Zehr's view of restorative justice as, among other things, a means by which victims' harms and needs are addressed, then the central role played by victims means that they are integral to the process. To be sure, victims may arrive at their conference full of retributive and bitter emotions, but this is usually no more than a normal reaction to the harm they have experienced. Only by acknowledging the legitimacy of these retributive emotions and permitting their expression can restorative justice be perceived as a mainstream alternative to the exclusive and impersonal punitive focus of the formal justice system. Without such an acknowledgment, restorative justice will remain limited to trivial disputes between people little affected by the crime or its treatment.

Restorative justice provides the time and space for victims and offenders to talk about more than the price to be exacted for the wrongdoing, and much of it is more salient and important to all players than the question of punishment. But the need for censure and reparation through the voluntary undertaking of a burdensome action, should be seen for what they usually are: the signal of an offender's remorse and an acknowledgment of the legitimacy of the victim's suffering. The restorative justice agenda need not, and should not, require victims to arrive in a "restorative" frame of mind. It is the work of a restorative justice encounter to engender emotions of remorse and forgiveness to the benefit of all participants. When that is achieved, then the restorative justice agenda has been fulfilled.

REFERENCES AND SUGGESTED READING

Braithwaite, J. (1999). "Restorative Justice: Assessing Optimistic and Pessimistic Accounts." In: M. Tonry (ed.), *Crime and Justice: A Review of Research*, vol. 25. Chicago, IL: University of Chicago Press.

Daly, K. (2000). "Revisiting the Relationship between Retributive and Restorative Justice." In: H. Strang and J. Braithwaite (eds.), *Restorative Justice: Philosophy to Practice*. Aldershot, UK: Ashgate.

Duff, R.A. (2002). "Restorative Punishment and Punitive Restoration." In: L. Walgrave (ed.), *Restorative Justice and the Law*. Cullompton, Devon, UK: Willan Publishing.

Mawby, R. and M. Gill (1987). *Crime Victims: Needs, Services and the Voluntary Sector*. London, UK: Tavistock.

McBarnett, D. (1988). "Victim in the Witness Box — Confronting Victimology's Stereotype." *Contemporary Crises* 7:279-303.

McCold, P. and B. Wachtel (1998). *Restorative Policing Experiment: The Bethlehem Pennsylvania Police Family Group Conferencing Project*. Pipersville PA: Community Service Foundation.

Retzinger, S. and T. Scheff (1996). "Strategy for Community Conferences: Emotions and Social Bonds." In: B. Galaway and J. Hudson (eds.), *Restorative Justice: International Perspectives*. Monsey, NY: Criminal Justice Press.

Shapland, J., J. Willmore and P. Duff (1985). *Victims in the Criminal Justice System*. (Cambridge Studies in Criminology.) Aldershot, UK: Gower.

Sherman, L.W., H. Strang and D. Woods (2000). *Recidivism Patterns in the Canberra Reintegrative Shaming Experiments*. Research School of Social Sciences,

Australian National University, Canberra (www.aic.gov.au/rjustice/rise/recidivism).

Strang, H. (2002). *Repair or Revenge: Victims and Restorative Justice.* Oxford, UK: Clarendon Press.

—— G.C. Barnes, J. Braithwaite and L.W. Sherman (1999). *Experiments in Restorative Policing: A Progress Report on the Canberra Reintegrative Shaming Experiments (RISE),* (www.aic.gov.au/rjustice).

Umbreit, M., R. Coates and B. Kalanj (1994). *Victim Meets Offender: The Impact of Restorative Justice and Mediation.* Monsey, NY: Criminal Justice Press.

Waller, I. (1989). "The Needs of Crime Victims." In: E. Fattah (ed.), *The Plight of Crime Victims in Modern Society.* Basingstoke, UK: Macmillan.

Zehr, H. (2002). *The Little Book of Restorative Justice.* Intercourse PA: Good Books.

Chapter 9.
Have Offender Needs And Perspectives Been Adequately Incorporated Into Restorative Justice?

by

Barb Toews and Jackie Katounas

After 20 years of criminal activity and prison time, it was a minor offense — as far as I was concerned — that brought me to my senses. After taking chairs from a friend who had stolen them from a hotel, I realized that I knew the victim. I had betrayed a friend, the pub owner. I had broken a trust and was ashamed.

I couldn't nark on my friend due to a code of ethics. Instead, I went to my pub-owner friend, said I was sorry and that I wanted to make amends by getting his property back for him — anonymously. That was one of the hardest things I have ever done. He accepted my apology and my intentions to put things right, no questions asked. Remaining friends, I continued to visit his pub.

After that incident, I didn't have the heart for crime. Despite a conscious decision to do something constructive with my life, however, I didn't know how to go about it. Struggling, I still contemplated, but never played out, criminal acts, and I continued to associate with other criminals. I finally decided that I needed to re-educate myself so I could communicate with, listen to and understand people who weren't like me.

This experience gave me first-hand knowledge that restorative justice can work. Now, more than eight years later, I have facilitated conferences between willing victims and offenders, and educated inmates about restorative justice through Hawkes Bay Restorative Justice and, more recently, became Restorative Justice Project Manager for Prison Fellowship New Zealand. Through my conference experiences within the degrading and desolate confines of the prison environment, I have witnessed numerous examples of reconciliation, forgiveness and healing. As an ex-inmate myself, I offer a unique experience to those who are imprisoned and bring a credibility to the work that many others cannot offer.

Jackie

I have had a different journey. Restorative justice has always been consistent with my faith and sensibilities of right/wrong, justice and peace. After years of mediating between victims and offenders in the juvenile arena, I began restorative justice work in prison with the Pennsylvania Prison Society, an offender advocacy and direct service agency. Through my work, I have seen and heard the strong desire from prisoners to have opportunities to "make things right" in a meaningful way often not afforded them in prison. I have discovered my greatest passion, and challenge, in exploring restorative justice from the offender's perspective.

Barb

We, as authors, come from different backgrounds and experiences yet have found ourselves on a similar journey, that of understanding and practicing restorative justice with men and women who have committed crimes and within prison.

Under the prevailing — and retributive — system, the state and offenders become the focus. Victims are almost entirely shut out. Restorative justice has sought to bring victims back into the "loop," making their experiences and needs central to the process. Victim centrality is a key restorative justice tenet.

The criminal justice system is often, and perhaps legitimately, considered offender-oriented. However the system, its processes and results, are rarely embraced by people who enter it as offenders. They do not view it as *their* system, feeling fortunate to be the subject of its attention. Seeking to punish and blame offenders, the system is rarely concerned with their needs. Restorative justice seeks to also bring offenders back into the "loop," making their experiences and needs central to the justice process.

However, without embracing offender centrality as a key restorative justice tenet, we risk overlooking or minimizing offenders' experiences and needs. While the total exclusion of offenders is unlikely, it can be difficult for restorative justice practitioners to fully appreciate the needs of offenders and to understand how they affect practice.

Through our work, we have observed that offenders need the following opportunities to:

- Express their remorse, sorrow and regret for the harms done and offer apologies to the victim.

- Have others, ideally including victims, accept their remorse as genuine, no matter how inadequately expressed.

- Tell their story — without justifying or excusing their offending.

- Gain greater insight into the effects of their offending.

- Have others, including victims, realize that they, offenders, may have come from a world in which they may have themselves been victims of violence, abuse, neglect, etc.

- Receive acknowledgment of their experiences with victimization and attention to their needs as crime victims.

- Experience personal growth and transformation and be able to demonstrate their new lives.

- Have opportunities to make things right and build relationships with their families and the broader community.

Perhaps surprisingly, offenders themselves identify these as their needs. One incarcerated man commented that "wanting to make peace with others is part of being human." Restorative justice provides the opportunity to be human through making amends and demonstrating accountability.

Another incarcerated man described restorative justice as "taking the slow lane." Restorative justice invites us to slow down and see, hear and feel all that is beside the road, including the experiences, joys and pains of the people we pass. However, despite the opportunities it offers offenders, we believe that current restorative justice practice is passing offenders by. This chapter introduces four "sights" that we have seen and heard while in the slow lane with offenders — offender personal experiences and worldview, prison experiences, community involvement and restorative justice values. Throughout the chapter, we introduce each of these four "sights" with a reflection (in italics) that emerges from our work with people who have committed crimes.

The victim's father started to interrogate the offender. "If you knew this vehicle was stolen, why didn't you ring the police?" When the guy tried to say, "I just couldn't do that," the doctor just couldn't understand he had a code of ethics of not "grassing" on friends. Then the victim's mother started to grill the offender's wife, saying "You can't tell me you didn't know what was going on. Why didn't you report it?"

I (Jackie) observed this interaction during a conference that I facilitated. Prior to this point, the offender had been forthcoming about how he had come to be friends with the man who stole the victim's car and how he had allowed this friend to use his garage to strip it. Yet, it was hard for the victims to listen or understand. The offender had, for much of his life, come from an offending culture, and associated with people who had committed crimes, experiences quite different from those of the victim. It was if they were strangers in need of a "translator."

Many offenders have grown up in environments guided by offending values and beliefs. Using words like "dog-eat-dog world" and "war," and describing crime as "no big deal, just part of life," these individuals suggest lives shaped by the following attributes:

- Violence, or survival of the fittest;

- Offensive and defensive relationships ("Get them before they get you"); and

- A struggle for respect ("No one speaks to me like that and gets away with it").

These experiences and worldviews are frequently perpetuated by institutional and societal victimization — for instance, racism, classism, un/under employment, lack of access to education, health care, or housing. While certainly not excuses for offending behavior, these experiences are nevertheless harmful, disempowering and disrespectful. James Gilligan (1996) suggests that violence is a form of justice to undo previous injustices, raising the possible link between one's experience with personal and institutional violence and his or her own commission of violence. Interestingly, this effort to respond to injustice with violence, in many ways mirrors the values and intents of the criminal justice system.

For some from this background, it may be difficult to show concern for others or to express a desire to attend to harms caused by crime. I (Jackie) was oblivious to the harm I was causing other people. I was living in a very selfish world, void of consideration for others. Nobody ever challenged me — "Jackie, do you know what you've done?"

Unfortunately, it seems that restorative justice, in its race to ask "Do you know what you have done?" turns a deaf ear to offenders' experiences. Perhaps, like the victim in the reflection, we, as practitioners assume that our own personal experiences and world views — often white, middle class, educated and male — are those of people who have committed crimes. The result may now be the exclusion of the experiences of the black or Maori, poor and undereducated people who populate U.S. and New Zealand prisons from our understanding and expectations of restorative justice.

With a whole life of experiences to untangle, expecting a conference to lead to lasting change may be unrealistic, for it may be little more than a one-time opportunity for healthy interaction. Some offenders, though feeling genuinely remorseful, may remain influenced by the attitudes and experiences that have shaped their life choices. If we believe James Gilligan, that violence is an attempt to undo injustice, we are encouraged to pay more attention to the violence and disrespect that permeates the lives of many offenders. This means addressing offender experiences with personal victimization, such as when they have been victims of crime, or responding to disrespectful social institutions, such as inadequate education or unfair economic opportunities.

Unfortunately, few restorative justice programs offer opportunities to explore these experiences with offenders or to determine their needs and apply restorative justice principles in light of them. As practitioners in a harms-oriented approach to justice, we may need to take a step back to listen, learn and expand our vision for restorative justice to include offender experiences. If that pub owner hadn't understood me, Jackie, would I have turned my life around?

It's Time To Take An RJ Break

During a prison-based restorative justice class, I (Barb) and a colleague invited the participants to brainstorm ways to do restorative justice in their everyday lives, including in their relationships with correctional officers. They generated many ideas, but it was this relationship, they said later, that was the most challenging to consider in a restorative way. Later, one participant created the mantra above to remind him to act restoratively.

This mantra suggests that restorative justice provides a respite from something that is the norm. For those who are incarcerated, that norm is the disrespect, violence and victimization that characterize the prison experience. Interestingly, these norms are similar to the values and beliefs that have shaped many offenders. Gilligan's theory would suggest that the violence of prison is an attempt to undo the injustice of the crime. Sadly, just as offender's violence rarely, if ever, achieves justice, prison and its violent atmosphere are unlikely to promote justice, particularly in forms of accountability, restoration and healing.

Meeting with one's victim or participating in other restorative activities may seem like a hiatus in an offender's life — a momentary opportunity for positive sharing and healing sandwiched between the hostility of their past and the ongoing hostility of their present. The reality of prison may make real personal change difficult, even if desires for accountability are real. After meeting with his victim, one prisoner responded, "I can't promise anything but I'll try," when asked about changing his life. While restorative opportunities may be beneficial in and of themselves, we encourage practitioners to appreciate this reality and to consider its impact on the offender.

Restorative justice, however, has more to offer than just a respite from everyday life. We are challenged to explore what restorative justice, as a philosophy, has to say about the prison environment itself. Our work has raised questions for us:

- Is restorative justice possible in prison without challenging the violent and punitive prison values and practices?

- Without challenging the prison environment, are we condoning violence and saying that harming offenders is OK?

- Is restorative justice about system and prison reform (and even prison abolition) or just about providing an alternative process that exists alongside the current system and prison practices?

- Is restorative justice about transforming people's lives to the fullest extent possible or only to the degree we allow while punishing them?

- Can restorative justice resist co-optation by the values and practices of prison?

- Does punishment and prison even have a role in restorative justice?

These questions encourage practitioners to expand their understanding of restorative justice, as a philosophy, in order to incorporate offenders' experiences with victimization and violence at the hands of the system. Certainly, this increased understanding will add new meaning to "doing" restorative justice in prison and contribute to the creation of new practices.

> One offender got a full-time job for the first time in his life. When the boss asked him to do a particular task, he walked off the job, too embarrassed to tell the boss he didn't know how to do it. Later picked up for another crime, I tried to talk to him about what happened with his job and he confessed. He had no comprehension about asking someone for help. He's due to get out very shortly and he's got another full-time job to go to — the same job.

I (Jackie) know that the offender was blown away that his boss would even consider taking him back. The boss is likely now to be more aware of the need to walk through job-related issues with this man. I am not sure, however, how the offender is going to deal with other struggles such as relationships with his past associates for whom crime and doing time is the norm. In many ways, the boss's understanding and commitment to this young man are unique. They reflect a rare dedication from a community member for an offender.

Many communities have embraced the idea that justice should address the needs of victims and hold offenders accountable. However, when it comes to offenders — particularly prisoners — the role and meaning of community seems to stop short. With three strikes against them the moment they leave prison, offenders often feel unwelcome in a community that has said, albeit indirectly, that they have paid their debt to society. Not trusted, offenders have to prove themselves over and over again to dispel suspicions that they will re-offend. All this means that offenders rarely receive the support that they need when re-integrating into community life. Many find themselves faced with difficult situations with the potential to respond with the same values that lead them to crime in the first place. Their needs are left unnoticed and unappreciated.

As practitioners, we regularly encounter the realities of limited community involvement. We are faced with the stereotypes and biases towards offenders that make it difficult to hear and see them as human beings with needs, hopes and fears. Offenders need the community to open itself to their needs, particularly at the point of reintegration.[1] Going beyond issues of accountability, the community has a responsibility to help offenders to receive and do what they need to be a productive member of society. This frequently means responding to offender experiences with personal and social victimization. If the community is better educated about restorative values and prepared to embrace offenders, it will be a more humane and open place for them to return.

What about the victims' obligations? Aren't they obligated to not hurt the offender, to not take revenge? Isn't restorative justice about how they respond to the crime, too?

During a prison-based seminar, a participant raised these questions after I (Barb) drew a frequently used triangle to represent the relationship between offenders, victims and community and their resulting obligations to each other. My co-facilitator and I were noticeably uncomfortable, perhaps defensive, in our response, believing that victims do not have obligations. While holding firm to this belief, I am open to the broader question behind it.

Restorative values include empowerment, respect, transformation, interdependence, dialogue and mutuality, to name a few. We see gaps where these values are given different weight if you are an offender, victim or community. For instance, we generally challenge offenders to change or show empathy for victims and community, yet rarely expect transformation or empathy on the part of the victim or community, particularly toward offenders.

As restorative justice practitioners, we have gone to increased lengths to ensure that victims are not revictimized by their participation in restorative processes. Sadly, we have not been as attentive to offender's concerns about revictimization, for example, by the process, a victim's hostile participation or by other participants, including process facilitators who may not understand the offender's experiences. For many offenders, the justice system has been hostile, unempathic and rarely concerned with their backgrounds and needs. Participating in a process where they may face the same attitude may seem no more restorative than the traditional system. We are not suggesting that anger should be excluded from restorative processes or that victims should be censured in their participation. Rather, we challenge practitioners to be respectful of an offender's concerns for safety.

We have heard offenders raise questions that suggest there we are not practicing restorative values to the fullest:

- If restorative justice is about accountability and empowerment, what can I do when I am not permitted to take any initiative to make amends, e.g., by initiating a victim-offender encounter?

- If restorative justice is about understanding the crime and people's needs for justice, why am I am supposed to understand the victim and community perspectives when my own experiences, needs and perspectives are ignored or minimized?

- If restorative justice is about healing, why are my experiences of victimization denied?

- If I am to accept responsibility, what do I do when I am not believed and thus not supported to do anything about it?

These questions challenge us to consider what it means for offenders to be a key justice stakeholder. We seem to offer them an opportunity to be accountable without considering that they may have something to offer us. Certainly, they have much to offer — their experiences, their personal needs, including those that have little or nothing to do with the victim, and their ideas for meeting those needs.

Sadly, we have typically not included offenders in the development, implementation and facilitation of restorative justice programs. While the increased participation and buy-in from criminal justice and corrections partners is valuable, these partners are control agents of offenders.

Without direct offender involvement, programs risk being developed from the perspective and culture of the system. Without seeing offenders as resources and inviting their active involvement, restorative justice will likely become something we *do to* offenders without being responsive to their needs, little better than the current system.

I (Barb) started my work with offenders in the fast lane. Not without internal tension, I shifted gears and slowed down. There are certainly times when I catch myself gaining speed and must remind myself to be aware of the sights. I (Jackie) am on the same road as a practitioner and, as offender, have been passed by as others sped along. For those who have committed crimes, the road before and after the crime is not a short, or quick, one. As practitioners, we are called to work with offenders as long as they are on the path, regardless of the speed and backward steps in the journey. Restorative justice cannot offer any guarantees about the impact on an offender's life. However, if we recognize them as key stakeholders in restorative justice, invite them to name their needs, and provide opportunities for accountability, empathy and justice, the end result will be a better society.

We invite you to move into the slow lane and join the journeys of those who have committed crimes. In order to do so, we challenge you to:

- Visit a prison and challenge yourself to embrace the humanity of those who are incarcerated there.

- Hold focus groups in prison in which you listen to and learn from men and women who have committed crimes.

- Invite people who have committed crimes to be part of the development team of restorative justice programs.[2] This may mean changing the way you "do business" to include people who are confined.

- Read prisoner writings. A few suggestions are at the end of the chapter.

- Explore Afrocentric, Maori and other cultural approaches to criminal and restorative justice to ensure that your programs are relevant to those that make up the majority of the prison population.

- Get involved in prevention programs and activities that address the social, cultural and economic root causes of crime.

- Challenge yourself to explore your own personal biases and stereotypes of offenders and what it means to walk the restorative justice talk with them.

Taking this slow lane may be difficult. You may gain knowledge that is deemed "unpopular." You may uncover new knowledge about yourself. Others may pass you by, arriving at their destination before you. But imagine the journey along the way, meeting new people, learning new experiences and creating a new vision for restorative justice.

Address correspondence to: Jackie Katounas, E-mail: <jackkat@paradise. net.nz> or Barb Toews, E-mail: <btoews@prisonsociety.org>.

REFERENCES AND SUGGESTED READING

Casarjian, R. (2001). *Houses of Healing, A Prisoner's Guide to Inner Power and Freedom*. Boston, MA: Lionheart Foundation.

Consedine, J. (1999). *Restorative Justice: Healing the Effects of Crime*. Lyttelton, NZ: Ploughshares Publications.

Gaines, P. (1997). *Moments of Grace, Meeting the Challenge to Change*. New York: Crown Publishers Inc.

Gilligan, J. (1996). *Violence: Reflections on a National Epidemic*. New York: Vintage Books.

Leder, D. (2000). *The Soul Knows No Bars: Inmates Reflect on Life, Death and Hope*. Lanham, MD: Rowman and Littlefield.

Parker, T. (1995). *The Violence of Our Lives: Interviews with American Murderers*. New York: Henry Holt and Company.

Pranis, K. (2001). "Not in My Backyard." *Conciliation Quarterly* 20(3):9-11.

Rideau, W. and R. Wikeberg (1992). *Life Sentences: Rage and Survival Behind Bars*. New York: Times Books.

Toews, B. (2003). "Restorative Justice Poses Challenges for Men Incarcerated in Pennsylvania." *Offender Programs Report* 7(1):1-12.

Zehr, H. (1996). *Doing Life: Reflections of Men and Women Serving Life Sentences.* Intercourse, PA: Good Books.

—— (1990). *Changing Lenses.* Scottdale, PA: Herald Press.

NOTES

1. Ex-offenders participating in a focus group with the Pennsylvania Prison Society affirmed the following as their needs at the point of parole: access to and assistance in getting health services, including addictions treatment, physical and mental health; assistance in becoming financially stable through meaningful employment, job training, education and financial management; safety; assistance in re-establishing or strengthening healthy relationships, including with family, friends, children and others in their communities of care; assistance in securing safe and affordable housing; clear feedback from the community about their expectations and needs and support in fulfilling those expectations and meeting the needs; willingness from the community and others to support and assist the offender in value/lifestyle changes and the reintegration process; assistance in rebuilding or developing personal and social life skills such as problem solving, crisis and stress management, hobbies, empowerment and decision making; support and assistance in addressing the personal, relational and social needs that are specific to that offender; opportunities to understand the needs of the victim and to attend to them to the extent possible; attention to community dynamics that contribute to crime and limit one's successful reintegration; and transformation of identity from "con" or "felon" to valued community member.

2. This point is the first of ten "signposts" for working toward appropriate offender involvement in restorative justice. These signposts, created by Lorraine Stutzman Amstutz and Barb Toews, are part of a restorative justice bookmark series available free from the Mennonite Central Committee, PO Box 500, Akron, PA 17501-0500; phone 717-859-1151.

Chapter 10.
What Is The Appropriate Relationship Between Restorative Justice And Treatment?

by

Gordon Bazemore and Dee Bell

Is rehabilitation restorative? No. Is restorative justice rehabilitative? Sometimes.

Treatment programs, no matter how effective, are not in themselves restorative. However, such programs, can be carried out in more or less restorative ways when these interventions also take into account, to the degree possible, the needs of victims and community.

Likewise, restorative justice can be rehabilitative. In fact, Braithwaite (2001) suggests, paradoxically, that restorative justice is often rehabilitative precisely because rehabilitation is not its primary purpose. That is, it can be rehabilitative because it doesn't frame the problem as something that is wrong with the offender that must be "fixed" by professionals. Rather, the "collective resolve" of the support group around the offender provides the solution and thus increases the likelihood of offender (and victim) reintegration. We will argue here that there are ways for restorative justice to maximize this potential for offender rehabilitation.

Restorative justice practice must focus most attention on involving and meeting the needs of victims first and communities second. However, failure to apply restorative justice to rehabilitative efforts abandons the offender to forces of punishment or risk management/ incapacitation — or to offender treatment programs which lack any connection to the victim or the community.

There has been, however, a great deal of ambivalence in the field about the role of rehabilitation in restorative programs. Though seeking change in offenders, most restorative justice practitioners are unenthusiastic about professionalized treatment models that seem to separate the offender from victim and community. It seems unlikely that the "strengths-based" assumptions of a restorative view of the offender can be easily reconciled with a "medical model" perspective that views the offenders primarily in terms of deficits and "thinking errors" (Maruna, 2001).

A Restorative Model Of Rehabilitation

We believe it is possible to develop a fully restorative model of rehabilitation that would outperform other models. This holistic approach would apply restorative principles to existing treatment programs, to the way decisions are made about obligations, to the way in which offenders are supported and supervised in the community, and to the way they are treated in residential facilities. This approach would ensure that restorative programs such as conferencing do not detract from offender reintegration goals. Additionally, this approach is based on the premise that rehabilitation is important, but not in isolation from a community or relational context: "whether focused on work and service or cognitive restructuring, interventions that do not ultimately build stronger relationships and positive roles for offenders in the community are unlikely to have long-tern rehabilitative impact" (Bazemore et al., 2000:15).

A holistic, relational model of restorative rehabilitation would have the following related core features (Bazemore and O'Brien, 2002; see also, Toews-Shenk and Zehr, 2001):

- a *collective* approach to offender reintegration that focuses on rebuilding or strengthening relationships damaged by crime, or on building new, healthy relationships;

- a *naturalistic* focus that does not always assume the necessity (or value) of formal intervention; and

- an organic process of informal support and social control that emphasizes the *community* role in offender transformation and increased reliance on the role of citizens as "natural helpers."

Such a model cannot be solely offender-focused, but it must articulate a role for all primary stakeholders in restorative justice: victim, community, offender and system professional. The justice system, its functions and agencies would be challenged to promote a seamless and resonant relationship between the various interventions that are concerned with offender treatment, risk management and public safety, sanctioning, victim support, and prevention. Working in congruence with each other, the goal for all intervention outcomes is repair, healing and relationship-building.

Finally, a restorative framework for rehabilitation should also be linked through the practice of relationship building with a community-level focus (Bazemore and O'Brien, 2002). *Networks* of relationships built up over time as a by-product of restorative responses have the potential to build *social capital* (Putnam, 2000) in the form of new and enhanced forms of informal social control and social support (Cullen, 1994).

Despite the relationship-building and naturalistic focus, this model would nonetheless include professional treatment as needed, but only those models empirically demonstrated to have the greatest likelihood of reducing recidivism for the specific type of individual (e.g., Lipsey, 1995; Andrews and Bonta, 1994). In other words, restorative justice advocates would use "effective treatment" programs that are adapted to ensure consistency with restorative justice principles.

We argue that restorative justice can improve the *effectiveness* of effective treatment and decrease the likelihood of recidivism and increase reintegration for offenders in these programs.

Restorative justice can be summarized as three principles (Van Ness and Strong, 1997):

- *The principle of repair.* Justice requires healing of victims, offenders and communities injured by crime or other harmful behavior. Interventions identify the damage to victims and communities resulting from by the actions of offenders with a goal of repairing this harm.

- *The principle of stakeholder participation.* Victims, offenders and communities should have the opportunity for active involvement in the justice process as early and as fully as possible. Since repair cannot be effectively achieved without input from those most affected by the crime, the extent and quality of repair is largely dependent on the quality and extent of stakeholder involvement.

Victim, offender, and community members must "own" and take responsibility for the decision-making process.

- *The principle of transformation in community and government roles and relationships.* In order to repair the harm of crime through an inclusive decision making process, we must change the role of justice professionals and the mandate of the justice system to ensure communities are allowed and encouraged to assume greater responsibility. This implies two goals: (1) changing the role of criminal justice professionals and the mandate or mission of justice systems and agencies to support community ownership of the restorative process; and, (2) increasing the capacity of citizens and community groups to address the harm of youth crime.

Principles Of Effective Correctional Treatment

The so-called "principles of effective correctional treatment" (ECT) (e.g., Andrews and Bonta, 1994) may be less familiar to the reader and are quite different from restorative principles. They have been developed empirically, for the most part derived from meta-analyses of program evaluations of treatment programs.[1]

The ECT, or "what works" literature, has made vital contributions to the treatment field. First, in response to the cynicism that "nothing works" (Martinson, 1972), ECT researchers have been able to demonstrate that under the right conditions, interventions *can* work to significantly reduce recidivism (e.g., Lipsey, 1995). Second, this research indicates that some correctional treatment models work better than others. In fact, this research has clearly demonstrated that many of the most popular criminal justice interventions — deterrence-based, punitive programs, aversive therapy, and shock confrontation programs such as Scared Straight, shaming/humiliation programs, as well as a range of benign but dubious therapeutic programs (e.g., insight-based counseling; psychotherapy, self-esteem enhancement) — often do more harm than good (Gendrau et al., 1994).

Recently some ECT advocates have argued that restorative practice may detract from the commitment to the principles of effective treatment (e.g., Levrant et al., 1999). Ironically, this is in part due to the misperception that restorative programs are based on assumptions similar to some of the above-mentioned *ineffective* programs. This criticism is also based on a concern about overloading the offender with excessive and irrelevant requirements. A more realistic fear is that the focus on victim needs and community participation may diminish the priority given to ECT principles.

While restorative justice advocates promote victim- and community-focused interventions for principled reasons independent of offender outcomes, a strong case can be made that restorative justice can actually *enhance* ECT principles.

Four core principles of effective treatment, when applied consistently, produce significant reductions in recidivism when compared with alternative correctional treatments. Effective correctional treatment: (1) relies on behavioral, intensive and multi-modal programming; (2) promotes positive clinical relationships; (3) targets criminogenic needs; (4) is responsive to the specific individual; and (5) avoids "over-consequencing." Each of these can be consistent with a restorative approach.

1. *Behavioral, Intensive And Multi-Modal Programming*

At the most general level, the correctional treatment programs most effective in reducing recidivism are those that provide rewards/incentives for positive behavior and are focused on positive outcomes, are intensive and structured, and incorporate more than one type of intervention (i.e., are multi-modal).

Truly multi-modal intervention programs could support restorative justice objectives by incorporating victim awareness and conflict resolution, for example, into treatment protocols. Such programs could also include apprenticeship components and restorative community service in which offenders and community members work together on projects that contribute to the common good. One primary intermediate measure of success in each of these would be the strength and quality of the relationship formed.

"Behavioral" programs within the ECT model have come to include cognitive restructuring programs which challenge destructive thinking patterns, or "thinking errors," that some argue distinguish criminal personality types from non-criminal types (Yochelson and Samenow, 1976). Though some of these programs have shown positive impact on recidivism (Ross and Fabiano, 1985), restorative justice advocates would object in principle — and perhaps on the empirical record — to what is often a demeaning, deficit-focused separation between offenders and non-offenders.[2] However, restorative justice could find ways to work around these problems, especially when it is reality-based and includes a strong dose of victim awareness and community input. These cognitive classes could be linked to some kind of reparative experience, grounding the program in actual harm rather the insular focus on cognitive deficits and "thinking errors." In this reparative experience, offenders gain the opportunity to practice pro-social actions, mirroring and deepening the cognitive program learning.

Restorative justice practitioners can also learn much from the general implications of the success of multi-modal approaches. Too often restorative programs seem to be one-shot interventions that are disconnected from any follow-up. While it is surprising that such short-term interventions as victim offender mediation and other forms of conferencing work as well empirically as they do in reducing recidivism (see generally, Umbreit, 2001; Braithwaite, 2002), the impacts are not as great as they might be. Imagine how much more impact restorative justice practices might have if they were part of a whole package of mutually reinforcing interventions rather than a half hour conference alone.[3] (Bazemore and O'Brien, 2003) We might then find impacts in such multi-modal restorative interventions equal to or stronger than those associated with ECT programs (Lipsey, 1995).

2. Positive Clinical Relationships

ECT advocates place great emphasis on the development of a positive clinical relationship between the offender and the primary treatment professional. However, this relationship is not likely sufficient to achieve reintegration. Relationships with family, friends, peers and supporters are more important. From a restorative justice perspective, the professional is most helpful when s/he takes action to strengthen these relationships. Seeing a similar process in good clinical models, we advocate a more strategic extension of this model to be inclusive of family, other peers and supportive community.

Restorative justice is grounded in the premise that crime is both a cause and an effect of weakened relationships. Restorative interventions focus on the repair of weakened or broken relationships, and help for victims and offenders to develop new ones, and in general promote right relationships in communities as a preventative feature. Maximizing the role of friends, family and other supporters and community members, good restorative justice practice creates more sustainable and impactful relationships than those between professional and client. In fact, prevention research confirms that young people will engage in pro-social lifestyles when given opportunities to acquire/practice new skills and productive behaviors, strengthen relationships and increase pro-social bonds (e.g., Saleebey, 2002).

Restorative justice adds the role of "natural helpers" or "community guides" (McKnight, 1995) in successful reintegration. While some ECT advocates appear to fear that nonprofessionals will diminish the relationship between the offender and the therapist, others seem comfortable with the idea of such naturalistic social support and the role of restorative justice processes in mobilizing such support (Cullen, 1994). They may also recognize the vital role of such supporters in encouraging offenders to attend and commit to treatment — the "collective resolve," as Braithwaite puts it (see also, Toews-Shenk and Zehr, 2001). Research on the resiliency of youth-at-risk supports the importance of these relationships. Such research indicates that those who grow out of patterns of criminal and high risk behavior — even when all other risk factors are held constant and irrespective of treatment and services — do so as a result of long-term, caring close relationships with one or more prosocial adults (e.g., Saleebey, 2002).

Strong, positive, interpersonal relationships may reduce the *need* for treatment, and should therefore be a consideration in risk and need assessment of a youth. It is also possible that excessive or inappropriate treatment may inadvertently *weaken* positive relationships and ultimately make matters worse in much the same way that any excessive use of rules and conditions of supervision may encourage criminal behavior by low risk offenders (Andrews and Bonta, 1994).

3. Target Criminogenic Needs

This principle affirms that scarce treatment resources should only focus on issues directly related to an offender's criminality. Factors that have been found to have little direct bearing on what motivates offenders to commit crimes (e.g., low self esteem, anxiety or depression) should generally not be part of the offender's supervision or treatment plan. While these factors may be related to an offender's overall well-being, emphasis on them can detract from the focus on those forces (e.g., substance abuse, criminal or delinquent peers) that tend to relate directly to criminogenic impulses. In fact, some misdirected or irrelevant interventions (e.g., Scared Straight) have been found to not only distract focus but also to increase recidivism.

Some ECT advocates would like to eliminate a number of obligations that restorative justice advocates believe should be part of what the offender does to make amends to victims and communities — regardless of impact on recidivism. Specifically, meeting with one's victim, paying restitution, completing community service, or attending a victim awareness class may be obligations that may or may not address criminogenic needs, but would be performed on behalf of the victim and the community. However, these obligations do address criminogenic needs in the broadest sense, e.g., the lack of relationships of support and reciprocity in the offender's life. Arguably they are not included in ECT's list of criminogenically-related needs because they are not part of the primarily-clinical list of "effective interventions," or they are incorporated in a very weak, even counterproductive, fashion (e.g., court-ordered community service in which the offender picks up trash on the highways).

Restorative justice adds a less pejorative, broader and more accurate reframing of criminogenic needs as an absence of pro-social relationships, effective guardianship, and social support. Viewing the problem as bigger than what is inside the offender's head, restorative justice takes into account the community context. For instance, a criminogenic need might be to rebuild a severed or weakened relationship with a grandparent or teacher.

The fact that these additional stakeholders are brought to the table through a restorative justice conference may present opportunities to engage them directly in the treatment process. The principle of stakeholder involvement makes reparative (and treatment) obligations meaningful and ultimately makes reintegration more likely by creating a context for the emergence of social support (Braithwaite and Mugford, 1994; Cullen, 1994). From the offender perspective, involvement means playing an active role in the solution to the problem that his/her crime has created. In the most effective restorative processes, the *problem*, rather than the offender, is placed in the center of the circle (Melton,

1997). At the same time, the offender becomes aware of his/her responsibility for the problem, that s/he is *capable* of making things right, rebuilding community connections and moving back into a pro-social relationship with the community.

4. *Responsivity*

This principle suggests that one size doesn't fit all. For effective correctional treatment, it is fundamental to perform risk and needs assessments in order to match offenders' needs and risks to the appropriate kind of intervention and even the type of therapist or treatment professional who can best address these needs.

Classification based on risk and need also plays a role in restorative justice programs. Compatible with the traditional correctional emphasis on public safety (Guarino-Ghezzi and Klein, 2000), restorative justice is also consistent with most efforts to restrict opportunities for victimization and harm based on probability of reoffending. Although traditional risk classification models fail to address the needs and interests of victims and communities, classification could conceivably be expanded to assess victim needs as well as community risks and needs and to involve these stakeholders in the decision making process (Dooley, 1999). Most importantly, by applying restorative justice principles to classification and case management, agencies can also turn over some decision making to communities and victims, freeing always scarce correctional resources for the supervision and management of more serious offenders (Karp and Walther, 2000).

5. *Avoiding Over-Consequencing*

This principle points to the importance of minimizing sanctions and requirements beyond those directly related to criminogenic needs. Most importantly, it is based on the well-documented finding that most youth in trouble get better without formal intervention of any kind and the finding that adding too many requirements in treatment or supervision plans for low-risk youth may actually increase the likelihood that they will reoffend.

While the fear that restorative practices may overload offenders with unnecessary requirements is a valid one, historically the greatest culprit of overloading has been professionally-based diversion and probation alternatives. There is certainly no evidence thus far that community members in restorative programs overload offenders with obligations. When they do so, I suggest that they are merely replicating what they think professionals would have them do. Indeed, restorative conferencing programs that provide volunteer community members with lists of treatment program referrals invite a professional "fix" because volunteers are made to feel that a more naturalistic solution is inferior to a professional one.

Commitment to the third core principle of restorative principles provides the best guidance. This principle suggests that we must maximize the community role while changing the government role to one of facilitator rather than as professional "fixer." In doing so, we reduce the problem of over-consequencing by minimizing the system role wherever possible and maximizing the community role. This, in turn, promotes the establishment of relationships.

Over-consequencing is likely to most affect restorative justice when system professionals refer cases where there has been little real harm or in order to add on restorative interventions along with a list of other interventions. In such cases, participants in a restorative conference may feel the need to "do something" when in fact that "something" could have been done by a police officer, offender and family on the street, by a teacher, youth and family in a school and so on.

"Net-widening" — the tendency to use interventions as add-ons rather than alternatives, thus widening the scope of governmental control — is another concern related to over-consequencing. Restorative justice reduces the reliance on professionals and programs which in turn reduces the primary causes of net-widening. In addition, restorative justice has attempted to strengthen "community nets" while challenging the hegemony of "government nets" (Braithwaite, 1994; Bazemore, 1999).

CONCLUSION

Many corrections practitioners recognize a number of potential benefits in a merger between restorative justice and effective treatment approaches (Rhine et al., 1997; Carey, 2000). However, some ECT advocates fail to acknowledge that rehabilitation is bigger than changing the attitudes, thinking, and problematic behavior of offenders. Restorative justice poses this question: what good is an initial change in thinking and behavior patterns if the offender's relationships with law-abiding adults and peers are weak or nonexistent?

A restorative model of rehabilitation does not, therefore, render treatment irrelevant. Efforts to repair harm and effective correctional interventions are not either/or propositions. Therapeutic interventions for offenders who evidence cognitive or behavioral patterns that limit their ability to form positive relationships could support the restorative goal of strengthening existing connections with positive peers and groups and building new ones. Treatment programs may also reinforce reparative obligations more directly by, for example, processing disruptive behavior that may occur as offenders engage in community service or other reparative projects. Treatment professionals may play an important supportive role in family group conferencing and other restorative decision-making processes (Hudson et al., 1996), and restorative justice practitioners would certainly do well to manage dialogue and interaction with offenders according to principles of effective treatment. Practitioners can ensure that offenders are not overloaded with requirements when determining restorative obligations (Braithwaite and Parker, 1999; Levrant et al., 1999).

In summary, restorative justice is compatible with ECT principles, but also offers a great deal of added value in three ways. A blend of restorative justice and effective treatment principles broadens the rehabilitative context to include victim and community; emphasizes the non-punitive accountability for harms in a way that reinforces reciprocity in human relationships; and connects the offender with informal supports and controls. In doing so, this blended approach builds on the assets of offender, community and victim.

Address correspondence to: Gordon Bazemore, Community Justice Institute, Florida Atlantic University, University Tower, 200 SE 2nd Ave., Ft. Lauderdale, FL 33315.

REFERENCES

Andrews, D. and J. Bonta (1994). *The Psychology of Criminal Conduct.* Cincinnati, OH: Anderson Publishing.

Bazemore, G. (1999). "After Shaming, Whither Reintegration: Restorative Justice and Relational Rehabilitation." In: G. Bazemore and L. Walgrave (eds.), *Restorative Juvenile Justice: Repairing the Harm of Youth Crime.* Monsey, NY: Criminal Justice Press.

—— and C. Erbe (2003). "Operationalizing the Community Variable in Offender Reintegration: Theory and Practice for Developing Intervention Social Capital." *Youth Violence and Juvenile Justice* 1(10):246-275.

—— and S. O'Brien (2002). "The Quest for a Restorative Model of Rehabilitation: Theory-for-Practice and Practice-for-Theory." In: L. Walgrave (ed.), *Restorative Justice and the Law.* Cullompton, Devon, UK: Willan Publishing.

—— L. Nissen, and M. Dooley (2000). "Mobilizing Social Support and Building Relationships: Broadening Correctional and Rehabilitative Agendas." *Corrections Management Quarterly* 4(4):10-21.

Braithwaite, J. (2002). *Restorative Justice and Responsive Regulation.* New York: Oxford University Press.

—— (2001). "Restorative Justice and a New Criminal Law of Substance Abuse." *Youth & Society* 33(2):227-248.

—— (1994). "Thinking Harder about Democratizing Social Control." In: C. Alder and J. Wundersitz (eds.), *Family Group Conferencing in Juvenile Justice: The Way Forward or Misplaced Optimism?* Canberra, AUS: Australian Institute of Criminology.

—— and S. Mugford (1994). "Conditions of Successful Reintegration Ceremonies: Dealing with Juvenile Offenders." *British Journal of Criminology* 34:139, 171.

—— and C. Parker (1999). "Restorative Justice is Republican Justice." In: G. Bazemore and L. Walgrave (eds.), *Restorative Juvenile Justice: Repairing the Harm of Youth Crime.* Monsey, NY: Criminal Justice Press.

Carey, M. (2001). "Infancy, Adolescence and Restorative Justice: The Application and Timing of Strategies in Promoting Organizational Change Toward Restoration." In: G. Bazemore and M. Schiff (eds.), *Restorative and Community Justice: Cultivating Common Ground for Victims, Communities and Offenders.* Cincinnati, OH: Anderson Publishing.

Cullen, F.T. (1994). "Social Support as an Organizing Concept for Criminology." *Justice Quarterly* 11:527-559.

Dooley, M. (1999). "Classification and Restorative Justice: Is There a Relationship?" *Topics in Community Corrections.* Longmount, CO: National Institute of Corrections Monograph.

Gendrau, P., F. Cullen and J. Bonta (1994). "Up to Speed: Intensive Rehabilitation Supervision and the Next Generation in Community Corrections." *Federal Probation* 58:72-79.

Guarino-Ghezzi, S. and A. Klein (1999). "Public Safety in a Restorative Justice System." In: G. Bazemore and L. Walgrave (eds.), *Restorative Juvenile Justice: Repairing the Harm of Youth Crime.* Monsey, NY: Criminal Justice Press.

Hudson, J., B. Gallaway, A. Morris and G. Maxwell (eds.), (1996). *Family Group Conferences: Perspectives on Policy and Practice.* Monsey, NY: Criminal Justice Press.

Karp, D., and L. Walther (2000). "Community Reparative Boards: Theory and Practice." In: G. Bazemore and M. Schiff (eds.), *Restorative and Community Justice: Cultivating Common Ground for Victims, Communities and Offenders.* Cincinnati, OH: Anderson Publishing.

Levrant, S., F. Cullen, B. Fulton and J. Wozniak (1999). "Reconsidering Restorative Justice: The Corruption of Benevolence Revisited?" *Crime & Delinquency* 45:3-27.

Lipsey, M.W. (1995). "What Do We Learn from 400 Research Studies on Effectiveness of Treatment with Juvenile Delinquents?" In: J. McGuire (ed.), *What Works: Reducing Reoffending.* New York: Wiley.

Martinson, R. (1972). "What Works — Questions and Answers About Prison Reform." *Public Interest* 32:22-54.

Maruna, S. (2001). *Making Good: How Ex-Convicts Reform and Rebuild Their Lives.* Washington, DC: American Psychological Association.

Melton, A. (1995). "Indigenous Justice Systems and Tribal Society." *Judicature* 70:126-133.

McKnight, J. (1995). *The Careless Society: Community and Its Counterfeits.* New York, NY: Basic Books.

Putnam, R. (2000). *Bowling Alone: The Collapse and Revival of American Community.* New York, NY: Simon and Shuster.

Rhine, E., A. Neff and G. Natalucci-Persichetti (1998). "Restorative Justice, Public Safety, and the Supervision of Juvenile Offenders." *Corrections Management Quarterly* 2:40-48.

Ross, R. and E. Fabiano (1985). *Time to Think: A Cognitive Model of Crime and Delinquency Prevention and Rehabilitation.* Ottawa, CAN: Academy of Arts and Sciences.

Rutter, M. (1985). "Resilience in the Face of Adversity: Protective Factors and Resistance to Psychiatric Disorder." *British Journal of Psychiatry* 147:598-611.

Saleebey, D. (2002). "The Strengths Perspective: Possibilities and Problems." In: D. Saleebey (ed.), *The Strengths Perspective in Social Work Practice* (3rd ed.). London, UK: Allyn and Bacon.

Stuart, B. (1996). "Circle Sentencing — Turning Swords into Ploughshares." In: B. Galaway and J. Hudson. (eds.), *Restorative Justice: International Perspectives*. Monsey, NY: Criminal Justice Press.

Toews-Shenk, B. and H. Zehr (2001). "Restorative Justice and Substance Abuse: The Path Ahead." *Youth and Society* (December) 33(2):314-328.

Umbreit, M. (2001). *The Handbook of Victim-Offender Mediation*. San Francisco, CA: Jossey-Bass.

Van Ness, D. and K.H. Strong (1997). *Restoring Justice*. Cincinnati OH: Anderson.

Yochelson, S. and S. Samenow (1976). *The Criminal Personality*. New York, NY: J. Aronson.

NOTES

1. Meta-analysis is a procedure aimed at providing an overall assessment of the strength of impact of a collective body of independent evaluations. The procedure yields an overall score (generally a phi coefficient) for a category of programs (e.g., counseling programs). Meta-analyses of treatment programs often compare the strength of one type of treatment model with another.

2. Our problem with such characterizations is that many of the thinking error types used to distinguish offenders fit equally well with many members of any faculty, or family, and many corrections professionals who work with offenders — in other words, theoretically and empirically, they don't help us understand criminality very well.

3. E.g., a circle or conference followed by a victim impact panel or victim awareness classes and community service performed with a conference participant, with regular follow-up mentoring and support from conference or circle participants.

Chapter 11.
What Is The Place Of Shame In Restorative Justice?

by

Gabrielle Maxwell and Allison Morris

John Braithwaite's (1989) theory of reintegrative shaming has been enormously influential in providing a basis for restorative justice in general and for some forms of conferencing in particular. This theory links shaming with effective crime control and Braithwaite, in his original text, argued that societies like Japan, which shamed effectively, had lower crime rates than countries which did not. With respect to family group conferences in New Zealand, Braithwaite subsequently (1993:37) linked them to traditional Maori conflict resolution processes that, he suggested, placed "great importance on ceremonies to communicate the shame of wrongdoing." He claimed that family group conferences had the effect of "bringing shame back into the justice process." More broadly, Masters (1998:134) has argued that shame is a critical component in the development of effective restorative justice. He suggested that communication between victims and offenders offers "a framework for shaming," and presented it as "almost inevitable" that restorative practices would lead to the shaming of offenders (1998:129). He quoted, in support of this, Retzinger and Scheff's (1996:330) description of a family group conference as "an automatic shaming machine."

We would not depict family group conferences in New Zealand as "bringing shame back into the justice process" nor as "automatic shaming machines." Nor do we see shaming as an essential part of restorative justice. In this article, we question these presumed linkages between shaming and effective crime control at both theoretical and empirical levels. First, we summarize briefly some of the psychological literature that suggests shame is a troublesome concept; it is difficult to define and cannot be assumed to have a single or uniform effect. Then we raise some general concerns about shaming and question how it can result in effective crime control for those most likely to come into the justice system. Finally, we draw on research on family group conferences in New Zealand that explored key factors affecting young offenders' re-offending (and reintegration), including the impact of shame, to examine whether or not shame reduced the likelihood of reoffending. But first, it is important to make clear what Braithwaite meant by "reintegrative shaming."

What Is Reintegrative Shame?

The distinction between "stigmatic shaming" and "reintegrative shaming" is crucial for Braithwaite's theory of crime control. Braithwaite is firmly opposed to stigmatic shaming and sees it as counter-productive and as likely to result in more crime.[1] Reintegrative shaming, on the other hand, is seen as likely to be effective in controlling crime (1989:4). Reintegrative shaming means that the offence rather than the offender is condemned and the offender is reintegrated with (i.e., included) rather than rejected by society (excluded). This is said by Braithwaite to be achieved through certain steps:

- disapproving of the offence;

- sustaining a relationship of respect for the offender and not la-beling the offender as bad or evil;

- not allowing the offending to be viewed as the offender's main characteristic; and

- re-accepting the offender through "words or gestures of forgive-ness" (1989:100).

Braithwaite also emphasized that the shame which mattered most was not "the shame of remote judge or police officer, but the shame of the people they most care about" (1993:37). If shaming is to be a part of restorative justice, therefore, it is crucially important to get it "right." The next two sections raise potential problems in achieving this.

Shaming As A Psychological Process

Sabini and Silver suggested that shame is effective in preventing "many of us doing things the world is better off without our doing" (1977:12). Psychological research presents a different and less clear-cut picture. Shame is seen by some psychologists as the feeling generated by the actual or imagined negative responses of others to our behavior and, importantly, early writers on shame linked it to national characteristics. For example, Benedict (1946) suggested that traditional group-oriented societies, such as Japan, were more likely to generate shame than peer-oriented societies, such as America, that were more likely to generate anxiety. Benedict saw both of these emotional responses as potentially negative, but the important point to make here is that the influence of shame, and the way it is generated, depended on cultural factors and not simply on certain situations. Also, Benedict noted that the people whose disapproval had the greatest impact — elders, peers or the self — varied culturally. Both of these findings raise difficulties for a general theory of shame.

However, it is not only culture that is a determinant. Within any particular culture or society, there will always be individuals who respond differently and members of different sub-groups — for example religious communities — may also respond differently. It is not surprising, therefore, that those who have attempted to understand emotional responses as the general reactions of all individuals have not always been able to do so. Tomkins (1987), for example, concluded that shame can be used to stand for a whole gamut of emotions that included embarrassment, contempt, ridicule, humiliation and feeling put down. The nature of these emotions is defined and experienced somewhat differently by different people depending on their past history as well as on their temperament. Such a formulation can explain the variety of mixed, and often confusing and inconsistent, research findings reported by those who have attempted to explore the concept of shame in research on responses to specific situations (cf. Tangney, 1991; Harris, 1999). Again, these findings raise difficulties for a general theory of shame.

While the underlying emotional experience appears to be elusive and variable, the consequences of being shamed are more easily described and, at the extreme, the consequences are almost always viewed as negative. Miller (1996:151) called shame the "bedrock of much psychopathology." Lewis (1971) suggested that the consequences of shame are often an inability to feel empathy, depression, powerlessness, anger and hostility to others. Nathanson (1997) suggested that, whatever form subjective experiences take, when shame (or one of its related emotions) is triggered the individual will engage in one of four patterns: withdrawal, attack of self, avoidance or attack of others. Olthof (2000) concluded, in a review of recent psychological literature, that inducing shame in an offender could lead to a desire to avoid being in such a situation again, but that it was potentially risky in that it could evoke further negative, anti-social and hostile behavior.[2]

Such negative views of shame are confirmed by the empirical research of Tangney and her associates. They related shame to: a lack of empathy (1991); maladaptive responses such as anger, including malevolent intentions; direct, indirect and displaced aggression; self-directed hostility and negative long-term consequences (1992); and to anger, aggression, suspiciousness, resentment, irritability, a tendency to blame others for negative events and indirect expressions of hostility (1996).

Of course, it could be argued that what is really being discussed here are the effects of stigmatic and not reintegrative shaming. Again this points to the importance of getting the shaming "right." However, if we link the findings of this section with the concerns raised in the next section, we are bound to conclude that we do not know for sure how to do this: the intent of the shamer cannot determine the effects on the shamed.

Some Concerns About Shaming

It is important to distinguish "the act of shaming" — others consciously taking steps to shame — and "feeling ashamed" — the internalization of shame. The former is probably best demonstrated in the various stigmatic practices currently in vogue in the United States mentioned earlier. No doubt, these practices can lead to offenders feeling ashamed. However, "feeling ashamed" can happen irrespective of the acts of others. Data from Maxwell et al. (2003) showed that some young offenders reported feeling very ashamed after their family group conference, although the researchers present at the conference did not record observing any shaming behavior on the part of those present. Conversely, attempts to shame — whether stigmatically or reintegratively — may not be noticed by the intended objects. Other young offenders in Maxwell et al.'s (2003) sample did not report feeling ashamed after conferences, although the researchers had noted statements made by others present at the conference that seemed intended to shame. Furthermore, despite intentions, shaming intended to be reintegrative might be viewed by the offender as stigmatic. In this case, the shaming would become, in Braithwaite's terms, "counter-productive."

In this context, Blagg's (1998) critique is important. He raises questions about how Australian aboriginals, who have experienced harassment on the street by the police and discrimination in everyday life by the dominant culture, can realistically be expected to see the processes of shaming as resulting in reintegration within communities. Indeed, we would extend Blagg's point to apply to all who are socially excluded — most young people, the unemployed, the poor and so on.

Braithwaite recognized the way shame has contributed to the destruction of indigenous (and presumably other socially excluded) communities. However, the issue now is the extent to which any shaming in these communities can become reintegrative; there has to be some doubt about this given their experience of policing and their experience of the criminal justice system more generally. Walgrave and Aertsen (1996) also question the value of shaming by official representatives of the community — for example, by police officers. It might, of course, be a different matter if indigenous and other socially excluded people were supported by communities of care and if any shaming was carried out, not by criminal justice or social work professionals, but by those whom these excluded groups respected, such as their family, elders or supporters. This is, of course, what Braithwaite advocated but it is not often what happens in practice. However, we would have reservations about this type of shaming too.

Shaming And Reoffending

As noted earlier, Braithwaite argued that reintegrative shaming was likely to be effective in controlling crime and that stigmatic shaming was likely to be counter-productive. We attempted to explore this by comparing the experiences of samples of young offenders who had family group conferences in 1990/91 and in 1998, then with respect to whether or not they were reconvicted in later years (Maxwell and Morris, 1999; Maxwell et al., 2003). These results indicate that family group conferences can have an impact on reoffending.

For example, with respect to the 1990/91 sample (Maxwell and Morris, 1999), we showed that there were significant relationships between reoffending and a number of variables describing the views of the young offender about his/her experience of the family group conference. These variables were as follows: meeting the victim and/or apologizing; feeling involved in the conference and participating in the decision making; agreeing with the conference outcomes; remembering the conference; completing the tasks agreed to; feeling sorry and that they had been able to contribute to repairing the damage to the victim; and, importantly in the context of this paper, not being stigmatically shamed or made to feel a bad person

The findings reported in Maxwell et al. (2003) replicated some of these results and added to them. Based on the young people's reports of their conference experiences, not being convicted as an adult seemed to be related to the following: feeling that they were involved in the conference and had participated in the decision; feeling that they were treated with fairness and respect; a sense of forgiveness indicated by the sense that those present had let them put the past behind them; being able to make up for what they had done; and forming an intention not to reoffend. In addition to these defining characteristics of a constructive (restorative) conference, one further finding was important: a feeling of being stigmatically shamed or excluded had a highly significant relationship with conviction as an adult (and with not experiencing positive life outcomes after the conference).

There are, therefore, consistent themes across both sets of findings. A sense of participation in the conference, repairing the harm to the victim and an avoidance of stigmatic shaming appeared to be important for both the 1990/91 and 1998 samples. However, new variables emerged in the analysis of the data on the 1998 sample: understanding what went on, a sense of forgiveness and forming an intention not to reoffend. Conversely, some of the variables which appeared from the analysis of data on the 1990/91 sample did not emerge from the analysis of data on the 1998 sample. The reason for this was that apologies to the victim, a sense of remorse, and agreement with the outcomes were reported by almost everyone in the second study, and so they did not emerge as important factors which distinguished those reconvicted from those not reconvicted. It is possible that a young offender feels a potentially reintegrative sense of shame as a result of what happens during a family group conference. However, our research suggests that such shame occurs not because of attempts by others to induce shame but because of recognition of the consequences for others of the offender's behavior. Thus, in our view, a better way of describing what the offender experienced is a feeling of remorse or empathy and we have no problems with attempts within conferences (or any other restorative justice process) to create these feelings.

CONCLUSION

One clear finding from all this is that a sense of being shamed, of being made to feel a bad person, that endures after decisions about how to repair damage are made, is likely to contribute to further reoffending. This, of course, is more like what Braithwaite meant by stigmatic shaming rather than reintegrative shaming, and might lead to the conclusion that reintegrative shaming could and should be a theoretical basis for both conferencing and restorative justice. However, taking into account the concerns we raised previously and other findings in our research on family group conferences in New Zealand, we do not conclude this.

We suggest rather that the inducement of shame is both risky and potentially counter-productive. Further research is clearly needed to explore how best to ask questions that define the subjective experiences of the young offenders who have experienced a restorative justice process and to determine how they are interrelated. For the present, this data suggests the elements that help define a constructive family group conference resulting in an intention not to reoffend include the following: being supported, participating in and understanding what is going on in the conference, being treated with fairness and respect and not being stigmatically shamed, agreeing with outcomes and taking actions to repair the harm, and feeling forgiven and able to put matters behind them are all. For us, the lessons from this for restorative justice are clear: As Braithwaite (1989:12) recognized, "shaming is a dangerous game" and one which, in our view, carries too many risks to be worth playing.

Address correspondence to: Gabrielle Maxwell, 63 Cecil Rd., Wellington, NZ. E-mail: <g.maxwell@paradise.net.nz>.

REFERENCES

Benedict, R. (1946). *The Chrysanthemum and the Sword: Patterns of Japanese Culture*. Boston, MA: Houghton Mifflin.

Blagg, H. (1998). "Restorative Visions and Restorative Justice Practices: Conferencing, Ceremony and Reconciliation in Australia." *Current Issues in Criminal Justice* 10/1:5-14.

Braithwaite, J. (1997). "Conferencing and Plurality: Reply to Blagg." *British Journal of Criminology* 37:502-506.

—— (1993). "Shame and Modernity." *British Journal of Criminology* 33:1-18.

—— (1989). *Crime, Shame and Reintergration*. Cambridge, UK: Cambridge University Press.

Harris, N. (1999). "Shaming and Shame: An Empirical Analysis." Unpublished Ph.D. thesis. Canberra: Australian National University.

Inkeles, A. and D.J. Levinson (1969). "National Character: The Study of the Modal Personality and Sociocultural Systems." In: G. Lindzey and E. Aronson (eds.), *The Handbook of Social Psychology* (2nd ed.). Cambridge, MA: Addison Wesley.

Karp, D. (1998). "The Judicial and Judicious Use of Shame Penalties." *Crime & Delinquency* 44(2):277-294.

Lemert, E. (1971). *Instead of Court: Diversion in Juvenile Justice*, Washington, DC: U.S. Government Printing Office.

Lewis, H.B. (1971). *Shame and Guilt in Neurosis*. New York: International Universities Press.

Masters, G. (1998). "The Importance of Shame to Restorative Justice." In: L. Walgrave (ed.), *Restorative Justice for Juveniles: Potentialities, Risks and Problems for Research*. Leuven, BEL: Leuven University Press.

Maxwell, G.M. and A. Morris (1999). "Understanding Reoffending: Final Report to the Social Policy Agency and the Ministry of Justice." Wellington, NZ: Institute of Criminology, Victoria University of Wellington.

—— V. Kingi, J. Robertson and A. Morris (2003). "Achieving Effective Outcomes in Youth Justice: Draft of the Final Report to the Ministry of Social Development." Wellington, NZ: Crime and Justice Research Centre, Victoria University of Wellington.

McCold, P. and B. Wachtel (1998). *Restorative Policing Experiment*. Pipersville: Community Service Foundation.

Miller, S. (1996). *Shame in Context*. Hillsdale: Analytic Press.

Moore, D. (1993) "Shame, Forgiveness and Juvenile Justice." *Criminal Justice Ethics* (Winter/Spring):3-24.

Nathanson, D.L. (1997). "Affect Theory and the Compass of Shame." In: M.R. Lansky and A.P. Morrison (eds.), *The Widening Scope of Shame*. Hillsdale, NJ: The Analytic Press.

Olthof, T. (2000). "Shame, Guilt, Antisocial Behaviour and Juvenile Justice." In: I. Weijers and A. Duff (eds.), *Punishing Juveniles: Principles and Critique*. Oxford, UK: Hart Publishing.

Retzinger, S.M. and T.J. Scheff (1996). "Strategy for Community Conferences: Emotions and Social Bonds." In: J. Hudson and B. Galaway (eds.), *Restorative Justice: International Perspectives*. Monsey, NY: Criminal Justice Press.

Sabini, J. and M. Silver (1997). "In Defense of Shame in the Context of Guilt and Embarrassment." *Journal for the Theory of Social Behaviour* 27(1):1-15.

Sherman, L., H. Strang, G. Barnes., J. Braithwaite, N. Inkpen and M. Teh (1998). "Experiments in Restorative Policing: A Progress Report to the National Police Research Unit on the Canberra Reintegrative Shaming Experiment." Canberra, AUS: Australian National University.

Tangney, J. (1991). "Moral Affect: The Good, The Bad and The Ugly." *Journal of Personality and Social Psychology* 61(4):598-607.

—— P.E. Wagner, D. Hill-Barlow, D.E. Marshall and R. Gramzow (1996). "Relation of Shame and Guilt to Constructive Versus Destructive Responses to Anger Across the Lifespan." *Journal of Personality and Social Psychology* 70(4):797-809.

—— and P.E. Wagner, C. Fletcher and R. Gramzow (1992). "Shamed into Anger? The Relation of Shame and Guilt to Anger and Self-reported Aggression." *Journal of Personality and Social Psychology* 62(4):669-675.

Tomkins, S.S. (1987). "Shame." In: D.L. Nathanson (ed.), *The Many Faces of Shame*. New York: Guilford Press.

Vagg, J. (1998). "Delinquency and Shame: Data from Hong Kong." *British Journal of Criminology* 38(2):247-264.

Walgrave, L. and A. Aertsen (1996). "Reintegrative Shaming and Restorative Justice." *European Journal on Criminal Policy and Research* 4(4):67-85.

Young, R. and B. Goold (1999). "Restorative Police Cautioning in Aylesbury — From Degrading to Reintegrative Shaming Ceremonies?" *Criminal Law Review* 126-38.

NOTES

1. Stigmatic shaming is a recognized part of conventional criminal justice systems; many of their rituals serve to signify the separation and segregation of defendants — by, for example, their placement in the dock or in stocks. There has, however, been a revival of stigmatic practices in sanctions in some jurisdictions (see Karp [1998] for a review of practices in the United States, including the use of placards and notices identifying offenders and warning the rest of us to beware).

2. Sociologists have also discussed the negative consequences of shame. Vagg (1998:250) suggested that shame could produce feelings of "humiliation, rage and desire for revenge rather than feelings of guilt and remorse," and labeling theorists (for example, Lemert, 1971) similarly argued that labeling or stigmatizing an offender increases the likelihood of subsequent deviant behavior. They introduced terms like "secondary deviance" and "deviance amplification" to capture this.

Chapter 12.
What Is The Place Of Punishment And Imprisonment In Restorative Justice?

by

Russ Immarigeon

> VORP is probably not answering the need for alternatives to in-carceration... Instead of avoiding problems created by the use of the prison system, another sentencing option has been imple-mented which pulls a different set of offenders deeper into the system of social control and inevitably increases cost (Dittenhof-fer and Ericson, 1983:346).

> Since the beginning of 1998, a "restorative detention" pilot proj-ect has been active in six Belgian prisons. In 2000, more quickly than expected, the policy makers saw to it that the restorative detention project had taken root in the Belgian penal establish-ment as a whole... (W)e must avoid the danger that imprison-ment, with all of its known disadvantages is "packaged as re-storative justice." The hijacking of restorative justice initiatives is a real threat, certainly when it concerns a possible new legitima-tion of imprisonment (Robert and Peters, 2002:95, 116).

Twenty years ago, British writer Martin Wright, who has worked for both the offender-oriented Howard League and the victim-oriented Na-tional Association of Victim Support Schemes, asked, "What can be done to reduce society's reliance on prisons, given the prevailing am-bivalent framework of attitudes (that) try to combine punishment with rehabilitation?" (Wright, 1982:77). At about this time, at least in the United States, the National Council on Crime and Delinquency had called for a moratorium on prison construction, an advocacy group called the National Moratorium on Prison Construction was organizing for "Jobs, Not Jails," and historian David J. Rothman told a conference group at the opening of the National Institute for Sentencing Alternatives that displeasure with the use of imprisonment and disenchantment with efforts to reform it had never been stronger.

Of these three organizations, only the National Council on Crime and Delinquency still exists. Stronger than ever, however, is the concept of restorative justice. Twenty years ago, when victim-offender reconciliation programs (VORPs) first appeared in Canada and the United States, restorative justice was not yet a term in the vocabulary of criminal justice reform advocates. Clearly, though, the overuse of imprisonment (as measured through high rates of incarceration and high gross numbers of prisoners), as well as the inherent legitimacy of imprisonment, was being seriously challenged as a method of sanctioning criminal offenders. It was in this context that the seeds of restorative justice were planted with small local efforts to bring victims and offenders together to informally counter routinely punitive court decisions. Those who started to establish VORPs were part of a larger movement of people displeased and disenchanted with the use of incarceration.

Like probation and other so-called "alternatives," restorative justice measures were first proposed with the hope that they would significantly challenge and replace incarceration as a dominant response to crime. But, as the restorative justice movement ages, its vision seems less focused on its relationship to incarceration, with the possible exception of those efforts to incorporate the use of restorative justice inside prisons or even to use it as a set of guiding principles for the operation of prisons.

In this article, I argue that restorative justice measures rarely divert anyone from imprisonment, particularly in the United States, although this also seems the case in Australia and Canada. Some evidence exists that New Zealand is using restorative justice as an alternative to detention, but even that evidence is weaker than one would hope for. Instead, restorative justice sentences commonly increase the burden of these sanctions on convicted parties. To some extent, extra consequences can be helpful, especially when they are directed toward victim, offender, or community "healing," but often they simply seem punitive or they fail to challenge the flow or hegemony of sanctions that rely on the use of incarceration. In addition, restorative justice sanctions or interventions are being used with persons who have committed less serious, and even minor, offenses. Or, as is the case with many prison-based programs, involvement with a restorative justice program is not meant to affect the length of sentence.

RESTORATIVE JUSTICE AS AN ALTERNATIVE TO PRISON

If restorative justice is being used anywhere as an alternative to incarceration it is in New Zealand, where the use of family group conferencing (FGC) for juvenile offenders was enabled when the Children, Young Persons and Their Families Act of 1989 was passed into law. I have spoken with academics, activists, and researchers familiar with New Zealand's experience with family group conferences and they inform me of the complexity of establishing the diversionary impact of FGCs. Umbreit, Coates and Vos (2002), for example, report that the number of juvenile court cases declined from 13,000 to 2,600 within a year of the Act. However, others report that the reduced number of juvenile cases is also partially because of other factors, such as an increase in the age of criminal liability (Newbold, 2003). At one point, I heard that New Zealand had closed six juvenile detention facilities because of the use of family group conferences. But, I have since been informed that, while some social welfare institutions for juveniles have closed in the past, again for a variety of reasons, New Zealand is currently in the process of building four new juvenile prisons and is being pressured to build more, in part because of juveniles being confined in local police stations (Dunstall, 2003; Newbold, 2003).

In New Zealand, statutory language appears at least to focus program and policy attention on the objective of reducing the use of incarceration through FGCs. Among the guiding principles of the youth justice section of the Children, Young People and Their Families Act (Section 208) are the following:

- criminal proceedings should not occur if other methods of addressing the problem are available;

- criminal proceedings should not be imposed simply to advance social welfare concerns of young people or their biological or extended family;

- measures that address offending behavior should strengthen the family unit and the young person and foster their ability to address offending behavior by family members;

- young people should be maintained in the community as much as possible;

- sanctions should involve the least restrictive alternative; and,

- sanctions should take heed of the interests of crime victims.

These principles, by and large, lay the groundwork for loosening reliance on incarceration and allowing a search for alternatives to incarceration.

Elsewhere, however, one finds little evidence of anything encouraging. When O'Brien (2000) searched American state statutes or codes for passages about restorative justice, she located supportive language in 19 states, but little about the use of imprisonment. Umbreit, Lightfoot and Fier (2002) conducted another national search for state laws pertaining to victim-offender mediation, the most frequent form of restorative justice. They found that statutory authority for such programs existed in 29 states. While these statutes covered issues such as funding, statewide monitoring commissions, training requirements, organizational structure, and eligibility, none specifically suggested the use of restorative justice as an alternative to incarceration. Interestingly, victim-offender mediation was not specifically mentioned in the statutes of four states that seemingly embraced restorative justice.

Research studies have also shed little light on the ability of restorative justice to divert or displace men or women from prison. Researchers typically say that restorative justice cases are too few in number to accurately measure such a result. Researchers also say that it is too complex a matter to decisively determine such a specific outcome, especially when other factors are at play. One noted researcher says that, at least in Australia, youth in court are rarely sentenced to detention and that "it is really through many incremental decisions over time that jail may be avoided" (Daly, 2003).

Rare is the study that makes an effort to gauge diversionary or displacement outcomes. In one such study in the early 1980s, Dittenhoffer and Ericson (1983) explored the possible net-widening effect of victim-offender reconciliation programs in Ontario, Canada. They discovered that some judges using this program stressed its punitive aspects and, not surprisingly, the sentences they imposed de-emphasized the use of restorative justice as an alternative to incarceration. Prosecuting attorneys stressed this even more so, with only probation officers being able to see and explore some of the wider objectives of the program, including its use as an alternative to incarceration. Still, the everyday functioning of probation officer activities mitigated the use of VORPs as alternatives to confinement. "VORP is probably not answering the need for alternatives to incarceration," concluded the researchers, who also despaired: "it is difficult even to imagine circumstances that might lead to substantial change" (Dittenhoffer and Ericson, 1983:346-347).

Other studies have also examined the use of restorative justice as a diversion measure or as an alternative to incarceration. Diversion, however, can mean several things, including diversion from arrest, prosecution, court, and community sentences, as well as from jail or prison. But diversion from prosecution, for example, does not necessarily mean diversion from incarceration, because prosecutorial diversion cases are often less serious offenses in which incarceration is not a likely outcome anyway. Notably, the program examined in the Dittenhoffer and Ericson study attempted to use VORPs as a post-conviction remedy for those cases in which incarceration was a possible outcome of normal court process, yet the program still failed to divert or displace offenders from imprisonment.

Umbreit, Coates and Vos (2002) reviewed studies that assessed the diversionary impact of victim-offender mediation, family group conferences, and sentencing circles. They found at least one study that established diversion from prosecution (Dignan, 1990) and one from court processing (Clarke et al., 1992). More promisingly, they also found a study (Coates and Gehm, 1985) that demonstrated that offenders in victim-offender mediation programs in Indiana and Ohio spent less time incarcerated than a control group; still, this group was also more likely to experience jail time than prison time in comparison to its non-victim-offender mediation counterparts.

Umbreit, Coates and Vos also show that studies of family group conferencing reveal evidence of less police intervention (Moore and Forsythe, 1995) and less court involvement (Maxwell and Morris, 1993). Few studies examine sentencing circles, but one of them (Native Counseling Services of Alberta, 2001) shows that even persons charged with assault offenses can be diverted from provincial and federal justice systems.

RESTORATIVE JUSTICE AS A PRISON PROGRAM

Prison-based restorative justice programs have also emerged in various locations across the country, as well as internationally. However, while these efforts may have some utility as a method of healing harms between victims and offenders (a significant achievement in itself), they have had little impact on the extent to which prisoners are confined. Indeed, most such efforts categorically exclude consideration of restorative justice programming as a mitigating circumstance to support early release from confinement.

Ten years ago, when I first surveyed the extent of prison-based restorative justice programming, I found nine promising programs located in penal settings in Canada, England, and the United States. These programs included the Face-to-Face programs in Manitoba, Newfoundland and Saskatchewan; the Victim-Offender Reconciliation Program in Graterford, Pennsylvania; the Victim-Offender Workshop at Ossining, New York; and the Restorative Justice Project in Madison, Wisconsin. Today, no accurate survey exists on the extent of these programs in the United States and elsewhere. However, Umbreit et al. (2003) have evaluated Victim-Offender Dialogue Programs in Ohio and Texas and report that similar initiatives are operating, or in the planning stage, in 15 states. Victim-offender meetings have expanded from Graterford to other prisons in Pennsylvania, and in Nebraska the OASIS program uses the Internet to enable victim-offender connections. So, while no comprehensive information is available about these programs, anecdotal evidence shows that many efforts are being made. Also, little information exists about whether these programs operate on either an individual, case-by-case basis, or on a more full-fledged basis. In New York State, for example, the mediation section of the Office of Court Administration is involved with approximately five cases a year, but these occur irregularly and little seems in place to establish these options routinely throughout the state prison system.

BARRIERS TO DIVERSION/DISPLACEMENT

Generally speaking, restorative justice measures have not lived up to their expectations or possibilities as an alternative to penal confinement. As I have suggested, such an outcome was an important aspect of original visions of restorative justice. Yet it has largely not come to be. Why is that? I propose four reasons in this article, but other reasons abound. It is important to note that the difficulties inherent in using restorative justice measures as an alternative to imprisonment are also embedded in the prospects of using other options, such as community service, restitution, or even rehabilitative programming, as a diversionary sanction.

Definition

Howard Zehr, as far as I know, is responsible for the first effort to conceptualize or define restorative justice as we know it (Zehr, 1985). Zehr speculated, "Restoration, making things right, would replace the imposition of pain as the expected outcome in new paradigm justice. Restitution would become common, not exceptional. Instead of committing one social injury in response to another, a restorative paradigm would focus on healing" (1985:15). He also asked, "(W)ill VORP be just another alternative program, an alternative that becomes institutionalized, ossified, co-opted until it is just another program, and perhaps not an alternative at all? Or will VORP be a means of exploring, communicating, embodying an alternative vision?" (1985:17).

A good, typical definition of restorative justice comes from a recent gathering in New Zealand:

> Restorative justice is a community-based process that offers an inclusive way of dealing with offenders and victims of crime through a facilitated conference. Restorative conferencing brings victims into the heart of the criminal justice process, and provides encouragement for offenders to take personal responsibility for their offending, the opportunity for the healing of victims and offenders to commence, and where appropriate, the application of more practical and helpful sanctions. It is a procedure (that) focuses on accountability and repairing the damage done by crime rather than on retribution and punishment. Restorative justice processes create the possibility of reconciliation through the

practice of compassion, healing, mercy and forgiveness (Ministerial Committee..., 1989).

A shortcoming of such definitions, however, is the absence of any explicit reference to penal diversion, de-institutionalization, or displacement. Incarceration is the institutional manifestation of the punitive impulse that restorative justice is designed and intended to challenge. I argue that restorative justice practitioners and theorists need to include this objective more consciously in debates and discussions of restorative justice. Without doing so, it seems likely that the issue will be left isolated and unresolved. In such a context, it also seems likely that restorative justice will challenge neither the practice nor the hegemony of incarceration.

Public, Professional, And Political Education

Public sentiments about crime and punishment (or non-punishment as the case might be) are not as harsh as people think, so while public education is necessary, it is not quite as necessary now as educational efforts on other fronts.

Criminal justice, corrections, and, more importantly perhaps, professionals working in the business, media, mental health, and social service fields, are in greater need of educational efforts. Practitioners may not be an especially active — or effective — lobby group, but they have direct experience working with offenders and victims. This knowledge provides fertile ground for support for restorative justice to grow. Moreover, at some point, it can be expected that their professional connections to the "problems" of criminal justice and corrections will resonate with those who wield budgetary and other sources of power.

Politicians, of course, are usually the last to fall into line. So, informing them directly about restorative justice is necessary, but public parties and practitioners may carry out this task best through their particular relationships with local, state, and federal political leaders. Projects that use restorative justice as an alternative to incarceration more likely than not need to influence, and gain support from, local leaders because these programs become part of their constituency.

Implementation

Putting restorative justice into practice, especially if it is to resemble best practice, is a daunting task. It is far more difficult than putting someone behind bars. But there are ways it can be done with some certainty. I suggest steps that may assure that those who receive restorative justice sanctions were actually jail- or prison-bound.

First, local data must be on hand to describe who is incarcerated. Programs must know the personal and criminal justice histories of their potential clients. They must also know the characteristics of local criminal justice practices, such as the decision-making and sentencing practices of prosecutors, defense attorneys, judges, and probation officers. Once programs identify who is likely to be incarcerated, then these cases can be targeted for attention.

Second, sentence planning or advocacy must be conducted on behalf of the potential restorative justice client. Jail- or prison-bound cases have to be identified and worked on. Restorative justice advocates or program staff should routinely interact with prosecutors, defense attorneys, judges, and probation officers to apply restorative justice to particular cases and to obtain judicial approval for such sanctions. Often times, sentencing advocates from a restorative justice program, a public defender's office, or a community treatment program must gather and prepare information for the sentencing court to show why and how a restorative justice sanction, and not jail or prison, is appropriate for the community and victims, as well as for offenders.

Research

We are in a stage of organizational development where the empirical evaluation of program initiatives has gained some ascendancy. Restorative justice, perhaps more than any other reform initiative in recent decades, has been subject to a sizeable, and growing, number of research evaluations, especially in Australia, New Zealand and the United Kingdom. Little of this research, however, focuses on the matters of diversion or displacement. Few researchers explore the question, "To what extent has restorative justice diverted or displaced men or women, boys or girls, away from detention or confinement?" Little descriptive data even exists on the number of programs that have the intention of using restorative justice, at least in part, as an alternative to imprisonment.

FUTURE PROSPECTS

Restorative justice's general future is relatively rosy. The restorative justice movement has produced a wealth of experience as well as a strong body of empirical and theoretical work that will give it visibility and viability well into the future. However, the key questions, at least in terms of the issues raised in this article, concern the extent that restorative justice measures are challenging and replacing traditional or current criminal justice practices and the extent that mainstream practices and policies are capturing or co-opting them.

To date, restorative justice is not being used as an alternative to imprisonment. Prison-based projects rarely result in the diminished use of incarceration, even in individual cases. Instead, they fortify the social order of prisons without challenging the hegemony of prison use. This is true in specific cases and in a larger number of cases, such as for offenders who commit non-violent crimes or drug-related offenses. In the U.S., examples exist that show that restorative justice is being used in cases that involve violent crimes, but these cases are exceptional. Nowhere is restorative justice being used in significant numbers as a matter of routine practice to divert or displace men and women from prison.

Thus, Robert and Peters (2003) are not being alarmists when they warn about "the hijacking of restorative justice." Without careful and conscious attention, restorative justice measures, like other alternative options, will be folded into the lap of the criminal justice system, where they will rest comfortably, effecting only the appearance of change over the general criminal justice landscape.

Address correspondence to: Russ Immarigeon, 563 Route 21, Hillsdale, NY 12529. E-mail: <russimmarigeon@taconic.net>. The author is interested in receiving new articles or reports or reader responses that support or counter the arguments made in this article.

REFERENCES

Clarke, S., E. Valente Jr. and R. Mace (1992). *Mediation of Interpersonal Disputes: An Evaluation of North Carolina's Programs*. Chapel Hill, NC: Institute of Government, University of North Carolina.

Coates, R. and J. Gehm (1985). *Victim Meets Offender: An Evaluation of Victim-offender Reconciliation Programs*. Valparaiso, IN: PACT Institute of Justice.

Daly, K. (2003). Personal communication to the author.

Dignan, J. (1990). *Repairing the Damage: An Evaluation of an Experimental Adult Reparation Scheme in Kettering, Northamptonshire*. Sheffield, UK: Center for Criminological Legal Research, Faculty of Law.

Dittenhoffer, T. and R.V. Ericson (1983). "The Victim/Offender Reconciliation Program: A Message to Correctional Reformers." *University of Toronto Law Journal* 33(3):317-347.

Dunstall, K. (2003). Personal communication to the author.

Immarigeon, R. (1994). *Reconciliation between Victims and Imprisoned Offenders: Program Models and Issues*. Akron, PA: Mennonite Central Committee U.S.

Maxwell, G. and A. Morris (1993). *Family, Victims and Culture: Youth Justice in New Zealand*. Wellington, NZ: Social Policy Agency and Institute of Criminology, Victoria University of Wellington.

Ministerial Committee of Inquiry into the Prisons System (1989). *Prison Review: Te Ara Hou: The New Way*. Wellington, NZ: Crown.

Moore, D. and L. Forsythe (1995). *A New Approach to Juvenile Justice: An Evaluation of Family Conferencing in Wagga Wagga*. Wagga Wagga, AUS: Centre for Rural Social Research.

Native Counseling Services of Alberta (2001). "A Cost-Benefit Analysis of Hollow-Water's Community Holistic Circle Healing Process." Ottawa, CAN: Aboriginal Corrections Policy Unit, Solicitor General of Canada.

Newbold, G. (2003). Personal communication to the author.

O'Brien, P. (2000). "Restorative Justice in the States: A National Assessment of Policy Development and Implementation." Boca Raton, FL: Florida Atlantic University.

Robert, L. and T. Peters (2003). "How Restorative Justice is Able to Transcend the Prison Walls: A Discussion of the 'Restorative Detention' Project." In: E.G.M. Weitekamp and H-J. Kerner (eds.), *Restorative Justice in Context: International Practice and Directions*. Portland, OR and Cullompton, Devon, UK: Willan Publishing.

Umbreit, M.S., B. Vos, R.B. Coates and K.A. Brown (2003). *Facing Violence: The Path of Restorative Justice and Dialogue*. Monsey, NY: Criminal Justice Press.

—— R.B. Coates and B. Vos (2002). *The Impact of Restorative Justice Conferencing: A Review of 63 Empirical Studies in 5 Countries*. St. Paul, MN: Center for Restorative Justice & Peacemaking (http://ssw.che.umn.edu/rjp).

—— Lightfoot, E. and J. Fier (2002). *Legislative Statutes on Victim Offender Mediation: A National Review*. St. Paul, MN: Center for Restorative Justice & Peacemaking (http://ssw.che.umn.edu/rjp).

Wright, M. (1982). *Making Good: Prisons, Punishment and Beyond*. London, UK: Burnett Books.

Zehr, H. (1985) *Retributive Justice, Restorative Justice*. Elkhart, IN: U.S. Office of Criminal Justice, Mennonite Central Committee U.S.

Chapter 13.
What Is The Role of Community In Restorative Justice Theory And Practice?

by

Paul McCold

One of the greatest challenges facing restorative justice, as it aspires to maturity, is to define the role of "community" in theory and practice. Community, difficult to define, may range from a local area or neighborhood to the world or international community, or from a geographic place to a group whose members have a common interest or occupation. The word "community" has very flexible boundaries that expand or contract, depending upon the context.

When restorative justice began in the late 1970s with mediated encounters between victims and offenders, the citizen volunteer mediator represented the "macro-community" and the interests of society in general. During the 1990s, the practice of restorative justice broadened to include family group conferences in New Zealand and Australia and peace circles among North American aboriginal populations. These practices brought new participants into restorative justice practice, the victims' and offenders' communities of care — family members, friends, neighbors, teachers, coaches and anyone else emotionally connected to a particular offense. This newer "micro-community" perspective defines the relevant community not as the wider society, but as those most directly affected by a particular crime (McCold, 2001; McCold and Wachtel, 2002).

The macro-community and micro-community are different populations with different needs. These two perceptions of community present restorative justice with an apparent conflict of interests, and have profound implications for the emerging restorative justice paradigm

(McCold and Wachtel, 1998; McCold, 2004). Can restorative justice simultaneously meet the needs of both?

After briefly reviewing these two views of community, this chapter presents a needs-based theory of restorative justice that distinguishes between the roles of the micro-community and the macro-community in restorative justice practice. This theory suggests that by focusing on *means,* that is, the restorative processes utilized and their participants, rather than *ends* or *outcomes,* the interests of both micro- and macro-communities can be satisfied.

DEFINING COMMUNITY

Micro-communities are our individual communities of care, comprised of those family members, friends and others with whom we have meaningful personal relationships. These are the people who, if given the opportunity, are most likely to share their perceptions and concerns with us, and whose opinions are most likely to influence our feelings and behavior. They provide the personal, emotional and material care and support we need to face problems and make difficult changes in our lives. The actions of each person in this community directly affect every other member. A network of relationships, the micro-community is not dependent on geography.

Macro-communities, on the other hand, are groups not defined by personal relationship, but by geography or membership. For example, when crime happens to someone within the macro-community, the direct effect of that crime will differ widely among the people in the neighborhood, city, state, church, club or professional associations within the community. Aside from those who may be part of a victim's or offender's micro-community, most macro-community members are likely to have little or no significant emotional connection to any specific crime.

From the micro-community perspective, crime harms *specific* people and relationships: victims, offenders and their respective friends and families. The emotional pain experienced by family and friends can be intense, sometimes even greater than the victim's. The trust between offenders and their families is reduced and they are likely to feel a strong sense of shame. The victim's family members often blame themselves for not protecting their loved one and may harbor rage toward the offender. In varying degrees, crime harms all of the members of each victim's and offender's micro-community. With its basic purpose as repairing harm, restorative justice suggests that, for "justice to be done" to its fullest extent, every person and every relationship in the victim's and offender's micro-community must be restored to well being.

From the macro-community perspective, crime creates *aggregate* harm and is not limited to specific individuals. The macro-community view is more concerned with the cumulative effect of crime on neighborhoods or society, and the resulting loss of a sense of public safety. From a neighborhood perspective, crime results in public fear of certain places which, in turn, reduces the public guardianship of those areas. This situation, then, further encourages crime and eventually leads to general neighborhood decay. People — especially young people — are more likely to commit crimes if they live in areas with high neighborhood disorder, high fear of crime and poor quality-of-life Therefore, crime is both caused by and causes dysfunctional neighborhoods. On a cumulative basis, this phenomenon impacts whole cities, regions and society-at-large.

Since crime also harms the wider community, the macro-community perspective suggests that, for "justice to be done" to its fullest extent, it is not sufficient in most cases to focus on the reparation of the specific harm done to specific individuals and their relationships. Specific actions must be taken to protect the neighborhood and society through, for instance, retraining or restraining offenders when necessary, and requiring payment or community service to compensate and benefit the wider community.

IMPLICATIONS FOR PRACTICE AND THEORY

Currently, restorative justice theory and practice is evolving along two paths — one focused on the role of the micro-community, the other focused on the role of the macro-community. These different views of community have led to conflicting goals and divergent practices of restorative justice.

Goal Of Restorative Justice

From the micro-community perspective, the primary goal of restorative justice is to repair the harm caused by the offending behavior. Other outcomes, such as reduced reoffending, are side-benefits, not goals, of restorative justice. To repair the harm means addressing the specific financial and emotional harm done to victims and their families, and their relationships with offenders and each other. In a restorative process, the individual victims, offenders and the members of their communities of care determine the measure of harm done and repair needed, instead of the court with its professional advocates and magistrates. The participants in a restorative mediation, conference or circle use their subjective experience and collective wisdom to determine what needs to be done. Thus, from a micro-community perspective, restorative justice is a process that brings together those directly affected by a specific crime to collectively determine how best to repair the harm.

In contrast, the primary goal of restorative justice, according to a macro-community perspective, is to repair the aggregate effect of crime and limit the potential threat posed to society by the offender's future behavior. Repairing the harm to individuals and their relationships is a secondary goal, at best. While the macro-community approach to restorative justice also seeks to remove professional advocates and magistrates from the process, it does not require an encounter that involves victims and offenders or their communities of care. Rather, it favors having citizens, representatives of the macro-community, deal with the offender.

The macro-community measures the reparation of this collective harm by the action taken by the offender to repair the harm to both the victim and the "victimized community." As discussed earlier, the community may also restrain and retrain offenders where appropriate. The development of offender competencies through meaningful accountability and public protection are considered as important as the reparations to individual victims. Because of the concern about both future harm to others and the protection of individual legal rights, the state, from a macro-community perspective, cannot depend upon the individual actions of those directly affected by crime to protect the public interests. Thus, micro-community processes are suited to handle only those cases without a compelling government interest.

Practice Of Restorative Justice

From the micro-community view, restorative justice should be primarily concerned with the *process* of how justice is done, who is involved, and who makes the decisions. The harm to relationships can only be addressed by the active involvement of those whose relationships are harmed. Therefore, from this perspective, the *means* are more important than the *ends*.

The macro-community view is primarily concerned with the *ends* — the specific actions that are taken to repair the harm — regardless of the process used to achieve them. Reparative sanctions might be imposed by the court or determined by a panel of citizen volunteers under the direction of criminal justice personnel. Whether or not victims and offenders agree to meet, offenders can be required to repair harm by paying into a general victim fund or through community service sanctions. They can provide unpaid work to local charitable organizations or participate in neighborhood beautification programs. From this perspective, such outcomes provide symbolic reparation to society and specific assistance to needy residents. Thus, offenders are collectively helping to rebuild neighborhoods harmed by crime. In contrast to the micro-community approach to restorative justice, this approach provides a set of general reparative outcomes for all cases, with only the specific amount of restitution or hours of community service adjusted for each individual case.

From a micro-community perspective, restorative outcomes cannot be predetermined since the circumstances and relevant justice stakeholders differ in each case. Cases should be diverted from the formal justice system as early as possible and to the maximum extent possible. Outcomes should be determined on case-by-case basis, with a unique community gathering to address each crime. Restorative programs operating at the micro-community level include family group conferences, community group conferences, peace circles, and sentencing circles, all involving those directly affected by the wrongdoing as participants in the decision making.

On the other hand, according to the macro-community view, local citizen volunteers, under the guidance of justice professionals, can symbolically represent the community. Those individuals directly affected by the offense can be involved, but they are not necessary in the process. Thus, justice can be standardized and handled efficiently, with many different cases processed by the same set of decision makers. Youth sentencing panels, community boards and youth offending teams are examples of programs operating at the macro-community level.

The interests of the micro-community clearly differ from the interests of the macro-community. The conflicting assumptions about the appropriate roles of the two types of community have created a divergence in restorative justice theory and practice, confusing the ends with the means of the restorative justice paradigm. Without guidance from an accepted theory of restorative justice, the roles of justice stakeholders — victims, offenders, family members and friends, neighborhood, society or government — are left to be determined by the most vocal advocates or by political expedience. To develop a more reasonable rationale for defining roles, we must clarify the meaning of restorative justice itself.

A NEEDS-BASED VIEW OF RESTORATIVE JUSTICE

The paradigm of restorative justice risks becoming "an *Alice in Wonderland* concept, in which it is made to mean whatever particular groups or individuals intend it to mean, irrespective of its defining characteristics" (Dignan, 2000:7). Restorative justice, however, is neither a clever invention nor a fad that follows popular whim. Rather, it represents the recent discovery of innate human adaptive processes that meet the needs of those harmed by wrongful behavior. Perhaps it might best be called a re-discovery, given that similar processes have existed in most human societies and continue in many indigenous cultures today. The emerging field of restorative justice is a modern manifestation of these ancient processes that has not yet reached a consensus in theory and practice.

Defining Restorative Justice

In 1996, some prominent restorative justice advocates participated in a research process[1] to test the degree of consensus on the meaning of the key concepts of restorative justice (McCold, 1998). There was general agreement on three concepts: (1) restorative justice views crime as a harm to people and relationships; (2) offenders have an obligation to make things right to those affected; and (3) victims and offenders are direct stakeholders, but others are affected as well. Beyond this, there was little agreement on who these other justice stakeholders are, what role they should play, or what reparation the offender owes to them. Importantly, there was no consensus on the primary goals of restorative justice or even what practices constitute restorative justice. To move towards consensus, I propose a needs-based theory of restorative justice, which relies upon responses best able to repair the harm caused by crime in both the micro- and macro-community.

Howard Zehr (1985) first described restorative justice as a new paradigm of justice based on the goal of healing rather than punishment. The harm caused by crime could be healed by meeting the *needs* of victims, offenders, and the community.

> Restorative justice is a process to involve, to the extent possible, those who have a stake in a specific offense and to collectively identify and address harms, needs, and obligations, in order to heal and put things as right as possible (Zehr, 2002:37).

Rather than asking, "What laws were violated?" "Who is guilty?" and "How shall they be punished?" restorative justice asks, "Who has been harmed?" "What are their needs?" and "How can these needs be met?" Drawing on work by Virginia Mackey,[2] in "Restorative Justice and the Role of Community" (McCold, 1996), I created a grid to elaborate on the role of the community in restorative justice. In "Toward a Mid-range Theory of Restorative Criminal Justice: A Reply to the Maximalist Model" (McCold, 2000), I revisited this grid to distinguish between and identify primary and secondary justice stakeholders. I specified the harms, needs and responsibilities (or responses to meet those needs) for crime victims, offenders, their respective friends and families, neighbors and government officials.

These five kinds of justice stakeholders can be divided into two groups (Figure 1). The *primary stakeholders* are victims, offenders and their respective families and friends who comprise the *micro-community*. They experience direct harm and have specific needs that require active responses. The *secondary stakeholders* are neighbors, officials and others who comprise the *macro-community*. The secondary stakeholders experience harm vicariously, out of concern for those who have been directly harmed and through the fears that such crime engenders. Therefore, their needs are aggregate and require a general and supportive response.

Figure 1: Restorative Justice Stakeholder Roles

	Harm	Needs	Responses
PRIMARY STAKEHOLDERS			
Victim(s)	direct	specific	active
Offender(s)	direct	specific	active
Families+	direct	specific	active
SECONDARY STAKEHOLDERS			
Neighbors+	vicarious	aggregate	supportive
Officials+	vicarious	aggregate	supportive

While the harm, need, and response may be different for each person, the three are logically interrelated. The role of each stakeholder in the justice process is related to the specific harm, need and response necessary to reduce or repair that harm. Even offenders, although they initiate the crime, inflict harm on themselves and those who care about them, engendering needs and requiring a response.

Primary Justice Stakeholders

The primary justice stakeholders are the victim, the offender, and their communities of care (Figure 2). Beyond physical injuries and/or property loss, victims are harmed by the loss of control they experienced from the offense and, as a result, need to regain a sense of personal power. They need an opportunity to take control, be heard and tell their story. Through personal involvement in the process and by playing a direct role in determining the outcome, victims repair the harm created by the crime and become healthy survivors.

Offenders harm more than their victims. They damage their relationships with their communities of care by betraying trust and create a negative relationship with the victim's communities of care. To regain that trust and repair the relationships, they need opportunities to behave responsibly — to do what they can to make right the wrong.

Figure 2: Primary Justice Stakeholder Roles

VICTIMS

Harm	Need	Response
physical	safety	protect self and others
	medical attention	seek necessary treatments
economic	restitution	be realistic about costs
emotional/relational		
loss of trust	safety to disclose (confidentiality)	find someone to trust
loss of faith	know justice will take place	take the time necessary/be patient
sense of isolation	social support and acceptance	to ask for and accept help
disbelief in experience	to tell their story, to be heard	to face their pain
	deminimization	expect others to take seriously
	deprivatization	willingness to break the silence/disclose
	truth telling	faith in your experience
cognitive shock	meaning	seek understanding
	answers to questions	to articulate the questions
enmity	to forgive, but not forget	acknowledge the pain under the anger
loss of control	empowerment over disposition of case	take opportunities to exert influence
self-blame	reassurance that it wasn't their fault	to forgive self
indignation	validation that it was wrong	reaffirm value system
fear	strategies for the future	take action to take control
	assurance it will not happen again, to self or others	participate in appropriate processes

continued...

OFFENDERS

Harm	Need	Response
diminished integrity	to be held responsible for our behavior	to own our behavior, admit it was wrong
disconnect from true feelings	to feel empathy	to learn how others were affected
	opportunities to express sorrow	connect to their true feelings
loss of standing	reconciliation with family group	behave responsibly toward community
loss of connectedness	social support and acceptance	to affirm importance of standards
loss of self control	a sense of control for the future	to face their responsibility to self
shame	regain a sense of self-worth	demonstrate responsible behavior, do the right thing
violation of true values	to have the deed separated from the doer	join in condemning behavior
diminished personal prospects	hope for the future	to learn and change
diminished social prospects	the skills and resources to prevent reoccurence	to ask for and accept help
moral debt/obligation to victim	reconciliation with victim, to be forgiven	demonstrate remorse concretely
	to experience a sense of justice	seek opportunity to demonstrate trustworthiness

continued....

What Is The Role of Community In Restorative Justice Theory And Practice?

COMMUNITIES OF CARE

Harm	Need	Response
economic	acknowledgement of costs	be realistic about expectations
emotional/relational sense of failure toward obligations	opportunities to help/way to be constructive	provide appropriate support/ take the time to listen
shame	reassurance that it wasn't their fault	help others to behave responsibly
loss of standing	to let others know they condemn the behavior	to not make excuses
loss of trust	to treat victims and offenders respectfully	not minimize or usurp responsibilities
indignation	reinforce boundaries of acceptable behavior	encourage responsible behavior
loss of sense of community	recognize communal responsibilities	participate in appropriate processes
vicarious victimization	acknowledge their own injuries	to keep their own feelings separate

– 165 –

Figure 3: Secondary Justice Stakeholder Roles

LOCAL COMMUNITY/TOWN

Harm	Need	Response
community values threatened	reassurance what happened was wrong	separate deed from doer/condemn behavior
order and predictability threatened	to know something is being done about it	ensure victim and others are safe, offending stopped
fear increased	steps are being taken to prevent its reoccurence	ensure responsive processes
incivility increased	that offenders will be held accountable	ensure fair process consistent with public safety
relationships injured	for "right relationships" to be restored (reconciliation)	ensure that every person matters
sense of community lessened	for the victim and offender to return to the community	ensure every person has a place to belong
faith in institutions weakened	reassurance that future harms are diminished	address local social causes of crime
sense of injustice	a sense that justice was done	provide restorative justice processes

SOCIETY/GOVERNMENT

Harm	Need	Response
diminished dominion	protect the rights of citizens (dominion)	ensure due process standards
disorder	empowered problem solving communities	support local capacities without stealing the conflict
failure of prevention	objective evaluation and monitoring	support research and oversight efforts
faith in institutions weakened	reassurance that future harms are diminished	address social systemic causes of crime
fear and prejudice increased	public educated in conflict resolution	rationalize justice expenditures
politically exploitable opportunity	respect the victims' needs	model integrity through responsible behavior toward citizens and employees
economic costs of crime	encourage policies to prevent and minimize harm	stop doing what does not work

Victims' and offenders' respective communities of care — friends, family and others with an emotional connection to either victim or offender — are also directly affected by the offense. Like victim and offender, family members need an opportunity to express how they were affected. They need acknowledgement of the wrong, as well as reassurance that something will be done about it, that constructive steps will be taken to prevent further offending, and that victims and offenders will have opportunities for reintegration into their communities and society. Families, especially, need chances to encourage the offender to behave responsibly, listen to the victim, support the restorative roles of the victim and offender and avoid either exaggerating or minimizing the harm.

Restorative justice sees crime as doing harm to people and relationships, creating different needs and, therefore, requiring different responses in each situation. The best way for individuals directly affected by a crime to reliably meet their needs is to participate in deciding what will happen. The very act of participating in a restorative process is what brings the most healing. So victims, offenders and their respective communities of care need to "own their conflicts" and stop the courts' professional advocates and magistrates from stealing the resolution of the conflict from them.

Secondary Justice Stakeholders

Secondary or indirect stakeholders have different needs than those directly affected (Figure 3). In the aftermath of crime, the local community and the wider society also want assurance that what happened was wrong, something was done about it, offenders were held accountable, relationships were restored, steps were taken to prevent its reoccurrence and that justice was done in every case possible. If the best way to do that is through restorative processes, then active macro-community responses, whether by courts or citizen panels, would only impinge on the direct stakeholders' chance to experience a reliably healing restorative processes.

So the most important role for secondary stakeholders, such as neighbors, citizens and officials, is to ensure that restorative justice processes are readily available to everyone and that they are supported and funded. The government has additional broader responsibilities to ensure fair process, inquire into the local sources of crime, and fashion an effective crime policy through well-funded research.

Of primary concern for all justice stakeholders is that the harmful behavior stops and everyone is safe. Of course, when dangerous and uncontrollable offenders need to be restrained and perhaps incarcerated, the macro-community's professional justice personnel and resources are required. However, in the vast majority of cases it appears that the macro-community needs can best be satisfied by restorative justice processes directly involving victims, offenders and their communities of care. The wider community and government should be supportive, rather than directive, and take care not to usurp this role from the direct stakeholders.

CONCLUSION

The future of restorative justice hinges on involving the micro-community directly in those restorative processes that provide healing. Reparation decided by a judge or a community panel actually interferes with healing as it deprives primary stakeholders of the opportunity to express their feelings, tell their story and collectively identify and address harms, needs, and responses. Such macro-community interference, although currently in vogue, is inconsistent with the essence of restorative justice.

We promote "family values," but do not value families in our response to crime. We have not recognized that an extended family community-of-care is the single most important social institution for the regulation of misbehavior. Families are those critical networks that provide the underlying structure of civil society. The potential for informal social control diminishes each time justice professionals or symbolic community representatives make decisions on behalf of those who will be most directly affected by those decisions.

Through restorative processes, the micro-community not only meets its own needs but also meets the needs of the macro-community — the wrongdoing is acknowledged, the offender is held accountable, relationships are reconciled, neighborhoods are strengthened, the potential for future harm is diminished and justice is done. Therefore, the focus on *means* — the processes utilized and their participants — rather than the *ends* or *outcomes,* best satisfies the needs of both the micro- and macro-community. The amount or nature of restitution or community service is less significant than the dynamic of the restorative process itself (Scheff, 1997; Strang, 2001).

As a means to restore public confidence and ensure the safety of all, it is the macro-community's ultimate responsibility to develop and support micro-community restorative processes involving all direct stakeholders. Restorative justice practices, facilitated by local organizations and supported by government, empower micro-communities to work through specific incidents and achieve resolution. A needs-based theory of restorative justice provides the road map for determining the appropriate community roles to successfully reintegrate both victims and offenders, strengthen family bonds, build caring communities and strengthen civil society (Braithwaite, 2002). The cumulative effect of all these individual micro-community restorative justice efforts is the most effective means to repair the aggregate harm caused by crime in society.

Address correspondence to: Paul McCold, International Institute for Restorative Practices, PO Box 229, Bethlehem PA 18016-0229. E-mail: <paulmccold@iirp.org>.

SUGGESTIONS FOR FURTHER READING:

Braithwaite, J. (2002). *Restorative Justice and Responsive Regulation.* Oxford, UK: Oxford University Press.

Dignan, J. (2000). *Restorative Justice Options for Northern Ireland: A Comparative View.* (Research Report 10.) London, UK: Home Office.

Mackey, V. (1992). *Restorative Justice: Toward Nonviolence.* Louisville, KY: Presbyterian Criminal Justice Program, Presbyterian Church (U.S.A.).

McCold, P. (2004). "Paradigm Muddle: The Threat to Restorative Justice Posed by the Merger with Community Justice." *Contemporary Justice Review* 7(1):13-35.

—— (2001). "Primary Restorative Justice Practices." In: G. Maxwell and A. Morris (eds.), *Restorative Justice for Juveniles*. Oxford, UK: Hart Publishing.

—— (2000). "Toward a Mid-range Theory of Restorative Criminal Justice: A Reply to the Maximalist Model." *Contemporary Justice Review* 3(4):357-414.

—— (1998). "Restorative Justice: Variations on a Theme." In: L. Walgrave (ed.), *Restorative Justice for Juveniles: Potentialities, Risks and Problems for Research*. Belgium: Leuven University Press.

—— (1996). "Restorative Justice and the Role of Community." In: B. Galaway and J. Hudson (eds.), *Restorative Justice: International Perspectives*. Monsey, NY: Criminal Justice Press.

—— and T. Wachtel (2002). "Restorative Justice Theory Validation." In: E. Weitekamp and H-J. Kerner (eds.), *Restorative Justice: Theoretical Foundations*. Devon, UK: Willan Publishing.

—— and B. Wachtel (1998). "Community is Not a Place: A New Look at Community Justice Initiatives." *Contemporary Justice Review* 1(1):71–85.

Scheff, T. (1997). *Emotions, the Social Bond, and Human Reality*. Cambridge, UK: Cambridge University Press.

Strang, H. (2001). "Justice for Victims of Young Offenders: The Centrality of Emotional Harm and Restoration." In: A. Morris and G. Maxwell (eds.), *Restorative Conferencing for Young Offenders*. Oxford, UK: Hart Publishing.

Zehr, H. (2002). *The Little Book of Restorative Justice*. Intercourse, PA: Good Books.

—— (1985). "Retributive Justice, Restorative Justice." *New Perspectives on Crime and Justice*. (Issue #4.) Akron, PA: Mennonite Central Committee Office of Criminal Justice.

NOTES

1. The Delphi method is a research process used extensively in futures research to make forecasts based upon expert consensus. A panel of experts is gathered and asked to present a scenario of the future developments in their field. Each person then responds to the scenarios, offering modifications or additional considerations. These are incorporated or responded to and another round is presented. Through iterative interaction and modifications, a consensus emerges.

2. Virginia Mackey (1992) used these questions to create a two-dimensional grid of restorative justice, with the harms, needs, and responses to meet those needs along one axis, and the justice stakeholders on the other axis — victim, offender, and community.

Chapter 14.
What Are The Dangers As Well As The Promises Of Community Involvement?

by

George Pavlich

RESTORATIVE JUSTICE'S COMMUNITY:
PROMISE AND PERIL

The concept of "community" occupies a central place in restorative approaches to conflict and crime. However, supporters of restorative justice embrace diverse definitions of the concept, with important implications for how they envisage effective practice.

Some view the community as contained within a geographical space; restorative justice is here developed as an element of local "neighborhoods" (Kurki, 1999; Shonholtz, 1988/9; see also Abel, 1982 and Hofrichter, 1987). For others, the community comprises individuals linked by common interests, values, goals and aspirations — extended families, sports clubs, community leagues — irrespective of geography. Included here is the idea that community could form around, and in response to, given incidents (McCold and Wachtel, 2003). From such perspectives, restorative justice emerges as group or community conference that "empowers" stakeholders harmed by a criminal event to negotiate restorative outcomes (Galaway and Hudson, 1996; Bazemore, 1998; see also Johnstone, 2002). Some analysts expand the implications of these conferences beyond the specific events, emphasizing how restorative practices help to preserve vital democratic structures (Braithwaite, 2002). The community is thus visualized as a collective comprising spontaneous interaction among free individuals. While distinct, it is nevertheless crucial to the democratic functions of formal state institutions (Shon-holtz, 1988/89). Accordingly, restorative justice is seen as a way to promote democracy by nurturing civil society's active participation in justice-related affairs (Strang and Braithwaite, 2001).

Still others envisage the community as an amorphous idea, a symbolic or imagined representation that both reflects and creates group identities. As an imagined symbol, it projects an ideal for our everyday interactions with others. From this vantage, restorative justice is enlisted to *transform* interpersonal relations for the better, and to provide a vocabulary for envisioning harmonious, peaceful communities (Bush and Folger, 1994; Morris, 2000; Pranis, 2003).

Despite these differences, restorative justice advocates all view the community in positive terms. It signifies aspirations to collective harmony that is the ultimate goal of restorative justice. It also offers a way to distinguish restorative practices from the state's adversarial, abstract and coercive system of justice (e.g., Zehr, 1990). But why is this concept so enticing? Bauman puts it thus:

> The word "community"…feels good: whatever the word "community" may mean, it is good "to have a community," "to be in a community." Company or society can be bad; but not the *community*. Community, we feel, is always a good thing…because of the meanings the word…conveys…"community" is nowadays another name for paradise lost — but one to which we dearly hope to return, and so we feverishly seek the roads that may bring us there (2001:1-3).

The uncertainties of our ethos may well enhance the appeal of claims to find a collective lost paradise.

With this in mind, the following chapter assesses the underlying promise and danger of restorative justice's appeals to community. The promise to redress injustice by revitalizing communal life is, no doubt, praiseworthy. It is, however, compromised when supporters appeal to fixed, or absolute, images of community. Here totalitarianism lies in wait, because rigid formulations of community create simulated divisions that isolate insiders from outsiders. In turn, through peculiar dints of human discourse, these constructed divisions often reappear as immutable realities. This offers privileges to insiders at the direct expense of, and without emphasizing responsibilities to, outsiders. Thus, instead of appealing to fixed images of community, I propose that Derrida's (2000) concept of *hospitality* offers a different way of thinking about how to live with others in the absence of fixed communities. To the extent that hospitality is centered on the host's welcome, it is attentive to totalitarian exclusions because it focuses on inclusive responsibilities to others. It provides, therefore, a promising exemplar through which to envisage just relations with others.

The Promise: Emphasizing Communality

> Who would not wish to live among friendly and well-wishing people whom one could trust and on whose words and deeds one could rely? For us in particular — who happen to live in ruthless times, times of competition and one-upmanship, when people around seem to keep their cards close to their chests and few people seem to be in a hurry to help us, when in reply to our cries for help we hear admonitions to help ourselves, when only the banks eager to mortgage out possessions are smiling and wishing to say "yes"[.] — the word community sounds sweet (Bauman, 2001:2-3).

Restorative justice's call for "community" is for many a "sweet" sound. It emphasizes collective rather than individual conceptions of, and responses to, crime or harm. Notwithstanding my own deep-seated reservations about the communitarian (re-)turn to community (see next section), there is considerable promise in restorative justice's emphasis on "community."

For one thing, the quest for community justice highlights the role that collective social relations play in creating crime, criminals and punishment. It emphasizes that effective responses to harmful events must extend beyond individual offenders and that responses must include afflicted community members (victims, family, etc.).

This challenges prevalent *neo-liberal* philosophies that assume the individual to be a primary unit for collective life, and then hold that individual responsible for wider social problems (e.g., crime, poverty, etc.). In direct opposition to this position, restorative processes directed towards the community emphasize the collective dimensions to such problems.

From my theoretical vantage, I am inclined to take this insight in a particular direction. Drawing on Derrida (1999) and Lévinas (1985), one might argue that the individual is always only a response to others. The "I" emerges as a particular kind of being ("my" identity) through responses evoked by interactions with others. In other words, the individual's shifting identity materializes through changing relations and responses to others. A *respons*ibility to others is therefore elemental to individual being. As response, the individual is not a self-sustaining, primary entity; it comes into being through responses to others.

With this in mind, collective arrangements evoke specific kinds of responses and thereby create particular sorts of individual identities (victim, offender, mediator, etc.). Therefore, to alter specific identities requires that we alter the patterns of collective being (perhaps as indicated by Pranis, 2003, or Morris, 2000). Restorative justice is most promising when it acknowledges that *a priori* individuals are never the root cause of crime, nor are they the fixed points of reference for communities. Destructive individual identities are the product of responses drawn from local collective formations. To change the former requires a change in the latter.

In any case, the promise of restorative justice is to affirm practices that embrace dynamic visions of communality. However, I would want to add an important caveat: community should never be seen as a fixed entity. To do so is, in effect, to petrify always changing collective relations according to the whims of a fashionable viewpoint at a given historical moment. Restorative justice, I suggest, compromises its promise when it takes any one image of the "community" to be universal or absolute.

Fixing Community: The Totalitarian Threat

> If by community one implies, as is often the case, a harmonious group, consensus, and fundamental agreement beneath phenomena of discord or war, then I don't believe in it very much and I sense in it as much threat as promise (Derrida, 1995:355).

I have elsewhere echoed Derrida's concerns about upholding a closed conception of community in restorative justice practice (Pavlich, 2001, 2002a, 2002b). Aside from the parochialism, exclusions, prohibitions and segregations associated with fixed notions of community, a perilous totalitarian threat haunts every attempt to ground restorative justice in community. This threat is palpably symbolized by the horrific fates of those excluded by Nazi, Stalinist, and Apartheid regimes. It is also evident in the genocide, "ethnic cleansing" and sheer hatred kindled by acts that create fixed borders, impervious boundaries, in "community" members' imaginings.

Of course, not all evocations of community necessarily lead to totalitarian disasters; it is just that discourses seeking to define community absolutely are poorly positioned to guard against despotic exclusions. The processes that separate insiders from outsiders to form a given community can anesthetize newly defined insiders, preventing them from empathizing with, or recognizing the distress attendant upon, the excluded (see S. Cohen, 2001).

The totalitarian threat is fundamental because there can be no such thing as a universal community. A community that includes everybody cannot be specified; quite literally, it is meaningless. Communities always have members and outsiders; to identify a community requires that we distinguish insiders from those who live outside that community — strangers, offenders, etc. (Bauman, 1997). This aspect of community ensures that members are made responsible to one another, but places less (if any) emphasis on being responsible to those who are cast as non-members. The unity (*unum*), being with (*com*), the identity, the common, is made present through successful exclusions that erect limits, brace borders, specify boundaries.

It is perhaps not surprising that community should be related to the Latin *municeps* (from whence we have "municipal"), which referred to those who were citizens of a Roman city (the *municipium*), but not permitted to be magistrates (Ayto, 1990). Restorative justice's community is like the citizen who serves the state but not as an entirely sanctioned official. The walled city may keep strangers out through the coercive forces of law's empires, but the community assists by carving supportive limits through its unique governance.

This is community's secret: communities are identified — implicitly or explicitly — by exclusion. Identifying a community absolutely does not encourage members to face responsibilities to the excluded. Derrida describes the problem thus:

Once you grant some privilege to gathering and not to dissociat-
ing, you leave no room for the other, for the radical otherness of
the other, for the radical singularity of the other (Derrida,
1997:14).

Leaving no room for the other is dangerous — one could again point
to the many lives exterminated by genocides whose tormented cries remained unheard simply because they emanated from realms of silenced
exclusion.

There is, one might say, a short leap from the promises of bordered
community life to the claim that one community is superior to, and
therefore uniquely capable of deciding the fate of, others. The latter haz-
ard provides a fertile breeding ground for the most perilous, irresponsi-
ble and tyrannical of exclusions. To the extent that restorative justice
practices emphasize the creation of boundaries and borders around
communities, they are implicated in the totalitarian effects — even if
unintended and unforeseen — that may arise when a responsibility to
the excluded is ignored.

Hospitality: Communality Without Community?

I have argued that an important positive effect of restorative appeals
to community is to have focused questions of justice about collective
rather than individual responsibilities. However, by approaching the
community as a definable entity, many restorative justice discussions do
not emphasize their responsibility to people who are excluded from
given definitions. The shadows of totalitarianism lurk close when pre-
defined community members do not actively confront their responsibilities to outsiders.

In more technical terms, the above analysis leads us to question,

...how the community can remain a place for communality while
at the same time being an open, interrupted community that is respectful of difference and resists the closure implicit within totalitarianism and immanentism (Critchley, 1992:219).

Several commentators have responded by formulating the community dynamically (e.g., Agamben, 1993; Nancy, 1991; Corlett, 1989).
These analyses recognize that the appeal to community is always an ethi-

cal matter that demands changing, open, and future-directed aspirations of how to be with others.

Searching for a way to grasp communality without reference to fixed communities could have important implications for restorative justice practice. To begin with, restorative justice could be recast as an always open-ended means of negotiating new communal forms that do not create violent, destructive and harmful individual identities in given contexts. Its role would be less *restorative* and more *revisionary*, focused on processes that continuously calculate new ways of being with others. Revisionary gatherings would actively seek alternative collective patterns that generate communally minded (as opposed to destructive) identities through the responses they draw.

And how might we conceive of such revisionary practices? Drawing on Derrida's (1999, 2000) work, I have elsewhere suggested a broad working analogy to guide the task: *hospitality* (see Pavlich, 2001, 2002b).

That is, one could use images of a welcoming host receiving guests as a guiding framework for developing revisionary practices directed to redressing injustice. The basic idea of hospitality could guide attempts to work out specific events and revision new ways of being with others in context. Images of a welcoming host could serve as a leitmotiv for processes that help affected parties come to mutual understandings of a specific situation, and negotiate future ways of being with each other.

Think of it this way. As host, one welcomes the other at a threshold that is always directed to the future (do we ever know quite how hosting guests will play out?). In that circumstance, the host welcomes the other as other, not as a member of a pre-specified community. At base, this is an inclusive gesture; but it does not require the host to yield mastery over the place where s\he receives guests.

The hosting image can be appropriated to guide various interactions, including those between victims, offenders, mediators, panels, etc. It depends on what sort of response is deployed. In all cases, however, one can use hospitality as an analogy to guide negotiations between host(s) and the other(s) who stands at the threshold of a given interactive space.

The host, as master of the space, has certain obligations that include welcoming and receiving the guest. Such gestures, if successful, open the way for effective discourse, enabling frank discussions of past events that could lead to mutually developed understandings of what has taken place. These understandings could serve as the groundwork for considering how the host and other might exist with each other in future, overcoming past discordance.

The host's welcome thus provides a ritualized lore for how to negotiate ways of being with others that do not depend on creating insiders and outsiders to a pre-defined community. It is, in the first instance at least, an inclusive model that provides a unique orientation. It demands that both host and guest be mutually responsible: the host is always a sort of hostage to the guest, just as the guest is no more than the responses to the welcome offered by the host.

This model could be adapted such that the agent of restorative (revisionary?) justice be viewed as a host who welcomes an other at the threshold of justice-related processes seeking new ways of being. The welcoming orientation is different from community justice in that it requires a host to meet the other as other, with the aim of opening up to future forms of collective being. It does not, for instance, demand that the other (offender) accept the rules of a conference that mirrors a pre-defined concept of community. Nor does it see its aim as "restoring" the auspices of a pre-defined community.

Instead, the revisionary host understands just how the welcome makes him/her hostage to the unpredictable responses of the other. At the same time, the guest identity is generated by the responses elicited by the host's welcome in a given context. The ensuing hospitality requires a negotiation that requires both host and guest to grapple with the contours of a given injustice, and to experiment with different ways of associating from those that have led to current circumstances.

These brief comments suggest that restorative justice's comforting, but potentially totalitarian, closures around community are potentially perilous. By contrast, the inclusive orientation of hospitality's welcome enables us to pursue laudable communal aspirations in the face of collectively destructive or harmful events. Moreover, it promises to do so without denying, or seeking to close off, the dynamism of our collective being. This approach offers no guarantees of justice. Its instinct is inclusive, democratic and remains constantly attentive to totalitarian closure. If no more is possible, no less is required to confront justice and the responsibilities of communal being.

Address correspondence to: George Pavlich (Ph.D.), Professor, Dept. of Sociology, University of Alberta, Edmonton, Alberta, T6G 2H4, Canada. Email: <george.pavlich@ualberta.ca>.

REFERENCES

Abel, R.L. (ed.) (1982). *The Politics of Informal Justice*. New York: Academic Press.

Agamben, G. (1993). *The Coming Community*. Minneapolis, MN: University of Minnesota Press.

Ayto, J. (1990). *Dictionary of Word Origins*. London, UK: Bloomsbury.

Bauman, Z. (2001). *Community: Seeking Safety in an Insecure World*. Cambridge, UK: Polity.

—— (1997). *Postmodernity and its Discontents*. New York, NY: New York University Press.

Bazemore, G. (1998). "Restorative Justice and Earned Redemption: Communities, Victims, and Offender Reintegration." *American Behavioral Scientist* 41(6):768-813.

Braithwaite, J. (2002). *Restorative Justice and Responsive Regulation*. New York: Oxford University Press.

Bush, R. and J. Folger (1994). *The Promise of Mediation: Responding to Conflict Through Empowerment*. San Francisco, CA: Jossey-Bass.

Cohen, A. (2002). "Epilogue." In: V. Amit (ed.), *Realizing Community: Concepts, Social Relationships and Sentiments*. London, UK: Routledge.

Cohen, S. (2001). *States of Denial: Knowing About Atrocities and Suffering*. Cambridge, UK: Polity.

Corlett, W. (1989). *Community Without Unity: A Politics of Derridian Extravagance*. Durham, NC: Duke University Press.

Critchley, S. (1992). *The Ethics of Deconstruction: Derrida and Levinas*. Oxford, UK: Blackwell.

Derrida, J. (2000). "Hospitality." *Angelaki* 5(3):3-18.

—— (1999). *Adieu to Emmanuel Levinas*. Stanford, CA: Stanford University Press.

—— (1997). *Roundtable. Deconstruction in a Nutshell: A Conversation with Jacques Derrida*. J.D. Caputo. New York, NY: Fordham University Press.

—— (1995). *Points . . . : interviews, 1974-1994.* Stanford, CA: Stanford University Press.

Galaway, B. and J. Hudson (1996). *Restorative Justice: International Perspectives.* Monsey, NY: Criminal Justice Press.

Hofrichter, R. (1987). *Neighborhood Justice in Capitalist Society: The Expansion of the Informal State.* New York: Greenwood Press.

Johnstone, G. (2002). *Restorative Justice: Ideas, Values, Debates.* Cullompton, Devon, UK: Willan.

Kurki, L. (1999). *Incorporating Restorative and Community Justice Into American Sentencing and Corrections.* Washington, DC: U.S. Department of Justice, Office of Justice Programs, National Institute of Justice.

Lévinas, E. (1985). *Ethics and Infinity.* Pittsburgh, PA: Duquesne University Press.

Morris, R. (2000). *Stories of Transformative Justice.* Toronto, CAN: Canadian Scholars' Press.

McCold, P. and B. Wachtel (2003). "Community is Not a Place: A New Look at Community Justice Initiatives." In: G. Johnstone (ed.), *A Restorative Justice Reader: Text, Sources, Context.* Cullompton, Devon, UK: Willan Publishing.

Nancy, J-L. (1991). *The Inoperative Community.* Minneapolis, MN: University of Minnesota Press.

Pavlich, G. (2002a). "Deconstructing Restoration: The Promise of Restorative Justice." In: E. Weitekamp and H-J Kerner (eds.), *Restorative Justice: Theoretical Foundations.* Cullompton, Devon, UK: Willan Publishing.

—— (2002b). "Towards an Ethics of Restorative Justice." In: L. Walgrave (ed.), *Restorative Justice and the Law.* Cullompton, Devon, UK: Willan Publishing.

—— (2001). "The Force of Community." In: H. Strang and J. Braithwaite (eds.), *Restorative Justice and Civil Society.* Cambridge, UK: Cambridge University Press.

—— (1999). "Preventing Crime: 'Social' versus 'Community' Governance in Aotearoa/New Zealand." In: R. Smandych (ed.), *Governable Places: Readings on Governmentality and Crime Control.* Aldershot, UK: Ashgate.

Pranis, K. (2003). *Peacemaking Circles: From Crime to Community.* St. Paul, MN: Living Justice Press.

Shonholtz, R. (1988/89). "Community as Peacemaker: Making Neighborhood Justice Work." *Current Municipal Problems* 15:291-330.

Strang, H. and J. Braithwaite (2001). *Restorative Justice and Civil Society.* Cambridge, UK: Cambridge University Press.

Zehr, H. (1995). "Justice Paradigm Shift? Values and Visions in the Reform Process." *Mediation Quarterly* 12(3):207-216.

—— (1990). *Changing Lenses: A New Focus for Crime and Justice.* Scottsdale, PA: Herald Press.

PART III.
GOVERNMENTS AND SYSTEMS

Government — State — System

These three words evoke a variety of reactions, even heated debates. For some, the words represent welcomed entities, leaders and allies in the work of creating societal harmony and justice. For others, the words represent oppression and structures that destroy social harmony and impede justice. For good or for bad, our lives are influenced on a daily basis by government and related systems. We cannot avoid it.

Consequently, restorative justice theorists and practitioners cannot avoid the influence of the state and its systems on the philosophy and practice of restorative justice. The question of the state's role in restorative justice hovers over almost every form of practice, at least in the criminal justice arena. There is no simple answer to an appropriate government role, however. For each positive argument about state involvement, a counter-argument may be offered. Some common "opposing" perspectives are summarized in the chart below.

The authors invited to respond to questions about governments and systems present a variety of perspectives. Vernon Jantzi explores the different roles, positive and negative, that a state may play in restorative justice, including that of the wrongdoer. Through a discussion of human rights and due process, Ann Skelton and Cheryl Frank suggest that the state offers safeguards that restorative justice is not necessarily designed to provide. Carolyn Boyes-Watson offers encouragement that system professionals can be personally and profoundly impacted by their restorative justice experiences. Guy Masters considers the role of legislation, and the resulting tensions, in promoting restorative justice practice. Yet, while many themes within this section seem hopeful about state involvement, there is no clear consensus on how this may appropriately happen, if at all.

Maximize state involvement	Minimize state involvement
As the facilitator of the criminal justice system, the state is in the best position to take leadership in adopting restorative justice values and principles. Without its ownership, true change can't happen. Change the system from within.	As a facilitator of the criminal justice system, the state is too ingrained in its current values and principles so that it gets in the way of restorative justice practice. With its involvement, true change won't happen. Challenge /counter the system from outside.
The system's professionals desire change, and restorative justice offers a welcome set of values, principles and ways to bring more humanity to their work. Their involvement should be embraced and encouraged.	The system's professionals will co-opt restorative justice because the pull of system values and principles are too strong to resist. For the integrity of the field, their involvement should be minimal.
System professionals are well suited to practice restorative justice in their jobs. They are not the enemy, and can learn new skills and new ways to partner with their constituents.	System professionals are allied professionals but not appropriate as restorative justice practitioners. They work within a system that maintains influence over them, limiting their ability to practice with integrity.
The recent surge in state involvement has brought restorative justice into the mainstream, making it more widely accessible. Legislation is being passed to promote restorative approaches. Restorative justice can't hide under a bushel.	The recent surge in state involvement has "McDonaldized" restorative justice, contributed to increased misunderstandings and turned restorative justice into a passing fad, subject to the whims of politicians and funders.

Whether excited, skittish or both about the question of a relationship between restorative justice and the state, we all have something to offer to the dialogue. We each bring valuable perspectives on questions such as these:

- Is restorative justice about system change. What are the possibilities and dangers of this approach?

- Alternatively, is restorative justice primarily about providing a different track, or alternative, to the current system? What are the possibilities and dangers of this approach?

- What are the forces (state or otherwise) that dilute or co-opt restorative justice? How can these be countered or minimized?

- What is the role — ideally as well as in practice — of state and community-based practices?

A dialogue on these and related issues is important. However, our dialogue cannot be solely based on our position regarding state involvement. Rather, we must identify and articulate those underlying assumptions, biases and inclinations that shape our current and individual perspectives. This may mean exploring those personal experiences that shape our attitudes toward the state and systems as well as toward community involvement — while at the same time respecting the experiences of others. It may even mean examining stereotypes that we carry about the "other."

Chapter 15.
What Is The Role Of The State In Restorative Justice?

by

Vernon E. Jantzi

Haiti's political collapse in the early 1990s powerfully underscored the importance of the state's role in the administration of justice. The glaring absence of the state meant that all across the country, but particularly in the more remote rural areas, villages and towns found themselves without a functioning judicial system or police force. They had no other choice but to cobble together whatever justice and police systems they could devise. In areas where restorative justice had been introduced as part of a larger peacebuilding strategy (Lederach, 1997), it soon became the only available orderly means to deal with wrongdoing. In many places villagers, reinforced with whatever training in mediation and restorative justice they had, functioned to the best of their ability as the justice system for over a year until the state could reestablish its presence in those areas. The return of the state was both a blessing and a curse, however. It was a blessing because it could now presumably guarantee a legitimate criminal justice system, but it was also a curse since local initiatives that had emerged from community ingenuity were replaced rather than incorporated or even used as foundations for the state system.

During the time that citizens struggled to maintain an emergency criminal justice system, people often yearned for the state to legitimate and support their efforts to deal with wrongdoing so that their agreements would be recognized beyond the small group of participants in the process. Villagers appreciated the opportunity to take greater control of political and social processes in their communities, but in most cases they never actually considered that what they were doing could or should replace the state's role in the administration of justice. They viewed their actions as stop-gap and complementary to the state. The state's role in providing an overall legal framework and legitimacy for local action was acutely missed.

The question in such cases is not whether the state has a role, but rather what its role should be. Even though civil society could mobilize resources and people to create an emergency justice system in a situation like Haiti's, it was unable or unwilling to sustain that system over an extended period of time. This was especially true once the presence of the state re-emerged in those areas where it had been absent. Would it have been possible for the state to return to the local scene in such a way that it would have built upon community-based restorative justice efforts and experience to strengthen the community — i.e., civil society — rather than to essentially replace what had been built in its absence?

The state's role in restorative justice, as the Haitian case illustrates, is indeed a civil society matter. Nations, multilateral institutions, NGOs (non-government organizations), academics, politicians and many others have underscored the importance of civil society in building and maintaining liberal democracy, a political ideology spreading across the world in one form or another in the wake of economic and cultural globalization. Civil society fosters the growth of social capital, the ability of social entities to identify and use the own human, economic and intellectual resources to address common problems (Jantzi and Jantzi, 2002; Wiarda, 2002).

Strang and Braithwaite (2001) as well as Crawford and Clear (2001) explore the multiple relationships between restorative justice and civil society. However, in such a relationships, what role does the state play? The Haitian case is an example of a state that missed an opportunity to function as an enabler to create infrastructure for civil society to empower itself further, a role that Bazemore and Schiff (2001) consider to be of vital importance. Experience in many other countries illustrates the state's multiple roles in relation to restorative justice: enabler, resource provider, implementor, guarantor of quality practice — and even offender. The offender role is particularly significant because rare is the state that has not crossed at one time or another from being guarantor of the rights of all its citizens to exploiter or abuser of at least some specific group of its citizens.

STATE AS ENABLER

The enabling role of the state — in which it provides legal frameworks for restorative justice alternatives and structures to devolve a certain level of responsibility to communities for addressing wrongdoing — constitutes one of its most significant roles in restorative justice. New Zealand exemplifies superbly the enabler role. The landmark enabling legislation known as the Children, Young Persons, and Their Families Act of 1989 propelled New Zealand to the fore among nations seeking to introduce restorative justice principles and processes into the criminal justice field on a national level (Consedine, 1999; MacRae and Zehr, 2004).

Rising crime rates in general, but especially among Maori youth, had led New Zealand to propose a new youth justice bill in 1988. Its defeat moved Parliament to set in motion a listening process intended to hear and take seriously Maori concerns and suggestions on crime and its treatment. As a result, the much more radical 1989 Act was presented and passed that contained a fuller recognition of Maori community justice, a process that included many elements central to restorative justice practice (Zehr, 2002). Judge Fred McElrea (1994), a leading New Zealand restorative justice proponent, noted that even though the authors of the 1989 Act did not frame it explicitly on restorative justice principles, it nevertheless ultimately embodied many essential features of what the field today would identify as restorative.

The 1989 Act is but part of a larger alternative justice movement in New Zealand, to varying degrees restorative, that over the years has sought to implement ways of dealing with offending behavior that differ from the primarily retributive approaches practiced by a Western-oriented, punishment and offender-centered criminal justice system (Jantzi, 2001). Other countries, particularly in Latin America (Cooper, 2001), have reformulated their national judicial and criminal justice systems to include penal mediation, a provision that establishes the legal basis for restorative justice, but unlike New Zealand they have not gone so far as to develop any particular system-wide program premised on restorative justice principles.

New Zealand's Children, Young Persons, and Their Families Act committed the state to structure a youth justice system based on family or community group conferencing for the vast majority of youth offenders. It introduced restorative justice at the community level throughout the nation. Nuclear and extended families of both offenders and victims became actors along with the state to actively create justice in situations where wrongdoing had occurred. Restorative justice practice became a legitimate community activity at the face-to-face level, a context in which it has historically functioned and where practice has been most highly developed, even though its principles are equally relevant at the more complex levels of social organization such as province, tribe or nation.

The enabling role of the state need not stop with initial legislation to establish restorative justice practice. Enabling legislation to strengthen or expand the reach of restorative processes continually evolves. New Zealand, for example, has continued to develop policy and supporting legislation over the past decade. It recently enacted changes in sentencing laws, The Sentencing Act 2002, that include provisions that oblige judges to take into account outcomes of restorative processes prior to sentence even if they did not occur within the state system (Bowen, 2002).

Even though the state played a major role in developing legislation and implementing restorative justice practice at the community level, debate persists in New Zealand about the role of the state (Jantzi, 2001). Restorative justice proponents and practitioners in *pakeha* (European ancestry) communities feel apprehensive about what some would call the progressive co-optation by the state criminal justice system of a peoples' movement for community-owned restorative justice. In addition, Maori and immigrant Pacific Islander communities worry that introducing borrowed and adapted indigenous practices and hiring indigenous practitioners into the national criminal justice system merely indigenizes the dominant system rather than developing a more culturally-appropriate indigenous system under the control of indigenous populations (Tauri, 1998, 1999). On the other hand, the state counters that its actions merely express its desire to support an alternative to the traditional Western criminal justice model and to provide a framework for community-based practice.

Local entities of the state can also play an important enabling role for restorative justice practices by enacting restorative legislation at the local level as a basis for eventual change at the regional and national levels. For example, restorative justice proponents in Fresno County, California have engaged local judicial and political entities in an effort to pass legislation that would mandate offering a restorative justice option to all offenders in that county before they are brought to trial (Claassen et al., 2001). Offenders or victims would have the right to opt for the regular court-based process if that were their choice, but all qualifying cases would be offered a restorative justice option first. Such local efforts point towards the possibility of a national system like the New Zealand case.

STATE AS RESOURCER

A common theme in the restorative justice community throughout the world is the lack of resources for programs at all levels. The advantage of national-level legislation is that the legislation frequently carries funding with it for program implementation. The entire youth justice system in New Zealand, for example, is funded by the state. Recently the nation completed a three-year pilot program for adults in which it subcontracted private providers to facilitate community conferences in cases diverted to a restorative justice process (Bowen, 2002). We see similar resourcing support in Australia (McDonald and Moore, 2001) at the provincial level and nationally in the South African Truth and Reconciliation Commission (Tutu, 1999) or national tribunals to address large-scale reparations for exploited and abused populations. The resource-provider role enables the state to gain and maintain a significant amount of power and influence in all programs, either through direct financing as in the case of state-run programs or via subcontracts with private providers for the facilitation of state authorized programs.

However, even though much of the support for restorative justice programming comes from the state, it is not necessary either that all practitioners be state employees or that they be primarily responsible to the state. New Zealand has experimented with a mixed model in which the state sets the standards and contracts practitioners from local service provider groups to facilitate restorative conferences and encounters. Though still heavily dependent on state contracts, the provider group, in theory at least, can engage in a variety of restorative justice activities that are not directly supervised by the state. The providers can also provide private-sector feedback to the state system.

STATE AS IMPLEMENTOR

Countries like Canada, New Zealand, Australia, the United Kingdom, Ireland, France and Spain all implement restorative justice programs of one sort or another. In many of these cases the state or its sub-national units play an implementing role. Financially, programs are more likely to be sustainable when directly administered by the state. However, a common criticism is that restorative justice programs simply become another tool available to the state in the administration of justice and leads to the marginalization of non-state actors. Another concern is that these arrangements do the least to prepare, involve and strengthen civil society. The push for autonomy by aboriginal groups and community pressure for greater control over the process relate directly to the issue of strengthening civil society. To what degree can funding and implementation be "unhooked" so as to foster greater community ownership of the process? For example, what accountability must communities have to the state if the funding for community-based programs comes primarily from the state?

State-implemented programs typically have a bias toward individualized cases, thus making it difficult to incorporate restorative justice initiatives into larger community and regional efforts to address the social context for crime. The ability of programs to contribute to the overall strengthening of civil society, and thus address some of the social causes for crime, is increasingly limited because it is difficult to achieve synergy between public sector bureaucracies and community social forces. The degree to which synergy occurs depends in part on whether a state decides to pursue short-term, narrowly-defined goals to address wrongdoing or whether it makes its approach to criminal justice part of an overall effort to alter the social roots of crime, inequality and marginalization (Jülich, 2003).

STATE AS GUARANTOR OF QUALITY PRACTICE

Restorative justice practice at every level is dynamic; it continually evolves and adapts to local particularities and challenges. As a result, it often finds itself subjected to pressures that arise around efficiency, cost and effectiveness. In most countries where alternative justice initiatives exist, they will fall at different points on the degree-of-restorativeness continuum as Zehr (2002) and others have suggested. As a result, issues of best practices continually arise. Rather than seeing this as a major problem, the state can serve as a guarantor or encourager of quality practice. This can be supported through activities to promote restorative practice broadly, but also by encouraging parties from different points on the continuum to enter into conversation with each other to explore together what has been learned as a community and how that can affect practice. In Canada, the restorative justice community has developed jointly a charter for restorative justice practitioners that sets mutually agreed upon practice standards (Law Commission of Canada, 2003). As discussed later in this book (chapter 21), a similar discussion is under way in New Zealand. Thus, the state can play the guarantor role without having to actually impose a set of standards.

New Zealand also has regularly convened palavers, known as *huis* in the Maori community, to address broad restorative justice issues of practice and policy. As in the Canadian case, this process has served to address quality of practice issues without having to impose government-established practice standards, though such standards do exist for government-sponsored programs. It also creates a venue where alternative justice matters, particularly restorative justice, can be discussed by practitioners who work at very different points on the degree-of-restorativeness continuum.

STATE AS OFFENDING PARTY

History has amply documented that the state is frequently an offender. Examples abound of national histories that include atrocities like genocide, slavery, ethnic cleansing, apartheid, female exploitation and forced relocation or internment, to cite only a few. Nations typically recognize the facts, but rarely offer appropriate repentance or restitution, thereby insuring that the harm becomes a negative national legacy (Biggar, 2001; Rigby, 2001).

The New Zealand government has acknowledged its role as an offending party and has taken positive steps to face the issue, though not to the entire satisfaction of all parties. The case in point revolves around traditional Maori lands. Current Maori land claims attempt to gain some recognition for past wrongs by the state against Maori ancestors during the colonial era and the disenfranchisement of various groups in later history (Gilling, 1993). Restorative justice principles would certainly apply in this situation, but how can the state be both a party to the wrongdoing and a facilitator of the restorative justice process? The answer is not straightforward. Certainly at a national level of wrongdoing, where often millions of people have been affected, frequently many years ago, it is not possible for restorative justice to function in the same way that it does in cases focused much more at an individual and community level. So, what are the differences and how do they relate to practice at the various levels?

The state as enabler and as offending party represent poles of a continuum of how the state relates to restorative justice. At the one end would be the state as creator of the legal base for programs to deal with individual cases, as has been the case with many types of victim-offender programs. Possibly because of this successful history, much discussion of the state's role has focused on this type of program designed to address specific, individual cases of wrongdoing. However, while certainly this is the most common expression of restorative justice, it is not limited to micro practice by any means.

Efforts like the Truth and Reconciliation Commissions in South Africa and or Rwanda's use of the traditional indigenous justice system represent efforts to implement practice that is to some extent restorative at the national level (Drumbl, 2002). In such situations, there are thousands or millions of stakeholders. The "victims" could be entire ethnic, religious, or racial populations, and the "offenders" may be large formal organizations like the military, the national government, economic units such as multinational corporations or even religious denominations, as in the case of Christian missionary efforts among North America aboriginal populations. So, even though restorative justice emphasizes the importance of right relations and the importance of putting broken relationships right, this does not limit application to what sociologists would call the level of primary relationships.

Individual-level restorative justice practice is the level at which most people likely become aware of the concept and experience it. Nevertheless, today restorative justice is practiced at all levels of social organization — from the individual level in the family, neighborhood or community to national-level processes focused on righting wrongs committed by the state or other large formal organizations. While the principles will remain relatively constant from level to level, practice will vary significantly. Whereas conferencing with individual victims, offenders and their respective support groups may be a typical practice at the primary level of society, at more complex levels the practice may involve non-governmental tribunals, commissions and, in some cases, even formal courts as in the New Zealand Maori land claims. What is clear is that the offender role of the state requires that its legislation stress reparational and symbolic elements in addition to economic restitution. The more complex the level of social organization, the more important the symbolic and ritual elements become because the personal emotional features present in face-to-face individual-level encounters are not present at the macro level. Thus a variety of ritual and symbolic acts, be they official apologies or token reparations, must create the emotional and political space for healing and restitution to begin to take place (Brooks, 1999).

PRACTICE IMPLICATIONS

The debate about the role of the state in restorative justice suggests a number of implications for practice ranging from the most micro to the most macro contexts. What follows is a sample of a much larger list that could be generated by restorative justice practitioners at any level of society if given the opportunity to reflect systematically on the practice implications of the topic.

- The state through legislation and budgetary allocations should seek ways to devolve responsibility for ownership and action to the community and larger civil society. This would be within an explicit policy by the state to use restorative justice as an approach to deal with crime, but also more importantly as part of a larger plan to strengthen civil society. Some persons would call this a national plan to build a just and sustainable society along the lines of the now somewhat maligned national or regional development plans.

- A variety of resources for restorative justice — legal, financial, process/practice and symbolic — can be generated at every level in society, in both the public and private sectors, that are important to implement restorative justice across the entire society. The state does not hold a monopoly on these resources even though at times that seems to be the case.

- The idea of a continuum of restorativeness suggests the need for more collaboration and discussion among groups at different points along the continuum as well as with the state. The *huis* or restorative justice palavers held in New Zealand in November and December 2002 exemplify how spaces can be created to bring together groups that rarely or too infrequently talk with each other.

- The state is present in some form at all levels of society. Restorative action takes place across a continuum of increasing social complexity, i.e., different levels of society. The state must recognize that restorative justice practice will not be the same at the different levels, though the basic criteria of restorativeness remain, albeit operationalized in different ways.

- Symbolic and ritual aspects of restorative action are always important, but become increasingly so as one moves from local to national-level wrongdoing. Thus clear symbolic actions, such as formally enacted apologies and reparations, need to be part of the state's actions for restorative justice when it has been an offender. Aboriginal autonomy issues are not limited to control of resources, but also represent issues of collective respect and dignity that the state needs to address.

- Practitioners must recognize that macro causes cannot be addressed using the primary-relationship-based models of analysis and practice used for many of the offences committed within a community. Social movement understandings, informed by restorative justice principles, should be used to address policy and practice where the state is more of a participant than an arbitrator, e.g., Maori land rights in New Zealand.

As the following chapters indicate, the role of the state in restorative justice is complex and contested. What is clear, however, is that as restorative justice continues to grow and spread, it is inevitable — and, I would argue desirable — that the government will have a role to play. The crucial questions have to do with what kind of role. What is the appropriate role of government in relationship to community initiatives?

How is this determined? What kind of accountability is required for both, and how can it be achieved? Such questions require, at minimum, an ongoing dialogue both within and between government and civil society sectors.

REFERENCES

Bazemore, G. and M. Schiff (2001). "Dangers and Opportunities of Restorative Community Justice: A Response to Critics." In: G. Bazemore and M. Schiff (eds.), *Restorative Community Justice*. Cincinnati, OH: Anderson Publishing.

Biggar, N. (ed.) (2001). *Burying the Past: Making Peace and Doing Justice after Civil Conflict.* Washington, DC: Georgetown University Press.

Bowen, H. (2002). "Recent Restorative Justice Developments in New Zealand/Aotearoa." Paper presented at the International Bar Association Conference 2002, Durban, South Africa, October 23.

Brooks, R.L. (ed.). (1999). *When Sorry Isn't Enough: The Controversy over Apologies and Reparations for Human Injustice.* New York, NY and London, UK: New York University Press.

Claassen, R., C. Tilkes, P. Kador and D.E. Noll (2001). "Restorative Justice: A Framework for Fresno." Fresno Pacific University, Center for Peacemaking and Conflict Studies, Fresno, CA. (Online at: http://peace.fresno.edu/docs/rjframe0201.pdf.)

Consedine, J. (1999). *Restorative Justice: Healing the Effects of Crime* (rev. ed.). Lyttelton, NZ: Ploughshares Publications.

Cooper, J.M. (2001). "Se abre una nueva oportunidad: Importando sistemas horizontales de justicia durante una época de Reforma Judicial." Revista *CREA* (Centro de Resolución Alternativa de Conflictos). Universidad Católica de Temuco, Temuco, Chie. Ano 1, No, 2, pp.91-103.

Crawford, A. and T. Clear (2001). "Community Justice: Transforming Communities Through Restorative Justice?" In: G. Bazemore and M. Schiff (eds.), *Restorative Community Justice*. Cincinnati, OH: Anderson Publishing.

Drumbl, M. (2002). "Restorative Justice and Collective Responsibility: Lessons for and from the Rwandan Genocide." *Contemporary Justice Review* 5(1):5-22.

Gilling, B.D. (1993). "The Maori Land Court in New Zealand: An Historical Overview." *Canadian Journal of Native Studies* 13(1):17-29. (Online at: http://www.brandonu.ca/Library/CJNS/13.1/gilling.pdf.)

Jantzi, V.E. (2001). "Restorative Justice in New Zealand: Current Practise, Future Possibilities." Final Report 2000-01 Sabbatical Leave, Eastern Mennonite University, Harrisonburg, VA, USA. (Online at: http://www.emu.edu/ctp/vern-newzealand1.html.)

Jantzi, T.L. and V.E. Jantzi (2002). "Strengthening Civil Society for Rural Development: An Analysis of Social Capital Formation in by a Christian NGO Programme in Bolivia." In: R. Hoksbergen and L.M. Ewert (eds.), *Local Ownership, Global Change: Will Civil Society Save the World?* Monrovia, CA: MARC Books, World Vision.

Jülich, S. (ed.), (2003). *Critical Issues in Restorative Justice: Advancing the Agenda in Aotearoa New Zealand.* Auckland, NZ: Centre of Peace and Justice Development, Massey University (Auckland) and Conflict Transformation Programme, Eastern Mennonite University, Harrisonburg, VA, USA.

Law Commission of Canada (2003). *Transforming Relationships Through Participatory Justice.* Ottawa, CAN: Law Commission of Canada.

Lederach, J.P. (1997). *Building Peace: Sustainable Reconciliation in Divided Societies.* Washington, DC: United States Institute of Peace.

MacRae, A. and H. Zehr (2004). *The Little Book of Restorative Justice, New Zealand Style.* Intercourse, PA: Good Books.

McDonald, J.M. and D.B. Moore (2001). "Community Conferencing as a Special Case of Conflict Transformation." In: H. Strang and J. Braithwaite (eds.), *Restorative Justice and Civil Society.* Cambridge, UK: Cambridge University Press.

McElrea, F.W.M. (1994). "Restorative Justice: The New Zealand Youth Court – A Model for Development in Other Courts?" Paper presented to the National Conference of District Court Judges, Rotorua, New Zealand, 6-9 April.

Rigby, A. (2001). *Justice and Reconciliation: After the Violence.* Boulder, CO: Lynne Rienner Publishers.

Strang, H. and J. Braithwaite (eds.), (2001). *Restorative Justice and Civil Society.* Cambridge, UK: Cambridge University Press.

Tauri, J.M. (1999). "Family Group Conferencing: The Myth of Indigenous Empowerment in New Zealand." Native Law Centre of Canada, *Justice as Healing Newsletter* 4(1) (Spring). (Online at: http://www.usask.ca/nativelaw/publications/jah/tauri.html.)

—— (1998). "Family Group Conferencing: A Case Study of the Indigenisation of New Zealand's Justice System." *Current Issues in Criminal Justice* 10(2):168-182.

Tutu, D. (1999). *No Future without Forgiveness.* New York: Random House.

Wiarda, H.J. (2002). "Civil Society and Third-World Development: Models, Philosophical Issues, and Cross-Cultural Validity." In: R. Hoksbergen and L.M. Ewert (eds.), *Local Ownership, Global Change: Will Civil Society Save the World?* Monrovia, CA: MARC Books, World Vision.

Zehr, H. (2002). *The Little Book of Restorative Justice.* Intercourse, PA: Good Books.

Chapter 16.
How Does Restorative Justice Address Human Rights And Due Process Issues?

by

Ann Skelton and Cheryl Frank[1]

This chapter explores the risks to human rights associated with restorative justice relating to both victims and offenders. It places the issues of risks to due process rights within a broader framework of human rights issues, and raises a challenge to restorative justice theorists and practitioners to broaden the discourse around human rights and restorative justice.

Rights Protected In The Standard Criminal Justice System

The purpose of a criminal trial is to establish the liability of the accused person and decide upon a sentence. This process is guided by the principles of a fair trial, or due process, the key elements of which are the presumption of innocence, the right to legal assistance and the right to have criminal charges and sentence determined by an independent tribunal. Defendants have a right to be placed on an equal footing with the prosecution in presenting their case. Proportionality also emerges as an important principle, which means that restrictions on individuals' rights should be proportionate to the aim that the infringement seeks to achieve (Akester, 2003). Every accused person also has the right not to be tried twice for any offence and to have a right of recourse to appeal or review to a higher court (Skelton, 1995).

The fair trial concept is offender-focussed, but in the past 25 years the rights of victims have also come to the fore. Strang (2001) records how the victim movement developed differently throughout the world, with some rights-based and others more support-focussed. The rights movement has focussed on reforming laws that are detrimental to victims, such as cautionary rules that prejudice victims, particularly women and children, and which weaken the impact of their evidence, and has fought for the protection of victims from prejudicial cross examination. The support-based movement has stressed victims' rights to be informed about the developments in their cases and to have an opportunity to make victim impact statements.

Risks To The Rights Of Offenders And Victims In Restorative Justice Processes

Risks To Victims

The promises made by restorative justice to victims are unique and ambitious; they include repair, healing, and the opportunity to tell their stories and to ask their questions. Yet studies indicate that victims participate in restorative justice programs far less than expected (Umbreit, Coates and Vos, 2001), notwithstanding the fact that many report high levels of satisfaction after participation (Umbreit, Coates and Vos, 2001; Hooper and Busch, 2001). The risks to the rights of victims within such programs are varied; they include coercion to participate, threats to personal safety, offender-biased proceedings and a lack of information about what to expect from proceedings.

Another risk is that restorative justice processes may leave victims without a remedy if there is a failure of offenders to follow through on agreements, especially with regard to restitution. Given the value placed on restitution by victims (Umbreit, Coates and Vos, 2001) this kind of failure may result in overall distrust in the potential of these processes to respond to victims' particular needs. There has been little discussion about the victim's right to bring civil proceedings being compromised by participation in a restorative justice process. Can we ask victims of crime to forfeit their right to use the civil process as a prerequisite to participating in a restorative justice process? If we don't do so, what about the risk to offenders who may be asked to pay compensation through a restorative justice process and later be sued through the civil process?

Risks To Offenders

Historically, the rights of offenders are more elaborately defined than those of victims. Restorative justice poses risks to these offender rights in at least five categories: coercion, "net-widening," outcomes, double jeopardy, legal representation and child offenders.

Because most current restorative justice processes require the offender to acknowledge responsibility before referral to a restorative justice program, the rights to be presumed innocent until proven guilty and to remain silent are no longer applicable. Some argue that the offender is voluntarily relinquishing these rights in order to benefit from the restorative justice option, but the extent to which these decisions are made voluntarily is in doubt. Plea bargaining, in which the offender gives up the same rights in order to benefit from reduced sentences, often puts offenders under stress as it makes them choose "between a rock and a hard place." So if the comparison is made with plea bargaining, then the risk of coercion in restorative justice processes is no greater. However, comparing current practice with the ideal, much can be done to reduce the risk of coercion, particularly concerning how the option is put to the offender. Training can ensure that practitioners are aware of offenders' rights, and develop skills to describe the options fairly, without "pitching" one too strongly.

"Net widening" refers to the tendency of criminal justice systems to be ever more inclusive, thus expanding control over their citizens. It can take many forms. Cases where there is insufficient evidence to sustain a conviction may end up being "dumped" on the restorative justice pile, along with petty cases that the prosecution considers not worth taking to trial, such as school cases that could have been dealt with in school, and family issues that could have been dealt with in the family. The value of a straightforward decision not to prosecute should not be overlooked, provided that the victim's views are taken into consideration. Roach (2000) raises concerns about how concepts such as responsibility and shame may be used to widen the net of social control.

The principle of proportionality in outcomes is a major factor in deciding on a particular sentence in a criminal trial. Warner (1994) asserts that in a criminal trial a sentence cannot be increased beyond a limit appropriate to the severity of the offence, on the grounds of possible future offending, nor on the grounds of the need to treat the offender.

However, these considerations may tend to influence outcomes of restorative justice processes.

Another concern relates to disparities in outcomes. Conference outcomes may be outside the range of penalties usually imposed by courts. Thus, there is a risk that not only will there be internal inconsistency in family group conference (FGC) outcomes, but in addition there will be disparity between FGC outcomes and court outcomes for similar offences (Warner, 1994). It might be argued that a victim-driven process will almost inevitably lead to more variation in outcome, but that the risks might be managed through standards ensuring restrictions on excessive penalties.

In most criminal justice systems, if a convicted person is of the view that his or her sentence is disproportionate, a remedy lies by way of appeal or review. One of the dangers of restorative justice processes is that there is often no procedural avenue open for review or appeal.

A fair trial includes the right not to be tried twice for the same offence. Known as double jeopardy, the risk may arise where a restorative justice process fails to reach an agreed outcome and the offender is then punished by the court for failure of the conference as well as for the offence (Kadar, 1992), or where an offender complies with the agreement to a certain point, and then fails to complete. While Warner (1994) points out that these situations are not true double jeopardy, they do entail risk. Warner gives an example of legislation which prevents the outcome of the mediation being presented back to court. This approach, however, may leave the victim with no remedy.

Whilst many restorative justice processes do allow parties to have legal representatives present, lawyers who have not been trained in mediation or restorative justice tend to hinder rather than help the process. Braithwaite (2002) points out that restorative justice is intended "to transcend adversarial legalism," and he therefore does not support a legal right of the accused to have a lawyer speak on his or her behalf at such proceedings. However, in New Zealand specially selected and trained youth advocates are successfully involved in family group conferences.

Due to their lack of experience, children are highly suggestible and are more likely to be coerced into making false admissions to avoid "more trouble," often guided by caring but misguided adults around them. Dumortier (2000) has recorded research that indicates that children also are often excluded from mediation due to their inability to pay material reparation.

Risks To Broader Human Rights Issues

Over and above the procedural rights detailed above, there are broader human rights issues as stake. Braithwaite (2000) has identified a number of international human rights values which have specific relevance to restorative justice, such as restoration of human dignity, property loss, and damaged human relationships. A survey of the literature regarding human rights and restorative justice suggests that equality is another important underpinning value. Problems of inequality surface in relation to issues such as social justice and power differentials.

A critique often levelled at restorative justice has been its inability to resolve questions relating to social justice (White, 1994, 2000; Skelton and Frank, 2001). This is an important issue. Economic, social and racial inequalities are deepening globally. It is likely that the rights of those who are disempowered, excluded and vulnerable due to these inequalities will be at risk in restorative justice processes. While it is not suggested that the criminal justice system is any better an arbiter of these social justice concerns, the broader ambitions of restorative justice dictate that these concerns be brought to the centre of the discourse relating to both theory and practice.

Related to social justice are concerns about the effects of power imbalances that frustrate the intentions of restorative justice interventions (Daly, 1996; Dumortier, 2000). These disparities, arising out differences such as race, culture, age and gender, pose a substantial threat to the protection and promotion of rights in restorative justice programmes. Daly (1996) quotes Razack, who suggests that "community has not been a safe place for women" and that "culture, community and colonialisation can be used to compete with and ultimately prevail over gender based harm." Hooper and Busch (1996) warn of the specific kinds of power imbalances that can result from violent relationships and how these can affect mediation sessions.

Mbambo and Skelton (2001) have raised concerns about the way in which children suspected of crimes in South African communities are sometimes violently victimised by communities that are angry about crime. Citing examples of children being painted, beaten and burned, they show that traditional ideas of "it takes a village to raise a child" may be mutating into "it takes a village to punish a child," and they suggest that restorative justice practice in South Africa will need to be underpinned by minimum standards. Issues of race and culture play themselves out in different, though equally problematic ways. (Umbreit and Coates, 2000; Umbreit, Coates and Vos, 2001; Gallinetti, Redpath and Sloth-Nielsen, 2003).

Given the power imbalances discussed above, coercion and the degree of voluntariness are a concern (Zehr, 1999 and Boyes-Watson, 2000). The assumption that coercion disappears once there is consent to participate in a restorative justice process is dangerous and denies the nuances relating to power that are present in all human interactions.

Managing Risks

Proposals that have been made to manage the risks to rights in restorative justice processes can be categorised into two types: those that promote the building of safeguards into internal programme procedures, and those that rely on the standardisation of restorative justice processes.

Strategies to provide rights protection within the internal processes of restorative justice interventions include the following: involvement of victims in programme design (Coward-Yaskin, 2002), strengthening systems for preparing participants, codes of conduct, improved training for facilitators of programmes, focused engagement and reflection by facilitators on issues such as race, culture and gender, and continual reassessment of the role of professionals (Blagg, 2001; Sandor, 1994; Umbreit and Coates, 2000; Young, 2001). While many of these will ensure some level of improvement in managing risks to the rights of participants, there is a need for oversight in order to ensure that high standards of service quality are maintained. In many models, the State is playing this role. This raises concerns of ownership, and requires us to reexamine the role of civil society in quality control (Strang and Braithwaite, 2001).

Both the United Nations and Council of Europe have recently drafted principles and standards relating to restorative justice. These deal with the availability of mediation; voluntary participation; the necessity for the parties to be evenly balanced; procedural safeguards; and the question of when legal advice should be available (Akester, 2003). Braithwaite (2001) fears that standardisation may crush indigenous empowerment and inhibit innovation, however, he concedes that there is some practice that is so obviously bad that we do need to act to eliminate it.

International and regional standards are not specific to the particular country context. Therefore, the possibility of standards being set in a more detailed manner in individual countries is also a consideration through legislation or codes of conduct. The more prescriptive such standards become, however, the more there is a danger that they begin to destroy the essence of restorative justice.

CONCLUSION

Human rights protection must be part of restorative justice practice. The criminal justice system emphasis on due process rights is, however, a rather narrow construct of rights. It is possible to give up the right to be presumed innocent through acknowledging responsibility and retaining one's human rights. Indeed, human rights such as dignity and equality may be enhanced through acknowledging responsibility in a restorative justice process, notwithstanding concerns about the limitations of restorative justice to deal with issues of social justice and power differentials.

In an attempt to be sensitive to human rights protection, restorative justice practitioners appear to be getting drawn into a confined discourse about due process rights and are answering to expectations that restorative justice processes must provide the same protections as courts. As due process rules were designed to deal with the specific dangers inherent in the criminal justice trial process, it is not particularly logical to mirror the rules in restorative justice processes.

Comparisons with the standard criminal justice process are more likely to be made when there is an interdependent relationship between the State and restorative justice programmes. Systems that run parallel and are not interdependent are more likely to set up their own rules for practice that promote restorative justice and human rights. A project in South Africa, for instance, has set up a code of good practice for its peace-making process, transcending rules of presumed innocence or legal representation. It promotes instead concepts such as "we create a safe and secure environment in our community, we do not gossip about our work or other people, we are consistent in what we do, our aim is to heal, not to hurt" (Shearing, 2001:21).

The way forward lies in broadening the discourse around rights. Human rights encompass a broader view but are based on an individualised approach. Countries with a history of indigenous conflict resolution evidence a more communitarian approach to rights. African philosopher Kwame Gyeke (1998) asserts that a communitarian ethos underpins African social structures. He believes that although this ethos gives prominence to duties towards the community, the existence and value of individual rights should be recognised by the community. Restorative justice theorists and practitioners may need to move beyond the focus on the individual and begin an evaluation of the rights of the individual within a more communitarian approach.

Address correspondence to: Ann Skelton, E-mail: <ann.skelton@up.ac.za>.

REFERENCES

Akester, K. (2003). "Restorative Justice, Victim's Rights and the Future." In: *Articles and Views on RJ*. Restorative Justice Consortium (www.restorativejustice.org.uk/article1.html#1).

Blagg, H. (2001). "Aboriginal Youth and Restorative Justice: Critical Notes from the Australian Frontier." In: A. Morris and G. Maxwell (eds.), *Restorative Justice for Juveniles: Conferencing, Mediation and Circles*. Oxford: Hart Publishing.

Boyes-Watson, C. (2000). "Reflections on the Purist and Maximalist Models of Restorative Justice." *Contemporary Justice Review* 3(4):441-450.

Braithwaite, J. (2002). "Setting Standards for Restorative Justice." *British Journal of Criminology* 42:563-577.

—— (2000). "Standards for Restorative Justice." A paper presented at the United Nations Crime Congress, Ancillary Meeting, Vienna, Austria.

Coward-Yaskin, S. (2002) "Restorative Justice." *Herizons* 15(4):22.

Daly, K. (1996). "Diversionary Conferences in Australia: A Reply to Optimists and Skeptics." American Society of Criminology Annual Meeting, 20–23 November 1996.

Dumortier, E. (2000). "Neglecting Due Process for Minors: A Possible Dark Side of the Restorative Justice Implementation." Free University of Brussels.

Gallinetti, J., J. Redpath and J. Sloth-Nielsen (2003). "Race, Class, and Restorative Justice in South Africa: Achilles Heel, Glass Ceiling or Crowning Glory?" Paper Presented at Second Annual Restorative Justice Conference, De Montfort University, Leicester, UK.

Gyeke, K. (1998) "Person and Community in African Thought." In: P.H. Coetzee and A.P.J. Roux (eds.), *The African Philosophy Reader*. London, UK: Routledge.

Hooper, S and R. Busch (1996). "Domestic Violence and Restorative Justice Initiatives: The Risks of a New Panacea." *Waikato Law Review Tamauri*. Volume 4. Special Issue on Domestic Violence (Http://www.waikato.ac.nz/law/wlr/special_1996/4_hooperbusch.html).

Kadar, E. (1992). "Victim Offender Mediation Programme." In: L/ Akinson and S. Gerull (eds.), *National Conference on Juvenile Justice*. Canberra: Australian Institute of Criminology.

Morris, A., G. Maxwell and P. Shepard (1997). *Being a Youth Advocate: An Analysis of Their Role and Responsibilities*. Wellington, NZ: Institute of Criminology, Victoria University of Wellington.

Mbambo, B. and A. Skelton (2001). "Preparing the South African Community for Implementing a New Restorative Child Justice System." Paper written for a conference on Repositioning Restorative Justice, held in Belgium on 16-19 September 2001.

Roach, K. (2000). "Changing Punishment at the Turn of the Century: Restorative Justice on the Rise." *Canadian Journal of Criminology* 42(3):249-280.

Sandor, D. (1994). "The Thickening Blue Wedge in Juvenile Justice." In: C. Alder and J. Wundersitz (eds.), *Family Conferencing and Juvenile Justice: The Way Forward or Misplaced Optimism?* Canberra, AUS: Australian Institute of Criminology.

Shearing, C. (2001). "Transforming Security: A South African Experiment. In: H. Strang and J. Braithwaite (eds.), *Restorative Justice and Civil Society*. Cambridge, MA: Cambridge University Press.

Skelton, A. (2002). "Restorative Justice as a Framework for Juvenile Justice Reform: A South African Perspective." *British Journal of Criminology* 42:496-513.

—— (1995). "Diversion and Due Process." In: L. Muntingh (ed.), *Perspectives on Diversion*. Cape Town: NICRO National Office.

—— and C. Frank (2001). "Conferencing in South Africa: Returning to our Future." In: A. Morris and G. Maxwell (eds.), *Restorative Justice for Juveniles: Conferencing, Mediation and Circles*. Oxford: Hart Publishing.

Steytler, N. (1988). *The Undefended Accused on Trial*. Kenwyn, Cape Town: Juta & Co. Ltd.

Strang, H and J. Braithwaite (eds.), (2001). *Restorative Justice and Civil Society*. Cambridge, UK: Cambridge University Press

Umbreit, M.S. and R.B. Coates (2000). "Multicultural Implications of Restorative Justice: Potential Pitfalls and Dangers." St. Paul, MN: Centre for Restorative Justice and Peacemaking, School of Social Work University of Minnesota.

—— R.B. Coates and B. Vos (2001). "Victim Impact of Meeting with Young Offenders: Two Decades of Victim-Offender Mediation Practice and Research." In: A. Morris and G. Maxwell (eds.), *Restorative Justice for Juveniles: Conferencing, Mediation and Circles*. Oxford: Hart Publishing.

Walgrave, L. (2001). "On Restoration and Punishment: Favourable Similarities and Fortunate Differences." In: A Morris and G Maxwell (eds.), *Restorative Justice for Juveniles: Conferencing, Mediation and Circles,* Oxford: Hart Publishing.

—— (2000). "How Pure Can a Maximalist Approach to Restorative Justice Remain?" *Contemporary Justice Review* 3(4):415-423.

Warner, K. (1994). "Family Group Conferences and the Rights of the Offender." In: C. Alder and J. Wundersitz (eds.), *Family Conferencing and Juvenile Justice: The Way Forward or Misplaced Optimism?* Canberra, AUS: Australian Institute of Criminology

White, R. (1994). "Shaming and Reintegrative Strategies: Individuals, State Power and Social Interests." In: C. Alder and J. Wundersitz (eds.), *Family Conferencing and Juvenile Justice: The Way Forward or Misplaced Optimism?* Canberra, AUS: Australian Institute of Criminology.

White, R. (2000). "Social Justice, Community Building and Restorative Strategies." *Contemporary Justice Review* 3(1):55-72.

Young, R. (2001). "Just Cops Doing 'Shameful' Business? Police-led Restorative Justice and the Lessons of Research." In: A. Morris and G. Maxwell (eds.), *Restorative Justice for Juveniles: Conferencing, Mediation and Circles*. Oxford: Hart Publishing.

Zehr, H. (1990). *Changing Lenses*. Scottdale, PA: Herald Press.

NOTES

1. The authors would like to acknowledge the assistance of Ashley Shearar with document searching and referencing.

Chapter 17.
What Are The Implications Of The Growing State Involvement In Restorative Justice?

by

Carolyn Boyes-Watson

There is no denying the fundamental incompatibility between the state system of doing justice and the principles of restorative justice. The state operates through impersonal and rationalized procedures administered by disinterested professionals with specialized legal, administrative and penal expertise. The goal is to punish, manage or rehabilitate people who violate the law in order to maintain control over its jurisdiction. Restorative justice, by contrast, seeks to delegate decision making and control to those individuals directly involved in the incident. The goal is to harness the power of relationships to heal that which has been harmed and to empower the community to engage in processes of repair, reconciliation and redemption in order to restore balance in the wake of harm. It is a political vision of a society aspiring to equality and non-domination for all its members based on an ethic of care. Restorative justice ultimately relies on love, not force, as a foundation for lasting peace within civil society.

It is sensible to be skeptical about state involvement in restorative justice. One need only reflect on previous criminal justice reforms — the penitentiary, the reformatory, the juvenile court, probation, diversion programs and community corrections — to see a dismal pattern of good intentions gone awry (Rothman, 1980). In each instance, the ideal vision of reformers was undermined by forces beyond their control and imagination. Likely pitfalls for state-sponsored restorative justice include: lip service for victims (Reeves and Mullay, 2000); re-victimization of victims

(Achilles and Zehr, 2001; Brown, 1994); the phenomenon of net-widening (Levrant et al., 1999; Polk, 1994); erosion of due process for offenders (Delgado, 2000; Warner, 1994); professionalization of the restorative process (Daly and Immarigeon, 1998); rationalization of the process (Umbreit, 1999); bifurcation of the system into a two-tier system based on race and class (Cunneen, 1997); and deeper penetration of the state into the community (Cohen, 1985). Some of these dangers may so likely be inevitable that future historians may look back and see terms like "community justice" and "restorative justice" as ideological masks for the continued extension of state power and control.

Despite the likelihood that state involvement will undermine the ideal vision of restorative justice, I believe our greatest hope for achieving restorative justice in modern democratic societies lies in growing state involvement in restorative justice. My optimism lies in the belief that the incompatibility between the institutions of the justice system and restorative justice may generate a kind of creative tension that opens space for the transformation of those institutions. It is worthwhile remembering that the implementation of restorative justice has been motivated by discontent with the legalistic-bureaucratic-punitive paradigm. A significant force for change has been people inside the system who are disillusioned and demoralized by its ineffectiveness and the harm it causes. I have hope for a "decolonization of the mind" (Cunneen, 2003:35) and an incremental shift in habits among those who make up the system. Any degree of system change will begin in the hearts and minds of individuals, both inside and outside of the system.

Peacemaking Circles And The Constraints Of State Justice

Three related but distinct features of the state criminal justice system provide enormous pressure and can be thought of as "constraints" on the implementation of restorative justice: constraints of sovereignty, organization and professionalism. These features bring up conflict when system professionals try to practice, yet consistently undermine, the values and ideal vision of restorative justice. The tension between this ideal vision and the current reality may, nevertheless, represent opportunities for institutional change.

This article draws on the ongoing research on the impact of peacemaking circles and principles of restorative justice within the Department of Social Services (DSS) and Department of Youth Services (DYS) in Massachusetts. Over three years ago, Roca, Inc., a Boston area community organization, championed restorative justice principles and incorporated peacemaking circles into its work with at-risk youth and communities. The resulting community-based collaboration intrigued practitioners inside the DSS and DYS and provided the catalyst for change. Both systems began to explore the use of the peacemaking circles internally and in their work with young people, families, other agencies and communities.

My research focuses on the impact of this collaboration on the systems themselves and the patterns with which they change and increase capacity to build community relationships. The ideas presented here are necessarily tentative as the system and its services providers are new to circles and restorative justice principles. Yet it is clear that these principles and practices challenge some of the fundamental assumptions guiding the state system and its interaction with the "clients," co-workers and the wider community. Tensions and conflict arise almost immediately. Will these be the "creative tensions" that generate organizational and institutional change?

The Constraint Of Sovereignty

Sovereignty concerns the political interests of the state regarding crime control, frequently understood as "law and order" and a key obligation of an effective government (Garland, 2001). With the rise of corrections the state has also claimed responsibility for the "reform" of the "offender/client" through treatment, programming, education and other services. The state claims "ownership" of crime and justice through control of both the process and meaning of justice.

This claim of both "crime control" and "corrections" has become problematic for the state. Formal institutions depend heavily on favorable societal conditions, such as economic opportunity and informal social control, for law and order. The state's capacity to reintegrate offenders, however, is severely limited when faced with the loss of millions of industrial entry level jobs and a concentration of poverty within racialized urban ghettos (Polk, 2001). The explosion in commercial private security and gated communities is one sign that the state cannot guarantee public safety. Despite being attractive to politicians at the polls, the promotion of punitive segregation of poor people was not an "easy" solution for those whose job it was to adjudicate, process, control, warehouse and supervise approximately 6.7 million American adults on probation, in jail or prison, or on parole in 2002 (U.S. Bureau..., 2002).

For the last three decades, the criminal justice system has searched for a new paradigm for itself and its relationship to the citizens of this country, often using "magic words" like "community," "neighborhood" and "reintegration" (Cohen, 1985:36). Despite the rhetoric, the system has continued to expand through state-controlled diversion and treatment programs in the community and the massive construction of prisons. Since new understandings of justice will not arise from within the system, state-sponsored restorative justice has the potential to be yet another form of "control talk" allowing the state to penetrate deeper into community.

Fortunately, restorative justice has evolved through the lived experiences of people who have been excluded from the discourse and structure of dominant justice systems, bringing to light new meanings of justice. As "rhetoric," the system can easily co-opt this meaning but as genuine practice the incorporation of restorative justice requires a journey of discovery. The challenge is to create genuine collaboration and dialogue with, but not contained within, the system.

The partnership between Roca, Inc., DSS and DYS created space for this kind of a journey to start. More than a "tool" within restorative "programs," circles are being used to invent new forms of collaboration based on shared understandings and principles. Judges, gang members, ex-cons, social workers, parents, police officers, youth, legislators, nuns, teachers, lawyers and business people routinely sit in circle, dealing with specific issues, sharing their experiences, reflecting on what can be done differently in the future and talking about issues of community, justice, despair and hope.

Moving toward restorative justice through its value for deliberative dialogue, these conversations transform the relationships between people, forging common identities beyond those that routinely divide and separate. It is hard to imagine another context where a 17 year old gang member, middle-aged white judge, 20-something police officer, pregnant teen, 50 year old ex-con, and 40-something high school principal share their experience of growing up and talk about what "community" and "justice" means to them.

These reflections generate discomfort with the system. According to the deputy commissioner of juvenile corrections, sitting in circle with people from outside the system "holds a mirror" to the juvenile correctional system and reflects what it is doing "through the eyes of the community, particularly the minority community." This challenges the system to think about "what we are *really* doing with kids." It opens a broader lens for defining "safety," assessing "risk," and thinking about what "effectiveness" means. The circles, though a work-in-progress, are creating long term, egalitarian working relationships between the hosting community and the system, the invited guest.

The Constraint Of Organization

The crime control industry is a system of loosely coupled formal organizations which employ people to "work" at doing justice. These organizations are structured to align the material and symbolic self-interest of the individual employee with the larger goals of the organization, control the worker's time and define their purpose. Whether lawyers, correctional officers, police, caseworkers or probation officers, this organization mediates the parameters of the paid employees' relationships to their "clients," the offenders or victims.

The concept of social capital refers to an invisible infrastructure of connections based on the "weak ties" of friendship, neighborliness, comradery and collegiality (Putnam, 2001). These informal connections are generally not the manifest purpose of the relationship. For instance, joining a bowling league creates both the opportunity to bowl and the by-product of connection and trust that the individual can rely on when in need of assistance or support. This latent function of the bowling league is more important to the community's well being than the bowling itself. Much of what we call "informal social control" is a latent function of relationships characterized by emotional bonds of identity, trust and reciprocity. The healing and transformative processes of restorative justice take place within the context of these informal relationships.

Formal bureaucratic systems structure relationships in such a way that they are impersonal, asymmetrical and fragmented in scope and duration, thus making it difficult to sustain latent functions. Organizational structure undermines the ability of employees and those served by them to form an emotional bond and develop a sense of reciprocity, trust and mutuality. "Clients" are viewed as bearers of deficits and problems rather than valuable sources of knowledge, skill and support. Interestingly, when in need of support or assistance, people in the community rarely turn to those who are "paid to care" (McKnight, 1995; Pranis and Bazemore, 2000). The impersonal, bureaucratic structure makes it difficult to provide the emotional and relational connections that support transformation, healing and accountability.

It is a humbling experience when system personnel reflect on the genuine limitations of their professional expertise and realize that they need to find ways to support, not replace, informal networks within the community. One social service director, admitting "that family looks to the family for help or to their church," indicated that her organization is "beginning to realize…that we should be looking to the family as well."

Circles offer systems a way for professionals to strengthen the social capital within the community and begin to "build a village" around a particular child or family. Though considered a part of that village, the system's role is less central and authoritarian and more supportive and empowering. The egalitarian structure of the circle helps professionals treat families and community members with respect and encourages them to listen more and to be less judgmental, attitudes routinely swept aside by professional systems. The director of the agency observes, "…we talk *at* the families, we talk *to* the families, we don't talk *with* the family or *visit* with the family. And many times you will hear a parent who is in a lot of pain really saying, 'you're not listening to me'…the circle process allows for that kind of listening…that kind of respect."

The use of peacemaking circles also can be a catalyst for change within the bureaucratic organization. Many system personnel use circles for internal organizational purposes, such as staff meetings, peer supervision and strategic planning, even before using them with clients. Because they operate on the restorative principles of respect, equality and honesty, circles offer a powerful antidote to the hierarchical habits of bureaucracy. When commissioners, department heads and line staff sit together in circle, the format encourages people to speak their minds and allows for a more open-ended exploration of issues. As the director and managerial staff of one agency have noted, the use of circles has created a greater willingness to speak more constructively about the conflicts and disagreements among the staff. The department head notices a discernable diminution in the culture of informal griping that has plagued the agency for decades.

The Constraint Of Professionalism

Restorative processes run counter to many of the norms of professionalism that privilege mental and technical expertise over other kinds of knowledge and experience and valorize intellectual problem-solving and the efficacy of coercion over compassionate caring and the efficacy of love. This ideology pressures system personnel to discount and distrust their own knowledge and wisdom and forces a separation between personal values and professional responsibilities.

In circle, each person participates as a full human being, speaking from their own experience, sharing stories about themselves, speaking about what matters to them and expressing emotions. Employees are often shocked to find out how little they know about co-workers because professional norms censor exposure of their personal life in the workplace. Knowing that a person runs a youth group, has a passion for music, or is the sole caretaker of elderly parents somehow never surfaces in the context of the work relationship.

Professionals more easily accept "being personal" with colleagues than with clients. A frequent concern of professionals about circle is that it is "inappropriate," "unprofessional," or "dangerous" to share personal information or stories about themselves with clients. In reality, such reciprocity threatens the status differential between professional and client. But this status differential is an obstacle to trust. One social worker observed, when asked personal questions by clients, "We are trained to say, 'We're not here to talk about me, we're here to talk about you.' But we ask our clients to reveal the most intimate details of their lives at a most vulnerable time in their lives. Would you do that with someone who wouldn't tell you what they did over the weekend?"

The restorative paradigm recognizes the journey toward healing as a central part of justice and the participation of family, community and system as supporters and witnesses as important to that journey (Zehr, 2002; Weingarten, 2003). Those who witness are empathetic observers who assist the victim and offender in their journeys. People who work in criminal justice routinely witness the trauma of victims, the suffering of offenders subject to state-sponsored punishment and the human suffering brought on by poverty, discrimination, neglect, abuse, violence, shame, humiliation and loss. In a sense, the system has "professionalized" the witnessing of trauma (Conner, 2003).

Yet professional norms reject an emotional stance of compassion or empathy. Instead, these norms idealize a kind of emotional detachment, objectivity and technical expertise and resist empathetic engagement with offenders or victims. To do otherwise is "unprofessional." The roles available to the systems professional are limited to that of the "zealous advocate" for victims or offenders or "technical expert" who dispassionately and objectively applies rational problem-solving skills to effectively manage a problem or a population.

System personnel are often unaware of the emotional impact of what they witness on themselves and their own lives. They may be expert in analyzing, discussing and even manipulating the emotions of others but they are often unaware of their own emotions. Weingarten (2003) refers to a pattern of toxic witnessing when people are exposed to violence on a regular basis but neither acknowledge or process what they see and experience. This kind of exposure leads people to psychological attitudes of "us versus them" and black-white moral judgments.

Those who are aware of the suffering they witness may nonetheless feel powerless to do anything to alleviate it. One young caseworker left a circle abruptly when she was moved to tears after listening to a young person talk about his life. Embarrassed and confused by her reaction, she feared her empathy and display of emotion was "unprofessional" and a dangerous display of weakness in her relationship with the inmates in the facility. She later confessed that "many times I want to cry...their lives are so sad... But I know I can't do that." Chronically demoralizing for systems professionals, this position leads to attitudes of cynicism, bureaucratic ritualism, apathy and numbness.

Professionals assigned the task of intentionally inflicting harm on other human beings have perhaps the greatest struggle. As advocates for either victims or offenders, justice personnel are trained to pursue the interests of their client at the expense of the person on the other side of the conflict. In the role of "warrior" the professional adopts tactics and engages in behaviors intentionally designed to diminish or harm the other person, usually by denying their full humanity and refusing to empathize with them as full human beings. A district attorney commented that: "If I thought of the people I prosecute everyday as real people like my own family, I couldn't do my job." Whether doing physical harm to people through restraining them in cuffs, strip searching them, locking them in a room or doing psychological harm by deliberately constructing an image of them as bad parents, dangerous predators or blameworthy victims, the system expects the professional to engage in acts of violence against other human beings on behalf of the public. They are routinely asked to violate the golden rule to treat others as you yourself would like to be treated. A juvenile correctional administrator reflects:

> ...we do the kinds of things you are not supposed to do to kids...and we do this everyday. It's easy for an organization like this to get ugly. [The circles are] a place for staff to talk about some of the things that they do and some of the things they experience.

With few other opportunities, circles offer a safe space for systems personnel to tentatively explore some of their feelings about the task the system has assigned to them and to talk about the demands of their work, their personal values and the tension they experience between the two. Circles help personnel to acknowledge the demoralized agenda of containment and control and find a way to deal with the pain of witnessing the lives of abandoned young people without succumbing to numbness, de-humanization and denial. According to the director of a detention facility, the use of circles has taught the powerful lesson that it is possible to be empathetic and still hold people accountable. Staff finds that they can open themselves to compassion and still be firm on security, the core responsibility of the job. This is a significant shift away from habits of social distance and objectification and in the direction of a more humanized and restorative approach toward young people in their charge, their co-workers and ultimately themselves.

CONCLUSION

The Native-American insight, "you cannot get to a good place a bad way," suggests that the state's adoption of restorative principles won't be achieved through the processes of hierarchical authority, rationalization, or centralization. It is not possible, as Einstein said, to solve a problem with the same consciousness that created it. For the state to embrace restorative principles and be in genuine partnership with the community, it will have to explore how to reform in a way that honors the values of restorative justice. In DYS and DSS, staff is invited to learn about peacemaking circles and the community offers the training to systems as a gift not a paid contract. It is, thus far, an exploratory process: some departments use it, others do not, some are cautiously trying it out for staff meetings, others are enthusiastically adopting it for programming and organizational purposes. Management has given permission for people to learn and explore the possibilities, but no authority figure is mandating staff to use circles and no one is telling people *how* to use circles. Most discussions about how to use circles are taking place in circle.

If restorative justice is practiced rather than preached in the criminal justice system, the goals, procedures and priorities of the organization will be transformed, as will the vision of the justice system and its relationship to the community. When people work; what they are rewarded for doing; how they act towards clients and co-workers; and what they define as success may all require change. There is widespread awareness of the need to re-think the relative roles of the system and the community in order to pursue restorative justice at a systemic level. But there is no roadmap for *how* to make these changes. That pathway lies in the collaboration and creativity between the community and the system as they work together to discover how to change.

Address correspondence to: Carolyn Boyes-Watson, Suffolk University, 41 Temple Street, Beacon Hill, Boston, MA 02114-4280. E-mail: <cwatson@suffolk.edu>.

REFERENCES

Achilles, M. and H. Zehr (2001). "Restorative Justice for Crime Victims: The Promise and the Challenge." In: G. Bazemore and M. Schiff (eds.), *Restorative Community Justice: Repairing Harm and Transforming Communities.* Cincinnati, OH: Anderson Publishing.

Bazemore, G. (2002). "Restorative Justice and the Future of Diversion and Informal Social Control." In: E. Weitekamp and H.J. Kerner (eds.), *Re-*

storative Justice: Theoretical Foundations. Cullompton, Devon, UK and Portland, OR: Willan Publishing.

Braithwaite, J. (2002). *Restorative Justice and Responsive Regulation.* New York: Oxford University Press.

Brown, J. (1994). "The Use of Mediation to Resolve Criminal Cases: A Procedural Critique." *Emory Law Journal* 43:1247-1309.

Cohen, S. (1985). *Visions of Social Control: Crime, Punishment and Classification.* New York: Polity Press.

Conner, C. (2003). "The Wounded Witness: Police. Lawyers, Judges and Community" (http://www.brc21.org/resources.html).

Cunneen, C. (2002). "Restorative Justice and the Politics of Decolonization." In: E. Weitekamp and H.J. Kerner (eds.), *Restorative Justice: Theoretical Foundations.* Cullompton, Devon, UK and Portland, OR: Willan Publishing.

—— (1997). "Community Conferencing and the Fiction of Indigenous Control." *Australian and New Zealand Journal of Criminology* 30(3):292-311.

Daly, K. and R. Immarigeon (1998). "The Past, Present and Future of Restorative Justice: Some Critical Reflections." *Contemporary Justice Review* 1(1):21-45.

Delgado, R. (2000). "Goodby to Hammurabi: Analyzing the Atavistic Appeal of Restorative Justice." *Stanford Law Review* 52:751-75.

Feeley, M.M. and J. Simon (1992). "The New Penology: Notes on the Emerging Strategy of Corrections and Its Implications." *Criminology* 30:449-474.

Garland, D. (2001). *The Culture of Control: Crime and Social Order in Contemporary Society.* Chicago, IL: University of Chicago Press.

Levrant, S., F.T. Cullen, B. Fulton and J.F. Wozniak (1999). "Reconsidering Restorative Justice: The Corruption of Benevolence Revisited?" *Crime & Delinquency* 45:3-27.

McKnight, J. (1995). *The Careless Society: Community and its Counterfeits.* New York: Basic Books.

Polk, K. (2001). "Positive Youth Development, Restorative Justice and the Crisis of Abandoned Youth." In: G. Bazemore and M. Schiff (eds.), *Restorative Community Justice: Repairing Harm and Transforming Communities.* Cincinnati, OH: Anderson Publishing.

—— (1994). "Family Conferencing: Theoretical and Evaluative Questions." In: C. Alder and J Wundersitz (eds.), *Family Conferencing and Juvenile Justice: The Way Forward or Misplaced Optimism?* Canberra, AUS: Australian Studies in Law, Crime and Justice, Australian Institute of Criminology.

Pranis, K. and G. Bazemore (2000). *Engaging the Community in the Response to Youth Crime: A Restorative Justice Approach.* Washington DC: Office of Juvenile Justice and Delinquency, U.S. Department of Justice.

Putnam, R.D. (2001). *Bowling Alone: The Collapse and Revival of American Community.* Carmichael, CA: Touchstone Books.

Reeves, H. and K. Mulley (2000). "The New Status of Victims in the UK: Threats and Opportunities." In: A. Crawford and J. Goodey (eds.), *Integrating a Victim Perspective within Criminal Justice Debates.* Aldershot, UK: Ashgate.

Rothman, D. (1980). *Conscience and Convenience: The Asylum and Its Alternatives in Progressive America.* Boston, MA: Little Brown.

Umbreit, M. (1999). "Avoiding the Marginalization and McDonaldization of Victim Offender Mediation: A Case Study in Moving Toward the Mainstream." In: G. Bazemore and L. Walgrave (eds.), *Restorative Juvenile Justice: Repairing the Harm of Youth Crime.* Monsey, NY: Criminal Justice Press.

U.S. Bureau of Justice Statistics (2002). Department of Justice website at: (http://www.ojp.usdoj.gov/bjs/correct.htm).

Warner, K. (1994). "The Rights of the Offender in Family Group Conferences." In: C. Alder and J Wundersitz (eds.), *Family Conferencing and Juvenile Justice: The Way Forward or Misplaced Optimism?* Canberra, AUS: Australian Studies in Law, Crime and Justice, Australian Institute of Criminology.

Weingarten, K. (2003). *Common Shock: Witnessing Violence Every Day: How We Are Harmed, How We Can Heal.* New York: Dutton.

Zehr, H. (2002). "Journey to Belonging." In: E. Weitekamp and H.J. Kerner (eds.), *Restorative Justice: Theoretical Foundations.* Cullompton, Devon, UK and Portland, OR: Willan Publishing.

Chapter 18.
What Happens When Restorative Justice Is Encouraged, Enabled And/Or Guided By Legislation?

by

Guy Masters

This chapter considers the extent to which restorative processes can be established through legislation. At the time of writing (September, 2003) numerous jurisdictions (certainly too many to list) have sought to increase the use of restorative approaches through legislation in a variety of ways. Restorative justice (RJ) is clearly highly popular with many governments. For example, the U.K. government have recently published a consultation document stating that it "aims to maximise the use of restorative justice in the Criminal Justice System" (Home Office, 2003:7), with the intent of expanding recent developments in youth justice throughout the adult system. Consequently, as restorative approaches have now been mainstreamed, *to some extent*, in several countries through legislation it is timely to consider the implications from some of these experiences.

Informal Beginnings

Many commentators (e.g., Van Ness and Strong [1997]; Wright [1996]) argue that before the introduction of centralised criminal justice systems the most common approach to dealing with offences was through methods recognisable as RJ, focusing on negotiated reconciliation and compensation rather than centralised punishment and/or assistance. However, the modern RJ movement is considered to have begun in Canada in 1974 with the introduction of "Victim-Offender Reconciliation Programmes" (Peachey, 1989). These first projects were established by practitioners seeking to introduce less confrontational approaches and provide opportunities for safe communication between victims and offenders. Early promising results inspired the establishment of similar programmes outside Canada (Zehr, 1990). These first programmes did not operate under any legislative basis, but were developed within existing systems. For example, in England, of four schemes developed in the 1980s, one sought to divert young offenders from prosecution, and three sought to affect the likely court sentence received by an adult offender, in some cases diverting them from a custodial sentence. However, evaluation identified that lack of statutory authorization left projects vulnerable to funding cuts and often struggling to secure referrals despite their positive results (Marshall and Merry, 1990; Umbreit and Roberts, 1996).

Developments In Theory And Practice

The growth of programmes was relatively slow until the 1990s, when something of a small revolution occurred. Inspired by the combined impact of the reforms in New Zealand in 1989 (which introduced Family Group Conferencing) and the high profile achieved by the development of Diversionary Conferencing[1] in New South Wales (Australia) in the early 1990s, many new programmes were established. Importantly, the RJ movement was transformed from having effectively one practice model (Victim Offender Mediation or VOM) to three. The development of Family Group Conferencing (FGC) is hugely significant. Firstly, while VOM had clearly demonstrated the potential for victims and offenders to meet and discuss an offence, FGCs went much further in devolving decision-making power, illustrating that comprehensive support plans acceptable to courts could be created through an RJ process. Secondly, FGCs were introduced by legislation to become the *core* forum through which decisions would be made about young offenders, either through diversion from prosecution or by informing court decisions. FGCs became the first *mainstreamed* RJ process in the world and New Zealand remains the only jurisdiction in which restorative processes inform almost the entire system.[2]

Further developments have taken place in Canada (Sentencing Circles), Vermont (Community Reparation Boards), and recently, in England and Wales (Referral Orders) that have advanced theory and practice. Sentencing circles in Canada involve several circles of participants in a restorative process: an inner circle made up of those close to the offender and the victim, and possibly involving criminal justice personnel, such as prosecutors and judges. Significantly, there is also an outer circle made up of local community members who also have the opportunity to comment (Stuart, 1997). In Vermont, reparation boards, made up of five to six community volunteers meet with offenders, and victims (if they wish) (Sinkinson and Broderick, 1998). These two processes are examples of how "the wider community" can now be directly involved. In summary, RJ has evolved from promoting encounters between victims and offenders, to advocating encounters which enable (1) communication between victims and offenders, (2) the community to be meaningfully involved, and (3) all these parties to comment on what response should follow an offence.

Legislating Community-Oriented Restorative Justice?

Writing about the early English experience with VOM, Marshall (1991:21) commented that: "The problem of arranging mediation between an individual victim and an individual offender was really quite minor compared to the problem of mediating between a reparation scheme and other agencies concerned with criminal justice." It would seem that a key issue is that for many within existing criminal justice systems, RJ represents a radically different approach. It is critical to acknowledge the difference between conceiving RJ as a *philosophy* that would inform how an entire criminal justice system would operate, compared to restorative processes being seen as a *desirable programme* for use with certain offenders at certain stages. The second option enables an existing criminal justice system to continue functioning largely unchanged, with a subset of offenders considered eligible for restorative approaches. An analogy is whether RJ represents a completely new toolbox, or whether it is simply another tool for use in some circumstances. It is this second option which enables prison populations to expand (as in England and the U.S.A.) alongside the expansion of RJ programmes.

I believe that it is this dilemma which informs much of the debate on whether RJ should be developed through *central legislation*, or *through local community activism*. Gordon Bazemore (2000) is one of the few commentators to consider this in any detail, identifying possible dangers for both approaches. Considering the slow growth of restorative practice in the U.S.A. compared to the rapid development in certain Australian states following legislation, Bazemore (2000:1) comments that he is convinced legislation is required to "advance" the development of restorative practice. However, he notes several concerns about the "legislative route."

First, legislation could be introduced that would be net-widening (Cohen, 1985) in effect: i.e., restorative practice would be introduced as means of dealing with a population of offenders who had hitherto escaped any formal attention. Second, "legislation may lead to an overly 'professionalised' practice that has little connection to the community and makes little or no use of volunteers." This possibility is only valid if latter RJ theory is accepted — that local communities should play an active part in criminal justice responses.

Third, "legislation may water down restorative justice by inviting traditional agencies to adopt, in order to receive funding, restorative language and add services without changing values and priorities." Bazemore's (2000) fourth concern is that legislation may be "overly specific" and "discourage creativity and continuous innovation." Taken together these two concerns appear difficult to overcome; to avoid the issue of "watering" down, legislation could prescribe what was acceptable practice, which may also discourage creativity.

Finally, for many RJ advocates, state involvement in promoting RJ may be highly undesirable. Nils Christie (1977) has been highly influential on this point, arguing that most states have established formal, professionalised, systems which effectively "steal" conflicts from the key participants. Consequently, for some, attempts by any government to legislate RJ may be perceived as only representing further attempts to maintain professional supremacy rather than devolve responsibility to local communities.

The remainder of this chapter will examine the development and impact of legislation designed to support the development of restorative processes in two jurisdictions. Bazemore's (2000) concerns will then be revisited to assess their accuracy.

CASE STUDY 1: NEW ZEALAND

The Children, Young Persons and their Families Act 1989 radically overhauled both New Zealand's existing child welfare and youth justice systems (see Hudson et al. [1996] for a full review). The new system is one which seeks to divert young people from prosecution and custody wherever possible, while not ignoring victim views. In practice, 80% of young people do not formally enter the system but are dealt with informally by the Police Youth Aid Division, which can include informal work such as apologies, compensation, or reparative work, etc. None of these young people are formally recorded as having entered the criminal justice system. Of the remaining 20% of offenders, one-half are referred to a diversionary FGC, resulting in non-prosecution. Only 10% formally enter the criminal justice system through a court appearance, almost all of whom can't be sentenced until an FGC has been convened (Maxwell and Morris, 1998).

This legislation took place within a social context of wishing to greatly enhance family and victim involvement, and consensus decision making, as well as diversion from both prosecution and custody. The proportion of young people appearing in court decreased from 67 per 1,000 prior to the legislation to 16 per 1,000, with custodial sentences also declining dramatically (Maxwell and Morris, 1993). FGCs were "reserved" for the most serious cases (effectively the "top 20%"), and long-term evaluation has illustrated that well convened FGCs can impact on recidivism, even, when other social and background factors would suggest that the FGC had little chance of success (Morris and Maxwell, 1999). Victim attendance nationally was 51%, however, Maxwell and Morris (1993) consider this to be primarily due to practice issues, with only 6% of non-attending victims reporting that they did not wish to be involved. (See Masters [2002a] for a full review of FGCs from a victim perspective.)

New Zealand is an example of how an ambitious alternative criminal justice philosophy can be successfully legislated, resulting in the significant use of restorative encounters while decreasing the use of court and custody. This achievement is even more noteworthy considering that these reforms occurred in a country not famed for any liberal approach to criminal justice (JUSTICE, 2000). However, these reforms were not based on RJ principles. Rather, they followed the successful piloting of FGCs, inspired in part by Maori approaches to conflict resolution and pressure from Maori activists about discrimination.

CASE STUDY 2: ENGLAND AND WALES

Early experimentation with victim-offender mediation began in the late 1970s in England with various projects coming and going during the 1980s and 1990s (Liebmann and Masters, 2000). Until 1998 no legislative basis existed for restorative processes to be attempted, though by the mid 1990s several FGC projects had also been established. In an evaluation of seven RJ schemes in England and Wales, operating in the absence of any legislation, David Miers and colleagues (Miers et al., 2001:vii) noted that:

> There was considerable variation in the nature of the schemes' work with victims and offenders. They engaged in activities ranging from, on the one hand, full-scale family group conferences and face-to-face meetings between victims and offenders to, on the other, general "victim awareness" sessions and initiatives in which offenders write letters of apology. Where contact with victims was not a high priority there are serious doubts as to whether they could reasonably be called restorative justice schemes at all.

Such a conclusion illustrates that one of Bazemore's (2000) concerns — that RJ will be "watered down," with traditional work simply being renamed — is as valid an issue in the absence of legislation.

The 1998 Crime & Disorder Act did not legislate any particular restorative process. However, a *Reparation Order* was introduced, and reparation was set to be a key element of other court orders. Neither legislation nor Home Office guidance mentioned RJ per se, but the "success criteria" for Reparation Orders strongly suggested that something akin to RJ was intended. Section 6.1 of the Home Office Guidance (2000) noted that reparation:

- will have a part to play in helping the victims of crime to come to terms with what they have suffered, and will have enabled them, if they so wish, to receive some practical recompense for the distress and inconvenience that has been caused to them; and

- will have helped the offender to understand the consequences of his or her thoughtless actions, to accept responsibility for them and to make amends.

According to the Crime & Disorder Act, before making any Reparation Order, courts must consider a report (prepared by newly created Youth Offending Teams), detailing the capabilities of the young person, *and* the wishes of the victims. In making a Reparation Order, courts should specify the nature of the reparative task and the number of hours they were to perform this task (up to a maximum of 24 hours). If reparation was to be direct to a victim, then the legislation requires that they should also be named in the Court Order. A Home Office guidance document (2000) gave a strong steer that direct reparation to victims was the preferred option in every case; however, when this was not possible, reparation should be made to the community instead.

While many Youth Offending Teams (YOTs) have established a wide variety of innovative community reparation projects, victim involvement, *nationally*, remains low. Jim Dignan's (2002) comprehensive assessment of four pilot reparation areas found that 86% of cases included in the evaluation had identifiable victims. Only two-thirds of eligible victims were actually consulted, one-half of whom agreed to accept some form of reparation. Direct reparation was made to a victim in 12% of all cases, with 9% resulting in mediation. However, Masters (2002b) argued that, similar to New Zealand, these low levels of victim involvement do not reflect a general reluctance amongst victims to participate, as two English projects, one primarily undertaking VOM, and another FGCs, are involving over 60% of victims. Both were providing services throughout the reformed youth justice system, but are comparatively very well staffed and highly committed to the delivery of restorative outcomes Masters (2002b).

What appears clear is that in the absence of any legislative requirement to actually *offer* restorative encounters to victims and offenders, these events appear rare. Some commentators (e.g., Mediation UK, 2001) have noted how the desire to deal with cases speedily at court has worked against the delivery of restorative encounters. The desire to sentence as speedily as possible appears to regularly result in courts delivering their judgements in the absence of any information about victims, in which case they revert to recommending community reparation. However, the key lesson here is that the legislation required the introduction of reparation, which it has achieved with great success to the benefit of communities. Restorative justice processes were *not* explicitly legislated by the Crime and Disorder Act, and have yet to materialise.

However, subsequent legislation, the Youth Justice & Criminal Evidence Act 1999, introduced a further new youth justice order, *The Referral Order*, which was explicitly intended, by government, to be a RJ process. Referral Orders are currently only available for young people appearing in court for the first time and pleading guilty. When a young person meets these conditions, courts can effectively discharge the offence, sentence the young person to custody, or make a Referral Order for between three and 12 months. Once a Referral Order has been made, it is the responsibility of the local YOT to arrange a *Community Panel Meeting*, to be attended by the young person (and a legal guardian if they are under 16). Though the court can order specific legal guardians to also attend, the YOT can also invite other adults "of good influence" and close to the offender to attend. A YOT Officer must be present, but only in an advisory role. The Panel Meeting is to be led by two volunteer members of the community. A seven-day training programme has been designed by the Youth Justice Board for volunteer panel members. The YOT is also responsible for contacting and inviting all victims to attend the Panel Meeting if they wish.

In the first year of full implementation (April 2002-2003), close to 30,000 Referral Orders were expected to have been made (20,356 were made from April to December 2002), representing 29% of all court orders made on young people in that time (Youth Justice Board, 2003). Over 5,000 community volunteers have been recruited to act as community panel members, a third of whom had never volunteered before. However, as with reparation, victim attendance at panels is generally low — the evaluation of 11 pilot Referral Order sites found that only 70% of victims eligible to attend were contacted, with 13% of all those eligible attending. Nevertheless, a small number of the pilot sites had higher victim attendance rates, reaching 41% in one area that received very few cases (21 in total), and 28% in a "bulk" area (137 cases). Newburn et al. (2002:42) note that the reason for greater victim attendance in some areas "is in large part due to the higher priority accorded to victim contact (notably in the first year of implementation)." It was also noted that less than a quarter of YOT staff involved in contacting victims and preparing them for panels reported having had any relevant training (Newburn et al., 2001:55).

CONCLUSIONS

To briefly return to Bazemore's (2000) views, these case studies illustrate that the legislation clearly has much *potential* to significantly increase the level of restorative practice within a criminal justice system. The results from England and Wales indicate that while the *reparation* initiative (to date) has not led to a great increase in the use of restorative encounters, these have expanded. However, as in New Zealand, the Youth Justice & Criminal Evidence Act, which legislated an actual process (the panel) that had to happen, has produced a great increase of at least partially restorative encounters, albeit with low victim involvement in many areas. All evaluations of recent developments in England and Wales have noted that victim involvement is a new area of work for many professionals, and it should not be too surprising that this area is in need of further attention. Thus, these early disappointing figures from the recent reforms in England and Wales reflect the difficulty of quickly establishing an effective national system, and steps are being taken to raise the standard of practice.

A concern of Bazemore (2000) was that legislation would simply lead to a re-branding of existing practice, "restorative" in name only to attract funding. While some evidence of this from England and Wales has been noted (Miers et al., 2001), legislation that specifies a process appears to be the most successful, and speediest, route to mainstreaming restorative encounters (a conclusion shared by Justice [2000]). However, Bazemore (2000) appears accurate with his concerns that legislation may stifle creativity, and attention needs to be paid at the drafting stage to ensure that competing priorities do not hamper practice. It has been noted that in England and Wales a (worthwhile) commitment to "speeding up justice," combined with a requirement to name victims receiving reparation in court orders, appears to have significantly impacted on the lack of victim involvement. Bazemore (2000) is accurate that legislation *without* localised support for its aims can render the development of effective practice problematic. The challenge for legislators is to require that restorative processes are used, while maintaining flexibility for practitioners in actual delivery.

Both pieces of legislation can be considered to have strengths and weaknesses, which depend on personal political perspectives. In New Zealand, the wider political context in which the reforms occurred called for a reduction in the number of young offenders formally entering the criminal justice system, and strong gatekeeping measures were implemented to achieve this. Conversely, in England and Wales, the Crime & Disorder Act 1998 *limited* the number of times a young offender could be diverted from prosecution to a maximum of twice, and commentators have warned of the net-widening implications of this system (Goldson, 2000). Bazemore's (2000) point about the danger of net-widening thus remains pertinent but not inevitable. Well structured legislation can not only restrict net-widening but reverse it. A strength of the Referral Order is that it illustrates how Bazemore's (2000) concern that communities and volunteers will be omitted is not a foregone conclusion.

My own view is that it is highly appropriate that RJ be formally supported by legislation for two linked reasons. First, it is unrealistic for the RJ movement to expect any government to fully devolve criminal justice decision making to the community in any but the simplest of cases. Careful legislation is required to ensure effective practice that has the backing of courts. Second, if restorative processes are to be mainstreamed throughout a criminal justice system, which must surely be a key aim for RJ advocates, then legislation will be required to that effect. This will be a significant success in any country, indicating that the value of RJ, and the inclusion of the community throughout the system, has been recognised. The challenge for reformers is to lobby for the wholesale reorganisation of criminal justice systems around RJ principles, rather than accept the introduction of restorative encounters at a single stage of a system as the ultimate aim for restorative justice.

REFERENCES

Bazemore, G. (2000). "Why We Need Restorative Justice Conferencing: A Discussion Paper." (Unpublished paper.) Fort Lauderdale, FL: Florida Atlantic University.

Christie, N. (1977). "Conflicts as Property." *British Journal of Criminology* 17:1-26.

Coates, R. and J. Gehm (1989). "An Empirical Assessment." In: M. Wright and B. Galaway (eds.), *Mediation and Criminal Justice*. London, UK: Sage.

Cohen, S. (1985). *Visions of Social Control*. Cambridge, UK: Polity Press

Davis, G. (1992). *Making Amends: Mediation and Reparation in Criminal Justice*. London, UK: Routledge.

Dignan, J. (2002). "Reparation Orders." In: B. Williams (ed.), *Reparation and Victim-Focused Social Work*. London, UK: Jessica Kingsley.

Goldson, B. (2000). *The New Youth Justice*. Lyme Regis, UK: Russell House.

Home Office (2003). *Restorative Justice: The Government's Strategy*. London, UK: Home Office.

—— (2000). *The Crime and Disorder Act Guidance Document: Reparation Order*. London, UK: Home Office.

Hudson, J., A. Morris, G. Maxwell and B. Galaway (eds.), (1996). *Family Group Conferences: Perspectives on Policy and Practice*. Leichhardt, NSW and Monsey, NY: Federation Press and Criminal Justice Press.

JUSTICE (2000). *Restoring Youth Justice*. London, UK: JUSTICE.

Liebmann, M. and G. Masters (2000). "Victim-Offender Mediation in the UK." In: T. Peterson (ed.), *Victim-Offender Mediation in Europe*. Leuven, BEL: Leuven University Press.

Marshall, T. and S. Merry (1990). *Crime & Accountability*. London, UK: Home Office.

Marshall, T. (1991). "Restorative Justice On Trial In Europe." In: H. Messmer and H-U. Otto (eds.), *Restorative Justice on Trial: Pitfalls and Potentials of Victim Offender Mediation — International Research Perspectives*. Dordrecht, NETH: Kluwer.

Masters, G. (2002a). "Family Group Conferencing: A Victim Perspective." In: B. Williams (ed.), *Reparation and Victim-Focused Social Work*. London, UK: Jessica Kingsley.

—— (2002b) "In or Out? Some Critical Reflections upon the Potential for Involving Victims of Youth Crime in Restorative Processes in England and Wales." *British Journal of Community Justice* 1:99-110.

Maxwell, G. and A. Morris (1998) *Understanding Re-offending*. Wellington, NZ: Institute of Criminology, Victoria University of Wellington.

—— (1993). *Family, Victims & Culture. Youth Justice in New Zealand*. Wellington, NZ: Social Policy Agency and Institute of Criminology, Victoria University of Wellington.

Mediation UK (2001). *The Rough Guide to Restorative Justice and the Crime & Disorder Act.* Bristol: Mediation UK.

Miers, D.M., S. Maguire, K. Goldie et al. (2001). *An Exploratory Evaluation of Restorative Justice Schemes.* London, UK: Home Office.

Newburn, T., R. Earle, S. Goldie et al. (2002). *The Introduction of Referral Orders into the Youth Justice System – Final Report.* London, UK: Home Office.

—— R. Earle, S. Goldie et al. (2001). *The Introduction of Referral Orders into the Youth Justice System.* (Second Interim Report. RDS Occasional Paper No 73.) London, UK: Home Office.

Peachy, D. (1989) "The Kitchener Experiment." In: M. Wright and B. Galaway (eds.), *Mediation and Criminal Justice.* London, UK: Sage.

Sinkinson, H. and J. Broderick (1998). "A Case Study of Restorative Justice: The Vermont Reparative Probation Program." In: L. Walgrave (ed.), *Restorative Justice for Juveniles: Potentialities, Risks and Problems for Research.* Leuven: Leuven, BEL: University Press.

Stuart, B. (1997). *Building Community Justice Partnerships: Community Peacemaking Circles.* Ottawa, CAN: Department of Justice.

Umbreit, M. and A. Roberts. (1996). *Mediation of Criminal Conflict in England & Wales. An Assessment of Services in Coventry & Leeds.* St. Paul, MN: University of Minnesota, Center for Restorative Justice & Mediation.

Van Ness, D. and K. Strong (1997). *Restoring Justice.* Cincinnati, OH: Anderson.

Wright, M. (1996) *Justice for Victims and Offenders.* Winchester, UK: Waterside.

—— and B. Galaway (1989). *Mediation and Criminal Justice.* London, UK: Sage.

Youth Justice Board (2003). "Members of the Public Take Action in Over a Quarter of Sentences for Young Offenders." (Press release, 4th April, 2003.) London: Youth Justice Board.

Zehr, H. (1990). *Changing Lenses.* Ontario, CAN: Herald Press.

NOTES

1. Also commonly referred to as "Restorative Conferencing."

2. FGCs are mandatory before all youth court sentencing except for murder and manslaughter offences.

PART IV.
PRACTICE AND PRACTITIONERS

Victim Offender Mediation — Family Group Conferencing — Peacemaking Circles

Whether practitioners or academics, most of us are familiar with these applications of restorative justice. Certainly, restorative justice is little more than a nice thought if we fail to practice it in real life. But what does it really mean to "do" restorative justice? Are these the only options? Are some better than others? What does "good practice" look like, and how do we ensure it? How do we know when we are off track?

Some argue that by definition, restorative justice requires a facilitated encounter between victims and offenders. Others contend that the application of restorative justice transcends encounters between victims and offenders, even in the criminal justice arena. Still others challenge us that we are truly doing restorative justice when we apply it in our everyday personal and professional lives or, as we shall see in an upcoming section, in cases of social injustice.

Differing perspectives on practice can certainly lead to conflict and confusion. A practitioner may doubt the integrity of another's work. Local practitioners' may not be able to agree on the best way to apply restorative justice within their community. One program may measure success by the number of meetings facilitated, while another evaluates its program on degrees of satisfaction experienced by victims or offenders, or even by changes in public policy. One program trains volunteers in facilitation skills, while another employs professionals to do community building. Programs may compete in promoting their models.

Much can be gained from a dialogue on questions such as these:

- To what extent are the various forms of practice responsive to the needs of victims, offenders and communities — and from the time of the offense through sentencing and beyond?

- To what extent do various forms of practice promote real involvement on the part of the victim, offender and community?

- What are possibilities and dangers of being committed to certain models or, on the other hand, of not adopting set, consistent models for practice?

- What are the possibilities and dangers of using volunteers, paid professionals or authority figures as dialogue facilitators?

- What are benchmarks for evaluating different practice models and for setting standards for good practice?

- What are the core features of "good" models and "bad" models?

The authors in this section explore these issues and more. Annie Warner Roberts contends that victim offender dialogue is the core of restorative justice. Wonshé explores practice by suggesting how the practitioners themselves as well as the environment in which practice takes place may impact how a program functions, who is served and how. Jim Boyack, Helen Bowen and Chris Marshall present a proposal for guidelines for good practice. Dave Dyck considers good practice and what it means for our personal and professional relationships. Carsten Erbe considers what being a "professional" means in this context and challenges the way in which professionals of various sorts currently function. Dave Gustafson also considers good practice and what the implications are for the types of cases we can and should be taking. Morris Jenkins and Barbara Raye challenge us to look at how the culture and gender of practitioners influence our "take" on restorative justice and, in turn, our practice.

In many ways, the themes raised by these authors point us back to the definition of restorative justice for it is difficult to know what to do or how to do it without knowing what guides us. Much of our dialogue is shaped by our visions for what restorative justice does and could mean for victims, offenders, communities and, perhaps, ourselves. In turn, exploration of our practice may offer insight into our definitions of and visions for restorative justice. It is through this movement back and forth between theory and practice that good practice is shaped.

Chapter 19.
Is Restorative Justice Tied To Specific Models Of Practice?

by

Ann Warner Roberts

As the Restorative Justice (RJ) movement has expanded, more techniques, models, practices, frameworks, and theories have been created. From the original application of the RJ philosophy to the criminal justice system, RJ has expanded to justice for families, schools, neighborhoods, communities, and even countries. On one hand this growth is positive, but it comes at a cost: RJ has become extremely amorphous. The core, "Restorative Dialogue,"[1] with its underlying principles and values, is at risk of being marginalized.

One Specific Model Of Practice

Originally, RJ was not only tied to one specific model of practice, it was virtually synonymous with the specific model of practice called Victim Offender Reconciliation Program (VORP) or Victim Offender Mediation (VOM). In fact, RJ was coined to refer to the principles and values underlying VOM, which, nearly three decades ago, evolved from an experimental practice in the criminal justice system — a new type of mediation, or Restorative Dialogue, between victims and offenders. The principles guiding Restorative Dialogue in response to crime or conflict are:

- repair of harm as much as possible,

- direct involvement of the parties,

- a problem-solving, collaborative approach, and

- consensual decision making.

Common values applied to Restorative Dialogue are generally understood as:

- respect among all parties,

- flexibility of the process, and

- empowerment of all parties.

VOM was regarded as a one-to-one mediation or meeting, facilitated by a neutral, impartial mediator or facilitator (often a community volunteer). Within a short time, VOM became more flexible, and often was multi-party, with several victims and/or offenders, family members and/or supporters. Next, this VOM model of practice became several models, and then a family of models. Later, RJ encompassed a systems-change model. With this growth, not surprisingly, has come an expansion in the definition of RJ, as well as conceptual confusion and conflict.

More Models Of Practice Emerge

After VOM, the next incarnation of Restorative Dialogue was the emergence of Conferencing, first in New Zealand, then in Australia, and then on to North America, Europe and beyond. Concurrently, Circles re-emerged as another similar model of Restorative Dialogue, adapted from indigenous cultures. And finally, Boards/Panels[2] were introduced as still another variation on a theme. The Conferencing, Circles and Boards/Panels expanded the practice focus with "community," in addition to the victim(s) and the offender(s), explicitly named as a primary stakeholder.

Face-To-Face/Direct And Indirect Dialogue

Along with Conferencing and Circles came another important issue — whether the process must be in-person. When everyone voluntarily wants to meet, and there is not a significant power imbalance, a face-to-face or direct Restorative Dialogue is usually the model of choice. With this method, there is enormous potential for healing and understanding. However, it also carries higher risk. For certain cases involving extreme violence and trauma, such as rape or domestic abuse, a face-to-face encounter might not be safely done and could lead to revictimization of the victim. Or a case where the victim might be violent or abusive could risk victimization of the offender. A person may prefer an indirect Restorative Dialogue[3] for individual or cultural reasons, such as someone who expresses her/himself better in writing. Examples of indirect encounters include: audio, video, letter, e-mail, fax or a shuttle process whereby the mediator/facilitator carries information back and forth. Therefore, an indirect encounter may be the appropriate process for a particular situation. And yet another model of Restorative Dialogue is added to the mix.

Both face-to-face and indirect processes have value, and research must help us learn when each is more likely to be most effective. Dialogue between practice and theory is a broad need in the field. Indeed, it is an imperative.

Practice To Theory; Theory To Practice

In short, RJ has changed over the last 30 years, from a single model practice to a multi-model, mixed practice in which the practitioner decides what is likely to work best in the situation. At its best, practice drives theory and theory drives practice. Originally, theory was grounded in practice, and early advocates and researchers helped shape later debates. For example, the various Restorative Dialogue practices — VOM, Conferencing, Circles and Boards/Panels — were positioned as individually "pure" and distinct, with the primary focus on the differences among models. On one hand, this was helpful for understanding and researching each model. On the other hand, it did not accurately represent what was happening in the world of practice. In reality, truly pure models did not exist as there was as much variety within models as among them. This is not RJ chaos, as some fear. This is, in fact, what the development of mature, evidence-based practice is all about. Yet this did not occur at first.

Confusion And Conflict

The initial focus on differences between and among models led to confusion and conflict that was detrimental to the field. In the practitioners' world, one particular tension arose early during the introduction of Conferencing, and did so both in the U.S. and England. Conferencing advocates maintained, "Conferencing is not VOM; these are completely different." VOM advocates felt dismissed: "why isn't our experience and proven expertise understood and valued?" Such tensions and misunderstandings resulted in anger, hostility and hurt feelings among practitioners, researchers and advocates. Conflict developed and became increasingly "positional" rather than "interest based." It became a case of "my model is better than your model." Subsequently, competition escalated, with a negative impact; the values and principles of RJ were seemingly compromised. Another ongoing controversy questions the superiority of the New Zealand model versus the Australian model — simply described as "private family planning time" versus the group staying together as a whole during Conferencing.

Adding to the tension within the RJ field was confusion and conflict about whether to use a written script or simply a brief outline in Conferencing. While the question can be debated on both sides, the issue could be likened to a cook preferring a recipe to a more flexible pinch of this and dash of that. The practice (and evaluation) question remains, "Is a script a useful tool, an unnecessary crutch or a bit of each?" Similarly, there were tensions with Circles. Advocates saw this new model as being the best model and, though unproven, used it as their method of choice. This is called "newism validity" of an emergent practice inside a scientific social movement. Research, evaluation and practice wisdom are marginalized to new practice.

The Needs-led, Multi-method Approach

Over time, there has been a gradual shift to moving beyond the focus on differences toward acknowledging similarities and overlaps between and among all the models. More and more hybrids were developed, as characteristics of each model were mixed and matched. For example, facilitators sometimes used a talking piece[4] to manage a Conference or multi-party VOM. VOM meetings sometimes invited community members as supporters, along with family and friends of the victims and offenders. Though the lines between models became blurred, Restorative Dialogue was the seed of each different approach. Experienced practitioners discovered that each case is different from the last and they must adapt models to people and their needs, not vice versa.

Thus, practice is evolving to what now may be called a needs-led, multi-method approach. For example, more than one meeting might be held for the same case. The first meeting might address issues between the victim and the offender in regards to the precipitating incident. A second follow-up meeting could address underlying issues relevant to the offender and family. More controversially, some practitioners say that the parties themselves should take an active part in designing their own dialogue process.

In retrospect, there is considerable irony about all the confusion and conflict since there may be little difference in the various models of Restorative Dialogue. Multi-party VOM and Conferencing (and to a lesser extent, Boards/Panels) can look similar if not identical. And clearly, there can be much overlap in practice between Conferencing (in all its incarnations) and Circles. All may have in common a more effective approach to problem solving, conflict resolution, right relationship and peacemaking. As any model can be retributive or restorative, it is critical that each be based upon RJ principles and values.

System Change Framework

As the numbers and types of Restorative Dialogue increased — from one specific model of practice (VOM), to multiple models (Conferencing, Circles, Boards/Panels), to indirect models, and then on to a multi-method, needs-led approach (combinations, hybrids, etc.) — the overall field of RJ continued to expand. For instance, the Balanced and Restorative Justice Project (BARJ), a national initiative funded primarily by the federal government, emerged to promote RJ principles as a framework for changing the criminal justice system as a whole.[5]

At this point, there was a massive influx of more models of practice placed within the definition and concept of RJ. These include, for example, restitution, victim impact panels, neighborhood accountability boards, letters of apology, community work service, community panels, community policing, and offender re-entry. Some models contain dialogue of one sort or another, but may or may not be restorative in its original sense. These models and programs are appropriate in a systems framework. However, without Restorative Dialogue as the core of RJ, the framework is in danger of not representing a true systems change, or at worst, of collapsing.

As the funding stream for RJ flowed more heavily, more and more models of practice claimed to be RJ — some accurately, some not. Indeed, some practices from within more formal, judicial structures call themselves "restorative," e.g., community, drug and teen courts. While some may be moving towards a restorative philosophy and practice, the mere fact that they are called "courts" raises suspicion that they are more adversarial than consensual, suggesting a difference from what we stand for and practice.

The focus on system change results in a troubling problem in that Restorative Dialogue is becoming marginalized, thus compromising the essential core of RJ. True, the extensive training courses for justice system professionals give attention to Restorative Dialogue, but this is a relatively superficial overview. While circle process is used within the training to explore issues, there is little depth in its use. A troubling development is the danger that restorative dialogue processes are being sidelined. Yet RJ as a live field is ever responsive to changing contexts, theories and practices. Our field yesterday is not at all like our field today. Nevertheless, it remains essential that Restorative Dialogue be kept at the RJ core in order to maintain the principles and values central to our understanding and ways of working: this is who we are, at base.

RJ TODAY

Today, RJ advocates, practitioners, policymakers and academics have yet to come together in a restorative fashion to resolve past and present conflicts and move beyond the anger, hostility and hurt feelings over models and practices. We have not yet told our stories, shown accountability for the harms caused, made amends, received support, and decided how to work together in the future. We have yet to do ourselves what we do daily with and for others. One wonders about the continuing impact of these ongoing disagreements on the major theories and models in our field.

As RJ field and practice continue to expand and evolve, there are always new ideas, experimentation and creativity, although less now in times of limited resources. Indeed, RJ must continue to innovate both philosophically and practically for the movement to thrive. If we are to have continued viability, one crucial area of focus is the place of RJ in our everyday lives.

Restorative Dialogue And Everyday Life

It is useful to accept the RJ philosophy as applicable to everyday life when reflecting upon the role of Restorative Dialogue. Central to the RJ philosophy is a concern for the most effective way for people to interact with one another in order to live in social harmony. It recognizes and operates on both the emotional level and rational or legal level. Furthermore, the RJ philosophy accepts that conflict and disagreement are inevitable, but offers a healthy model for turning such events into opportunities for learning, mutual understanding and cooperation. RJ may not be limited to, but *must* include Restorative Dialogue.

Restorative Dialogue must be present in our own lives and those of all people because it is as much about everyday life as it is about criminal justice decision making. Obviously, Restorative Dialogue can be appropriate and effective in schools, neighborhoods and the workplace. It offers a philosophy, perspective and process useful in any situation where there is any type of harm that leaves individuals feeling victimized or hurt and in search of solutions. In order to maintain the integrity of the RJ field, we must ask ourselves: "Are we using Restorative Dialogue in our own lives, and within our own organizations and our own field?" We must model the model and practice the practice of Restorative Dialogue.

CONCLUSION

With funds shrinking, we are once again seeing an increase in competition between and among individuals, groups and organizations over limited resources. Long-established programs are struggling for survival. In order for us to become a more integrated movement, collaboration is needed to advocate for the transformation of justice. Hope is on the horizon. There are plans for the early RJ practitioners to come together in Restorative Dialogue.[6] Conceived as a Circle of Understanding, its goal is to mend past harms and gain understanding. This is our opportunity to practice our central way of understanding and working — through Restorative Dialogue. Can we do otherwise and still claim to be practitioners of RJ?

EPILOGUE

Which Approach Should I Use?

To the reader new to RJ, all of this may be too abstract. A short case example demonstrates that any number of different Restorative Dialogue approaches could be applied in a given situation. Remember that what seems "obviously" good may not be perceived that way by interested theoreticians or practitioners. Remember too that research and evaluation may effectively contribute to the debate on "which approach should I use?" And most of all, remember that it is the parties themselves who must have the most say in what the process to be used. It is their conflict, their property, their Restorative Dialogue.

Restorative Dialogue In Practice: A Case Study

One way to illustrate the flexibility and overlap of the multiple models is to take an actual case and present hypothetical options as a restorative response.

> After a series of verbal fights, David (18), violently assaulted Steve (18). The result was serious injuries to Steve's face, requiring extensive reconstructive surgery. After the assault, David pled guilty to a third degree felony charge. Leading up to the assault, David and Steve's younger sister had a short relationship which, was unacceptable to Steve's family and, as result, they broke up. Subsequently, David and Steve had heard rumors of serious threats to each other, and were angry and upset.

> The actual outcome was that David went to court and was sentenced to: (1) indefinite probation, (2) financial restitution for medical costs not covered by insurance, (3) anger management class and (4) referral to the local Victim Offender Mediation (VOM) program. After having separate preparation meetings with a mediator/facilitator, a classic one-to-one VOM between David and Steve was held. Each very movingly told his story about what happened, and the devastating impact it had on their own lives and those of their families.

> David spoke about how his father, a military officer, had always told him it was OK to defend himself and his honor with his

fists. He said he had no idea that he was so strong and could inflict that amount of physical damage. Further, David expressed strong remorse, saying he had learned his lesson and does not plan on anything like this ever happening again. Steve talked about past behavior of which he was not proud. After discussing how difficult it is for guys to verbally express feelings, they both talked about racism in their school, yet believed the incident was not racially motivated (one youth is African American and the other is Caucasian). For the future, they agreed to greet each other if they run into each other socially. Additionally, they agreed to each tell their friends that there was peace between them and that hostilities should end.

As the conference came to a close, David and Steve spontaneously offered each other a handshake. David looked Steve squarely in the eye and said, "Are you really OK now?" David gave an emphatic "yes." There was no written agreement because they felt it not necessary.

The above resolution was "successful" for David, Steve and their families. However, numerous other Restorative Dialogue processes could have been possible in response to this particular crime:

- If the parents or siblings had wanted to participate, a multi-party rather than a 1:1 meeting could have been used.

- If there was a broader community impact, such as racial tension, a Circle Sentencing could have been facilitated to include the youth, their supporters, the judge, prosecutor and defender (albeit in non-professional roles as community members), school personnel and other affected community members.

- If David and his family had needed additional assistance from social services, the VOM could have been held first and then followed by Conferencing for only David and his family to address other challenges facing them specifically.

- If the program and the judiciary were in agreement, the case could have gone directly to a VOM with a recommendation to the court for disposition. Or, in a more radical route, it could have gone to a VOM with no court process on the condition that the resulting agreement was completed, and David stayed law-abiding while on probation.

From this list, it is clear that there is no one right or correct or best response. When solidly based on RJ values and principles, all of these variations on Restorative Dialogue process have the potential to be successful. Yet a good question remains:

Why did this case use VOM rather than a Conferencing or Circle? Because the practitioner judged this process to be the most fitting for the situation and the parties wanted this option. Certainly, any of these options were available during case assessment. It was their conflict, their property, their Restorative Dialogue.

Address correspondence to: Ann Warner Roberts, 1496 Chelmsford, St. Paul, MN 55108. E-mail: <aroberts@umn.edu>.

REFERENCES AND SUGGESTED READING

Bazemore, G. and M. Umbreit (2001). "A Comparison of Four Restorative Conferencing Models." *OJJDP Juvenile Justice Bulletin,* February issue.

Marshall, T.F. (1998) "Restorative Justice: An Overview." St. Paul, MN: Center for Restorative Justice and Peacemaking (ssw.che.umn.edu/rjp).

Pranis, K., B. Stuart and M. Wedge (2003). *Peacemaking Circles: From Crime to Community.* St. Paul, MN: Living Justice Press.

Roberts, A.W. and G. Masters (1999). *Group Conferencing: RJ in Practice.* St. Paul, MN: Center for Restorative Justice and Peacemaking, in collaboration with Restorative Justice Consortium UK, Mediation UK (ssw.che.umn.edu/rjp).

—— and G. Masters (1999). "The Practice of Family Group Conferencing; American-British Collaboration Identifies Key Implementation Issues." *Offender Programs Report* (July/August):19-26.

Schiff, M. and G. Bazemore (2002). "Understanding Restorative Conferencing: A Case Study in Informal Decision-making in the Response to Youth Crime." Washington, DC: National Institute of Justice (www.barjproject.org).

Umbreit, M. and S. Stacey (1996). "Family Group Conferencing Comes to the U.S.: A Comparison with Victim Offender Mediation." *Juvenile and Family Court Journal* 47(2):29-38.

—— and H. Zehr (1996). "Restorative Family Group Conferences: Differing Models and Guidelines for Practice." *Federal Probation* 60(3):24-29.

Zehr, H. (2002). *The Little Book of Restorative Justice*. Intercourse, PA: Good Books.

NOTES

1. "Restorative Dialogue" is an umbrella term referring to a process that brings people together in dialogue to gain understanding and repair the harm caused by a crime or conflict. Based upon specific values and principles, it includes VOM, Conferencing and Circles. Boards/Panels may also be included, although their structural design may inhibit the "restorativeness" of the encounter.

2. Boards/Panels often use a seating arrangement where participant(s) are seated on one side of a table or bench and Board/Panel members are seated on the other side — or oppositional, as in a magistrate's court. Thus, the structural design itself may set up an adversarial mode. The mediators/facilitators are in a literal "face-off," with the participants before any dialogue even begins. Conversely, in VOM, Conferencing and Circles, participants and mediators/facilitators are usually seated around a table or in a circle. Psychologically, this may create a more cooperative atmosphere — one that is conducive to collaboration and a consensual mode of problem solving and conflict resolution.

3. Anecdotally, there seems to be more indirect work being done than is being reported in the U.S. Why is this the case? It may possibly stem from the perception that indirect encounters are somehow inferior to face-to-face, and therefore are not considered "real" RJ, or counted in data collection. Despite this apparent bias against an indirect encounter in the U.S., it should not be overlooked. Interestingly, programs in several European countries report a much higher usage of indirect dialogue, despite designing their initial practice after the U.S.

4. Simply put, the function of the "talking piece" is to designate who may speak in the circle. As the talking piece passes around the group, each person may speak or pass in turn. A talking piece can be any object that is appropriate to the occasion; often the facilitator/keeper chooses a talking piece that is meaningful to the individual and/or the group. For example, an elementary teacher uses a plastic dinosaur for a playground conflict. Another uses a stone with a carved maze. Or, in Native American, First Nation and other indigenous cultures, an eagle feather or other

item with sacred symbolism is generally used. For more detailed information, see Pranis et al. (2003).

5. To learn more, please see website at www.barproject.org/.

6. The logistics for the RJ circle of understanding are being coordinated by Dan Van Ness, Prison Fellowship International, Centre for Justice and Reconciliation. The goal is to meet in 2004.

Chapter 20.
How Does The "Who, What, Where, When And How" Affect The Practice Of Restorative Justice?

by

Wonshé

During the past months, I have been exploring the real world of restorative justice in the United States. As part of this inquiry, I participated in numerous dialogues among people working in organizations expressly designed for restorative justice as well as other organizations or agencies that were implementing restorative justice. I participated in advisory and steering committee meetings for developing programs in high-risk victim offender dialogue and for reintegration of sex offenders into community. I took part in a variety of restorative justice training/workshops. I observed several reparative panels in which I was asked to offer critique of their process, and I attended regional restorative justice conferences. I also conducted personal interviews with many individuals who define their work as restorative justice.

In the following chapter I offer my personal observations not as definitive conclusions or answers but as encouragement to further critical examination of and discussion within the field.

(Re)searching For Restorative Justice

The more I witnessed, the more I felt like Dorothy in the Land of Oz[1] journeying to find restorative justice. Like her, I was surprised to discover the man behind the curtain maintaining the grand projection. I wanted to click my heels and go home, back to the nurturing, loving and respectful community in which I had been living, where restorative justice is modeled as a way of life.

But I am not Dorothy. So I continued as I have done in my life journey as a midwife, trusting my skills to navigate the terrain: my seasoned ability to see essence dwelling within a form, a keen perception of unborn potential, and devotion to guarding vulnerable processes from interference. I sought to use "engaged understanding" to discern ways in which to challenge problems and issues in the way restorative justice was being implemented without falling into moral judgment about them. Remembering that there are no maps to restorative justice, my compass was a vision for a natural process of relationship, with its own cardinal ordering and sense of timing.

My inquiry reflects my restorative justice education that took place in a peacebuilding context. There I learned that restorative justice begins with respect, that it asks for compassion and recognition of our common humanity and that it challenges us to understand and stay true to its philosophy and principles. In addition, I learned that restorative justice is not only a way of work; it is a way of life. These biases influence how I understood what I saw and experienced during my journey — for instance, my response to ideas of what restorative justice is and is not, its ultimate goals and the ways in which programs were developed and by whom.

After running through what seemed like a maze of risk-factoring, policies, procedures and flow charts, I began to feel deep concern about whether all this "restorative justice process" translates into practice guided by compassion, understanding, healing or recognition of our common humanity. So, I walked from the center of the maze to its margin, stopped, and turned around.

When I did, I saw a tribe made up of various clans building a bridge between the criminal justice system and community. The clan that was the most visible and audible called themselves the "systems people." They were in the center of construction, hurriedly moving around as though they were in charge, busily — sometimes frantically — carving out pathways, passing out blueprints and soliciting volunteers. The next clan I noticed was much quieter and moving at a slower pace. They didn't have a name that held them together, but were connected by heart and spirit. With some systems people among them, they were crafting new and more effective building tools. While some were building, others talked with communities and shared the information with those near the bridge.

As these groups worked on this bridge, it sounded as though they were communicating from different "time zones," or regions of understanding; for some the day was just beginning, while others were moving into evening. I saw that what we *understand* about restorative justice affects its practice differently from what we *know*. The societal and cultural contexts in which we live, our intersections with history and our worldviews contribute to our region of understanding.

Colonization Of — And By — Restorative Justice

Pivotal to all my concerns about what is taking place in the field of restorative justice is the tendency for systems-influenced people to "colonize" it and how this process impedes the vital need for autonomy. The current system, based on punishment, fears and control, is but one expression of a larger thought system infused into everyday culture that influences us all. Organizations based on such values are incongruent with, and often undermine, values of restorative justice that begin with respect, seek reconciliation and are based on love.

One specific example can be seen in the different hierarchies of the justice system and of restorative justice. The justice system operates within a hierarchy of *power* in which there exists only one recognized source of power. Because there is only one source of power, there is always fear of losing it, so controlling power is essential. Within this hierarchy the way to generate power is to accumulate it and hold onto it. The more powerful people are, the greater is their ability to control the less powerful.

Restorative justice, however, operates within a hierarchy of *skill*. Within a hierarchy of skill there are multiple sources of power recognized, available at different times in varying capacities and drawn upon based on need. Sharing power with another so that they are more powerful is the way is to generate more power — which is necessary to sustain the whole.

Negotiating a shared reality between these worldviews is a challenge. In my observations, it often appeared that the justice system was taking over restorative justice and the community. However, my story of the tribes building the bridge invites us to see restorative justice as a bridge between the criminal justice system and the community, rather than a part of, or alternative to, the criminal justice system. In this view, restorative justice should be allied with, but not assimilated into, criminal justice and remain autonomous in its ability to serve community but not to govern it.

Colonization is a force that has existed over time throughout the world, and still exists today. In its most rudimentary sense it is a process of uprooting one thing and replacing it with something else. For example, conquerors may try to uproot (if not clear-cut!) a people's culture — their language, religion, spirituality, ritual and art — and replace it with their own. Then the people who have to assimilate into the conqueror's culture experience weakened autonomy and ultimately are rendered dependent. Often cultural symbols become curiosities to be collected by the conqueror. Sacred objects become artifacts and when taken out of context forfeit their meanings.

We have to remember that colonization is a part of our own history in the United States, and that we need to include an examination of this history in any claim that restorative justice is rooted in indigenous teachings. Without acknowledging how these teachings were lost in the first place, we can never honestly evaluate the ways in which we choose to resurrect them. We are faced with the question whether restorative justice is wholly and authentically translating and implementing indigenous teaching in our present historical context, or is it once again collecting artifacts for our own interest and curiosity — a form of colonization.

First Nation artifacts — for example circles and talking pieces — are clearly becoming popular in restorative justice practice. My concern is whether we are actually doing the work of Circles when we don't understand their meaning. I am concerned about using "talking pieces" without understanding or honouring the process that gives it meaning. Without embracing the meaning, we cannot practice with integrity as we forget the origins of these gifts and leave behind the vital elements for personal transformation contained in their meanings.

What is traditionally known as a "talking stick," is now popularly referred to as a "talking piece," so that any random object can be used in its place. The talking stick, generally a naturally occurring piece of wood — or stick — is given meaning in varying ways, often represented by the way it is ceremonially adorned. The talking stick is passed among individuals in Circle, in what is called a "round." During each round the one who holds the talking stick is the only one to speak, while all others listen without responding. In this way the talking stick holds meaning as a symbol of respect and the opportunity to "speak one's truth" without interruption. Meaning can also be contained in its place of origin or the many places it has been carried, conveyed by the one who gifts it to the Circle Keeper, or enkindled by Circle Keepers themselves. The many hands that hold it also infuse meaning into each unique talking stick.

I believe that in order to facilitate a journey of transformation for another individual, the facilitator must have experienced the journey himself or herself. The philosophy and principles of restorative justice must *live* in the facilitator. Buddhist teaching would call this "mindful participation." First Nation teaching would call this "walking your talk." Even in China, acupuncturists have to receive treatment themselves for five years as part of their education. Kathleen Denison (1991:4) affirms this belief when she proposes that "...restorative justice needs to be operative within us, in our own inner world, before we can implement it within the criminal justice system."

When we follow the roots of restorative justice back to First Nation people we see that "restorative justice" was not named as such. It was not a program they went to or a model they followed. Rather, it was a thread woven into the fabric of their lives and an expression of values shared by and maintained by community. We need to honor the intricacy and richness of their culture without romanticizing it or losing the original meaning of restorative justice. Otherwise, we risk misinterpretation and distortion in our practices.

Language

Language not only expresses *what* we think; it shapes *how* we think. I am concerned that both justice systems people and restorative justice people use language characterized by naming, categorizing, generalizing and stereotyping. This language presents biases and worldviewing as universal truths. This is reflected in such statements as "sex offenders will never recover and will always have to be in treatment" or "sexual assault cases can never be brought to a victim-offender dialogue." Language, including that of restorative justice, often has subtle and not so subtle punitive overtones. For instance, people talk of "paying" — not "giving" — back; "admitting" — not "accepting" — responsibility; and "admitting" — not "feeling" — remorse. I have even heard comments such as: "Restorative justice only works for good people who've made a mistake — the rest of them can go to jail." Even terms that refer to relationships such as "investment," "buy in," and "stakeholders" sound more like parties in a financial transaction than people cultivating relationships.

This language and its hurry to categorize continue to create separate societies — victim societies, offender societies — where we lock individuals into rigid identities. Violence is a hurried approach. Building relationships with compassion, empowerment and journeying take time. As practitioners, we clearly need to challenge ourselves to be more creative and consciously develop a language that corresponds to the values and principles of restorative justice and authentically expresses them.

Cloning Restorative Justice Programs

There is a tendency for organizations, when creating new programs, to duplicate the policies, procedures and forms of other existing programs. While it is valuable to look to other established programs for information, I am concerned about duplication, particularly when the program is system-initiated. I think it is imperative to evaluate programs on their understanding of fundamental restorative justice principles and not assume that these programs are ideal just because they exist. Restorative justice accepts ambiguity and paradox and requires diversity. Cloning or copying shortchanges its creative process and interferes with innovation, a vital element of any organization. Further it begins to standardize restorative justice in a way that threatens its autonomy and discounts variance in community composition. A fundamental assumption of restorative justice, after all, is that it must be rooted in its context.

Institutionalizing Volunteerism

It seems appropriate that the majority of people doing restorative justice work, a community process, are community volunteers. Some programs even emphasize that it "means more" when volunteers donate their time freely. However, my concern is about other dynamics taking place and about the consequences not recognized. For instance, I see a pervasive "poverty consciousness" among restorative justice programs, expressed with the repetitive mantra, "We have no money." Poverty, however, is not simply about one's lack of access to currency; it is also about seeing no other way out. I wonder if dependency on the volunteer is becoming restorative justice's way out. This may have many implications.

Volunteerism is a form of charity that, on the surface, is all the things we know it to be: generosity, kindness, benevolence, goodwill and positive social action. Through volunteering, I as a privileged individual can make a change by sharing my resources to offer relief from the pressure of financial hardship. I feel good about myself for giving, and with the subsequent praise and recognition my privileged position is made more secure and my social status is elevated. Moreover, the organization's financial stress is temporarily relieved. However, it is often only symptomatic relief. It usually does not incite me to take further action or to deal with the structural and systemic problems that create the organizational "poverty" in the first place. Interestingly, this is parallel to a current lack of attention within restorative justice to the structural and systemic harms that contribute to crime. Comfort and reliance in using volunteers lends itself to the institutionalization of charity and the consequent shortcomings.

The question of *who* our volunteers are requires serious examination. First, there is a distinct separation between those who can financially afford to volunteer and those who cannot. This has a direct influence on restorative justice programs and their practice. As a community practice, restorative justice's volunteer population should reflect the characteristic *natural* diversity — including but not limited to race, class, and economic positions — of the community it serves. In a culture where time is money, however, it is often only those of privilege and affluence who have time to give to restorative justice programs. One resulting consequence is that the program establishes a fairly homogenized volunteer base whose worldviewing and ethnocentricity does not prepare them to deal with certain community issues. These, in turn, greatly influence the particular restorative justice practice being implemented. It can even cause a programmatic breakdown because volunteers expect the "other" — victim or offender — to meet them where they are, as volunteers, instead of meeting the "other" where they are. Such ethnocentricity is evidenced, for example, in a desire to have economic diversity on one's board yet holding meetings during the workday, thereby excluding those who cannot afford to take time off during the workday.

Talk Therapy

While issues of limited funding and volunteer time continue, "trainings" are proliferating. These trainings frequently attempt to cover complex information in very little time. An equally important issue is the orientation toward *training* people to do restorative justice work rather than *educating* them.

Related to this, I have observed a prevalent psychotherapy influence in training for certain victim-offender dialogue and family group conference programs. In this approach, the goal is to "get to the affect" or "moment of conversion" for the offender, i.e., a point where the offender not only "feels" but also *expresses* that feeling to the satisfaction of the therapist/facilitator. The goal of expressing remorse in a specific way reflects an ethnocentric approach to facilitation and how the culture of talk therapy speaks to specific populations (usually Western, privileged and white). Expecting a certain correct way for an offender to behave shifts attention away from the experience as theirs to that of the facilitator's. This practice discounts cultural and ethnic variance and the distinct ways people experience emotion; the offender is expected to adapt to the therapist's worldviewing. This approach to facilitation may not be appropriate for the community as a whole.

Rather than focus solely on training about psychological processes as a way to facilitate, I suggest providing education about the cycle of trauma and its relationship to violence. Education about the trauma cycle prepares a facilitator to navigate the complexities of victim-offender dialogue more wholly than training in any style of therapy.

Victim Offender Dialogue

Over all, victim offender dialogue seems to be implemented less frequently with adults and, with even less frequency, in severe or violent crimes. Some feel adamant that sex offenses or domestic violence should never be accepted for dialogue due to the potential for offender manipulation of the process and participants, revictimization of the victim, and facilitator unfamiliarity with the issues pertaining to these crimes. Interestingly, this familiarity often seems to belong to systems people and therapists, indicating elite access to this information.

I argue that a refusal to do these cases limits our ability to serve the community, denies dialogue to a distinct population of people, and creates an "elite" who can "afford" it. In essence, restorative justice becomes a process governed by experts. Instead of using sound principles of discernment to determine the appropriateness of each case, these experts tend to make categorical decisions about who can and cannot participate in dialogue. In reality, however, in "lower high risk" cases there will be individuals for whom it is not appropriate to engage in dialogue and, in "higher high risk" cases, there will be those who are fully ready to begin this process. Further, a categorical refusal to accept certain crimes denies the opportunity to maintain high facilitator training standards. I suggest increasing the scope of training — combined with appropriate oversight and advice — so that facilitators are equipped with the necessary information to responsibly deal with the specific variances of this population and to serve the parties.

Cycles Of Organizational Abuse

Perhaps the most significant and disturbing part of my exploration of restorative justice is my discovery of a cycle of mistreatment within a restorative justice organization. The patterns of behavior were identical in many ways to those of domestic violence or substance abuse: a repeated cycle of abuse, apology, honeymoon, abuse. I have observed the following dynamics in the organization's cycle of abuse:

- Hierarchies of power that reinforce "managers" and "directors," not hierarchies of skill that nurture emerging "leaders."

- Relationships based on dependency rather than autonomy.

- Patterns of habitual behavior and automatic reactions, rather than natural and healthy responses.

- Repetitive and redundant behavior that starves the natural process of creativity, variance and diversity.

- Censorship of honest communication which fosters resentment, dishonesty, mistrust and unhealthy competition, rather than an environment that develops trust, honesty, camaraderie and support for and among staff.

This pattern of behavior is particularly destructive when it is rooted in the organization's leadership. In addition to weakening organizational relationships, this type of leadership detrimentally influences each individual member's receptivity to his or her contributions to the agency, even when those contributions are sound and/or innovative. It also overshadows the leader's valuable contributions and insights to the organization and impedes the other members' ability to respect and trust that leadership. Often staff leaves as a way to resolve the conflict. But it does not end the conflict, for as new staff is hired there is nothing to compel the leader to change and the cycle continues.

Just as there are patterns to abusive behavior, there are patterns in the responses to it. Such responses include lowered self-esteem and confidence, increased self-doubt and a sense that no matter what one does, it will never be good enough. All in all, this dysfunction contributes to an unhealthy work environment and inefficiency. It also undermines the organization's work and its integrity, and that of the field as whole. Perhaps most critically, it undermines the relationships between organizational members. Inevitably, talented and committed individuals leave their jobs, no longer willing to participate in the cycle of abuse. The organization not only loses their skills and dedication but also then has to redirect energy away from the necessary program tasks toward filling these positions. This is hardly consistent with restorative justice values and principles.

CONCLUSION

From this experience I have learned that there is something powerful about innocence and about honoring naiveté. When seeing the world through an open heart, certain truths are revealed that, when embraced, become our allies and lead us toward other truths. For me, this measure of naiveté and the knowledge I've received through my graduate studies offered me an invaluable learning experience. For without heart, I could not have opened to compassion, which in turn leads to understanding. And without knowledge I would have had no structure in which to place this understanding. Understanding what we know — be it great or small — is wisdom. I believe that true education happens when small wisdoms are gathered and nurtured to grow into larger ones.

My experiences with "systems-people" have convinced me that they are a distinct clan unto themselves. I have learned to appreciate their way of seeing and being, as they have been patient with my critical and discerning inquiry. Some have offered me countless explanations and helped me understand this foreign world in which I found myself. Others were genuinely interested and open to my thoughts.

I hope that my perspectives and experiences also cause you to stop, turn around, consider to which clan you belong and think about what that might mean.

Address correspondence to: Wonshé, Post Office Box 6124, Boulder, CO 80306. E-mail: <wonshe@boulder.net>.

REFERENCES AND SUGGESTED READING

Denison, K. (1991). *Restorative Justice in Ourselves.* Akron, PA: Mennonite Central Committee, U.S. Office of Criminal Justice.

Leu, L. (2001). *Nonviolent Communication Workbook.* Las Crescenta, CA: Center for Nonviolent Communication.

Nhât Hanh, T. and A. Kotler (1989). *Being Peace.* Berkley, CA: Parallax Press.

Rosenberg, M. (2000). *Nonviolent Communication: A Language of Compassion.* Encinitas, CA: Puddle Dancer Press.

Ross, R. (1996). *Return to the Teachings: Exploring Aboriginal Justice.* Ontario, CAN: Penguin Press.

Witten, D. (1999). *Enlightened Management: Bringing Buddhist Teachings to Work.* Rochester, NY: Park Street Press.

NOTES

1. For those unfamiliar, I am referring to scenes from a classic U.S.-made film, *The Wizard of Oz*, in which Dorothy, having journeyed to find the grand and all-knowing wizard, discovers instead a man behind a curtain projecting an image onto a screen. She discovers too a power to "click her heels to go home."

Chapter 21.
How Does Restorative Justice Ensure Good Practice?

by

Jim Boyack, Helen Bowen and Chris Marshall

THE NEW ZEALAND EXPERIENCE

Restorative justice in New Zealand is a self-sown, community-based initiative which has recently gained official sanction through the passage of three pieces of ground-breaking legislation in 2002 — the Sentencing Act, the Parole Act and the Victims' Rights Act. All three Acts make explicit mention of restorative justice and place an expectation on state agencies to accommodate, encourage and support restorative justice processes.

The New Zealand movement is self-sown in that it arose out of dissatisfaction in the Maori community with the way in which they and their young people were treated by social agencies and the criminal justice system. Maori families (*whanau*) and wider tribal groups (*hapu*) felt sidelined and alienated by court processes. Young offenders were either given a meaningless admonishment by the court before being sent on their way to reoffend, or they were corralled into punitive institutions which removed them from any positive social influence from their *whanau*. The *whanau* is fundamental to Maori identity and self-esteem, and Maori sought ways in which *whanau* could play a more meaningful role in rehabilitating and reintegrating young offenders. Out of this discontent grew a lengthy consultation process which resulted in the 1986 *Puao-te-Ata-tu Report* (New Zealand Department..., 1986). This, in turn, spawned the Children, Young Persons and Their Families Act 1989, a progressive piece of legislation which required all young offenders to attend "Family Group Conferences" (FGC).

The adult restorative justice movement sprouted from *ad hoc* experiments in conferencing for adults inspired by the FGC model. The first conferences were facilitated in 1994 by volunteers who believed that the youth justice model had application in the adult court. The first restorative justice community group, *Te Oritenga*, was founded in 1995. It consisted of social workers, ministers of religion, teachers, lawyers, and various other community-minded people, and was encouraged in its work by sympathetic judges and lawyers.

The group soon came to realise that there were differences between its evolving model of adult conferencing and the FGC model. The primary distinction was that adult conferences were victim-centred, whereas the FGC was primarily oriented toward the offender's reintegration into his *whanau* or community. Another distinction was that attendance at the adult conference was voluntary for both victim and offender. In the youth court jurisdiction, all young offenders were required by law to attend FGC, and the conference took place whether or not victims wished to participate. In the adult equivalent it was decided that since it was a victim-focused process, conferences should not be held without victims being present.

The adult conferencing model continued to evolve over the years through open-minded, self-critical discussion within local restorative justice groups and throughout the national movement as a whole. In 2000, the essentials of adult conferencing as it then functioned were captured in the *New Zealand Restorative Justice Practice Manual* (Bowen et al., 2000) produced by the Restorative Justice Trust. That same year, this practical guide was put to the test in a privately-funded six-month pilot of restorative justice cases at one of the local courts in Auckland.

The groundswell of community support for restorative interventions in the criminal courts prompted the New Zealand government in 2001 to fund a four-year national restorative justice pilot scheme, at a cost of $4.8 million, in four district courts in the land. The architects of the pilot project endorsed the existing model of adult conferencing which the restorative justice community had developed, with a view to evaluating conference process and outcomes over the course of the pilot.

From the outset, restorative justice providers in New Zealand have been conscious of the need to develop processes to monitor and improve facilitation practice. Such processes initially focused on prompt debriefing by co-facilitators after the conference, with key practice issues being referred to plenary group meetings for further debate. The limitations of these processes soon became apparent however. Co-facilitators were sometimes less than honest with each other. When reporting back to the group, the emphasis tended to be on what went well rather than on an honest appraisal of how the conference could have been better facilitated. This was understandable, since no objective blueprint existed against which good or bad practice could be measured. In the absence of this, experienced facilitators offered supervision to the co-facilitators after they had debriefed.

With the launching of its pilot scheme and the passage of restorative justice legislation, the New Zealand government has now entered a domain previously occupied only by community volunteers. The government has a legitimate concern to guarantee safe and effective practice, and to ensure credible application of legislation requiring courts and the Parole Board to take restorative justice processes into account. Accordingly in May 2003 the Ministry of Justice published a discussion paper, "Draft Principles of Best Practice for Restorative Justice Processes in Criminal Courts," and called for public submissions.

Meanwhile the restorative justice community itself had been debating how to ensure good practice among restorative justice providers. Over a relatively short period of time many new providers had emerged all around the country, working in different communities and with their own models of facilitation. In light of this growth, some believed the time has come for the establishment of a national accreditation body, which could prescribe acceptable standards of practice. Others argued that restorative justice processes in New Zealand are still too new and culturally diverse to implement formal accreditation procedures. While minimum standards are important, the challenge is, in John Braithwaite's words, "to craft open-textured restorative justice standards that allow a lot of space for cultural differences" (Braithwaite, 2000).

After wide-ranging dialogue and discussion over two years, the Restorative Justice Network in New Zealand has opted for a values-based approach of defining standards of good practice. Such an approach, the Network believes, permits flexibility of practice while at the same time furnishes precise and workable guidelines for determining whether specific processes are truly restorative in effect. In June, 2003, the Network adopted the following statement drafted by us. While it is still a work in progress, it represents, we believe, a viable fresh approach to the task of ensuring good practice.

RESTORATIVE JUSTICE VALUES AND PROCESSES

1. Introduction

(a) Restorative justice is a generic term for all those approaches to wrongdoing which seek to move beyond condemnation and punishment to address both the causes and the consequences (personal, relational and societal) of offending in ways that promote accountability, healing and justice. Restorative justice is a collaborative and peacemaking approach to conflict resolution, and can be employed in a variety of settings (home, business, school, judicial system, etc.). It can also use several different formats to achieve its goals, including victim-offender dialogue, community or family group conferences, sentencing circles, community panels, and so on.

(b) For the purposes of this document, "restorative justice" refers to a process whereby those affected by an incident of wrongdoing come together, in a safe and controlled environment, to share their feelings and opinions truthfully and resolve together how best to deal with its aftermath. The process is called "restorative" because it is concerned primarily with restoring, insofar as is possible, the dignity and well-being of those harmed by the incident.

(c) From this it follows that justice processes may be considered "restorative" only inasmuch as they give expression to key restorative values, such as respect, honesty, humility, mutual care, accountability and trust. The values of restorative justice are those values that are essential to healthy, equitable and just relationships.

(d) It cannot be emphasised too strongly that *process* and *values* are inseparable in restorative justice. For it is the values that determine the process, and the process that makes visible the values. If restorative justice privileges the values of respect and honesty, for example, it is crucially important that the practices followed in a restorative justice meeting exhibit respect for all parties and give ample opportunity for everyone present to speak their truth freely. On the other hand, as long as these values are honoured, there is room for a diversity of processes and a flexibility of practice.

(e) It is this emphasis on deep human values and virtues on the one hand, and flexibility of practice on the other, that affords restorative justice such cross-cultural utility. Different cultural and ethnic communities may employ different processes in order to actualize common restorative values and achieve similar restorative outcomes.

(f) For this reason, it is unwise to restrict "best practice" to a single prescribed process or set of procedures to be followed in every setting. It is more helpful to:

- specify the values and virtues that inspire the restorative justice vision;

- describe how these ideals find expression in concrete standards of practice;

- identify the skills practitioners need in order to initiate and guide interactions that express restorative justice values;

- affirm that restorative justice values and principles should shape the nature of relationships between restorative justice providers and all other parties with a stake in the field, including government agencies which contract restorative justice services from community providers.

2. Core Restorative Justice Values

The vision and practice of restorative justice are shaped by a number of key values which distinguish restorative justice from other, more adversarial approaches to justice and conflict resolution. The most important of these values include:

- *Participation:* Those most affected by the incident of wrongdoing — victims, offenders, and their communities of interest — ought to be the principal speakers and decision-makers in the process, rather than trained professionals representing the interests of the State. All present in a restorative justice meeting have something valuable to contribute to goals of the meeting.

- *Respect:* All human beings have inherent and equal worth irrespective of their actions, good or bad, or of their race, culture, gender, sexual orientation, age, beliefs or status in society. All therefore deserve to be spoken to and treated with respect in restorative justice settings. Mutual respect engenders trust and good faith between the participants.

- *Honesty:* Truthful speech is essential if justice is to be done. In restorative justice, truth entails more than clarifying the facts and establishing guilt within strict legal parameters; it requires people to speak openly and honestly about their experience of offending, their feelings and their moral responsibilities.

- *Humility:* Restorative justice accepts the common fallibility and vulnerability of all human beings. The humility to recognize this universal human condition enables victims and offenders to discover that they have more in common as flawed and frail human beings than what divides them as victim and victimizer. Humility also enables those who recommend restorative processes to allow for the possibility that unintended consequences may follow from their interventions. Empathy and mutual care are manifestations of humility.

- *Interconnectedness:* While stressing individual freedom and accountability, restorative justice recognizes the communal bonds that unite victim and offender. Both are valued members of society, a society in which all people are interconnected by a web of relationships. Society shares responsibility for its members and for the existence of crime, and there is a shared responsibility to help restore victims and reintegrate offenders. In addition, victim and offender are uniquely bonded together by their shared participation in the criminal event, and in certain respects they hold the key to each other's recovery. The social character of crime makes a community process the ideal setting to address the consequences (and causes) of the offence and to chart a restorative way forward.

Adopted by the New Zealand Restorative Justice Network, June 2003.

Address correspondence to: New Zealand Restorative Justice Trust, Helen Bowen and Jim Boyack, Trustees, P.O. Box 105 410, Auckland, New Zealand. E-mail: <helen@bowen.org.nz>; <jim@boyack.org.nz>.

REFERENCES

Bowen, H., J. Boyack and S. Hooper (2000). *"The New Zealand Restorative Justice Practice Manual"* (www.restorativejustice.org.nz.)

Boyack, J., H. Bowen and C. Marshall (2003). "How Does Restorative Justice Ensure Good Practice – A Values-Based Approach." Adopted by the New Zealand Restorative Justice Network, June 2003.

Braithwaite, J. (2000). *Standards for Restorative Justice*. Vienna, Austria: United Nations Crime Congress, Ancillary Meetings.

New Zealand Department of Social Welfare (1986). *Puao-te-Ata-tu (Day Break): Report of the Ministerial Advisory Committee on a Maori Perspective for the Department of Social Welfare*. Wellington, NZ: Department of Social Welfare.

New Zealand Ministry of Justice (2003). "Revised Principles of Best Practice for Restorative Justice Processes in the Criminal Court" (http://www.justice.govt.nz/). October 2003.

Chapter 22.
Are We – Practitioners, Advocates – Practicing What We Preach?

by

David Dyck

She will be just fine with a bit of additional support, thought the hiring committee. Compassionate, eager to learn and candid about her own potential weaknesses, Shelly impressed the interviewers and was hired as a victim support worker at *Community Justice Services.*

It became clear before long, however, that Shelly would need more than a little help. On several occasions during her first week, she had to leave work early, devastated by hearing about the painful circumstances of people's lives. She felt that she could not handle more than three or four phone calls a day. "I worked for over 15 years in a field that didn't give me much exposure to human beings," she explained to co-workers, "so I must admit that I'm a little concerned about how I'll adjust to this position, even with my new degree." By week two, Shelly was giving out her home phone number to distressed victims and, exhausted, she once lost her temper with an angry caller.

Needless to say, Shelly's mentors, Terry and Ray, were becoming concerned. From day one, they had determined to handle the situation in a manner that was in keeping with the restorative values of the organization. During her first weekly check-in meeting, they created empathic space for Shelly to share about how she was experiencing her new work. They were honest yet gentle in sharing their own concerns and helped Shelly identify strategies to overcome the challenges she was facing. In the ensuing weeks, they put the ideas into practice, holding confidential feedback sessions with Shelly and offering her additional time role-playing appropriate responses to distressing situations. At the three week mark, Shelly and her mentors reviewed her strengths and areas which still needed work and agreed that an initial decision regarding continuing employment would need to be made in the next two weeks.

At the end of her training period, Shelly, with a shaky voice, thanked everyone for their support and announced her decision to resign. Although Terry and Ray had done everything they could to help Shelly succeed, in the end, it was not enough for her to retain her job. It was enough, however for her to retain her dignity and the program its integrity. While the meeting was not without discomfort and tears, the relationships and sense of mutual respect were very much intact.

For over a year, the conflict between colleagues at *Redwood Victim-Offender Services* had been escalating, and it was now at the point of needing outside intervention. When asked about the possibility of working towards healing, one employee's response was as unequivocal as it was striking: "As far as I'm concerned," Mike's eyes were hard, "this is a clear cut case. We're *never* going to work this out. The only solution is for her to go! Sometimes things are just wrong and some people will *never* change — period. Yeah, I know we get offenders and victims together, but that's different! *This* is complicated," he concluded.

This sentiment was typical of most *Redwood* employees in relation to those on staff they considered to be their enemies. While Mike's attitude might appear to be at odds with a restorative orientation, he was one of only two employees who even acknowledged the apparent inconsistency between what he encouraged his clients to do with their painful situations and what he himself was willing to try.

While the names and some of the details have been altered, the above stories are based on real dynamics I have encountered repeatedly over the years while working with agencies that claim restorative justice as a grounding philosophy. They also illustrate two ends of a continuum of effectiveness that currently exists when it comes to "practicing what we preach." The question of how well we, as practitioners and advocates of restorative justice, are practicing what we preach in our lives and in our programs — what I refer to as "congruency" — is the focus of this chapter. The question itself implies that the answers matter and that we have an obligation to live out restorative justice values in terms of how we pursue program development and delivery, and respond to conflict within our organizations and personal lives. Furthermore, they suggest that the effectiveness, credibility, and promise of the field as a whole depend, at least in part, on our ability to become living examples of the principles we espouse.

A FRAMEWORK FOR THIS CHAPTER

Given my agreement with these propositions, this paper elaborates on what congruency means and why it matters, expands on the notion of a continuum of effectiveness, and proposes some means of improvement. I should acknowledge that this essay, rooted in personal experience and informal discussions with colleagues, is intended as but one more contribution in the ongoing discussion of these issues.[1]

Before continuing, we must first address the thorny issue of who "we" are and what exactly we are "preaching" about. It is difficult to measure — at least to everyone's satisfaction — whether we are practicing what we preach when both "we" (i.e., who is staking a claim in restorative justice) and what we are "preaching" about (i.e., how these groups define the basic assumptions and core practices of this philosophy) are as diverse as they currently are. Whose definitions and behavioral standards should be used? While I agree with Howard Zehr that achieving a final consensus on these matters is probably not necessary, realistic, or even desirable, they *do* have critical implications for how one evaluates congruency between what we preach and what we practice (Zehr, 2002). For the purposes of this essay, I will consider the following to be defining principles of restorative justice:[2]

- Restorative justice is a way of seeing harmful actions, *but it also has implications for how we see and respond to conflict more broadly.*

- It involves the identification of needs and responsibilities that rise from a harmful action, so that things can be put right to the greatest extent possible and involves, to the extent possible, those who have a stake in the matter at hand.

- It includes processes that offer support for healing to those who have been affected by harmful acts and simultaneously holds those who inflicted the harm accountable for their actions, supporting them to take responsibility.

- Restorative practices are those which reflect a concern for such values as respect, inclusion and self-determination, equality, truth-telling, listening and understanding, humility, responsibility, safety, healing, renewal and reintegration.

- *Processes which provide opportunity for a facilitated encounter or face-to-face dialogue between stakeholders are <u>one</u> expression of restorative justice.*

- *At the same time, <u>any</u> <u>process</u> that demonstrably reflects a concern for the above values and goals may correctly be understood to be restorative.*

It is the last two points where differences arise and which are particularly germane to a discussion of congruency. For if restorative justice continues to be primarily understood in terms of facilitated face-to-face meetings,[3] it will by definition preclude as restorative any activity which does not involve or take such an encounter as a core aim. It will also indict any practitioner who engages in efforts which do not involve the pursuit of such dialogue to be failing to practice what s/he preaches. By comparison, a definition which considers facilitated encounter potentially valuable but ultimately *not always appropriate* leaves room for a much broader application of restorative principles. It suggests that any situation — including everyday ones that do not necessarily warrant the assistance of a third party facilitator — can be approached restoratively as long as the activities undertaken are aimed at engendering empowerment, healing, the acceptance of responsibility, and accountability to the full circle of stakeholders.[4] As such, a broader definition promotes a broader practice; it promotes congruency.

What about the related question of what behavioral standard to use to evaluate congruency? For those whose definition of restorative justice is tethered to a particular application (e.g., facilitated, face-to-face conferencing), assessing congruency is only a matter of evaluating the degree to which they follow their model or script when in session. But for those whose definition is based on dynamic principles and broad applicability, assessing congruency entails nothing less than examining all aspects of their lives — the professional-programmatic,[5] the personal-relational, and the social-structural.[6] While all represent legitimate means of measuring congruency and are ultimately interconnected, I will focus on the personal-relational sphere in the remainder of this chapter. My reasons for doing so are twofold. Firstly, it is in this sphere — as reflected in the story about the *Redwood Victim-Offender Services* — that I have personally experienced some of the most profound "gaps" between our rhetoric and our practice.[7] Secondly, it is my sense that this area has received less attention than the others in materials published to date.

What Does Practicing What We Preach Mean In Our Personal Relationships?

Practicing what we preach in the personal-relational realm involves intentional effort to put the values of restorative justice into practice in *all* of our roles and daily interactions. Whether one is a conference facilitator, a prison guard, a victim companion volunteer, an elder, a parent, or a postal worker, one can choose to approach all challenges in human interaction from a grounding in restorative justice. The following questions can serve as initial guides in any situation in which harm has been done or someone perceives harm as having been done: Who, if anyone, has been hurt? What are their needs? Who is responsible to begin to address those needs? Who has a stake in this situation? What are the broader issues involved? What are the best processes to involve these stakeholders in an overall effort aimed at healing, change, and/or resolution?[8] *A practitioner or advocate is giving faithful expression to restorative justice whenever they explore these questions with authenticity, appreciating their relevance to all aspects of their daily life.*

Does this mean we need a spotless track record of "successfully" applying the questions to be deemed to be practicing what we preach? On the contrary, we know there will be many times we fail to walk our restorative talk. My own experience is that my failure is sometimes a subtle one of degrees and at other times is miserably obvious to all. On the other hand, while perfection is not realistic, improvement is. And improvement is dependent on a willingness to be held accountable and supported in tangible ways, such as that modeled by a group of practitioners in British Columbia, Canada who recently developed *A Charter for Practitioners of Restorative Justice* (Abramson et al., 2003).[9] A "continuous work in progress," this document commits the signatories — in a rather public way — to hold one another accountable to live their lives as examples of restorative principles (2003:1).

Why Bother?

Besides the intrinsic rewards of personal growth it spawns, practicing what we preach in our personal relationships matters because those who pursue it are much more likely to provide effective service and contribute to the maturation of the field than those who do not. Those who are willing to continue to work intentionally at taking responsibility for their mistakes or acknowledging their contribution to a difficulty, listening to another's perspective, admitting the complexity of a situation, identifying and sharing their own needs and feelings respectfully, moving beyond the impulse for revenge, being open to feedback, acknowledging others' pain, and standing up for themselves appropriately are simply in a better position to guide others in these tasks than those who do not work intentionally at these things.

There is substantial, though largely anecdotal, evidence that there is a correlation between "walking the talk" in our personal lives and general effectiveness in programming. My experience and my conversations with colleagues suggest that organizations like the *Community Justice Services* described earlier generally demonstrate:

- higher rates of satisfaction among the people they serve;

- greater effectiveness at meeting their stated program goals and objectives;

- higher percentages of staff and volunteers who demonstrate core competencies;

- greater openness to ongoing learning and development;

- higher levels of contribution to the field in terms of publishing and giving leadership in other ways (e.g., serving as board members on professional associations and in offering training at conferences, etc.);

- better intra-program relations and higher levels of satisfaction among staff, volunteers, and board members as evidenced by lower turnover;

- better relations with members and partners in the community. [10]

A Continuum Of Congruency In The Field

If we accept the basic proposition that personal congruency matters and is likely to have practical implications for overall effectiveness, it is in our best interest to discover why some do better than others. First, however, let us return to answer the question — are we practicing what we preach? While representing ideal types which are likely to be un-achievable in reality, the following continuum provides a way to begin to visualize this question, prompting reflection regarding where we cur-rently "are" and the direction we need to move.

Figure 1: A Continuum of Personal-Relational Congruency

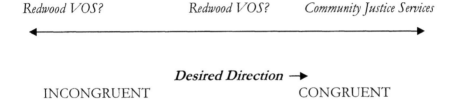

At the far right of Figure 1 labeled "congruent" are those practitio-ners whose day to day actions seem largely consistent with the values of restorative justice. The story of *Community Justice Services* illustrates this end of the continuum. At the left end, labeled "incongruent" are those with relatively little awareness/conscious commitment to personal con-sistency. They regularly take actions in their relationships that are at odds with restorative philosophy. In the middle are those who have some level of awareness of the importance of practicing what they preach, but whose actions in relationships do not yet consistently reflect restorative principles. If the stance taken by Mike in the story of the *Redwood* agency is typical of the way in which the agency deals with in-terpersonal difficulty, then *Redwood* could be seen to be an example of the "incongruent." However, if there are also instances where more healing, collaborative approaches are embraced, then *Redwood* would be better understood as an example of the middle.

In light of the above description, where might the reader place her/himself and/or his/her program? Given that the continuum assumes none of us have "arrived," what steps might s/he and her/his colleagues take to begin to move further in the right direction?

WHERE TO FROM HERE?

My experience is that there is at least one relatively common denominator among those who are comparatively effective at practicing what they preach: persons whose practice is based on values which they connect to a larger, cohesive world view, not just a particular application, are *more likely* to conceive of the possibility of applying restorative justice to their relationships.[11]

For example, the worldview that leads Terry and Ray to offer practical support in a variety of forms to the victims, offenders, and other community members at *Community Justice Services* also compels them to respond to their new co-worker, Shelly, with flexibility, compassion, transparency, inclusion, and respect. There is congruency because both responses are born of an overarching vision for their community and a dynamic sense of how all of their actions might tie in. In short, it leads them to practice what they preach.

By contrast, the vision at *Redwood Victim-Offender Services* is static, defined and confined by a particular model (in this case, victim-offender mediation). It lends itself to compartmentalization and contributes to the staff's failure to see that restorative justice is relevant to their interaction with one another. For if restorative justice is, by definition, the mediations they lead, then it is not the conversations they have with their spouses or children or colleagues.

Whenever we hear sentiments such as "restorative justice…is clearly not suited for every victim, or even for every offender," it is a sign that the philosophy is probably being reduced to a particular application (Mika et al., 2002:10). An understanding rooted in a panoramic vision would claim precisely the opposite; restorative justice is suitable for every victim, every offender, indeed for every challenging situation. An orientation towards healing, the taking up of responsibilities, support for all, and the involvement of those with a stake in the situation *is always relevant*.[12] It is particular expressions of restorative justice — such as face-to-face meetings — which are definitely *not* suited to every situation. This distinction is critical because it is precisely this tendency to confuse particular applications with the overarching philosophy that works against our ability to "see the bigger picture" and, therefore, achieve or even perceive the possibility of applying the principles in our daily lives.

A Few Practical Suggestions

If we accept that practicing what we preach in our personal relationships involves re-connecting restorative justice to an overarching vision, the question arises as to how to go about this. I offer the following suggestions:

(1) *Be clear and consistent with our language.* As teachers and writers, we need to offer definitions of restorative justice that are not tethered to particular applications and which consistently stress dynamic values and broad applicability.

(2) *Invest time and money in education that explores the underlying values and origins of this philosophy.* An overemphasis on teaching particular models and techniques works against personal-relational congruency. By "origins," I refer to identity groups whose historic worldviews form the seedbeds in which the philosophy now broadly known as "restorative justice" first began resurfacing in programmatic forms some 30 years ago. First Nations worldviews and those of the historic peace churches have been particularly critical in terms of placing the work within a larger frame of reference and meaning.[13]

(3) *Give students and new practitioners (at all levels — e.g., board members, staff, and volunteers) opportunities to explore the way in which the values of the field resonate with their own deepest individual and communal convictions.* That is, provide opportunities for them to reflect on their own experiences of conflict and pain, to consider what values they wish to express in such situations and from whence they arise, and to consider where these values resonate with or are in tension with the values of restorative justice. For example, when considering our response to the specific, day-to-day conflicts and harms in our relationships with coworkers, friends, and family, we might ask ourselves the following questions: What core values do I want to express in this situa-

tion (e.g., winning, showing respect, holding my ground, "owning" my part of the problem etc.)? Why are these values important to me? Where do they come from? Do my actions thus far reflect my core values? If yes, in what specific ways? If no, what might I do differently from this point forward? These questions lend themselves to individual reflection and/or small group discussion in restorative justice trainings.

(4) *Give students and practitioners opportunities to apply restorative justice principles to non-criminal case studies, including issues that arise in their personal lives.*[14]

(5) *Explore and hone the tools of analysis, communication, and interpersonal peacebuilding associated with the field of conflict transformation and seek out a better understanding of the relationship between crime and conflict.*[15] While most restorative justice practitioners and advocates have training in third-party facilitation models for criminal justice matters, relatively few have put as much energy into learning and practicing models of one-to-one, personal conflict resolution.

(6) *Model a commitment to improved congruency through the development of practices designed to offer mutual support and accountability in intentional ways.* At the programmatic level, create time to participate in team "circles" whereby we "check-in" to receive and provide feedback regarding our interactions with our co-workers and others.

(7) *Develop organizational conflict resolution protocols that reflect restorative values.*[16] These protocols should provide clarity on expectations, options and processes for responding to conflict and incidents of harm and reflect a commitment to timely responses.

(8) Finally, *participate in processes (e.g., research projects, organizational "audits" etc.) designed to help us assess the degree to which our actions reflect our principles and/or to "close the gap" between the two.*[17]

CONCLUSION

Clearly, there is much more that could be said in response to the question of whether or not we are practicing what we preach in the field of restorative justice. We have seen that the question requires giving attention to defining our core assumptions and practices and have realized, once again, that a broad, definitive consensus probably will not be achieved on these matters. And just as restorative justice cannot and probably should not be defined for the field as a whole lest we lose some of the vitality that accompanies diverse perspectives, so too congruency between ideals and practice probably can not be too definitively measured for our field as a whole.

At the same time, this in no way means we should not continue to ask and explore the question! For even if definitions and measures of our effectiveness at practicing what we preach will continue to be difficult to "pin down," we know consistency to see it and certainly miss it when it is absent. For this reason, it is incumbent on all of us — individually and collectively — to continually take stock of the degree to which *our* actions are consistent with *our* espoused values, recognizing the danger of trying to set up standards for the field as a whole, but sharing and comparing our perspectives in a spirit of vigorous dialogue and continuous improvement nonetheless.

Address correspondence to: David Dyck, 264 Home Street, Winnipeg, MB R3G 1X3 Canada. E-mail: <dcdyck@mts.net>.

REFERENCES

Abramson, A., C. Bargen, S. Bergen, D. Burnell, M. Egan, L. Elliot, D. Gustafson, D. Hale, B. LeClair, A. McCormick, J. Osborne, M. Ouelette, A.P. Moosmann, A. Powter, L. Steer, J. Stevulak, E. Stutzman and B. Warhaft (2003). "A Charter for Practitioners of Restorative Justice." (Please see http://www.sfu.ca/cfrj/fulltext/charter.pdf.)

Bargen, C. (2003). Interview with the author on June 12.

Barg-Neufeld, D. (2003). Interview with the author on May 28.

Claassen, R. (1993). *Discipline that Restores*. Fresno, CA: Center for Peacemaking & Conflict Studies.

Department of Justice, Canada (2003). Please see website entitled "Restorative Justice" at the time of publishing found at: ⟨http://canada.justice.gc.ca /en/ps/voc/rest_just.html⟩.

Dugan, M. (1996). "A Nested Theory of Conflict." *A Leadership Journal: Women in Leadership — Sharing the Vision* 1(1)(July):9-20.

Dyck, D. (2000). "Reaching Toward a Transformative Training and Practice of Restorative Justice." *Contemporary Justice Review* 3(3):239-265.

Gilligan, J. (1997). *Violence: Reflections on a National Epidemic.* New York: Vintage Books.

Lederach, J.P. (2000). "'Revolutionaries' & 'Resolutionaries': In Pursuit of Dialogue." In: C. Schrock-Shenk (ed.), *Mediation and Facilitation Training Manual: Foundations and Skills for Constructive Conflict Transformation* (4th ed.). Akron, PA: Mennonite Conciliation Service.

—— (1997). *Building Peace: Sustainable Reconciliation in Divided Societies.* Washington, DC: Endowment of the United States Institute for Peace.

Mika, H. (1992). "Mediation Interventions and Restorative Justice: Responding to the Astructural Bias." In: H. Messmer and H.-U. Otto (eds.), *Restorative Justice on Trial.* Dordrecht, NETH: Kluwer Academic Publishers.

—— M. Achilles, E. Halbert, L. Stutzman Amstutz and H. Zehr (2002). *A Listening Project: Taking Victims and Their Advocates Seriously.* (Harry Mika is corresponding author: ⟨harry.mika@cmich.edu⟩.)

Nader, L. (1993). "When is Popular Justice Popular?" In: S. Merry and N. Milner (eds.), *The Possibility of Popular Justice.* Ann Arbor, MI: University of Michigan Press.

Peachey, D. (1999). *Doing the Work, Telling the Story: An Examination of MCC Canada's Ministry in Restorative Justice.* Winnipeg, Manitoba, CAN: Mennonite Central Committee Canada. (Please contact James Loewen at ⟨James_Loewen@mennonitecc.ca⟩ for more information.)

Ross, R. (1996). *Returning to the Teachings: Exploring Aboriginal Justice.* Toronto, CAN: Penguin Books Canada.

Sharpe, S. (1998). *Restorative Justice: A Vision for Healing and Change.* Edmonton, CAN: Edmonton Victim Offender Mediation Society.

Sullivan, D. and L. Tifft (2001). *Restorative Justice: Healing the Foundations of Our Everyday Lives.* Monsey, NY: Criminal Justice Press.

—— and L. Tifft (2000). *Restorative Justice as a Transformative Process: The Application of Restorative Justice Principles to Our Everyday Lives.* Voorheesville, NY and Mt. Pleasant, MI: Mutual Aid Press.

Yantzi, M. (1998). *Sexual Offending and Restoration.* Waterloo, CAN and Scottdale, PA: Herald Press.

Yngvesson, B. (1993). "Local People, Local Problems, and Neighborhood Justice: The Discourse of the 'Community' in San Francisco Community Boards." In: S. Merry and N. Milner (eds.), *The Possibility of Popular Justice.* Ann Arbor, MI: University of Michigan Press.

Zehr, H. (2002). *The Little Book of Restorative Justice.* Intercourse, PA: Good Books.

—— (2000). "The Path to Justice: Retribution or Restoration?" In: C. Schrock-Shenk (ed.), *Mediation and Facilitation Training Manual: Foundations and Skills for Constructive Conflict Transformation, Fourth Edition.* Akron, PA: Mennonite Conciliation Service.

—— (1990). *Changing Lenses: A New Focus for Crime and Justice.* Scottdale, PA and Waterloo, CAN: Herald Press.

NOTES

1. Those individuals named were comfortable being identified, others who offered perspectives informally preferred anonymity.

2. As adapted from numerous sources (Zehr, 2002, 2000; Sharpe, 1998; Yantzi, 1998). This definition is not comprehensive, but is instead intended to highlight particular elements which are often not included and which have direct implications for a discussion of congruency. See the italicized points in particular.

3. Examples of writings that make this assumption include Tony Marshall as quoted in Zehr, 2002; Sharpe, 1998; and Department of Justice Canada website, 2003.

4. This is true provided these activities reflect a commitment, *in some concrete form,* to the full range of restorative principles as defined above. For example, practitioners working with victims can still be accountable to offender needs (and vice-versa) by including offenders and their advocates on the steering committees of their programs, providing information to victims about the full range of options available in regards to the offender, and building partnerships with those working with the offender.

5. Mika and co-authors (2002) argue that practicing what we preach at the programmatic level involves assessing the degree to which we give voice to victims throughout all levels of program governance and delivery. Mika et al. present a consensus among victim advocates in the United States that restorative justice

practitioners have, to this point, largely failed in this regard. On a more hopeful note, Mennonite Central Committee Canada's *Victim's Voice* program is in the process of implementing a "Registered Victim Companion" program and a "Contracting Safe Justice" program. The former aims to match victims with trained volunteers who provide support, and the latter negotiates the terms under which a victim who wishes to meet with her/his offender might do so, beginning with the victim's needs and timeline rather than that of the court. For more information, contact Wilma Derksen at <wld@mcc.org>.

6. For more exploration of the social/structural dimension, please see Sullivan and Tifft (2000, 2001), Dugan (1996), Dyck (2000), Lederach (2000, 1997), Mika (1992), Nader (1993) and Yngvesson (1993).

7. After interviewing over 80 Canadian restorative justice practitioners and advocates, Dean Peachy (1999) wrote: "People who have devoted their working lives to building bridges and reconciliation are not immune to rivalry. I heard respondents disparage the work of colleagues... The dynamic was most noticeable among some who have been working longest in the field. What struck me was not that people disagreed...but rather that people who exemplified respect when dealing with victims and offenders failed to convey a similar respect when speaking about colleagues with whom they disagreed" (1999:24).

8. Adapted from Howard Zehr's guiding questions of restorative justice (Zehr, 2002). Expanding restorative justice's applicability means enlarging the scope of the guiding questions as well. The more nuanced application of restorative justice to everyday conflict situations implies the possibility of intervention prior to a clear incident of harm and/or working with situations in which each party believes him/herself to be a "victim" and yet are seen by others as "offender."

9. See further *A Charter for Practitioners of Restorative Justice* at (http://www.sfu.ca/cfrj/fulltext/charter.pdf).

10. While there are studies which explore effectiveness using many of these indicators, new research may be needed to correlate them with the degree to which practitioners "practice what they preach" in their personal lives.

11. Many of Dean Peachey's interviewees expressed fears that "government adoption of restorative justice will result in it simply being appended to the existing system...without a deeper examination of attitudes, assumptions, and goals" (1999:19). My experience suggests that there is indeed something of a correlation between government initiated projects and a shallower understanding of the principles; with this comes a corresponding relatively weaker ability on the part of practitioners to practice what they preach.

12. I am not arguing for comprehensive restorative justice "systems" in the sense that I believe that restorative justice processes inevitably yield experiences of healing or that large scale applications could be constructed that are completely free from the use of coercive power. Rather, I am suggesting that restorative justice as a paradigm is a "compass" (Zehr, 2002:6) that can always help us discern in which direction healing is more likely to be found. Even when coercive power must be used, the compass guides us to use it respectfully and reasonably, mindful to rely on it as little as possible (Claassen, 1993). In this sense, then, restorative "systems" (i.e., in families, schools, workplaces, communities of worship, criminal justice) are indeed possible. Indeed, to the extent that there are groups in which an orientation towards healing and cooperative values guide all workers, volunteers, and other stakeholders in all of their varied yet compatible activities, such systems already exist.

13. Please see Rupert Ross's *Returning to the Teachings* and Howard Zehr's *Changing Lenses*.

14. For sample exercises of this nature, please contact the author at <dcdyck@mts.net> or at (204) 925-3410.

15. Some practitioners simply ignore the broader issue of conflict altogether while others misleadingly use the terms "crime" and "conflict" interchangeably (for an example, see Abramson et al., 2003:1). For the purposes of this essay, it is perhaps enough to suggest that while crime and conflict are not the same thing (conflict is the *a priori* condition consisting of differences plus tension and need not involve harms at all), they are closely related inasmuch as it is unresolved conflict which often gives rise to incidents of harm which, in turn, spawn more conflict.

16. For an example of such a policy, contact Mediation Services of Winnipeg regarding their *Respectful Workplace Policy*, <info@mediationserviceswpg.ca>.

17. For more information on such a process being developed collaboratively by *Mennonite Central Committee Canada (MCCC)* and *Menno Simons College*, contact James Loewen, *Restorative Justice Desk, MCCC* at <James_Loewen@mennonitecc.ca>.

Chapter 23.
What Is The Role Of Professionals In Restorative Justice?

by

Carsten Erbe

There comes a time when every movement sells out to the ideals that it once opposed. Our culture is littered with examples of movements gone astray, from the baby boomers living indulgently in the 1980s, to Ben and Jerry's selling out to corporate interests in Europe, to the inclusion of professional athletes into the Olympics. All are examples of when a movement is no longer truly representative of what it claims to be. Although restorative justice is merely in its infancy, with limited broad-based appeal, I fear this movement is in danger of crossing this irreversible threshold.

For all intents and purposes restorative justice developed as a community-based movement established in direct opposition to the large-scale, institutional way of doing business. It rejected notions of experts and the consolidation of professional power, and ventured to explore — or revive — a more communitarian and assessable means for community members to take back power that institutions stole from their lives. From the Maori in New Zealand, to the Tlingit of the Yukon, restorative justice provided a means by which traditionally marginalized groups rejected conventional institutional thought and replaced it with a more humanistic, collective way of doing business. At its basis was the community's independent spirit, exercising a humanistic and communal approach lost in the development of modern Western society.

While there were many forces that contributed to the creation of restorative justice, it is clear that the movement's central ideal is to retain control of community issues within the community. This is an understood tenet of restorative justice advocates, professional and community alike, and relates to all aspects of the process, including the operation, ownership, and control of restorative justice. While seemingly idealistic, the basis of this tenet is that for the movement to be "real" it has to be in and of the people. Otherwise the movement will be co-opted by the same institutional and professional processes that rendered the mainstream system useless in the first place. Restorative justice is therefore as much about the ownership of the process, as it is about focusing on the harm caused by a crime, involving the stakeholders in the event, and changing government/community relations (Van Ness and Strong, 2002).

If one looks at the recent developments of the restorative justice movement it has sharply turned away from this most fundamental of core values. The process, and its development, are being taken over and promoted by a new class of power brokers, many of whom have limited community involvement and practical knowledge of restorative justice. These professionals, whose knowledge and "expertise" often come from textbook knowledge of the subject, seriously threaten to undermine the validity of the movement and turn it into the bland, ineffective version of the system we already have.

Just as the criminal justice system has ignored the victim's perspective for so many years, these faux advocates ignore the true role that the community should have in the development of the movement. While the community is always presented as the driving force of the movement, the real power still exists in the venues that it always has — mainstream institutions. In its current form, this has presented itself by professionals shaping the instruction and debate around restorative justice implementation, and using mainstream mediums and venues to foster this discussion. Whether oblivious to these forces or not, these professionals have functioned to undermine the capacity of the movement in becoming truly grassroots and legitimized among community members.

The real demon in the development of the modern restorative justice movement is bureaucratic structures and the organizational culture/thinking around it. This specifically relates to the belief that professionals are in a better position to make decisions for those who are directly impacted by social events in their own lives. This of course is one of the things that restorative justice is trying to change, but as the movement pushes forward it seemingly works to undermine the reforms it wishes to promote. As restorative justice is not developing in a vacuum, it is bound to take on the institutional structures and ways of thinking around it. This is not to suggest that restorative justice is predetermined to fail, but rather that it is bound to repeat institutional failures without strategies to guard against it.

The knowledge about the misdirection of movements through processes of co-optation is nothing new in modern age. One of the most profound thinkers about the process was the German sociologist Robert Michels, who coined the term "Iron Law of Oligarchy." Michels proposed that internal democracy could never be sustainable in organizations or movements which claimed it to be its stated objective. Small groups of individuals would inevitably seek the control of the process and become more interested in maintaining their newly elevated status than in serving the democratically-based ideals and principles that led them to the position of power in the first place. The inevitability of this phenomenon was the "Iron Law" and was demonstrated by Michels in the context of the political movements of his time (Michels, 1962). Other sociologists have since applied this concept to other movements and mechanisms of reform with repeatedly the same results. The parallels to the development of restorative justice are uncanny and suggest that this "law" is gaining a foothold in restorative justice and the professionalization of the movement.

From this perspective is it is clear that blind trust should never be given to institutions and its professional staff to implement restorative justice. The track record of any formal institution to implement any meaningful positive change is marginal at best. Restorative justice, with its demands of community ownership of its problems and grassroots participation, can never exist within bounds of institutional control. The power dynamics of the entity do not permit this, and vigilant attention must remain to ensure that these principles do not get co-opted by bureaucratic processes or its representatives.

THE RESTORATIVE JUSTICE MOVEMENT TODAY

While communities are a part of the restorative justice process unfolding across the country, they are not primarily front-and-center of the restorative justice movement. Despite their diversity and collective brilliance, communities are slowly being pushed aside by this new batch of restorative justice professionals. Many of these individuals, in all likelihood, had never heard of the concept a few years ago, yet have passed themselves off as experts and leaders in this field, with many becoming a main point of referral for those interested in restorative justice. This is a perilous situation, for without a comprehensive understanding of the process and its workings, the collective discussion around restorative justice is bound to be inferior and cater more to the needs of institutions than to community members.

To envision where restorative justice is heading in the future, it is important to look at the types of people who are driving the process across North America. It is important not to belittle the contribution of these individuals, but rather to see where the erosion of restorative justice is occurring and how to impede this process. So despite the cynical overtones, the real focus is not on name calling, but rather figuring out who is in a position of power and deciding how to curb this dynamic in the promotion of the community driven ideal.

Academic Superstars

This first group of people who are controlling and driving the direction of restorative justice are a group of individuals I call "academic superstars." This group is composed of a small group of university professors and academics, who, through their written contribution to the field, are universally known within the field of restorative justice. While these individuals are unquestionably intelligent, insightful, and have a great deal to contribute, they are not necessarily the individuals most appropriate to lead a grassroots movement. Their knowledge of the subject matter comes from intellectually dissecting components of the restorative justice process, which often fails to adequately represent the knowledge and skill that comes from those closer to the work. Furthermore, these individuals typically come from a position of power and inherently represent these interests whether they want to or not. This generally puts them in a position to dominate the discussion about the topic and direct conversation to their perspectives, as opposed to that of the disenfranchised people, communities, and cultures their work is supposedly trying to represent.

Within this dynamic, certain academic superstars' work has become so closely associated to the models of restorative justice practice they discuss that there is little separation between their perspectives and the subject matter as a whole. As restorative justice is "new" in academic contexts, this is to be expected. Nevertheless, it is important to note that the individuals rarely invented the perspectives or the models that they discuss. While they need not explicitly take credit for this, they are often given it and the platform that requires their "expertise." While it is not necessarily the fault of the individual who is in this position, they often fall prey to this role and in the process the notion of an "expert" is born.

While there is no doubt a place for all of these individuals to contribute to the development and discourse of restorative justice, academics should take a secondary role to community members themselves. For the most part academics have ignored their own role in the development of restorative justice and the impact that their actions have in the community at large. This issue has not been addressed even though it's probably one of the most influential of all. If we ever lose sight of this we are bound to merely create a new justice system that simply mirrors the one we are trying to replace.

Established Guard

The second group involved in driving and formulating discussion around the implementation and development of restorative justice is the "established guard." This group is composed of the current mainstream criminal justice system as well as those in political office. While these individuals represent just a small proportion of the entire criminal justice system and political community, there are many in the established guard who have made it their mandate to change the focus of the criminal justice system and to do justice in a more holistic and balanced fashion. While these sentiments should be applauded, they also must be examined as to how many in the group wish to invoke this change.

Many of the established guard state that they want restorative justice to be something truly different and something which will transform the system. While these objectives are seemingly sincere, in practice many of these individuals still want to control how restorative justice will take shape in their jurisdictions. This is often done through the belief that they can establish restorative justice through the implementation of various practices or models, or through the initiation or various policies and procedures within their jurisdiction. While this approach may be useful in getting the process started, it promotes the belief that change requires their agency to be front-and-center for those changes to occur and that these changes will be envisioned without any meaningful input from community members. The community is therefore shut out once again, with its full potential and capabilities not being explored, and with its role mitigated to what the established guard states it can do and cannot do.

Many of the established guard fail to recognize that restorative justice is more than a process of simply doing business differently. Restorative justice to its fullest extent is as much about the state relinquishing control over criminal justice issues as it is about the focus on the harm of the crime and the focus on accountability of the offender to the victim. The movement is not about the community participating in the sanctioning of the offender, or the system allowing for community involvement. Rather, it is about the community taking ownership of its problems and being equal partners with mainstream criminal justice institutions. It is thus a more fundamental transition of power, with a strong element of de-constructionism at its basis.

Johnnies On The Spot

The third main group that is influential in the direction of restorative justice movement are "Johnnies on the spot." These are individuals who, primarily through good luck and fortune, happened to be in areas where restorative justice developed and took hold within their community. Often these individuals have had a more influential role which should not be ridiculed or mocked. Their contribution helped establish various programs and practices and organized community efforts within their community. In numerous occasions these local accomplishments have catapulted these individuals into the national spotlight and thrust them into superstardom within the field of restorative justice. They have become the de facto voice of their community efforts and have sometimes transferred this stature to their own personal gain and promotion. While it would be wrong to suggest that this is the only reason they have become involved in this process, it does point out that the focus is on their "brilliance" as opposed to the community context from which these practices arose.

In many instances these Johnnies are soon offered positions with national organizations in their field, or start consulting on a broader level on how other communities can replicate the work that the Johnny did in his/her community. While this makes sense to a degree, the Johnny soon becomes removed from the context that gave him or her notoriety in the first place. Over time their work becomes founded on a recollection of how things occurred as opposed to how they are currently unfolding within an ever-changing process. They also often become placed in a position to speak for the community from which they come, even though their real ties to the community are increasingly severed. Current attention is often more focused on building new ties within their places of work or building their new stature as an "expert" for the greater network of institutions which they are trying to impress. Unhealthy at best, the process becomes focused on one group of know-it-alls striving to replace another.

Often associated with the rapid assent of the Johnnies is the process by where the Johnny is thrown in a position to talk and give his/her opinion on topics that are out of his/her range of experience. In many instances, the Johnnies are then asked for their opinion on legislation reform or organizational development even though they might have no background in these fields. Often their voice grows beyond their range, again with little understanding of how certain systems and organizations work. This not only affects the quality of information given but also hampers true community reflection on how institutions can act and function. The Johnny thus becomes more a token symbol of community opinion rather than a true impetus for change. The end result is that it is business as usual, with the only changes being the dominance and influence of the Johnny irrespective of what he/she might say.

Issue Hijackers

The final group that has increasing clout in the development of restorative justice includes those who I call "issue hijackers." These are individuals or groups who are interested in promoting restorative justice for causes or issues which are not necessarily related to the needs of the offender, victim or community. Restorative justice for these individuals is merely a venue to spread the word about a belief system or social cause that they feel important, but does not fit the individual basis or context of each criminal event. Restorative justice therefore becomes an opportunity to hijack the conversation and discuss issues they feel important. In promoting these positions the process loses much of its power and contorts the discussion to topics restorative justice never was designed to address.

There are many instances where issue hijackers are at work. As restorative justice has gained popularity as a movement, it has become a venue to promote discussion around such topics as systemic racism (Moore, 2001), spirituality and religious beliefs (Hadley, 2001), the death penalty (Floridians for Alternatives to the Death Penalty, 2002), and even counter-terrorism efforts in Afghanistan (Kaleidoscope of Justice, 2001). All of these discussions are justified through carrying the principles around restorative justice to the extreme or exploring the deeper roots of the restorative justice movement. While discussion around these topics may be valuable in and of itself, it is questionable to what extent restorative justice has to do with any of them. Restorative justice is essentially a micro-level community-based process which can only speak to the social issues of a specific group. Restorative justice may or may not have relevance to these broader issues and it may weaken the strength of the process by making it a forum to discuss any and all social issues.

The vast majority of issue hijackers are not knowingly engaging in the activity in which they earn this dubious label. As concerned professionals, social organizations, and religious groups, they are contributing to the discussion and development of restorative justice by the only means they know. This should be encouraged as everybody has a voice and typically has something to valuable to contribute. Nevertheless, the restorative justice movement is about the balancing of perspectives, and no one topic regarding its development or implementation should prevail. When it does, it is a red flag of the issue hijackers at work and of their attempts to co-opt the discussion around issues or perspectives often only they believe important.

WHERE TO FROM HERE?

It is clear that restorative justice offers great promise to the criminal justice system and to those affected by criminal events. Even with the concerns I have raised, the restorative justice movement offers an improvement to the justice system and will increase the power that ordinary citizens have over their own lives. The real question, nevertheless, is how far this movement is going to develop and whether or not it will truly transform the way that people interact after a criminal event.

For restorative justice to reach its fullest potential it must be put back into the hands of the community. While this is easier said than done, there are certain things that can push in that direction. As a starting point, the process and its terminology must be couched in the simplest terms possible. Restorative justice is not a complex machine, so it must not sound like it takes technical knowledge to understand or to which one can contribute. Restorative justice is simply about the human experience and should promote a discourse that is inclusive in nature and not prohibitive to those "in the know."

Restorative justice mechanisms should also be primarily housed outside of the traditional reach and bureaucratic structure of the mainstream criminal justice system. For the community to truly embrace the concept of restorative justice they must have true ownership over it and have real input on how it will take shape. Centralized mechanisms of power, which criminal justice systems are, stifle creativity and make those who work within it blind to the goal of maintaining their power. While this may be more subtle than in past years, this force is still existent and will ultimately work against the objectives of promoting community restorative justice.

Furthermore, those who are actively involved in restorative justice practices should be the sole educators of how to implement restorative justice processes. Teaching others about restorative justice processes and mechanisms requires more than textbook knowledge of the subject. Teaching implementation skills for interested community members requires the skills of those who have lived it and have the interpersonal skills to convey their experience to others. This will help weed out the pretenders and ensure that education about restorative justice is grounded and accessible to all.

Finally, restorative justice should always maintain the central focus on bringing the offender, victim and community together to resolve the criminal event which brought them there in the first place. While there are many factors which may shape the quality of the encounter or play into the societal reasons of why certain people are involved, these must be addressed on a case-by-case basis. Restorative justice is therefore not inherently about one social issue, but rather, about the factors the participants believe to be pertinent to the resolution of the event. Promotion of this perspective should keep the movement centered and out of the hands of those who wish to contort the discussion to a viewpoint or issue they wish to discuss.

Collectively we must actively take steps that curb the influence of professionals on the development of restorative justice. We cannot just contend that restorative justice is for the victim, community and offender, while others who are peripheral to this dynamic determine how it will function and operate. While there is certainly a role for professionals and academics alike, their role must be tempered with humility and the recognition that for restorative justice to truly be different, it must be allowed to unfold in an unorthodox direction as compared to other movements in the past. This will ensure that restorative justice achieves legitimacy among the people, reach its greatest height and potential, and impede those who wish to promote it for their own benefit and gain.

Address correspondence to: Carsten Erbe, RR2 Rolla Road, Dawson Creek BC, V1G 4E8, Canada. Fax: 250-782-2230. E-mail: <carstenerbe@ hotmail.com>.

REFERENCES

Floridians for Alternatives to the Death Penalty (2002). (http://www.fadp.org/.)

Hadley, M. (2001). *The Spiritual Roots of Restorative Justice*. Albany, NY: State University of New York Press.

Kaleidoscope of Justice (2001). "Terrorist Attacks: Restorative Justice Responses." *Kaleidoscope of Justice: Highlighting Restorative Juvenile Justice* 3(Winter):1.

Michels, R. (1962). *Political Parties: A Sociological Study of the Oligarchical Tendencies of Modern Democracy* (Zur Sociologie des Parteiwesens). New York: Free Press.

Moore, C. (2001). "Restorative Justice When the System is the Offender." *MSC Conciliation Quarterly* 20(3) (Summer).

Van Ness, D. and K.H. Strong (2002). *Restoring Justice* (2nd ed.). Cincinnati, OH: Anderson Publishing.

Chapter 24.
Is Restorative Justice Taking Too Few, Or Too Many, Risks?

by

David L. Gustafson

...[M]y point is Restorative Justice needs to be rooted in values like: creating no further harms, safety, listening, validating, and empowering people to seek healing and restoration in their own way and timing. It needs to flow out of developing relationships between the clients and the practitioners. People respond to being honoured and loved and you can't fake this... RJ done well requires a huge time commitment and a consistent care. When doing RJ in cases of serious crime it can be life risking and consequently life changing. So full of risks and rewards. The hardest pain imaginable faced and the biggest relief!!!!" ["Margaret," survivor of violent sexual assault[1]].

"Is Restorative Justice taking too few, or too many, risks?" It's difficult to answer, since I don't see restorative justice as a program, or a person or a group of people; I see restorative justice as a way of life. Those of us who believe in restorative justice as a way of living don't take enough risks in living restoratively, in that we often succumb to peer pressure. I make this same critique of myself: there are times when I'm being observed that I revert to being the hardcore convict, acting out of a role. Every one of us gets out of bed every morning and puts on a mask — some of us, several masks, [which assist] survival or impression management. Amongst a group of our peers we will sometimes move away from a restorative stance for fear of ridicule; to continue acting restoratively would be to risk vulnerability and to take the risks we all need to take"* [Gordon Alcorn, Chair, Inmate Committee, Ferndale Institution[2]].

"WHEN YOU COME TO A FORK IN THE ROAD, TAKE IT" — YOGI BERRA

During the 6th International Conference on Restorative Justice held in 2003 in Vancouver, British Columbia, Howard Zehr, during one of the plenary sessions, invoked Yogi Berra[3], quoting him as having said: "'When you come to a fork in the road, *pick it up*.'" Gordon Bazemore, in his luncheon address the following day, good-naturedly offered his view that Berra had actually said: "When you come to a fork in the road, *take it*."

Either way, the question suggested to me by the editors clearly marks a fork in the road. With trepidation I decided to pick it up. And, approaching the fork, I decided to follow the advice of two others of my American heroes — Bazemore and Berra — and "take the fork." "Is restorative justice taking too few or too many risks?" The answer to the question can only be "Yes."

For the most part, research literature surveys such as that done by Jo-Anne Wemmers and Marisa Canuto for the Canadian Department of Justice (Wemmers and Canuto, 2002) indicate impressively high satisfaction levels among victims and offenders participating in restorative justice programs. But surveys of that literature also continue to highlight concerns on a number of themes that definitely need to be heeded.

The majority of my colleagues in victim service agencies, for example, are cautiously optimistic about the potential of restorative justice programs to serve their constituencies well. But most would also have at least a few anecdotes to share that illustrate "unsafe" practices or situations in which well meaning but insufficiently competent practitioners created secondary victimization for vulnerable people. I share the concern: I, too, have seen practitioners working with case referrals at even the "minor" diversion offence levels who set out without due caution, without sufficient respect for the difficulty of some of the terrain, without awareness of or commitment to the set of values, principles and ethics that would orient them, without experience and without much reference to the maps provided by earlier explorers. In such cases, yes indeed, I believe too many risks are being taken.

As one of the "greybeard loons" of this movement, I acknowledge that I probably have far too much personal investment in it all going well. But, that aside, I share the concern of stakeholder groups that insufficiently skilled or careless practice could put vulnerable people at risk, trigger past trauma or create new harms. Each such example increases the risk that restorative justice as a movement may be seen as ill-conceived and inadequate to the task of dealing with matters of any real consequence. The question, then, becomes: "Are restorative justice practitioners taking too few or too many risks *given the competencies they offer in relation to the needs of those referred to them?*"

That question, obviously, is extremely relevant at both ends of the offence seriousness scale. At the upper end of that scale, however, the primary problem so far is not one of rapid proliferation of programs and of concerns that they are taking cases beyond their capabilities. In my experience, where such programs exist, there are usually highly competent people involved. The concern is that so few such programs exist. Too few jurisdictions appear prepared to take the risks involved in developing the capacity to handle cases involving severe trauma. This leaves far too many people to deal with far too much pain, especially when part of the relief they seek could well be found in the healing approaches that restorative justice at its best offers.

The agency for which I work[4] began to research and develop restorative models for use in the most serious crimes in the Canadian Criminal Code as far back as 1989. What we heard from both victim and offender respondents ran counter to what we had been led to believe we would hear. The majority (82%) of victim respondents — all of whom had suffered severe trauma — indicated that they felt a need to meet and to dialogue with those who had offended against them. They indicated that they would participate in a program such as interviewers had described as soon as such a service could be implemented. Similarly, despite being instructed that program participation would not factor into early release decisions or sentence reductions, the majority of offender respondents (87%) indicated that they would choose to meet with the victims of their offences. Offenders' reasons included (Gustafson and Smidstra, 1989):

(1) a sense of the moral rightness of having to be held to account directly by those they had harmed;

(2) concern to release victims/survivors from fears about their intentions toward them upon release;

(3) hope of changing the stereotyped view portrayed by the media: "to be seen [by the victim] as human," rather than as the "ravaging 'animal' portrayed in court"; and,

(4) hope of finding an appropriate forum in which to offer and to negotiate meaningful symbolic and practical amends, including financial restitution.

The Gustafson and Smidstra (1989) study's findings and the program development suggestions of the anticipated user groups led to the implementation in the Pacific Region (British Columbia and the Yukon) of Canada's Victim Offender Mediation Program (VOMP) in 1990. Since then, victim offender mediation or mediation/dialogue programs dealing with traumatic criminal offences have been implemented in only a handful of other jurisdictions. American programs now exist (usually under the aegis of the state-level department of corrections, office of the victim advocate, or victim services divisions) in Pennsylvania, Texas, and Ohio. Similar programs, I understand, are also being initiated in New Hampshire, Alabama, Louisiana and California.

While there is keen interest in many parts of the world, only a handful of similar government-funded and authorized programs appear to have been established, worldwide, in over a decade. I recall Prison Chaplain Rev. David Hilderman, following a presentation of one of our program's case studies at an international conference in 1995, asking, "If this sort of healing is possible, for victims of crime and prisoners alike, how can it possibly be conscionable for our governments not to provide such a resource for those who seek it?" There were 89 countries represented there. Many of us continue to wonder about the answer to David's question.

At this level of harms, in matters involving serious crime and severe trauma, are government gatekeepers, funders and competent restorative justice practitioners taking too few risks? In most jurisdictions, I believe, the answer continues to be "Yes." We will, apparently, have to take both roads from the fork.

Refining The Question

One of the first tasks, in my view, is to refine the question. Restorative justice, it seems to me, isn't actually *doing* anything; that is, it isn't an operant in ways the question might suggest. Restorative justice is a profound yet pragmatic philosophical approach to crime and conflict. A cornerstone set upon a foundation establishes the line of the adjacent walls of a building. Similarly, an increasingly well articulated set of values and principles establishes the lines of this "new" approach to an ancient dilemma: *how to define and do justice* so that justice is done, and seen to be done, by the impacted parties and the public at large.

Outcomes and appearances are both important. True justice can neither be so punitive that it becomes simply vengeful, nor so lenient that it appears unconcerned about harm caused. Many[5] have begun to wonder if adversarial processes, punishment and deterrence theories can ever accomplish what we hope for justice. Some of our finest thinkers have led us to ask: "How can it be that any attempt to do justice should create new harms which are of one piece with the violence of the original harm?" As societies we've begun to ask whether there be a place for peacemaking, for advocating for the meeting of the needs of both aggrieved and aggressor, for founding justice processes not on foundations of "punishment and deterrence" so much as upon the foundation of an ethic of care?

There is nothing new about this foundation: the tenets of restorative or "relational" justice are rooted in the world's ancient civilizations. What is new is the cornerstone: the clear, modern articulation of restorative values and principles which establish the direction lines, the next level lines and the plumb lines against which specific program processes can be designed, built, utilized and evaluated. While restorative justice as a philosophical approach is not an operant (anymore than the cornerstone is the builder), the practitioners — mediators, conferencing facilitators, circle keepers — *are* the operants; the builders. How those practitioners define restorative justice, how they interpret (or misinterpret) the values and principles that have been established, how they put into practice their understandings, the degree of competency they bring to the work — all of these things have a great deal to do with the outcomes their practice will produce.

Praxis

Following the conference mentioned earlier, I invited Howard Zehr to stay on to help host a "Palaver on Praxis," a day-long gathering of about 60 knowledgeable folk with interest or involvement in "the marriage of restorative justice theory and practice." The group included representatives from the judiciary, victim services, crime prevention, prosecution, human resources, aboriginal justice and policing. There were students, educators, trauma counselors, trauma survivors, community restorative justice program managers and facilitators.

We began by identifying what were, for this group, issues of critical concern in restorative justice. Of the 13 "critical issues" identified, concern for ensuring "good practice" was listed more than twice as often as the next nearest items.[6] Much of the day's discussion was focused on the specifics of "good practice." Key elements listed included these:

- safety: the paramount commitment, borrowing from the doctors' Hypocratic Oath, to "First, do no further harm";

- completely voluntary involvement of all participants;

- commitment to preparation of and meaningful follow-up with all participants;

- recognition:
    o that healing requires time;
    o that individuals' needs vary vastly, requiring flexibility;
    o that understanding and awareness of cultural differences can be crucial; "'Make no assumptions' needs to be a watchword";

- need for adherence to principles such as Zehr and Mika's "Fundamental Principles" (Zehr, 2002), Susan Sharpe's "Touchstones,"[7] and practitioner values/ethics sets such as the British Columbia Charter for Restorative Justice Practitioners;[8]

- demonstrated, caring commitment to each individual participant is an indicator of the degree to which stated, notional values become realized values; and,

- competence of mediators and facilitators.

It is of interest that the elements of good practice listed by participants in the palaver so closely echoed those listed by respondents in the restorative justice program research literature as key "markers" in programs that were supported and drew high praise from participants. Wemmers and Canuto (2002), for example, indicate that restorative justice approaches have significant support from victims of even violent crimes where program participation is entirely voluntary, the program practitioners competent and the programs professionally and ethically run.

Practitioner Competency

Competency is not simply a matter of paper credentials, important though the latter may be. Competency is the confluence of knowledge, honed skills, character, personality traits, attitudes and experience. Ron Claassen, Founding Director of the Fresno, California VORP, looks for competencies among his trainees reflective of their grasp of "the art, skills and *spirit* of mediation..." (Claassen, 1992). Jacquie Stevulak, respected director of a North Vancouver, British Columbia mediation/conferencing program, counsels: "Hire for the heart; teach the skills." It is difficult to define intangibles, but not impossible to observe or assess for them.[9]

Complexities in cases increase dramatically as the scale of seriousness of the criminal offence increases. Thus it is crucial that there be clear differentiation between diversion programs taking referrals of relatively minor matters and those programs designed to work with cases involving highly traumatic, severe interpersonal violence. Facilitators working in cases involving interpersonal violence require a degree of competence considerably beyond that required of those working with less serious offences. This is especially true of sexual offences and the entire range of criminal offences with power-based components. In some cases those power dynamics are blatant, and relatively easily recognized. However, in the far greater percentage, as in incest cases for example, these dynamics are incredibly subtle and often hidden from even the individuals themselves. Education and experience in working with these dynamics are imperative for anyone working with these clientele; this includes thorough-going grounding in the victim experience, trauma and the post-traumatic syndromes.

In many cases, survivors of crimes such as these have had little or no meaningful therapy. Boundaries need to be negotiated, in terms of survivor expectations and what practitioners can provide. Referral to other support services may be required (or much preferred), but survivor participants often look to us to provide part of the therapeutic support they need for the journey. It helps to have, among the members of the practitioner team, the professional clinical credentials for the task.

The Needs Of The Offender Participant

In most jurisdictions, restorative justice practitioners who work with serious criminal cases clearly involving severe victim trauma will likely be working with them at a post-incarceration stage, in prisons. In our experience, an average of four years has elapsed between the time of the prisoner's sentence and time of referral, and many of those cases will involve working in maximum security environments. It is crucial, therefore, in addition to understanding the victim/survivor trauma, that facilitators have understanding of offender trauma. Further, they must be familiar with other complexities of work with prisoners, such as the risks involved for that prisoner in participating in such programs and the preparation steps that are a part of assessing, minimizing and managing those risks.

To attempt to create conditions that enable victim healing and empowerment, while creating situations that create new harms for the prisoner, cannot be ethically supported. Potential risks for the prisoner participant can include the following: psychological "melt-down"; suicide; new institutional charges if they "act out" their expression of anxiety and need for additional support as they enter (or exit) the process; and exposure to harms at the hands of other prisoners (especially non-involved co-accused who may see the participant to have "ratted out" or violated some other aspect of the "con-code" through their involvement). Truly restorative processes will seek to bring healing to both parties, advocating not for one party over the other but, rather, for healing, transcendence and well-being for both.

CONCLUSION

A few years ago my co-director and I wrote:

> Virtually around the globe, programs which fall under the caption of "restorative justice" are experiencing tremendous growth. For those of us who have advocated for and supported many of these developments for over two decades, this represents an exciting shift. Still, some of us have been laboring in the fields between

criminal justice systems and community alternatives for long enough that we temper our enthusiasm and optimism with skepticism on many fronts (Gustafson and Bergen, 2000).

It is precisely because we have seen such potential for restorative justice processes across the spectrum of cases that we are so concerned to see the current movement built upon solid foundations, staying true to its values and principals cornerstones. That will mean commitment on the part of practitioners, program overseers, governments and funders to ensure that they are emulating best practices. It will require training to the level of competency required by the work in which they are engaged and increasing program capacity only as they have prepared competent practitioners to serve the needs of those participants. Lack of practitioner competence, at either end of the offence seriousness scale, can turn participant involvement into a perilous journey. Ensuring that practitioners are competent to facilitate at the level demanded by the case is crucial to the safety of program participants; it will become increasing crucial to the credibility of the entire field.

If we as restorative justice practitioners are deeply committed to safe, responsible, ethical, principled practice, if we are clearly aware of the limits of our competencies, then taking reasonable risks — so long as that is done cautiously, with stakeholder consultation and in concert with the program participants themselves — should be encouraged. Given the availability of relevant training, growing numbers of participant applicants and the immensity of the need, are we taking too many risks? Within the limits of caveats I've noted, not nearly.

Address correspondence to: David L. Gustafson, Co-Director, Fraser Region Community Justice Initiatives Association, 101 20678-Eastleigh Crescent, Langley, BC V3A 4C4 Canada.

REFERENCES

Claassen, R. (1992). "VORP Mediators Are Skillful Volunteers." *Conciliation Quarterly* 11(Summer):4.

Gustafson, D.L. and S. Bergen (2000). "Vision and Values for Community Accountability Programs." Paper prepared for the Ministry of Public Safety and Solicitor General of British Columbia, Community Programs Branch.

—— and H. Smidstra (1989). *Victim Offender Reconciliation in Serious Crime: A Report on the Feasibility Study Undertaken for the Ministry of the Solicitor General.* Ottawa, CAN: Solicitor General Canada.

Sharpe, S. (1998). *Restorative Justice: A Vision for Healing and Change.* Edmonton, CAN: Victim Offender Mediation Society.

Wemmers, J. and M. Canuto (2002). *Victims' Experiences With, Expectations and Perceptions of Restorative Justice: A Critical Review of the Literature.* Montreal, CAN: International Centre for Comparative Criminology, University de Montreal.

Zehr, H. *The Little Book of Restorative Justice.* Intercourse, PA: Good Books.

NOTES

1. Personal correspondence with VOMP program client, August, 2003.

2. Personal interview, July 9, 2003.

3. Yogi Berra is a famous American baseball hero. Being a word person rather than a sports nut, I know Berra best for his witty "Yogi-isms," some of which find their way into this article.

4. Fraser Region Community Justice Initiatives Association in Langley, BC, Canada, is a non-profit/charitable organization established in 1981. Our programs include a therapeutic mediation/dialogue program working with prisoners and criminal trauma survivors in matters as serious as armed robbery, manslaughter, sexual assault, serial rape, first- and second-degree murder and multiple murder offences.

5. Including many judges, prosecutors, police and legislators. The Law Commission of Canada is doing some excellent work in these regards, animating discussion in Canadian Communities, most often from a restorative/transformative justice framework. See their web site at (www.lcc.gc.ca/).

6. Items tied for second in terms of frequency were: "doing restorative justice in a punishment-based and bureaucratic culture"; and "the role of spirituality."

7. In Susan Sharpe. *Restorative Justice: A Vision for Healing and Change,* (Edmonton Victim Offender Mediation Society, 1998), p.48.

8. In 2002, a group of restorative justice practitioners in British Columbia, Canada, began to meet together informally to discuss what was perceived as a growing problem: burgeoning numbers of community programs, established with some clear government policy criteria regarding what sorts of cases they could accept, but without what was felt would be helpful shared principals, values, and ethics sets. The first consensus draft (May, 2003) can be seen at: (http://www.sfu. ca/cfrj/fulltext/charter.pdf).

9. Our agency has long used competency-based assessments for those working with us on cases referred by prosecutors and probation at a diversion level.

Chapter 25.
How Do Culture, Class And Gender Affect The Practice Of Restorative Justice? (Part 1)

by

Morris Jenkins

The issues of racism, classism and sexism have plagued the criminal justice system's response to criminality in the United States. Restorative Justice is one proposed response to crime that may overcome these problems. This chapter explores the cultural sub-component of race and discusses how restorative justice has attempted to deal with the issue of race and racism within the movement. The primary focus of the chapter will be racism as it impacts African Americans, because African Americans and their communities are disproportionately represented as offenders and victims of crime within the largest population centers of the United States. The chapter specifically considers alternative explanations for African-American crime and examines responses to crime within the African-American community that can enhance the restorative justice approach.

The criminal justice system is criticized as being ineffective in dealing with crime, the needs of the victim, and the rehabilitation of the offender. Persons of color have additional criticisms about the criminal justice system, and often feel victimized by both offenders (many of whom are African American) and by the perceived and real discrimination that occurs throughout the criminal justice system (McCoy, 1993; Johnson, 1993; Weitzer, 1996; Miller, 1996). Even though community members feel victimized by "criminals," many in the African-American community feel that submitting a fellow brother or sister to the criminal justice system may be an inappropriate response (Austin, 1992). Current responses to crime and delinquency within the African-American community, grounded in the substantive criminal law and driven by recent expansion in police powers, have led to a disproportionate number of African Americans in prisons and jails in the United States (Leiber, 2002). Restorative justice is a process that is a paradigmatic shift in the approach to crime that could possibly deal with this issue. It seeks to "humanize" the participants in their quest for justice and requires that the community becomes an active participant, empowering its members to deal with crime and delinquency (Bazemore, 1994; Umbreit, 1995; Zehr, 1990). This community participation may also offset some of the problems associated with racism.

The shift towards restorative justice occurs within a society where institutional racism is the foundation for the power imbalance between Whites and Non-whites. Restorative justice scholars and practitioners have recognized that there are multicultural concerns in the movement and believe that institutional racism is a deterrent to an effective restorative justice process (Umbreit and Coates, 1999). However, within the African-American community there is a distrust, and at best apprehension, of approaches to crime that appear to come from the Eurocentric framework. Even though much of the literature states that the restorative justice process has its roots in non-European cultures (Benham and Barton, 1996; Vyas, 1995; Melton, 1995; Yazzie, 1997), there are very few academic and popular articles on restorative justice within the African Diaspora (Stern, 2001; Elechi, 1999; Elechi, 1996). These works illustrate key differences and in some cases similarities to the principles of restorative justice. An example of this approach is illustrated in the Kpelle tribe in Liberia (Benham and Barton, 1996:632):

> [an] informal form of dispute resolution is the moot or house palaver found among the Kpelle of Liberia....[D]isputes are settled formally in official and unofficial courts of town chiefs or quarter elders, or informally in associational groupings such as church councils or in moots. Because the formal court hearings are coercive in nature, they do not provide the best forum for cases involving ongoing relationships. The moot, on the other hand, is an informal airing of grievances that takes place in the home of the complainant before an ad hoc group of kinsmen and neighbors.

These practices were and are being used by people of African descent throughout the Caribbean and South America (Chung and Chang, 1998; Adeleke, 1998). In addition, especially during the times of *de jure* segregation, many of the problems within the African-American community were handled by an informal moot (Brown, 1994).

This history suggests that we should "go back to the future" by understanding the impact of racism and the African diaspora in order to create a culturally-specific restorative justice approach. As first steps to go "back to the future," the following should take place within the restorative justice movement:

(1) Use of culturally-specific theories to explain crime and social harms and develop a culturally specific response to the harm.

(2) Redefinition of community.

(3) Assurances that the "State" is not a dominant participant in the process.

(4) Education and training on the issues of race and racism that include alternative theories.

(5) Active research on this issue using non-European methodologies.

As I discuss these points in the remainder of the chapter, I will explore both the Eurocentric and Afrocentric approaches.

Culturally-Specific Theories To Explain And Respond To Crime: Afrocentric Theory

Traditionally and unfortunately, male-centered and Eurocentric criminological theories are used to explain criminal behavior. The foci of these explanations for Black criminality have typically included genetic inferiority, culture of poverty, or racial oppression (Cross, 2003; Lundy, 2003; Edmondson-Bell and Nkomo, 1998; Herrnstein and Murray, 1994; Morris, 1989; Corcoran et al., 1985; Wilson, 1978). These explanations reflect many of the biases that society holds towards African Americans. Unfortunately, they also help shape criminal justice policies. These theories are taught in educational institutions where future policy makers and criminal justice professionals internalize them. Schiele (1996:285) puts it like this:

Eurocentric theories of human behavior reflect concepts of human behavior developed in European and Anglo-American culture. The practice of using Eurocentric theories to explain the behavior and ethos of African Americans can be inappropriate because a major assumption of the Afrocentric paradigm is that social science theories are derived from the specific experiences and cultural perspectives of the theorist.

For example, contrary to the assumptions of both the race oppression and culture of poverty theories, African Americans do not desire the same individualistic objectives and goals as European Americans.

Afrocentric and Eurocentric theory differ in four fundamental principles; these fall in the areas of cosmology (worldview), axiology (values), ontology (nature of people), and epistemology (source of knowledge). From the Eurocentric perspective, the dominant worldview focuses on control. Key values include materialism and individualism. People are fundamentally competitive, operating in a "dog eat dog" world. Knowledge is derived through the scientific method. From the Afrocentric perspective, however, worldview focuses on the "oneness with others." Relationship with the community is valued. There is a belief in the goodness of people and that individuals work together. Spirituality pro vides a primary source of knowledge (Warfield-Coppock, 1995).

Afrocentric theory is a culturally-specific approach that can be used to both explain why the harm occurred and serve as a foundation for a restorative justice response to the harm, suggesting the need to explore offending from an African-centered ideology. The crux of Afrocentric theories about black criminality is that structural pressures, combined with dysfunctional Eurocentric cultural adaptation to those pressures, play out as unacceptable behavior in African-American communities.

After exploring the social problem through an Afrocentric lens, the remedy or solution of the problem should be grounded in an "African"-centered approach (Semmes, 1981). The primary focus is not retribution for the criminal act, the rehabilitation of the offender to a perfect Eurocentric citizen, or even the compensation of the victim. The Afrocentric approach does not ignore these concerns; however the liberation of the community is the primary concern. A true understanding of one's culture is needed to achieve emancipatory literacy: the ability to conceptualize the world in ways consistent with one's history and to apply that knowledge as one's personality and situation requires (Harris, 1992:155).

"Afrocentric theory is a theory of affirmation. It is a theory conceived to generate new knowledge and to pursue the path of liberation" (Bekerie, 1994:133). This in turn would lead to individual and collective liberation and freedom. From a restorative justice perspective, the concept of liberty in the African-American community ensures that all participants are aware of their personal responsibility to the larger body of African people. Emancipation means that all participants are aware of their responsibilities in relation to such concepts as unity and self-determination. The primary focus of restorative justice, then, is to move the participants from a "survival" orientation to a "liberation/empowerment" orientation.

Umbreit and Coates (1999), as well as Arrigo and Schehr (1998), argue that there are serious multicultural implications and concerns that must be addressed under the restorative justice model. One's understanding and application of the principles does not depend on one's skin color. Two of the Afrocentric principles, worldview and values, are deeply embedded in the restorative justice approach to crime, delinquency and other social harms. Both restorative justice and Afrocentric theory focus on the community.

The need of the community, which includes the victim, offender and significant others, is emancipation. Due to the fact that both the restorative justice and Afrocentric paradigms focus on community liberation or emancipation, it is imperative that the traditional Afrocentric approach provides the overarching framework for the restorative justice model in the African-American community. Pattison (1998) states that culturally-appropriate programs for minority juvenile offenders are not only a moral right, but also a legal right.

One example of an Afrocentric process that is transferable to a restorative justice process would be "rites of passage" (Delaney, 1995; Harvey and Rauch 1997; Warfield-Coppock 1992; Gavazzi, 1996). Under the "tough guy" scenario, the primary "community-based" socialization agent is the criminal justice system, more specifically detention centers, jails and prisons. In other words, the rite of passage for many young African-American males into the Eurocentric culture occurs in prison (Miller, 1996). Ritualism is a process that is not only used in traditional African cultures; it is an integral aspect of the American legal culture. For example, the trial is a ritualistic process that follows a procedure that must fall within the guidelines of the court's rules. There is a script that all of the players must follow and the judge is the director of the ritual. The concept of ritual is also important under the restorative justice paradigm, especially within the framework of the "alternative dispute resolution" that is used under this approach (Delaney, 1995; Warfield-Coppock, 1992). Within this framework, the ritual dictates that participants move from their positions in the dispute to a situation where they can discover each other's interest and come to a resolution. The notion of "community" is an integral part of this process and ritual. An Afrocentric restorative justice approach to these concepts could be facilitated through a rite-of-passage process facilitated by an elder who is well grounded in Afrocentric theory. Through this process, the offender would learn that being materialistic or a "tough guy" is counter to the Afrocentric principle of community emancipation. The elder would also ensure that the "victim" and all other participants are aware of the principles of Afrocentric theory and make attempts to follow them.

Because most of us are trained to deal with disputes and conflicts from a Eurocentric perspective, all of us, White and Non-white, tend to be individualistic in our approach to dealing with problems, including crime. Certainly, Afrocentric theory is not a "Blacks only" approach. Asante (1983) claims that, in many cases, Whites have a better understanding of the theory than many African Americans. However, a foundation in Afrocentric theory and its processes can improve the restorative justice process for non-European American cultures (Jenkins, 2003; Warfield-Coppock, 1992; Harvey and Rauch, 1997).

Redefining Community

The term community has various meanings and connotations within the culture of the United States. Under the law, community is defined by geographic boundaries. The village, town, city, state and the country have identifiable boundaries and each represent an aspect of the term community. Within towns, there are sometimes areas identified by geographic boundaries that are identified as communities. These neighborhoods are considered communities by both the legal and political structures, as well as by extra-legal definitions. The concept of community policing, for example, assumes that there are distinct boundaries that make a community.

Community is also defined by culture. Individuals belong to various communities defined by their ascribed and achieved positions within society. For example, lawyers are members of the "bar community" and medical doctors are members of the "medical community." This community identification is as strong, and sometimes, stronger than the bonds that occur within a geographic community. In the United States, because of the concept of race, there are various racial and ethnic communities. Many times these communities extend past the boundaries of the geographic communities. The bonds within these communities may also be as strong as the bonds in a geographic community.

Within certain cultures, community also includes one's history and heritage. Within these communities, ancestors are a vital component of the community. The adage "if you don't know where you came from, you won't know where you are going" is applicable to cultures that subscribe to this component. Again, the bond between these individuals and their ancestors can be as strong as the bonds in a geographic community. In addition, certain cultures have an additional or other spiritual component to their understanding of themselves and their comprehension of the concept of community.

Because community may encompass all of these definitions, a paradigmatic shift should occur in the understanding of community. Community is a "socio/cultural environment" in which one physically, mentally and spiritually resides. Within the "socio/cultural environment" there are individuals who are (or are perceived as) oppressors and other individuals who are the oppressed, though these labels may change depending upon the circumstances. In addition, the environment itself is (or perceived as) the oppressor or the oppressed (Vides, 1995).

Because most criminal offenses tend to be intra-racial, a culturally- (in this case race-) specific definition of community would be appropriate. However, since the Afrocentric approach to restorative justice includes the concept of spirituality, the definition of community should include one's history and heritage, as well as one's religious or spiritual belief. In this approach, all community members, oppressed or oppressor, are responsible not only to current members of the community, but also to the ancestors that preceded him/her.

Reduction Of "State" Participation

With its roots in individualism, the Eurocentric approach to dealing with crime ultimately means that the individual is responsible for his or her actions; the system must reform the individual, or the "individual" must compensate another "individual." It also assumes that the voice of the community is the same as the voice and values of the state. In addition, under most Eurocentric legal paradigms, the rule of law trumps the concept of justice. The primary goal remains social control and the punishment of the individual who violates the statute (Nunn, 1997).

Unfortunately, this system wrongly assumes that the broader community voice represents the African-American community. The result is mistrust of the criminal justice system by many African Americans. The recent events covered by the mainstream and popular media — including the O.J. Simpson trial, the Susan Smith situation in South Carolina, the Charles Stuart fiasco in Boston and the Rodney King trials — have highlighted this mistrust.

If the state or agents of the state remain a dominant participant in the restorative justice process, African Americans will continue to mistrust the process. The restorative justice process will be perceived as simply an expansion of the social control mechanism of the criminal justice system. In addition, the participation of the state as a dominant player is contrary to both the restorative justice and Afrocentric primary focus on the community. Agents of the state could be participants; however they should not act out their roles, or be perceived as doing so, as criminal justice or legal professionals.

Education And Training

Education and training on racism and culturally-specific approaches to restorative justice must occur in both formal and informal educational settings. Within higher educational settings, criminal justice, pre-law and other majors in the social sciences are taught the dominant, and typically Eurocentric, theories on crime and delinquency. The voices of communities, practitioners, and scholars of color, especially African Americans, are usually not heard. The exposure to restorative justice, coupled with alternative culturally-specific theories to crime in formal educational institutions, would allow for more academic debate and research that would test the viability of both restorative justice and Afrocentric theories. This author believes that this would also lead to more participation of African Americans and others within the restorative justice movement. Training sessions should include exercises and workshops that not only identify personal and participants' biases, but methods to determine both the facilitators' and participants' grounding in Afrocentric (or other culturally-specific) theory. The addition of the Afrocentric perspective will enhance intercultural communication and increase the tolerance for alternative worldviews (Schreiber, 2000; Kershaw, 1992; Nagan, 1993).

Research

Current research methodologies under the Eurocentric perspective have "...led to a hegemony of knowledge and of knowledge validation (especially apparent in academia) that omits or marginalizes the indigenous worldviews of people of color" (Schiele, 1996:286). Even within the Eurocentric research framework, using multiple or "triangulation" methodologies and approaches are assumed to lead to more reliable and valid conclusions (Schreiber, 2000). This suggests that including Afrocentric perspectives in research will lead to increased reliability and validity. Due to cultural differences and other concerns, an Afrocentric approach to restorative justice will at minimum enhance the value of research for African-American constituencies. Participatory research from an action perspective could also engage African-American offenders, victims and other community members and thus become a valuable tool for the recruitment of African-American facilitators.

Studies have shown that restorative justice has been successful from the viewpoint of both victims and offenders (Umbreit et al., 1994). However, additional research is needed, using an Afrocentric approach to measure whether Afrocentric values are present in the restorative justice process and to determine its effectiveness. The addition of the Afrocentric perspective to the existing research can only improve society's understanding of restorative justice. This approach will also ensure that community liberation will be the primary focus in the Black community as well as in other disenfranchised communities in the United States.

CONCLUSION

Some scholars and practitioners assert that an Afrocentric approach would promote separatism (Wilkinson, 1995). However, others counter that a healthy separatism, which involves the social and economic improvement of the race or ethnic group, is necessary for a truly multicultural society (Hing, 1993). Still others suggest that an Afrocentric approach addresses the power relationship between the races in order to have effective intercultural communications (Asante, 1983). Because of the intra-racial nature of much crime, the offender (oppressor), victim (oppressed), and the community (socio-cultural environment) tend to be of the same race or ethnicity. All three have a vested interest in the outcome of the restorative justice process. A facilitator, regardless of race, who is trained and grounded in Afrocentric theory could ensure that basic principles of both an Afrocentric theory and restorative justice are met. However, the use of an Afrocentric restorative justice process would also increase the number of African-American facilitators.

While this chapter focused on the African-American community, other culturally-specific approaches — whether racial, ethnic, religious, or gender — may be useful in other situations. Oybade (1990:234) maintains:

> Afrocentric perspective does not aim to replace Eurocentricity as a universal perspective. Indeed, Afrocentricity recognizes the validity of other non-hegemonic perspectives — Asia-centered, America-centered, and even Europe-centered in its non-hegemonic form. It would allow for a pluriversal perspective...looking at the world from different centers rather than from a single angle is necessary if we are to have a better understanding of this diversified and multicultural universe.

The addition of alternative perspectives, including an Afrocentric approach, would only enhance the concept of restorative justice.

Address correspondence to: Morris Jenkins, Department of Criminal Justice, University of Toledo, Toledo, Ohio 43606. E-mail: <mjenkin4@utnet.utoledo.edu>.

REFERENCES AND SUGGESTED READING

Adelke, T. (1998). "Black Americans and Africa: A Critique of the Pan-African and Identity Paradigms." *International Journal of African Historical Studies* 31:505-536.

Arrigo, B.A. and R.C. Schehr (1998). "Restoring Justice for Juveniles: A Critical Analysis of Victim-Offender Mediation." *Justice Quarterly* 15:629-666.

Asante, M.K. (1983). "The Ideological Significance of Afrocentricity in Intercultural Communication." *Journal of Black Studies* 14:3-19.

Austin, R. (1992). "The Black Community, Its Lawbreakers, and a Politics of Identification." *Southern California Law Review* 65:1769-1817.

Bazemore, G. (1994). "Rehabilitating Community Service: Toward Restorative Service Sanctions in a Balanced System." *Federal Probation* 58:24-35.

Bekerie, A. (1994). "The Four Corners of a Circle: Afrocentricity as a Model of Synthesis." *Journal of Black Studies* 25:131-149.

Benham, A. and A.B. Barton (1996). "Alternative Dispute Resolution: Ancient Models Provide Modern Inspiration." *Georgia State University Law Review* 12:623-651.

Brown, E.B. (1994). "Negotiating and Transforming the Public Sphere: African American Political Life in the Transition from Slavery to Freedom." *Public Culture* 7:107-146.

Chung, A.Y. and E.T. Chang (1998). "From Third World Liberation to Multiple Oppression Politics: A Contemporary Approach to Interethnic Coalitions." *Social Justice* 25:80-100.

Corcoran, M., G.J. Duncan, G. Gurin and P. Gurin (1985). "Myth and Reality: The Cause and Persistence of Poverty." *Journal of Policy Analysis & Management* 4:516-536.

Cross, W.E. (2003). "Tracing the Historical Origins of Youth Delinquency & Violence: Myths & Realities about Black Culture." *Journal of Social Issues* 59:67-82.

Delaney, C.H. (1995). "Rites of Passage in Adolescence." *Adolescence* 30:891-897.

Edmondson-Bell, E. and S.M. Nkomo (1998). "Armoring: Learning to Withstand Racial Oppression." *Journal of Comparative Family Studies* 29:285-295.

Elechi, O.O. (1999). "Victims under the Restorative Justice Systems; The Afikpo (Ehugbo) Nigeria Model." *International Review of Victimology* 6:359-375.

—— (1996). "Doing Justice Without the State: The Afikpo (Ehugbo) Nigeria Model of Conflict Resolution." *International Journal of Comparative and Applied Criminal Justice* 20:337-355.

Gavazzi, S.M. (1996). "Culturally Specific Programs for Foster Care Youth: The Sample Case of an African American Rites of Passage Program." *Family Relations* 45:166-174.

Harris, N. (1992). "A Philosophical Basis for an Afrocentric Orientation." *The Western Journal of Black Studies* 16:154-159.

Harvey, A. and J.B. Rauch (1997). "A Comprehensive Afrocentric Rites of Passage Program for Black Male Adolescents." *Health and Social Work* 22:30-37.

Herrnstein, R.J. and C. Murray (1994). *The Bell Curve: Intelligence and Class Structure in American Life.* New York: Free Press.

Hing, B.O. (1993). "Beyond the Rhetoric of Assimilation and Cultural Pluralism: Addressing the Tension of Separatism and Conflict in an Immigration-driven Multiracial Society." *California Law Review* 81:863-914.

Jenkins, M. (forthcoming 2004). "Afrocentric Theory and Restorative Justice: A Viable Alternative to Deal with Crime and Delinquency in the Black Community." *Journal of Social and Societal Policy.*

Johnson, S.L. (1993). "Racial Imagery in Criminal Cases." *Tulane Law Review* 67:1739-1764.

Kershaw, T. (1992). "Afrocentrism and the Afrocentric Method." *The Western Journal of Black Studies* 16:160-168.

Leiber, M. (2002). "Disproportionate Minority Confinement (DMC) of Youth: An Analysis of State and Federal Efforts to Address the Issue." *Crime & Delinquency* 48:3-46.

Lundy, G. (2003). "The Myths of Oppositional Culture." *Journal of Black Studies* 33:450-467.

McCoy, C. (1993). "From Sociological Trends of 1992 to the Criminal Courts of 2020." *Southern California Law Review* 66:1967-1991.

Melton, A.P. (1995). "Indigenous Justice Systems and Tribal Society." *Judicature* 79:126-133.

Miller, J.G. (1996). *Search and Destroy: African American Males in the Criminal Justice System.* New York: Cambridge University Press.

Morris, M. (1989). "From the Culture of Poverty to the Underclass: An Analysis of a Shift in Public Language." *The American Sociologist* 1989:123-133.

Nagan, W.P. (1993). "Africa's Value Debate: Kaunda on Apartheid and African Humanism." *Saint Louis Law Journal* 37:871-882.

Nunn, K.B. (1997). "Law as a Eurocentric Enterprise." *Law and Inequality* 15:323-370.

Oliver, W. (1989). "Black Males and Social Problem: Prevention through Afrocentric Socialization." *Journal of Black Studies* 20:15-39.

Oyebade, B. (1990). "African Studies and the Afrocentric Paradigm: A Critique." *Journal of Black Studies* 21:233-238.

Pattison, B. (1998). "Minority Youth in Juvenile Correctional Facilities: Cultural Differences and the Right to Treatment." *Law and Equality Journal* 16:573-599.

Schiele, J.H. (1996). "Afrocentricity: An Emerging Paradigm in Social Work Practice." *Social Work* 41:284-292.

Schreiber, L. (2000). "Overcoming Methodological Elitism: Afrocentrism as a Prototypical Paradigm for Intercultural Research." *International Journal of Intercultural Relations* 24:651-671.

Semmes, C.E. (1981). "Foundations of an Afrocentric Social Science: Implications for Curriculum-building, Theory, and Research in Black Studies." *Journal of Black Studies* 12:3-17.

Stern, V. (2001). "An Alternative Vision: Criminal Justice Developments in Non-Western Countries." *Social Justice* 28:88-104.

Umbreit, M.S. (1995). "Holding Juvenile Offenders Accountable: A Restorative Justice Perspective." *Juvenile and Family Court Journal* Spring:31-42.

—— and R.B. Coates (1999). "Multicultural Implications of Restorative Juvenile Justice." *Federal Probation* 63:44-51.

—— R.B. Coates and B. Kalanj (1994). *Victim Meets Offender: The Impact of Restorative Justice and Mediation.* Monsey, NY: Criminal Justice Press.

Vides, M. (1995). "Suffering: An Interfaith Conversation." *Center for Women & Religion Newsletter* April, 1995.

Vyas, Y. (1995). "Alternatives to Imprisonment in Kenya." *Criminal Law Forum* 6:73-102.

Warfield-Coppock, N. (1995). "Toward a Theory of Afrocentric Organizations." *Journal of Black Psychology* 21:30-48.

—— (1992). "The Rites of Passage Movement: A Resurgence of African-centered Practices for Socializing African American Youth." *Journal of Negro Education* 61:471-482.

Weitzer, R. (1996). "Racial Discrimination in the Criminal Justice System: Findings and Problems in the Literature." *Journal of Criminal Justice* 24:309-322.

Wilkinson, J.H., III (1995). "Race and Remedy in a Multicultural Society: The Law of Civil Rights and the Dangers of Separatism in Multicultural America." *Stanford Law Review* 47:993-1026.

Wilson, W.J. (1978). *The Declining Significance of Race: Blacks and Changing American Institutions.* Chicago, IL: University of Chicago Press.

Yazzie, R. (1997). "Aboriginal Systems of Restoration for Victims: Implications for Conventional Systems of Justice." Paper presented at the International Conference of Justice without Violence: Views from Peacemaking Criminology and Restorative Justice, Albany, New York.

Zehr, H. (1990). *Changing Lenses: A New Focus for Crime and Justice.* Scottdale, PA: Herald Press.

Chapter 26.
How Do Culture, Class And Gender Affect The Practice Of Restorative Justice? (Part 2)

by
Barbara E. Raye

PERSPECTIVE

I have used a power analysis in my work since reading *The Ugly American* (Lederer and Burdick, 1998) and its application to what in the mid-60s was a raging battle between the United States and Canada over U.S. involvement in the Canadian economy. But there was also the prohibition of women as "altar boys" in my then-church and my replacement on our speech team because "girls can't win national competitions." And the first woman to be allowed in the racing "pits" at the Indianapolis 500. And the first woman to be allowed to run the Boston marathon, the first woman on the U.S. supreme court, the first woman rabbi and Episcopal priest, and the first woman vice-presidential nominee on a major party ticket. All of which have happened in my lifetime. We still are seeing and hearing about the first woman something or other. And we still are seeing and hearing about the first "Black" or first "American Indian," or first "Hispanic" as modifiers for individual achievements.

As a girl in a family who raised its own chickens for food, felt the stares of others while buying groceries with food stamps, and knew the impossibility of college, travel, or buying things "new" rather than "second hand," I can also express the experience of class. The experience of poverty stays with you — regardless of any subsequent education or wealth. Knowing deep down that you are in a place no one in your family has ever gone before keeps you a little off guard. It also keeps you vigilant to the slights in respect that occur when determinations of worth, knowledge, or skill are based on the superficial issues of clothing, vocabulary, or style.

In our criminal justice system, people of color — especially African Americans and Native Americans — are systematically and universally disproportionately arrested, charged, convicted, and incarcerated. Discrimination by race in the United States criminal justice system is rampant and appears at every point of measurement. Yet the number of persons of color in our field of practice, leading our organizations, or receiving services from us is dismally under-representative.

Restorative justice isn't a new concept *"discovered"* by religious, peace-driven, middle class and educated white men of the early 1960s. We are grateful to them and we respect, honor and benefit from their work, life learning and teaching. But we cannot give them credit for starting or discovering the processes, values, and beliefs of restorative justice. They have, however, newly named them, and we have repeated and assimilated their language into our own. It is a good language in that the words have meaning, value, and truth. I am proud to use it and to claim myself as a part of the restorative justice movement.

However, the processes of circles with talking pieces and the belief in interconnection and power balance/harmony within relationships and with the earth are deeply indigenous and feminine. Mothers have known — deeply and perpetually — about the need to handle conflict within relationships in a respectful, balanced, face-saving, listening way. Native American and African peoples have built on indigenous and tribal practices to find nonviolent ways to address horrendous harm. Harm comes to them from the outside as a result of United States domination as well as from historical tribal traditions and internalized oppression. Women have needed to understand how to stay in relationship — even with their oppressors — to make sense of and to live in a Western culture built on and sustained by systematic subjection and discrimination based on gender.

EXPERIENCE

In 2000, I was invited by restorative justice leaders to a *new* training on "circle process." I found that I knew the process well from the women's movement almost 30 years earlier and one I have used in my family, teaching, and community work since that time. It was a feminist process then — based on deep listening and respect for each individual's experience and perspective. The process used the ritual of talking pieces of symbolic and emotional importance and focused conversations to guide knowledge and personal action through values of empowerment, healing, and re-connection. I now hear the voices of Native-American representatives on the board of a restorative justice organization asking how we are demonstrating respect for their community when we want to bring an outside person to conduct "circle training." We are using a process that is theirs to claim, to offer, and to welcome.

In order to approach restorative justice with authenticity and integrity, the principles that we use with clients must be visibly and actively practiced in our living and work with others in the field. So, how can we explain the absence of Native-American practitioners of restorative justice processes? How can we explain the absence of indigenous and African-American practitioners? How can we explain the absence of women's names as founders, leaders, and "experts" in processes that have been theirs for generations? How can we explain the increasing professionalization of a field despite its claims to be bringing justice back to a locus of power in the community?

The biases of gender, race, and class affect us as a sub-culture within the larger Western worldview. We are all products of our environment and come to any place as a result of our predispositions and experiences. These experiences are all we have and all we can have. Therefore it is not surprising that we find the results of gender, race, and class bias in our own organizations and practices.

Three specific areas need our attention: (a) selection and recruitment of facilitators, (b) the referral of cases, and (c) practitioners' understanding of offending, victimization, responsibility, shame, and trauma to ensure effective social change.

Selection And Recruitment Of Facilitators

When we hire trainers and mediation process facilitators we look for communication skills (use of language/words), "presence," education/training, appropriate attitudes (expressed in ways that reflect our values), some knowledge about boundaries, professionalism (in a good way), self-care under stress, and willingness to work as a volunteer (or entry level person) in our organizations. We then seek good background references and something we call "fit" with what we think our clients need or prefer.

Every one of these criteria can be defended. I am not suggesting that we are motivated to be biased. I am suggesting, however, that every criterion listed above can be used to exclude people as well as to include them. They hold bias. Differences in the selection of words, connotative meanings, accents, cultural traditions, experiences, worldviews, and histories get screened out. Our desire for organization "success" overrides the desire to take the risk of inclusion. The compelling question is why we experience inclusion as risk? Why do we fear it?

The result is organizations that look generally alike inside, that work with clients that look like them, and that hire trainers and facilitators who are similar to them. This often excludes those who might be most able to teach us and enrich our work and practice. The occasional person of genuine diversity often feels isolated, tokenized, and powerless. S/he often lives a "closeted" or dual (bi-cultural) life. We lose those who might best be able to build the relationships with the clients who have been least served, had the least access, and often experienced the greatest degree of harm.

Referral Of Cases

When making any type of referral, each of us wants to refer people to a place (or person) we know and have confidence will produce the desired results *and not subvert our own positions or interests.* Often restorative justice "cases" are referred to us by court services, police officers, probation officers, or prosecutors. Just as in recruitment, the referral system has built-in bias. Referrals are made to people with whom we've already built relationships through, generally, a shared language, education, and social and professional structures. The referral system is exclusive and narrow when we rely only on those with whom we already have relationships.

Courts will not refer to programs that fail to respect the authority and boundaries of the courts. Lawyers don't refer to people they see as competitors. They refer only to those who demonstrate respect for the role and authority of lawyers and willingly supplement cases of mutual interest (or are willing to do the work they, as attorneys, don't really want or can't effectively do anyway).

This is the heart of gender, class, culture, and race bias within our referral networks. Poor people don't go to lawyers to get referrals. African Americans don't seek referrals from the criminal justice system. And women don't usually first ask legal or "system" professionals for referrals for services. Non-English speaking people, legal or illegal immigrants, and refugees don't first seek help from the very system of which they try to stay clear on a daily basis. The access points, communication styles, cultural values, bias and experiences of these groups require them to use different entry points than those we provide.

But imagine where referrals would come from if these same people were practitioners? Referrals would come from the people and through word of mouth. We would have no oxymoron of "mandated mediation." We could change the system we have strived to change. We could indeed change the locus of power — the "place" where restorative justice is practiced. Restorative justice could then become the dominant cultural value, practiced in community-by-community and for community. It is only by taking the risk of moving beyond our biases and existing relationships that we can fulfill our own vision.

Practitioners' Understanding Of Offending, Victimization, Responsibility, Shame, And Trauma

Experience alone does not teach us wisdom nor instill in us the compassion and deep understanding that is part of transformative/relational justice. There are too many examples to the contrary where the experience of oppression breeds oppression rather than understanding and advocacy for others. Many peace-loving and -living, and respectful people hold the values and skills to guide restorative justice processes.

One does not have to be female to provide services to women — and thank goodness that today's women can receive quality services while we continue to overcome past experiences with discrimination. The contribution of social sciences in studying and understanding the dynamics of victimization and trauma has informed and enriched our practice without measure. Neither do I think one needs to have committed murder to understand the rage ignited by the experience of disrespect that often precedes violent action.

I believe that every one of us can "touch" the experience of the other by calling upon our own experiences and extrapolating from them. This ability is essential for everyone in our work. Battered women who stayed in their relationships fearing for their lives could touch the experience of war draftees who stayed fearing for their lives. Both saw no honorable or value-acceptable way to leave. Feeling they had no other options, both paid dearly (physically, emotionally, psychologically) for the choices they made.

But "touching" is not living or knowing. We cannot understand the experience of others without asking them and being open to truth different from our own. And one does need to have an emotional as well as intellectual understanding of an experience for her or him to believably say "I know." How can systems change and new values and processes become inculcated without such understanding and *"knowing?"*

My early work in domestic violence and child abuse situations reinforced that we needed to *"know"* that — save for circumstances — we could and would act in the same ways as both the offender and the victim. Without this "knowing" we could not build a relationship on acceptance and dignity of each individual human being. We too quickly made referrals to family services and established "recidivism" rates for victims using shelters. We got trapped in cycles of either blaming the victim or rhetoric of "learned helplessness," both of which were violations of our values and harmful to those we served.

In the early anti-violence and anti-racism movement, many attempted to use guilt and the obligation of privilege to create male and/or white groups to take on the work. We insisted that the dominant and privileged must work to undo the systems of oppression that they created and from which they benefited. But in hindsight we have to ask: How can male only groups address the issues of woman battering? How can white-only groups address the issues of racism? How can the wealthy really make substantive and sustainable changes that address the issues of class? Isn't it these groups of people who, without our equal partnership, have created our current situation?

I assume that the people who built our social services and criminal justice systems had the good of the community at heart. They did their best. But by continuing an exclusive process we cannot conceivably think we have the insight, wisdom, experience, and *"knowing"* to create something new or to recognize when our creation wasn't new at all! This is the most important part. *Without the voice of experience, we cannot know if the change we've proposed will make a difference in how people experience their lives.*

Personal experiences of class, gender bias, culture, and race might inform us and cut short the barriers to understanding. Shared experiences provide some common language and emotion and requires less "undoing" of previously held thoughts in order to reach genuine understanding and connection. Those who experience the issues of class, racism, and gender bias should be getting bonus points on their applications rather than being conspicuously absent or invisible. They (we) are essential in our policy, governance, activism, public awareness, and programmatic leadership.

Our work and movement cannot become whole without *BEING* whole. We cannot build relationships without *BEING* in relationship. Effective recruitment, retention, training and education, referral processes and sources, and quality practice require the *"knowing"* that comes from experience in order to be genuinely inclusive. Without this inclusion we cannot fully address the issues and meet the needs of those affected by them.

MOVING FORWARD

How do we address the issues of gender, class, culture, and race bias in our own field? How might we address and honor those whose experience and wisdom have informed us and our current understandings yet remain silent voices and invisible faces in our memory and written history? How might we ensure access to the processes most known to the people most harmed by our retributive and militaristic system of justice?

We have learned that the reclaiming of root values and early cultural practices are paths to healing for many offenders of color, for therapeutic processes, and for peaceful maturing and change in our relationships. We must now reclaim them in our work, our practice, and our policies.

It is the feminine, Native American and African elements of our current leaders' souls and their unity with all of us that are being expressed in their restorative justice work. They are committed to international and inter-racial work. They are attempting to live in harmony and equality with their female partners, colleagues and children and to influence their own organizational systems. In doing so, they are expressing their femininity, Blackness, and Color. We should celebrate them and honor the spirit that is showing up within them.

However, we must not allow them to speak for us. We must not negate our own knowledge, experience or wisdom — which perhaps predates their own. We must not diminish the language we used in the past as we embrace today's language of restorative justice. We must not assume nor project greater wisdom or insight on our leaders than we each hold deep in our own memories. Women must speak their truth and use their power while welcoming male colleagues to their femininity. People of color must claim what they know from earlier experiences — from their cellular memory — while welcoming and celebrating the "color" that is emerging from white colleagues in the field.

Two recent conversations reinforce this command for me. One was with Stephanie Autumn,[1] who is working with Native American communities and reservations in Minnesota. She notes that people of color have been excluded from program funding and organizational structures of leadership and power. This exclusion isn't because they do not use, need, or want "restorative justice" programs and services. Rather they did not know that what they held deep in their hearts and practiced in their systems was called such a thing. She asked, "How would we even know that these words applied to what we do and have done for generations?"

A second conversation with Repa Meka,[2] executive director of a Minneapolis-based program for urban African-American youth occurred after a presentation on chaos and complex adaptive systems theory and how it might apply to working with youth. After listening to the Anglo expert, Meka quietly said: "That's it? We as people of the earth, as people of oppression, have known and lived this knowledge forever." Dee Hock, former international executive of VISA, acknowledges Repa's wisdom in the beginning of his book *Birth of the Chaordic Age* (2000), when he pokes fun at the scientific "discovery" of complexity/chaos theory.

We, too, need to use care when claiming the "discovery" of restorative justice. As people of the earth who need to understand power and oppression in order to survive, who simultaneously experience love for and subjugation by their intimate partners, and who are connected out of a spiritual sense of power to all life have known and lived restorative justice for quite some time.

TAKING ACTION

What do we do about it?

As individuals we must:

(1) Acknowledge that our systems of justice and our practice/profession of restorative justice both have biases of class and discriminate against the equality of women and persons of color.

(2) Seek and implement processes of inclusion and balance in our families, organizations, profession, and communities.

(3) Use our power to include lay community persons, women and persons of color on our boards, staff and training teams and as speakers, teachers and service outreach consultants. And also as directors, managers, and leaders with power.

(4) Refrain from requiring a single path for certification into the field or practice. What we know and value is also already known and valued by others who we have not yet taught or trained — and when we meet them, we need to welcome them.

(5) Assume that we have much to learn from those who do not speak our language and that they may have learned what we know through different means than we have taken.

(6) Celebrate the feminine and the color in all of us — that essence of spirit and connection that comes forth in the values and practice of restorative justice.

(7) Listen — listen — listen to the voice of victims of violence and oppression when they say we must change our words,

practice, or understanding and include them and what they know.

(8) Invite lay community members, women, and people of color to write their stories. And then those of us who are lay community members, women and people of color need to accept the invitation and claim what we know.

(9) Resist the temptation of competition or separation between us — join, rejoice in the voice of peace from wherever it comes!

(10) Share what we know. Some of us know how to maneuver and change the systems of this country and how to use both skill and privilege to make a difference. Others know the content to replace the current system or make it more equitable, more effective, and produce more peaceful results. We are mutually obligated to share that knowledge with others.

(11) Be open and accessible for dialogue and learning. Take the risk to speak, to be bold, and to be wrong. Then invite restorative dialogue from others and stay in relationship with them as we learn together.

As a movement we must:

(1) Reclaim and distribute the voices and wisdom of those who came before us — who have informed us but remain silent or invisible.

(2) Engage in dialogue around the issues of class, race and gender to set an international agenda for correction.

(3) Wage change — insist on services that have no disparity of access, participation, or results. And insist that processes are adapted to the cultural context of those we serve.

(4) Set affirmative action goals — and meet them. Seek opportunities to make affirmative choices for inclusion.

(5) Create co-learning programs of exchange system-wide — worldwide.

(6) Apply principles and practices of restorative dialogue in our organizations and communities — long before there is a victim or offender.

(7) Launch and study experimental programs that have the potential to transform our laws, justice system practices, and current public attitudes.

(8) Show up everywhere poor, colorful and feminine — whether we are white, male or somewhere emerging in between.

I wish us all the wisdom and the power to become who we already are — and to be in joyous relationship and creation with each other.

Address correspondence to: Barbara E. Raye, Center for Policy, Planning, and Performance, Victim Offender Mediation Association, 5004 Cedar Avenue South, Minneapolis, MN 55417. Fax: 612-874-0253. E-mail: <braye@effective.org>.

REFERENCES AND SUGGESTED READING

Adams, M., R. Castaneda and X. Zuniga (eds.), (2000). *Readings for Diversity and Social Justice: An Anthology on Racism, Sexism, Classism, Anti-Semitism, Heterosexism, and Ableism.* New York: RoutledgeFalmer.

Fadiman, A. (1998). *The Spirit Catches You and You Fall Down: A Hmong Child, Her American Doctors, and the Collision of Two Cultures.* New York: Farrar, Straus, and Giroux.

Hock, D.W. (2000). *Birth of the Chaordic Age.* San Francisco, CA: Berrett-Koehler Publishers, Inc.

Lederer, W. and E. Burdick (1998). *The Ugly American.* New York: W.W. Norton.

Macro International Inc. (1997). "Study of Race, Class, and Ethnicity." Final report submitted to Corporation for National Service, Office of Evaluation, Department of Evaluation and Effective Practices.

Menchu, R. and E. Burgos-Debray (ed.), (1987). *I, Rigoberta Menchu: An Indian Woman in Guatemala.* New York: Verso.

Rothenberg, P.S. (2000). *Invisible Privilege: A Memoir About Race, Class, and Gender.* Lawrence, KS: University Press of Kansas.

Thomas, R.R. (1992). *Beyond Race and Gender: Unleashing the Power of Your Total Work Force by Managing Diversity.* New York: AMACOM.

NOTES (and resource persons)

1. Stephanie Autumn, Minnesota Restorative Justice Campaign, Legal Rights Center, 1611 Park Avenue South, Minneapolis, MN 55404.

2. Repa Meka, Freeport West, 2219 Oakland Avenue, Minneapolis, MN.

PART V.
INDIGENOUS AND RELIGIOUS TRADITIONS

A feather is passed from person to person, giving each speaker an opportunity to tell of their story. A prayer is raised, requesting healing for both victim and offender.

Some readers may be intimately familiar with these practices, finding them grounded in their traditions. They may in fact use these practices daily as part of their expression of their culture and identity. Others, however, may find such rituals foreign, yet rich with meaning. They may embrace and incorporate them into their lives as expressions of their identity. Still others may experience such rituals negatively. They may have rejected such traditions or feel that others are inappropriately borrowing them.

Restorative justice as a field has often claimed links to various indigenous and religious traditions. Certainly, there is evidence that the field as a whole has been influenced by such approaches. Many non-indigenous communities are today using some forms of peacemaking circles that entered the field from Canadian First Nation people. Talking pieces are regular features in many practitioners' processes. Similarly, some practitioners use spiritual or religious language to reflect on their motivation for their work and to describe participants' experience in restorative processes. Many programs seek partnerships with faith-based organizations.

While there is some obvious validity to claims of religious and indigenous roots and influences, the reality and integrity of such claims is by no means uncontested. Nor is the understanding and application of these traditions and practices a simple matter. More is involved than a specific set of practices or instructions. Indigenous and religious approaches are contextual, grounded in specific worldviews, cultures, histories and belief systems. Removing these approaches from their context may carry risks — for example, co-optation, romanticism, colonization — that are detrimental to those who own these traditions, to those who practice them outside of these traditions and, ultimately to those who experience them as participants.

The authors in this section represent both caution and hope regarding the use of these traditions. Chris Cunneen argues that restorative justice and its practitioners have not adequately understood the historical context of indigenous peoples, and suggests that therefore practice has a colonizing effect. Matt Hakiaha, reflecting on the New Zealand experience, argues that while New Zealand's approach was inspired by Maori tradition and concerns, there are significant problems in the state's adaptation of the indigenous practices in its legislation. Mike Batley explores spirituality, especially the Christian tradition, and its expression in restorative justice, suggesting a natural link between the two.

As indigenous and religious approaches are increasingly claimed and even incorporated into restorative justice theory and practice, we are challenged to engage in clear dialogue about the links. This dialogue will not be easy for there is much to discuss and core beliefs are often involved. For example, we might consider such questions:

- To what extent can those of us from other backgrounds truly understand the context and meaning of indigenous and world religious traditions and their practices?

- What are the perceptions and concerns of indigenous/religious peoples about restorative justice? Are we prepared to really listen to them and take them seriously?

- To what extent is it fair to characterize and claim religious and indigenous roots for restorative justice?

- What are the possibilities and dangers — to indigenous/religious peoples, practitioners, and stakeholders — in claiming these roots?

- When indigenous/religious approaches have been adapted, to what extent have practices remained true to those traditions? To what extent has this led to co-optation and neo-colonization?

- Is restorative justice, as some have claimed, an inherently spiritual process? If so, how should it respond to various and often conflicting religious traditions? What is an appropriate role for the secular state?

These are contentious issues, requiring many things from each of us: humility; an openness to the historical experiences, present realities and future dreams of other groups; a willingness to learn from other people and to let go our need for control; and an awareness of personal, perhaps unacknowledged, biases. Once again, such dialogue can benefit from each of us, individually, reflecting on our motivations for exploring or practicing restorative justice. This may include naming the values by which we live, our beliefs about people and relationships, our assumptions about the world and even about the manner in which we learn. We may find in such reflection that some of our traditions or belief systems are consistent with restorative justice – but also that some are not. Careful reflection and dialogue may increase our understanding of our practice and enhance relationships with our indigenous and faith-based allies. The following chapters, hopefully, will encourage such reflection and dialogue.

Chapter 27.
What Are The Implications Of Restorative Justice's Use Of Indigenous Traditions?

by

Chris Cunneen

Restorative justice is often seen as drawing on the justice processes of indigenous peoples, particularly in Australia, New Zealand and North America. Indeed restorative justice often lays claim to an indigenous "authenticity" as part of its search for its roots; Daly has termed this claim as a "myth of origin" (Daly, 2000). This claim of authenticity is said to separate restorative justice from current Western justice processes that are based on retribution, deterrence and rehabilitation. Based on local traditions, restorative justice programs have also been developed in Africa for both the more mundane law and order offences, as well as attempts to deal with crimes against humanity and genocide (Roche, 2003; Drumbl, 2003).

Often the claims which link restorative justice practices to indigenous peoples are trivializing and patronizing. They deny the complex effects of colonial policies which have, at various times, sought to exterminate, assimilate, "civilize," and Christianize Aboriginal peoples. This colonization has occurred through warfare, the establishment of reservations, the denial of basic citizenship rights, the forced removal of children and forced education in residential schools, the banning of cultural and spiritual practices, and the imposition of an alien criminal justice system. They also deny the complexity and variations in indigenous dispute resolution processes (Zellerer and Cunneen, 2001:246-247).

There is an unspoken assumption that indigenous people in the settler colonies of Australia, New Zealand and North America represent all indigenous people. Yet, according to the United Nations High Commission on Human Rights (2003), there are an estimated 300 million indigenous people in more than 70 countries worldwide. In other words, broad generalizations about the inherent nature of indigenous societies or cultures are bound to trivialize complexity. Why should we expect commonality between distinct indigenous societies from Africa and the Middle East, across South, Southeast and East Asia to the Pacific, South America, North America and the Arctic circle?

Indigenous peoples in the settler colonies of Australia, New Zealand and North America have been highly critical of the current criminal justice system and the colonizing impact it has on indigenous communities (Cunneen, 2001; Havemann, 1999). However, we cannot assume that the vision of justice is the same for restorative justice advocates and indigenous peoples. Much of the discussion that follows relates to the problems associated with state-sponsored restorative justice programs. However, community-based restorative justice programs may be faced with similar problems if they fail to acknowledge the specific historical and cultural experiences of indigenous peoples.

There is rarely any discussion of the similarities and differences between restorative and indigenous justice. The assumption is that they are one and the same, falling under the umbrella of restorative justice (Zellerer and Cunneen, 2001:248). Often a brief reference is made to the fact that some restorative initiatives, such as family group conferencing in New Zealand and circle sentencing in Canada, were derived from indigenous practices of resolving conflict. Little critical discussion about the nature of the relationship between the process itself and indigenous political aspirations for self-determination typically follows such observations.

Indigenous Human Rights

Despite their cultural differences, indigenous peoples do share common problems related to the protection of their rights as distinct peoples. They have sought recognition of their identities, their ways of life and their right to traditional lands and resources (United Nations High Commission on Human Rights, 2003).

The best starting point for understanding the relationships between human rights and restorative justice is in the United Nations Draft *Declaration on the Rights of Indigenous Peoples*. This Declaration contains a number of basic principles, including self-determination, which directly impact how restorative justice programs might develop respectful of Indigenous rights.

The draft Declaration affirms "the right of Indigenous people to control matters affecting them." Article 3 describes the right of self-determination as involving the free choice of political status and the freedom to pursue economic, social and cultural development. Article 4 provides that "Indigenous peoples have the right to maintain and strengthen their distinct political, economic, social and cultural characteristics, *as well as their legal systems*" (emphasis added). Article 31 sets out the extent of governing powers of Indigenous peoples, which include the right to autonomy, or self-government in matters relating to their internal and local affairs. Taken together, it is clear that the Declaration provides the basis for Indigenous people to maintain cultural integrity and exercise jurisdiction over various justice matters, if they so choose.

A central problem in the way restorative justice programs have developed has been that Indigenous rights have been ignored, in particular the right to self-determination.

Restorative justice programs *may* fit with indigenous claims to greater autonomy and control over the exercise of justice systems. However, indigenous human rights should be seen as integral principles to the development of restorative justice programs. This is in contrast to development practices based on an assumption that restorative justice is somehow fundamentally more suitable to indigenous peoples than other forms of justice.

Restorative Justice And Indigenous Peoples In A Global Context

Much restorative justice talk presents *itself as* an alternative approach to justice; as something outside the justice paradigms of retribution, deterrence and rehabilitation. Proponents paint restorative justice as the list of "good" things, different from these other forms of justice (Daly, 2000). Yet, restorative justice has been as much a globalising force as traditional Western processes. The potential to overrun traditional indigenous customs and laws is as real with restorative justice as it is with the retributive or rehabilitative models. There is a need to understand the historical context in which restorative justice is being promoted and introduced. For indigenous peoples, that historical context has been shaped through colonial expansion and the development of nation states.

The State, Policing And Punishment

Some of the core critiques of restorative justice revolve around its relationship with the state. There is a concern that restorative justice advocates embody both a naivete about the nature of politics and a positive and hopeful view of state power. This issue is particularly important to indigenous people because the development of the nation state has been at the expense of indigenous claims to land, resources and autonomy.

Thus, there is a need to understand the nature of the relationships between colonised peoples and the state. There often is an assumption in restorative justice that this relationship is not problematic as the state is seen as representative and legitimate. There is little recognition that a restorative program initiated and controlled by the state may be viewed with suspicion by indigenous peoples. There is no reason to believe that a state-sponsored restorative justice program will necessarily be seen as legitimate. It may be viewed as an imposed form of control which undermines existing indigenous practices of governance.

In this context it is worth remembering that restorative justice programs have often been state-controlled and introduced without consultation with indigenous organizations. While the creation of restorative programs through law and centralized operations may be seen as an achievement by proponents, it may create specific problems for marginalized indigenous communities who seek to maintain and develop their own justice initiatives.

A major issue stemming from the relationship between restorative justice and the state has been the question of the role of police in restorative justice processes, as well as the broader issue of criminalization. In many jurisdictions, the police exercise significant discretionary powers over restorative justice programs. Police determine who will participate in conferencing programs, and play a key role in the facilitation of the conferencing process and the agreement that is reached.

Indigenous, racial and ethnic minorities may have good reason to be skeptical that police can be independent arbiters in a restorative justice process. When police use discretionary powers, there is the danger that minority youth will receive adverse or more punitive decisions or be classified as "unsuitable" for restorative justice. There is indeed some evidence in Australia that this discrimination is occurring. Aboriginal young people are less likely than non-Aboriginal youth to be referred by police to youth conferences and are more likely to be referred to court (Cunneen, 2001:132-143).

We also need to think about where restorative justice fits within the overall patterns of punishment used by the criminal justice system. O'Malley (1999) has discussed the development of a "bewildering array" of penal policies based on discipline, punishment, enterprise, incapacitation, restitution and reintegration — policies that appear mutually incoherent and contradictory. In this sense, restorative justice may be part of a complex set of sanctions. How those sanctions are decided upon and applied becomes critical. Current trends in penal policy reflect a movement towards the prediction of risk: the development of "techniques for identifying, classifying and managing groups assorted by dangerousness" (Feeley and Simon, 1994:173).

The emphasis on actuarialism, i.e., the prediction of risk, and policies of incapacitation are not contradictory with the way restorative justice practices have developed. Rather both practices can be seen as complementary strategies placed within single systems of justice. Indeed risk assessment becomes a tactic for separating those who benefit from restorative justice practices from those who are channeled into more punitive and incapacitating processes, such as "three strikes" and mandatory imprisonment. Predicting risk becomes critically important for indigenous and other minorities and determines whether they are going to receive any benefit from restorative justice programs. As noted above, the evidence already indicates that indigenous youth are selected out of the opportunity for restorative justice programs and channeled into more traditionally punitive approaches.

Colonialism And Community

A concept at the core of restorative justice has been "community." Yet "community" is neither a natural set of relations between individuals nor a natural social process providing the foundation for all society. Communities are always constructed on the broad terrain of history and politics.

Colonial policies were directly responsible for constructing community in the interests of the colonizers. For example, many indigenous communities have formed directly as a result of policies of the forced relocation of tribal groups. Distinct rural and remote indigenous communities, as well as minority communities *within* first world cities, have been created under these conditions. History and current politics have shaped the position of indigenous and other minority communities in relation to the dominant society. What then does "community" mean in these situations and how does it impact on relations with the police, the criminal justice system and the state more generally? Importantly, where does restorative justice fit within these relations and processes?

Cultural Difference And The Aboriginal Domain

Despite the impact of colonialism, indigenous people have maintained distinct cultures. For example, the concept of the "Aboriginal domain" refers to the social, political and cultural space of Aboriginal people — a space that maintains the dominant social and cultural life and the language of indigenous people. The "Aboriginal domain" provides a point of resistance to colonizing processes and insulates minority cultural, social and political space from being overtaken. This is where indigenous knowledge, culture and governance reside (Cunneen, 2002).

Restorative justice assumptions often show a lack of understanding of indigenous governance and lack of recognition of cultural difference between indigenous people and the dominant society. There is an assumption that indigenous and restorative justice processes for resolving conflicts are one and the same. This is not necessarily the case. There are processes and sanctions that a restorative model uses that may seem culturally inappropriate to indigenous peoples. Many restorative approaches focus on bringing the parties together to confront and resolve the problem through the use of a neutral mediator. There are a variety of sanctions used by Indigenous peoples that include temporary or permanent exile, withdrawal and separation within the community, and restitution by kin. Many of the sanctions are based on avoidance rather than confrontation between offender and victim. Conversely, there may be aspects of indigenous justice that are seen as inappropriate to a restorative model. Restorative justice has had a tendency to romanticize indigenous dispute resolution and avoid mention of the use of physical sanctions or processes that involve social avoidance or banishment (Zellerer and Cunneen, 2001:250).

Subjectivity And Identity

How do people experience the restorative justice process? Subjectivity and identity go to the heart of restorative justice. Indigenous people, like all people, will subjectively experience the restorative justice process through the lens of their culture. Yet there are often assumptions made that all individuals will experience the restorative justice process in a certain way irrespective of their gender, class, race, ethnicity, or age. Restorative justice has tended to limit subjectivity to simplified notions of "offenders" or "victims," with little attention to the profound difficulties that underpin these labels.

"Victim" and "offender" are often understood as uncomplicated and homogenous categories of self. The assumption is that we all subjectively experience these categories in identical or, at least, similar ways without any inherent complexity. Can we assume that indigenous peoples will experience the restorative process in a similar way to non-indigenous peoples? The fact that some indigenous cultures use separation/banishment between offender and victim suggests that subjective experiences of a restorative justice model will be quite different to non-indigenous participants. There is ample evidence of the difficulties and disadvantages indigenous people face in the formal legal process (Cunneen, 1997). These difficulties partly derive from cultural and communicative (verbal and non-verbal) differences. These same difficulties may also be experienced in restorative programs, particularly where the dominant players in the process are traditional figures of non-Indigenous authority (such as police, welfare, juvenile justice, etc).

Indigenous Women

The complexity of the relationship between women and restorative justice has been well identified (Stubbs, 2002). A particular focus has been whether restorative justice can respond adequately to crimes of violence against women as well as other instances of gendered power imbalances. Indeed, the basic premise of restorative justice, that the harm between victim and offender is to be repaired, must be questioned as an outcome sought by women seeking intervention, support and protection against violence (Stubbs, 2002:51).

It is also fundamental to recognize the diversity of women's experiences that vary based on such lines as class, indigeneity and race/ethnicity. For example, it is important to remember that colonial processes were profoundly gendered in their design and have resulted in "deep colonizing" effects (Rose, 1996). One result of this process has been the valuing of men's knowledge over women's knowledge. Western legal traditions continue to impact gender relations in indigenous societies by treating men's knowledge as universal and women's knowledge as particular and sectional. These traditions often exclude or denigrate women's knowledge because it is defined as "partial."

It is important for restorative justice advocates to recognize that the long-term consequences of these gendered processes have not been well understood and that there is little understanding of the complex way gendered patterns of knowledge and culture have shifted due to colonization. We do know that there is often inadequate attention paid to the voices of indigenous women (Zellerer and Cunneen, 2001). Gender interests impact on the ability of indigenous women to develop and use restorative justice programs. There is no inherent reason to believe that restorative justice practices will reinstate the voices of indigenous women.

OUTCOMES AND POSSIBILITIES

Restorative justice provides us with an opportunity. It is important to explore the *possibilities* of restorative justice, and to rethink key concepts in the light of the colonial experience. Given the massive over-representation of indigenous and racial minorities in the criminal justice system, such a task is both a moral and political imperative.

Specifically in relation to indigenous peoples, such a rethinking is necessary to respond to the demands of "differential citizenship" (Havemann, 1999:472). This represents a new notion of citizenship based on collective rights for peoples, grounded in self-determination, as well as the traditional individual rights based on freedom from arbitrary state intervention and freedom from racial discrimination.

It was noted previously that a potential result of the introduction of restorative justice is the greater division in existing criminal justice system responses. There is substantial evidence in Australia that indigenous young people are discriminated against by police in their decisions to use diversionary options. The Australian example suggests that the entrenchment of unequal treatment and racism in the criminal justice system may be exacerbated by restorative justice programs (Cunneen, 2001:132-143).

Related to this issue is whether the difficulties and disadvantages particular groups face in the formal legal process are resolved by the restorative justice process. Will the racism, sexism and biases of the criminal justice system be removed, modified or left untouched by restorative justice? Indeed, will greater separation between justice options serve to compound existing oppressions?

We also need to ask whether the vision for reform is the same between restorative justice proponents and indigenous people. For example, to what extent are indigenous interests in promoting self-determination consistent with restorative justice aims? The compatibility of these interests is not always self-evident. Perhaps part of the problem is the lack of clear definitions or theories of justice underpinning much of the restorative justice literature, and the lack of a clear linkage with the emancipatory aims of oppressed groups. What is required of restorative justice practitioners is a commitment to building links with indigenous peoples and their organizations. Restorative justice programs need to develop and maintain organic ties with Indigenous peoples that are respectful of cultural difference and differing political aspirations. It is particularly important to avoid easy assumptions that indigenous people will participate in, and benefit from, restorative justice programs which have been designed as a generic policy for all offenders and victims.

Address correspondence to: Chris Cunneen, Institute of Criminology, University of Sydney Law School, 173-175 Phillip Street, Sydney, NSW 2000, Australia. Fax: 61-2-9351-0200. E-mail: <chriscu@law.usyd.ed.au>.

Chris Cunneen

REFERENCES

Cunneen, C. (2002) "Restorative Justice and the Politics of Decolonisation." In: E. Weitekamp and H.J. Kerner (eds.), *Restorative Justice: Theoretical Foundations*. Cullompton, Devon, UK: Willan Publishing.

—— (2001). *Conflict, Politics and Crime*. Sydney, AUS: Allen and Unwin.

—— (1997). "Community Conferencing and the Fiction of Indigenous Control." *Australia and New Zealand Journal of Criminology* 30(3):292-311.

Daly, K. (2000). "Restorative Justice in Diverse and Unequal Societies." *Law in Context* 17(1):167-190.

Drumbl, M. (2003). "Justice on the Grass: The Promise of *Gacaca* for Post-genocide Rwanda." Paper presented to the International Association of Genocide Scholars, Irish Human Rights Centre, NUI, Galway, 7-10 June 2003.

Feeley, M. and J. Simon (1994). "Actuarial Justice: the Emerging New Criminal Law." In: D. Nelken (ed.), *The Futures of Criminology*. London, UK: Sage.

Havemann, P. (1999). "Indigenous Peoples, the State and the Challenge Differentiated Citizenship." In: P. Havemann (ed.), *Indigenous Peoples in Australia, Canada and New Zealand*. Auckland: Oxford University Press.

O'Malley, P. (1999). "Volatile and Contradictory Punishments." *Theoretical Criminology* 3(2):175-196.

Roche, D. (2003). *Accountability in Restorative Justice*. (Clarendon Studies in Criminology.) Oxford, UK: Oxford University Press.

Rose, D.B. (1996). "Land Rights and Deep Colonising: The Erasure of Women." *Aboriginal Law Bulletin* 3(85):6-14.

Stubbs, J. (2002). "Domestic Violence and Women's Safety: Feminist Challenges to Restorative Justice." In: H. Strang and J. Braithwaite (eds.), *Restorative Justice and Family Violence*. Cambridge, UK: Cambridge University Press.

United Nations High Commission on Human Rights (2003). *Indigenous People and the United Nations System. An Overview*. (Leaflet No 1.) (http://www.unhchr.ch/html/racism/indileaflet1.doc), accessed 22 March 2003.

Zellerer, E. and C. Cunneen (2001). "Restorative Justice, Indigenous Justice and Human Rights." In: G. Bazemore and M. Schiff (eds.), *Restorative Community Justice: Repairing Harm and Transforming Communities*. Cincinnati, OH: Anderson.

Chapter 28.
What Is The State's Role In Indigenous Justice Processes?

by

Matt Hakiaha

My response to this question is based upon the history of my own people in Aotearoa/New Zealand, a history that has been documented within several important manuscripts. Briefly these manuscripts are referred to as The Declaration of Independence of New Zealand (1835), the Treaty of Waitangi (1840) and The New Zealand Constitution Act (1852). Although the treaties are specific to Aotearoa/New Zealand, the issues these raise have relevance to other people as well.

In the eighteenth century, Aotearoa/New Zealand started to experience an influx of settlers or *pakeha* (Europeans). With the increase of settlers came lawlessness and strained relationships with *Tangata whenua* (indigenous peoples) as the settlers failed to comply with any of the Native laws (*Tikanga Ture*) and as they inveigled themselves into the lifestyles of the Maori. This included dubious land sales that robbed Maori of their heritage.

In 1835, a new threat to Maori and the British appeared on the horizon, when the French were looking to trade and settle in Aotearoa/New Zealand. In response to this threat, the British crown, along with 34 northern chiefs, signed the Declaration of Independence, declaring New Zealand an independent state under British rule. The Declaration of Independence clearly mandates Maori to take control of their own affairs, both at a micro and macro level.

The Treaty of Waitangi, signed in 1840, has always been held as paramount by the *Tangata whenua*, and for some, considered the founding document for their country. The treaty promised protection of Maori customs and cultural values and the rights of Maori to possess and control that which is theirs. This included the ability of indigenous peoples to develop and establish their own community justice independently of the state.

Between 1842 and 1844, Lord Stanley suggested that certain Maori institutions be incorporated into the system (Lord Stanley, 1842b). He directed that legislation be framed in some measure to meet Maori practices, including punishment for desecrating waahi tapu (sacred places, cemeteries) (Lord Stanley, 1842a) and made provisions that, in crimes between Maori and non-Maori, interference depended on Maori request (Legislative Council, 1844). The New Zealand Constitution Act, which followed in 1852, was a liberal measure that demonstrated a willingness of legislators to allow Maori and non-Maori the ability to give effect to a parallel bicultural legal system (Joseph, 2000).

These three documents — the Declaration of Independence, the Treaty of Waitangi and the New Zealand Constitution Act — were never given the opportunity to flourish. They were violated, breached or left dormant, never realizing their full potential.

Since 1840, Maori have demonstrated their disdain for the governments' failure to comply with these documents, particularly with the provisions found within the Treaty of Waitangi. It appeared as if their cries and protests went unnoticed until, in 1975, the government decided to incorporate the Treaty of Waitangi into the New Zealand Constitution and over the following years to incorporate Maori philosophies and values into New Zealand legislation, including the Children, Young Persons and their Families Act of 1989.

However, the government and/or its respective agencies continue to establish and develop policies that impact Maori positively or adversely without consultation with them. Unless the Treaty of Waitangi in particular is honored, I predict that Maori will continue to be marginalized, aggrieved and perhaps confronted with further alienation from their land, *tikanga* (customs) and *kawa* (protocols pertinent to respective *whanau* [family], *hapu* [sub-tribe] and *iwi* [tribe]).

With this history, I believe that indigenous communities should be given the opportunity to pursue a justice system that is either independent of or parallel to the legal system.

Maori are increasingly and disproportionately represented — 62% by year 2010 — in New Zealand prisons. For years, Maori in general and their respective tribal leaders, both men and women, have cried out, *"Let*

Maori take care of their own. "This statement should be taken in its broadest sense including legislation, policy, consultation, programs, practices and appropriate and adequate resources.

In recent years there have been a number of experiments aimed at reviving aspects of traditional practice for dealing with sex offenders through "marae justice." This process involves holding judicial hearings on *marae* (Maori cultural and community centers) and in dealing with young offenders on the *marae* (Consedine and Bowen, 1999).

More recently, New Zealand laws have introduced Maori belief systems into legislation. The Children Young Persons and Their Families Act of 1989, has gained global attraction because of its innovation and, I suspect, its use and acknowledgement of indigenous imperatives. Some have termed it the first restorative justice system institutionalized within a Western legal system.

While these are signs of progress, there are risks to state involvement in designing indigenous justice. One such risk is the idea of partnership. While one of the principles contained within the Treaty of Waitangi advocates partnership, *Tangata whenua* continue to be skeptical with crown and crown agency relationships as they do not treat *Tangata whenua* as equal partners. This inequity of partnership continually plays out when the crown and its respective agencies have total control of three key characteristics which Maori believe should contribute to equity: consultation, resources and adequate timeframes

The Department for Corrections' recent *Maori Strategic Plan for the Years 2003 – 2008* (2003) lists "Building Partnerships with Maori" as one of its key themes. This conveys a readiness to develop a stronger and more meaningful relationship between themselves and *whanau, hapu* and *iwi.* However, there is cynicism among Maori regarding the theme of partnership, particularly since this very government department is in the process of building four new prisons that undoubtedly will house large numbers of Maori.

For the *Tangata Whenua,* partnership should reflect equity of the following:

(1) Resources.

(2) Adequate and reasonable consultation.

(3) Adequate and reasonable timeframes.

(4) Acknowledgement and acceptance of Maori imperatives, within all spheres of the Maori world view (*Te Ao Maori*).

(5) Acknowledgement and acceptance of *whanau, hapu* and *Iwi*.

(6) Acknowledgement and acceptance of changes within the Maori world view (*Te Ao Maori*).

Another risk in New Zealand has been the use of Maori words in legislation, such as *whanau, hapu* and *iwi*. This is evidenced in Section 4 of the Children, Young Persons and their Families Act. While these may be considered as minor inclusions, the legislation does not give a legal definition, nor should it. However, without an understanding of the meaning of these words, bureaucrats may develop policies that violate the true intention and *wairua* (spiritual matters) of the word.

There are fundamental and generic belief principles within the Maori cosmology that were practiced in the past and continue to remain. These principles include:

- *Whakapapa* - Genealogy.

- *Whanau* – Extended family.

- *Wairua* – Spiritual.

Maoris fear that the state's use and incorporation of Maori words in legislation and policies may lead to the dilution, bastardization and disenfranchisement of these revered and sacred principles. Because of their fears, Maoris may withdraw and become noncommittal about legislation. This, in turn, often results in non-Maori being critical of Maori for not accepting their assistance.

With a high number of Maori residing in the cities spread across New Zealand, a large number of them have been cut off from their communities, thus disenfranchised of cultural imperatives with loose or no ties to their *whanau, hapu* and *iwi*. Should they have the misfortune to appear in the criminal justice system, those individuals will be dealt with by professionals, often non-Maori or Maori raised in a non-Maori environment, who may actually have a more in-depth knowledge of cultural imperatives than the offender or defendant him or herself. This often leads to sense of shame and in turn contributes to low self-worth, low self-esteem and the perpetration of myths such as "I am slow and have nothing to offer," myths that were previously held by prior generations.

Donna Durie Hall in her article, *Restorative Justice: A Maori Perspective* (1999), argues that differences between Western adjudication and traditional, indigenous justice can be explained by the use of two symbols, a triangle and a circle. The triangle represents the hierarchical nature of Western law as a pyramid of power. The circle shows equality in relationships and implies that discussion within the circle promotes the respect required for decision by consensus (Consedine and Bowen, 1999).

Although Maori society clearly displays a hierarchical structure within its infrastructure — e.g., *Arikinui* (paramount chief), *ariki* (high chief), *rangatira* (chief) — this does not mean that all parties were void of horizontal "inter" and "intra" relationships. Inter- and intra-relationships were unavoidable due to genealogical links that forced a process of ongoing discussion and debate. Often these processes that included large numbers would take days if not weeks. Consequently, crown agencies often found these processes time consuming and daunting. A Maori proverb that has been held in high regard is often quoted at such processes: "*Te kai a Te Rangatira, he korero* — The food of chiefs is discussion." I suppose for Maori, while there is the circle of equality in relationships that implies consensus, nevertheless within that circle is the map of *whakapapa* (genealogical table of *Tuakana* and *Taina* — senior and junior relationships).

If we are to truly understand and practice indigenous justice, we need to understand the belief systems that are at the heart of the Maori milieu and the Maori need to be absorbed in a justice system that reflects quality and equity.

The processes of traditional, indigenous justice create a shift in the discourse from cognition or "head thinking" to affect or "heart feeling" (Consedine and Bowen, 1999). The traditional processes invite micro systems to move to macro, allowing the engagement of centrifugal processes to enact. Often these processes were time consuming and often a strain on already diminished resources. Whilst these traditional paradigms may prove time consuming and sometimes costly, outcomes nevertheless may prove effective and salient to all parties concerned.

Maori culture is fraught with emotion and action. Maori are a tactile people. A common yet respected practice amongst most if not all Maori is the *hongi*: the spiritual encounter with another person, pressing the tips of each others nose with their respective noses. Finding its origin in the creation of the first humankind, it is believed and taught that the Maori god/creator gave new life to the first human being by breathing the breath of life into their nostrils. (A similar story is found in the biblical genesis of Adam.) Hence, when Maori meet each other, they *hongi*, i.e., they may kiss as well as shake hands. Similarly, involvement within the local and or *whanau, hapu kapa haka* (dance group) is a place where each group is given the opportunity to display their points of view through dance. Topics may include their genealogy and history or current issues that affect the group such as health, education or land issues. Maori need that medium to vent and display their thoughts and feelings. Our current criminal justice system does not provide or allow the medium for Maori to vent and voice in a style that is conducive to Maori culture.

The current restorative justice system in New Zealand (for youth justice and a few pilot adult projects) does open the door for such matters, but often true expression may still be denied. With regard to macro and micro, Maori hold the view that you are not an individual on your own but that you belong to *whanau, hapu* and *iwi.* Hence when the opportunity for a *whanau* gathering is called, this may mean numbers from 10 to 50 for one family group. Because the *whanau* may be spread out geographically, time restraints, along with financial restraints, may place a burden on distant *whanau* in terms of travel, cost and numbers that could attend. This inevitably hinders the support and process, in turns affects the outcome.

Indigenous paradigms in my mind are more effective because they allow for the following:

(1) Large numbers of support people.

(2) Opportunity to vent true feelings.

(3) Reminders of their heritage, history and genealogy.

(4) Opportunity for reparation from a wider base.

(5) Opportunities to meet the victim and their *whanau.*

(6) Acknowledgement of each parties *tapu* (worthiness/sacredness).

(7) Restoration of each parties *tapu* (worthiness/sacredness).

Of course, the society we live in today bears no resemblance to the times when Maori were dominant. The social and religious structures that the Maori practiced prior to colonization were different, as were the outcomes for breaches of *tapu.* Because of this, some scholars hold the view that Maori or indigenous imperatives have no place in our society.

However, if we want to decrease our Maori prison population as a nation we need to consider first the voice and belief systems of the *Tangata whenua*. In spite of the negative effects of colonization on the indigenous people, they have had some systems that have maintained their dignity for the last 200 years. One of those belief systems is the strength of the *whanau*. If we have weak and ineffective *whanau*, then we perpetuate this pattern of weakness. However, when we have strong and effective *whanau*, we can continue to produce strong and effect *whanau*. From this comes overall social and personal health. The underpinning to all this is the fact the Maori belong to a strong and positive nation that has a wonderful heritage and history (*Whakapapa*).

The restorative justice system of New Zealand potentially allows and invites a merger between the two cultures, while at the same time giving the opportunity for other cultures to be included. It also allows the Crown to have an input, albeit from the sidelines. However, it often does not allow full scope for Maori cultural expression and needs. Because criminal justice matters affect the very fabric of both Maori society and non-Maori society, it very difficult to manage one overall system. Thus some Maori have advocated one system for Maori and another system for non-Maori.

At minimum, current frameworks and policies need to be reviewed with some urgency. Maori communities and the state need to continue to be in dialogue regarding the state's role and the betterment of Maori in the current criminal justice system. The state needs to understand that their system is failing Maori. The idea that "one size fits all" needs to be dispelled. It must be recognized that not all Maori are the same. Each *iwi* and *hapu* is unique and carries its own tribal and *hapu* DNA. The state needs to acknowledge the validity of Maori processes as cultural imperatives and give them the control of their own decision-making processes. Last but not least, the state needs to empower Maori and provide them with the appropriate resources.

In the meantime, practitioners need to be vigilant in continuing their working partnership with the *Tangata whenua*. They must remind themselves that, as a given, Maori clients should have the right to consult and work with Maori workers.

Address correspondence to: Matt Hakiaha, E-mail: <matth@iconz.co.nz>.

REFERENCES

Consedine, J. and H. Bowen (1999). *Restorative Justice: Contemporary Themes and Practice.* Lyttelton, NZ: Ploughshares Publications.

Declaration of Independence of New Zealand (1835).

Department for Corrections (2003). *Maori Strategic Plan for the Years 2003 – 2008.*

Durie Hall, D. (1999). "Restorative Justice: A Maori Perspective." (Reprinted from *LawTalk*, October 1997.) In: H. Bowen and J. Consedine (eds.), *Restorative Justice: Contemporary Themes and Practice.* Lyttelton, NZ: Ploughshares Publications.

Joseph, R. (2000). *Laws and Institutions for Aotearoa/New Zealand.* Te Matahauariki Research Institute, University of Waikato.

Legislative Council (1844) "An Ordinance to Exempt in Certain Cases Aboriginal Native Population of the Colony from the Ordinary Process and Operation of the Law." Ordinances, Session lll, No. XVIII.

Lord Stanley (1842). Colonial Office Records 209/14 at 202 (23 August).

—— (1842). Memorandum (23 August).

Ministry of Justice, Children Young Persons and Their Families Act (1989).

New Zealand Constitution Act (1852).

Treaty of Waitangi (1840).

GLOSSARY

Aotearoa: Land of the long white cloud. New Zealand.

Hapu: Sub-tribe.

Hui: Gathering of people.

Iwi: Tribe.

Kawa: Protocols.

Maori: Name used to describe the Indigenous people of New Zealand.

Marae: A complex where people gather. The complex may consist of a sleeping hall (*Whare Tipuna* – ancestral home) and dining hall (*Whare kai* – eating hall). Both of these buildings will carry an ancestral name belonging to that sub-tribe or tribe. The complex will have ablution blocks, and/or a church and/or a cemetery. It also means a piece of land situated in front of the *Whare Tipuna* – ancestral home.

Ranagatiratanga: Self-determination. Governorship.

Tangata Whenua: People of the Land – Indigenous people.

Tikanga: Customs.

Tino Ranagatiratanga: Chieftainship.

Ture: Native laws.

Waahi tapu: Sacred place. Cemetery.

Wairua: Spiritual matters.

Waitangi: Small town located in the Northern part of the North Island of New Zealand. Place where the Treaty was signed. Crying Waters.

Whanau: Extended family.

Whakapapa: Genealogy.

Chapter 29.
What Is The Appropriate Role Of Spirituality In Restorative Justice?

by

Michael Batley

In identifying this question as a critical issue, editors Howard Zehr and Barb Toews note that many people have found restorative justice processes to be spiritual experiences. This includes people who would regard themselves "religious" in the sense of believing in the Creator and practicing a specific faith, but it also includes people who would definitely place themselves outside such a category. What are we to make of this and how does it impact on our practice of restorative justice?

In attempting an answer to these questions I intend to "unpack" the terms "spiritual" and "spirituality" and then to explore the links these concepts may have with restorative justice concepts. Building on this, I will explore what this may mean in practice. I will suggest some possible pitfalls and outline some models for practice that may guide us in avoiding them.

As with many of the issues raised in this book, the subjects dealt with are substantial and easily justify more comprehensive treatment than is possible here. I also need to acknowledge that I am writing from a background of involvement in mainstream Christian tradition and, as a result, the following discussion draws mainly on this stream. I have taken this approach not because of any disrespect for other religions but simply because mainstream Christian tradition is my own frame of reference and because I am not particularly qualified to explore the topic from other perspectives. I should also like to acknowledge the influence of a number of colleagues in the process of writing this chapter — it would not have been possible without them.

"SPIRIT," "SPIRITUAL" AND "SPIRITUALITY"

In beginning to explore this terrain, the various uses of the word "spirit" listed by C.S. Lewis (1947) are useful:

- The chemical sense, for example "spirits evaporate very quickly."

- The (now obsolete) medical sense, which regarded certain fluids in the body as "the spirits." This is the origin of certain phrases we still use such as "being in high spirits."

- The opposite of "bodily" or "material." In this sense, all that is immaterial (emotions, passions, memory) is spiritual. The words "soul" and "psychological" could also be used for this sense.

- The ability and need of every human being to relate to a spiritual super-being. In this sense the word is used generically for relating to the supernatural. It needs to be distinguished from the way Christian writers use the word, for example, "to be spiritually re-born," referring to a new relationship with God.

Clearly, restorative justice processes have much to do with emotion and psychological dynamics. Indeed, the presence of emotion is regarded as one of the valuable elements of an encounter (Van Ness and Strong, 2002). However, the assumption I will make for this chapter is that "spirituality" refers to the supernatural element of the nature of human beings. I will deal only with this dimension, and not with emotional or psychological aspects.

Used this way, the term "spirituality" refers to the way we as human beings experience and relate to the supernatural (see Keating, 2000) — a further dimension of our need and ability to do this. From a specifically Christian perspective, spirituality is concerned with the "inner transformation of will, mind, and emotions into likeness to Christ's will, mind and emotions — (it is focused) on the transformation of the inward person" (Willard, n.d.:26-27). However, how this transformation happens, and how narrowly or holistically spirituality should be understood, is a matter of much debate.

Cannon (1994) suggests that there are six different ways transformation happens and spirituality manifests itself:

- Using sacred liturgy and ritual;

- Right action, focusing primarily on responding to the Gospel in conditions of injustice and suffering;

- Cultivating an attitude of devotional surrender to the grace of God;

- Becoming of a conduit of God's word and power, experiencing healing and miracles;

- Meditative contemplation — individual prayer and meditation; and,

- The prayer of faith seeking understanding and wisdom at a more rational level.

Cannon's concern is that the above approaches often tend to be viewed as mutually exclusive, resulting in a narrow understanding of spirituality. Instead, he argues, they should be seen as complementary. Similarly, de Beer (1998) stresses the need to move away from a narrow spirituality based on only one of the above approaches towards a holistic and balanced spirituality that draws on more than one of the approaches. A narrowly-focused spirituality is further characterized by a privatized view of the Gospel that separates the secular from the sacred. It also tends to spiritualize important concepts (for instance, homelessness and social injustice are not related to sin or salvation), and to individualize responsibility while ignoring the social context.

A holistic spirituality stands in contrast to these positions and is characterized by the following features: humility, a relational character, cooperation and mutuality, the sacredness of life, acceptability, inclusiveness and structures that allow for dialogue. Drawing on the work of Dorr (1998), de Beer goes on to present the well-known text from Micah 6:8 as a corrective to a narrow spirituality:

> This is what Yahweh asks of you, only this:
> > That you act justly
> > That you love tenderly
> > That you walk humbly with your God.

The concept of "acting justly," indicates that we should envisage and work for social justice, equality and *shalom* (see below) in the social-political-economic spheres of society. While the concept of "loving tenderly" refers to living in community, and "walking humbly before God" to our personal relationship with God, "a proper balance and integration of all three is the basis for a truly Christian spirituality and this is more important than ever in today's world" (p. 302). These authors suggest that we cannot fully experience God without balancing all three dimensions. While Dorr and de Beer are writing from a specifically Christian point of view, this concept would seem to be congruent with the Jewish concept of "halakhah," which seeks to apply the divine will to specific mundane circumstances and thus designates the correct way, the required action (Seltzer, 1980).

RESTORATIVE JUSTICE AND SPIRITUALITY

This brings us to one of the foundational arguments of the modern exposition of restorative justice among Christians, that justice should be rooted in a proper understanding of Biblical justice and the concept of *shalom* (Consedine, 1999; Zehr, 1990). Restoration, and making things right, rather than retribution, is identified as the keynote of Biblical justice. It has, of course, become one of the corner stones of our current understanding of restorative justice. Jim Consedine highlights the following dimensions of this:

- The concept of *shalom* refers to physical well-being, including adequate food, clothing, shelter, and wealth; a right relationship between people; and the acquisition of virtue, especially honesty and moral integrity.

- The concept of covenant, a binding agreement between parties, is the foundation of recognizing the dignity of each person within the context of their community.

- Justice is tested by its outcome, its substance rather than its procedure.

- Jesus states clearly that justice should be based on principles of forgiveness and reconciliation, that retaliation plays no part (Consedine, 1999:150-151).

This seems to relate directly to the concept of "acting justly," and suggests that we have found a clear link between what we understand restorative justice to mean and a crucial dimension of spirituality.

McDonald and Moore (2001) offer another possible link between restorative justice and spirituality in their perspectives on the critical aspects of "community conferencing." They suggest that during a conference:

- A group of people, affected by conflict, begin to understand themselves as a community with a common purpose.

- A collective experience of shame marks the transition from a focus on problems past and present to a focus on possibilities in the future.

- A point of understanding-that-runs-deeper-than-cognition is reached that involves individual and collective emotional transformation.

- Personal emotional transformation is interwoven with the interpersonal transformation of relationships.

Earlier, we saw that spirituality is concerned with "inner transformation of will, mind, and emotions...the transformation of the inward person." It is significantly apparent that both spirituality and a restorative justice process are concerned with personal and emotional transformation.

Why might this be so? When responding to a conflict or crime incident, we are dealing with a situation that touches the heart of the human condition and experience. Something has gone wrong; someone has not behaved as they should and others have been harmed in the process. What do we do with this situation? Viewed from a perpetrator's point of view, the values and principles of restorative justice — such as accepting responsibility, offering an apology, making a commitment to change behavior and make restitution — show us the way out. From the point of view of a person who has been harmed, this might include receiving these changes, growing towards healing and perhaps coming to the point of being able to offer forgiveness. In short, this process deals directly with our need for redemption and healing, both at an individual level and at a societal level. Together, these principles constitute some universal truths about justice and encourage transformation.

A modern secular mind may find it somewhat difficult to accede to the idea of "universal truth." However, C.S. Lewis (1990) has pointed out that there are many common moral values among religions that are very distant from each other. Writing in another era and from a different point of departure, Stephen R. Covey (1989) suggests that values are things that are important to us, reflecting the way we would like things to be. "Principles, on the other hand, are the way things are. They are natural laws that cannot be broken... We can only break ourselves against them" (pp. 24, 33).

The idea that restorative justice principles constitute universal truths about justice seems further born out by the fact that they are also found in indigenous justice practices. These principles include:

- We are interconnected. In South Africa we speak of the concept of *ubuntu* to refer to the "connectedness" and identity of an individual within a tribe and people group. An individual is accountable to, responsible for and interdependent on his or her community. This includes concepts of respect, individuality and uniqueness, implying the individual's role, position and contribution to a community and the importance of nurturing this role.

- Conflict or crime disturbs the entire community's peace and harmony. In order to make things right again, the community, victim and perpetrator are involved in the restoration process.

- The supernatural always played a part in the indigenous understanding of justice. Traditionally, violation of tribal law often entailed a violation of the "the balance of nature," which had to be reconnected.

- The use of mediators or facilitators to assist in the resolution process; this often included the king, chief or headman.

- The bringing of symbolic or actual reparations (National Association of Child Care Workers and Technikon Natal, 2001; Consedine, 1999).

Similarly, Michael Hadley (2001) has shown that the roots of restorative justice can be found in most major religions.

Since it seems that restorative justice reflects clear principles not unique to any specific faith or religion, I suggest that we should view them as universal principles of justice. This also means that the principles are simply there — we cannot change them or make them whatever we want them to be. Furthermore, these principles cannot be separated, at least in a Christian context, from the concept of spirituality. This is an objective reality irrespective of whether we place ourselves within this framework or not. Perhaps this goes some of the way to explain why some people who do not regard themselves as religious experience restorative justice processes as "spiritual." By participating in such a process, they are "acting justly" and therefore experiencing the Creator and the fact that the Creator is concerned about these human experiences.

WHAT DOES ALL THIS MEAN IN PRACTICE?

In the light of the above discussion, my judgment is that one cannot separate restorative justice as it is currently known and understood from the concept of spirituality. Restorative justice is by its very nature something spiritual — the two are entirely entwined with each other. If the principles of restorative justice represent "the way things are" in justice, then it is critical that we continue to nurture our understanding of these principles. Our practice of justice will be ineffective to the extent that our understanding of the principles is limited or dulled. If Steven Covey is correct that "principles...are natural laws that cannot be broken... We can only break ourselves against them...," we begin to see that this is a critical issue of no small magnitude. How do we nurture and inform our understanding of these principles to ensure that we do what we can not to violate them? I submit that we need to turn to the spiritual roots, to the religious faiths from which they come.

However, as Shenk (1999:160) suggests,

> postmodern consciousness is creating a new outlook on religious experience. While religion is positively regarded by postmodern people, notions of truth and absolute claims are offensive to post-modern sensibilities. Postmodern people have been characterized as "seekers," people on a quest, unabashedly searching for spiritual answers. But it is a quest that assumes cultural and religious pluralism to be normative.

In Europe and America, and in those countries that have inherited the "Christian civilization" of the West, the prevailing culture has become increasingly pluralist and increasingly secular. These societies now accommodate people who adhere to a range of religious faiths as well as many who do not adhere to any at all. Given that this is the context in which many (although not all) restorative justice practitioners operate, what are the practically acceptable ways of turning to the spiritual roots of the justice principles and applying them?

A brief look at some historical perspectives may provide us with some direction.

In his book *Issues Facing Christians Today*, John Stott (1990) addresses the question of whether Christians should impose their views. In a pluralist society, this is surely one of the first questions that arise for both Christians and non-Christians alike. Stott identifies three alternative responses from history:

- Imposition — a crusading attempt to coerce people by legislation to accept the way of a particular faith. He suggests that, in regards to Christianity, Prohibition — the legal ban on alcohol in the United States from 1919 to 1933 — is an illustration of this.

- A "laissez-faire" approach — not interfering or trying to influence others in any way. How the lack of widespread resistance to the Nazis contributed to the Jewish holocaust is an example of the type of consequence this approach may have.

- Persuasion — engaging people directly and through social action and commending the benefits of morality and principles by way of demonstrating their validity.

It is clear that the approach of persuasion is the only viable way in which applications from religious and indigenous traditions can be presented to influence our practice of restorative justice.

In a given secular and pluralist context, restorative justice practitioners from different religious traditions would need to find ways to conceptualize restorative justice in language and terms on which they can agree. The critical aspects identified earlier by McDonald and Moore could be useful as could the framework developed by van Ness and Strong (2002):

Encounter [p.56]	Amends [p. 81]	Reintegration [p. 100]	Inclusion [p. 125]
Meeting	Apology	Acknowledging human dignity and worth	An invitation
Narrative	Changed behavior	Providing material assistance	Acknowledgement that the person invited has unique interests
Emotion	Restitution	Offering moral and spiritual direction	Recognition that he or she might want to try alternative approaches
Understanding	Generosity		
Agreement			

In working with such a framework, a return to the spiritual roots of these values and elements would inform our understanding of them and our ability to apply them. Practitioners would be able to draw on their various traditions in this process to explore, explain and name these elements. All religions have much to offer on these subjects. To illustrate this further, note the perspective offered by Archbishop Desmond Tutu (1999:218-219) when writing on his experiences in chairing South Africa's Truth and Reconciliation Commission. Tutu writes from a Christian perspective but speaks in a language that all can understand.

> Forgiving and being reconciled are not about pretending that things are other than they are. It is not patting one another on the back and turning a blind eye to the wrong. True reconciliation exposes the awfulness, the abuse, the pain, the degradation, the truth…. Forgiveness does not mean condoning what has been done. It means taking what has happened seriously and not minimizing it, drawing out the sting in the memory that threatens to poison our entire existence. It involves trying to understand perpetrators and so have empathy, to try to stand in their shoes

and to appreciate the sort of pressures and influences that might have brought them to do what they did.

This perspective could be regarded as part of "offering moral and spiritual direction."

As practitioners from different backgrounds engage one another in this process, I suggest that they should not pretend that they have no differences. They should certainly be able to agree on fundamental principles of restorative justice, though they may have significant differences in interpretation, application and language as they return to their spiritual roots. I believe the key to dealing with such a situation is to nurture mutual respect and to find "anchored expressions"[1] of their faith in their practice. These expressions should be true to their spiritual roots, and should seek to learn from one another in this attitude of mutual respect.

This moves us away from the purely rational understanding of the principles to the question of what role spirituality should play in the way that restorative justice is practiced. This does not mean that overtly religious practices or rituals are required to apply restorative justice principles. These may or may not be meaningful. What is really required is that practitioners be well integrated with the principles and have the courage and skills to act accordingly. Umbreit and Greenwood (1997) suggest that a mediator should bring a non-judgmental attitude and a positive demeanor, and be present in a calm, centered manner. This approach seems to represent the kinds of appropriate practical applications that would be nurtured by a spiritual awareness of restorative justice principles.

A further dimension of this process is how the structures within which we practice restorative justice impact on our functioning. In our experience in South Africa (a country that has become rapidly more secular over the past 10 years) this issue has proved critical. Local houses of worship (or other faith communities), as opposed to those that represent the collective, certainly have a role to play in restorative justice processes. This could be in facilitating victim offender conferences, but is likely to be most active in providing material, moral and spiritual support to both victims and offenders. We have concluded that a "church-based organization" (a structure whose identity is closely tied to that of a local faith community) is not the appropriate structure to play a more active lobbying role closely linked to the criminal justice system. A church-based organization seems to increase the perception that an "imposition" approach is being followed. A faith-based organization is more practical for this role as it is independent yet at the same time fosters a strong faith-based ethos.[2] This can provide a platform for a number of houses of worship or other faith communities and individuals to collaborate around restorative justice practice issues and to develop their own "anchored expression" of restorative justice.

CONCLUSIONS

Against the backdrop of the above discussion, let me offer some conclusions:

(1) Restorative justice is by its very nature spiritual. To ensure that we do not stray from this reality, we should nurture our understanding and our practice of the fundamental principles by turning to their spiritual roots, as defined by various faith and religious traditions.

(2) We should not allow the prevailing secular mindset to suggest that there is no difference between "psychological" and "spiritual." Both are equally valid and important.

(3) Both the above conclusions are essential if we are to maintain an awareness of the universal principles of justice as "the way things are," and to ensure that we do not "break ourselves against them."

Address correspondence to: Michael Batley, Executive Director, Restorative Justice Center, PO Box 29516, Sunnyside, Republic of South Africa 0132. Fax: 27-12-4408303. E-mail: <mike@rjc.co.za>.

REFERENCES

Cannon, D.W. (1994). "Different Ways of Christian Prayer, Different Ways of Being Christian." *Mid-stream* 33(3):309–334.

Consedine, J. (1999). *Restorative Justice: Healing the Effects of Crime*. Lyttelton, NZ: Ploughshares Publications.

Covey, S.R. (1989). *The Seven Habits of Highly Effective People*. London, UK: Simon and Shuster.

de Beer, S.F. (1998). "Towards a Theology of Inner City Transformation." Unpublished Doctor of Divinity thesis, University of Pretoria.

Dorr, D. (1984). *Spirituality and Justice*. Maryknoll, NY: Orbis Books.

Hadley, M. (ed.), (2001). *The Spiritual Roots of Restorative Justice*. Albany, NY: State University of New York Press.

Keating, T. (2000). *Open Heart Open Mind*. New York, NY: Continuum Publishing.

Lewis, C.S. (1990). *The Abolition of Man*. Glasgow, UK: William Collins and Sons.

—— (1947). *Miracles*. Glasgow, UK: William Collins and Sons.

McDonald, J. and D. Moore (2001). "Community Conferencing as a Special Case of Conflict Transformation." In: J. Braithwaite and H Strang (eds.), *Restorative Justice and Civil Society*. Cambridge, UK: Cambridge University Press.

National Association of Child Care Workers and Technikon Natal (2001). *Restorative Conferencing: Philosophy and Practise Training Manual*. Durban, South Africa.

Seltzer, R.M. (1980). *Jewish People, Jewish Thought*. New York, NY: Macmillan Publishing.

Shenk, W.R. (1999). "The Church in Pluralistic North America." In: D.W. Shenk and L. Stutzman (eds.), *Practicing Truth: Confidant Witness in our Pluralistic World*. Scottdale, PA: Herald Press.

Stott, J. (1990). *Issues Facing Christians Today*. London, UK: Marshall Pickering.

Tutu, D. (1999). *No Future without Forgiveness*. London, UK: Rider.

Umbreit, M.S. and J. Greenwood (1997). *Criteria for Victim-sensitive Mediation and Dialogue with Offenders*. St. Paul, MN: Center for Restorative Justice and Mediation, School of Social Work, University of Minnesota.

Van Ness, D.W. and K.H. Strong (2002). *Restoring Justice*. Cincinnati, OH: Anderson Publishing.

Willard, D. (no date). "Spiritual Disciplines in a Postmodern World." *Radix Magazine, Inc.* 27(3):26-27.

Zehr, H. (1990). *Changing Lenses*. Scottdale, PA: Herald Press.

NOTES

1. Thanks to Carl Stauffer for this expression.

2. In South Africa, this distinction between a church-based and faith-based organization is important. Church-based refers to an organization that is directly linked to a specific church and, for instance, is part of the church management structure. Faith-based refers to an organization that seeks to integrate its practice with a faith perspective, but is autonomous from any specific local church congregation or denomination.

PART VI.
SOCIAL JUSTICE

Justice For Individuals...Or For Society?

Restorative justice emerged as an effort to address a specific type of wrongdoings — those which, for better or worse, we call "crimes." Soon restorative approaches began to spread to other spheres such as schools, workplaces, and more recently, even mass wrongdoing.

Some of the words we use to describe crime — disrespect, power imbalance, harm — also characterize social injustice. We disrespect Muslims when our laws subject them to intense scrutiny because of their skin color, garb and religious beliefs. We create power imbalances when inner city schools are not adequately funded and the students of these schools are later not able to compete in the economy. We do significant harm to those who are caught in the crossfire of a war for which they did not ask. Just as with crime, it is the people behind the problem who are hurt and seek justice. As with crime, such situations raise questions of harm, accountability and healing, and some argue that a restorative "lens" must be brought to bear in these arenas.

But does restorative justice also speak to ongoing and systemic injustices? Is it, as some have claimed, primarily a "mid-level theory" to address wrongs between individuals and groups? Could it — should it — say something to both our social and economic systems and, on a more "micro" scale, how we live our lives? Are restorative justice theorists and practitioners remiss if we do not address these arenas?

Some contend that restorative justice has no place in the broader social arena. They suggest that it is a crime-specific response developed specifically for victims, offenders and communities. They raise concerns that restorative justice, used as a peacebuilding tool, will minimize, if not sacrifice, individual victim and offender experiences and needs for the sake of a large-scale societal response.

Some see current attempts to use restorative justice in cases of social injustice as mere tokens. They suggest that without consciously expanding the vision of restorative justice beyond the individual victim and offender experience, the philosophy and its practice will have little impact on the creation of right relationships in the broader social context. They contend that, as currently practiced, restorative justice is shortsighted in its drive to respond to the results of violence without dealing with the cause.

The authors in this section suggest that there is room for more attention to the social justice applications of restorative justice. Bonnie Lofton contends that restorative justice does not sufficiently challenge the existing socio-economic systems and that it should be doing more in that arena. Dennis Sullivan and Larry Tifft offer a vision of how we might incorporate restorative justice values into our daily lives, thus helping to address systemic issues. Both authors challenge us to look beyond criminal justice borders.

However, the fundamental question remains — is restorative justice about societal relationships and transformation? There are many interrelated issues to engage:

- To what degree could and should restorative justice focus on micro- and/or macro-relationships, harms and justice?

- What are promises and dangers of either limiting or expanding our definitions of restorative justice to include or exclude expressions of social justice?

- Does restorative justice as currently applied ignore social justice issues ignore, address or even contribute to the causes of crime?

- What would a social justice approach to restorative justice look like in practice?

- In what way might micro-practice be positively influenced or co-opted by macro-practice and vice versa?

Once again, as we wrestle with these questions we have to listen to both others and ourselves. Indeed, own personal reflections may uncover those times when we sought justice only to not receive it or to be dissatisfied with its result. It is from such experiences that we can find common ground and, perhaps, a path with which to continue this dialogue.

Chapter 30.
Does Restorative Justice Challenge Systemic Injustices?

by

Bonnie Price Lofton

THE LIMITATIONS OF RESTORATIVE JUSTICE

Before discussing the limitations of restorative justice, I want to be clear that I agree with the authors in this anthology who explore its merits. I, too, recognize that restorative justice represents a vast improvement over the purely legalistic, retributive approach now used by most Western court systems. Nevertheless, I see four limitations to restorative justice:

(1) It fails to address the socio-economic roots of crime, therefore it is not preventative.

(2) It buys into the status quo's definition of crime as that which occurs between individuals, and thus fails to address the larger, more destructive crimes perpetuated systemically.

(3) On the level of small-time crime, it adopts the status quo's labels, calling those accused of a particular crime "offenders" and those hurt by that crime as "victims," instead of addressing the reality that this particular offense did not arise in a vacuum. In fact, it is statistically probable that the offender has also been a victim.

(4) If properly done, it is so time-consuming that it offers too little spread over too huge a problem — like putting a too-small bandage on a system that is hemorrhaging crime from a gaping wound.

First, I will focus on each of these limitations under its own numbered subhead. Then I will switch to a wider lens and ask the broad question "Where to Next?"

1. The Socio-economic Roots Of Crime

Elliott Currie, who worked for the National Commission on Causes and Prevention of Violence in the 1960s and who has written several books on the same subject, noted that there is "an astonishingly linear relationship" between poverty and youth crime. "The worse the deprivation, the worse the crime," he said (1985:146), offering supporting statistics from the United States, England and Denmark (pp. 148-151). "Around the world, at every level of economic development, increasing equality goes hand in hand with lower risks of homicide" (p. 169), wrote Currie.

After more than 30 years of treating and studying criminals as a forensic psychiatrist, James Gilligan (2001:101-102) summed up his findings thus:

> Violent criminals are not violent because they are dumb, out of touch with reality, or unable to recognize hypocrisy, dishonesty, and injustice when they see it. They are violent precisely because they are aware of the hypocrisy, dishonesty, and injustice that surrounds them and of which they have been victims. This does not mean that they respond to those conditions in a rational or just way, or that we should tolerate and permit their violence — which affects their fellow victims much more often than it does their oppressors. But it does mean that we cannot expect to stop the kind of violence that we call crime until we stop the kind of violence that I have called structural... By this I mean the deaths and disabilities that are caused by the economic structure of our society, its division into rich and poor. Structural violence is not only the main *form* of violence, in the sense that poverty kills far more people (almost all of them very poor) than all the behavioral violence put together, it is also the main *cause* of violent behavior.

If we acknowledge that the people we label "criminals" spring from the oppressed, deprived stratum of society, then these so-called criminals are the original victims, though it is unpopular to view them as such. Most commonly, they also perpetuate the cycle of victimization within their own class.

Many criminologists point out that outright poverty is not the only spark for crime in America. It is also a natural outgrowth of the incessant marketing of the "American Dream." Our economy is fueled by persuading consumers that they need more and more goods to be a success. Only a fraction of the population can afford this addiction to the consumer economy. The rest, especially the most deprived, either "fail" at playing the consumer game, or they play at any cost — even at the cost of what we call crime.

If we as a society would eliminate the obvious sources of criminal behavior — deprivation and inequality — we would preempt the need for restorative justice in criminal justice cases. Restorative justice practitioners often raise awareness of the causes of crime, but they offer no strategy for eliminating these causes.

2. The Whitewashing Of White Collar Crime

Restorative justice practitioners define "crime" as being primarily those crimes perpetrated by one individual on another. The larger crimes — the ones that hurt more people much more severely — stay as hidden under restorative justice as they do under the current retributive system.

I am referring to the relatively faceless crimes of ruining people's pension plans in the name of greed for a few, of forcing the public to pay unnecessarily high prices (as in the case of Microsoft's monopoly on the Windows operating system), and of finding other ways to work the system to accumulate far more wealth than anyone can possibly need while others are suffering from want.

Why isn't it a crime that Catherine Reynolds of Washington, DC managed to parlay her running of a so-called non-profit foundation for student loans into $48 million for herself and $20 million for a Catholic priest in just seven years? During that time, she paid herself $600,000 a year for running the non-profit, plus use of a company Mercedes and $94,000 in expenses. She won for her financial manipulations a seat near President Bush at a charity event, while the person who stole a car won a jail sentence (Montgomery, 2002:C01).

We find another example in Charles Bazarian. Bazarian was convicted of swindling $20 million from two California Savings and Loans and of skimming at least $100,000 from a low-income Housing and Urban Development project. He also participated in defrauding a Florida bank of $7.5 million. For his nearly $30 million in illegal gains, Bazarian served less than two years in prison and paid less than $18,000 in fines (Reiman, 1998:130). Such a light sentence would be regarded as heaven-sent if it were given to a cocaine-addicted prisoner who netted perhaps $1,000 in pawned merchandise from several robberies and who sold drugs to support his habit.

Government agencies track the number of rapes or property thefts that occur annually in each community of the United States. Yet there isn't a public agency that regularly collects statistics on white collar crime. For that matter, there isn't an agency — an Agency for Peace, for instance —that addresses the maiming and deaths resulting from our nation's production, distribution, and use of armaments. In short, there are *legal* mechanisms that permit pursuing the "American way" and profits, regardless of the toll this pursuit takes on humans here and elsewhere. Yet well-organized opposition to these mechanisms is non-existent.

Restorative justice practitioners mainly focus on those involved with illegal drug use, acts of one-on-one violence, and relatively minor theft and street crime. As a result, big power-abusers are not only free of the label "offender," but are also free to continue doing what they have been doing, including profiting from a system which gives rise to hundreds of thousands of small-time criminals.

3. Simplistic Labels: "Victim" And "Offender"

When a law has been broken, we Westerners seek to identify the "bad guy." If there is a victim, that person is usually viewed as the "good guy."

These labels are simplistic. Aside perhaps from a tiny minority of evil-born people, most so-called street criminals (and white collar ones) have sprung from their environment. Gilligan marshals impressive evidence showing that most street criminals — the "bad guys" in our justice system — are in fact victims themselves. They are victims of structural violence, of being assaulted by material deprivation in a consumer society, poor education, lack of opportunities, and social humiliation. They often have untreated mental and physical disabilities. These "bad guys" were victims long before they became labeled as criminals who victimized other people.

Reiman wryly noted that "capitalism makes us more capable of preying on our fellows without moral inhibition or remorse" (1998:161). We can see this at all levels of society, from the former chairman of General Motors who resisted shatter-proof windshields and effective bumpers in GM cars, to the teen who steals cars from shopping center parking lots.

Until we have a healthy social system, we gain nothing from pointing fingers at each other, trying to stick the label "offender" on particular persons for particular acts. All of us are unhealthy to one degree or another in this system, and we all need to help each other to heal and to create an equitable, compassionate society. The question is how we do this.

Howard Zehr states that "crime undermines a community's sense of wholeness, and that injury needs to be addressed" (1990:188). I argue that we should invert this statement in order to recognize that crimes *emerge* from a community's lack of wholeness, and it is that lack that should be addressed.

If we accept this view, then restorative justice needs to evolve away from the labels "offender" and "victim." Such labels support the myth that crime is entirely the result of the isolated decisions of a single individual, rather than a manifestation of a flawed society. Such labels support the status quo in that they hold the individual responsible for harms without looking at all the factors that gave rise to those harms or seeking ways to heal all the harms experienced, not just one particular harm that we've chosen to label as a "crime."

4. Restorative Justice Is A Medium-term Intervention

Restorative justice is clearly effective at easing the pain of individuals and facilitating their restoration to productive living. Lamentably, it takes time and is limited to relationships within a small circle.

Among Canada's native peoples, an offensive act often serves as the occasion to examine and address all the relationships and circumstances surrounding that act. Such peoples commonly use meetings in which community and family members sit in a circle to contemplate the circumstances that gave rise to a "crime."

Such careful attention to the whole picture allows the structural roots of troubles to surface. Regrettably, circle participants can do little with their new-found insights. Even if circle work empowers local communities, these communities have little control over the forces that permit unemployment and economic cycles that disproportionately affect them. The participants in restorative justice tend to be relatively powerless individuals. They are not the world's corporate tycoons, the government leaders, the wealthy power-brokers.

Furthermore, while it is possible to do a circle intervention for a particular person, it is unlikely that we could find enough community members in, say, the state of Minnesota to work with the 123,000 people on probation in a given year, not to mention those incarcerated (Minnesota Department of Corrections, 2001:Table 1). If each of those on probation received just one restorative justice conference or circle session, Minnesotans would have to hold 337 meetings on each day of the year, with no weekends or holidays off, just to process those 123,000 people.

As long as our society fails to address the causes of crime — and how we define crime — we will be flooded with dysfunctional people whom we have chosen to label as criminals. Restorative justice tries to handle this flood without closing the floodgates. For every person saved by a healing circle, 10,000 more will appear.

WHERE TO NEXT?

In its Universal Declaration of Human Rights (1948), the United Nations set forth standards similar to Gilligan's preconditions for eliminating crime. Article 25.1 states that "[e]veryone has the right to a standard of living adequate for the health and well-being of himself and his family, including food, clothing, housing and medical care and necessary social services, and the right to security in the event of unemployment, sickness, disability, widowhood, old age or other lack of livelihood in circumstances beyond his control."

Countries that come closest to meeting this standard, such as Sweden and Denmark, , have the lowest rates of crime, argue Gilligan (2001) and Currie (1985). So how do we get to the social order envisioned in 1948 by the United Nations?

With the discrediting of the Communist and Socialist movements since the Second World War, there seems to be no focused, organized group of people pushing for a socioeconomic system that will uphold the United Nations Declaration of Human Rights. In his widely circulated book, *Rich Christians in an Age of Hunger* (1997), Christian theologian Ronald J. Sider (1997:147) calls for dissent from the free market system:

> It is idolatrous nonsense to equate justice with the outcome of a pure laissez-faire economy. It is false to think that market economy, if freed from all government interference, would create what the Bible means by justice. Masses of poor folk lacking capital are unable to afford even basic necessities. Concentrated wealth threatens democracy. Materialistic messages and practices corrode moral values, family life, and God's creation.

But Sider's solutions are largely individualistic. He calls for living more simply, keeping a base income and then giving away most of the rest, and fasting regularly.

Such personal changes could be a starting point, but they aren't enough, says sociologist Charles Derber (1998:329): "Leaps in personal and moral awareness...are necessary for major political change. But to assume a political form, they must bring about not only changes in the consciousness and behavior of individuals, but an educated collective change to economic and political institutions." Derber (1998:331-332) outlines four steps necessary to translate personal awareness into social change. He says Americans have to:

(1) Realize that personal change is not enough;

(2) Undertake the discipline of serious education in the workings of the corporate economy and how it contributes to our problems;

(3) Lay out the alternatives — from public chartering of the corporation to employee ownership to the construction of a social market — that can bring a more just social order while preserving the dynamism of the economy; and,

(4) Commit to the social movements that can bring these more just institutions into being.

David Gil (2000:83) notes that "durable, major systemic changes" tend to be preceded by "lengthy, evolutionary processes" in which a new vision of the future motivates and inspires a growing number of people.

Clearly, we are somewhere in the "lengthy, evolutionary process" from big-time corporate capitalism to something else. It is not premature to start trying to figure out what that something else should be, and to try to coordinate our activities so that all of those advocating for the "losers" under the current system are moving in the same direction.

Restorative justice practitioners can play a positive role in this process by continuing to offer humane options in what some thinkers call the "crisis-intervention" stage of societal transformation (see Lederach, 1998). The more people who put on the restorative lens — i.e., the more people who look at offenses in terms of the harms caused and of the need for healing — the sooner we will move toward developing a just, peaceful society. As such, restorative justice is a hopeful compass, pointing the way out of the dismal swamp of our current criminal justice.

But restorative justice offers no more than a compass on our journey to a healthy society, so let's not stop at this crisis-intervention stage. At least some of us need to move beyond restorative justice concepts into educating ourselves in the workings of the corporate economy. Our aim, as Derber (1998) explained, should be to develop a more just social order while preserving the good parts — especially the dynamism — of today's economic system. We must start to define what that system would look like and how we might get there.

If we succeed in 10, 20 or even 50 years, we will find that restorative justice as we know it today will be less necessary, because the system itself won't be fostering one-on-one crime and violence.

To get to this new society, we will need to expand out of the justice studies arena and join with other dissenters from the status quo, such as those from the environmental, human rights, feminist, and development fields. Moving with cautious urgency — that is, with *urgent* consciousness that suffering and permanent damage are occurring now, but with *cautious* knowledge that ill-considered change may be worse than no change at all — we need to launch a worldwide discussion on what is the best possible socioeconomic system and how to get to it. Finally, we need to find and join social movements that come decently close to upholding our ideals. There is indeed strength in numbers.

REFERENCES

Currie, E. (1985). *Confronting Crime: An American Challenge.* New York: Pantheon Books.

Derber, C. (1998). *Corporate Nation.* New York: St. Martin's Griffin.

Gil, D.G. (2000). "Rethinking the Goals, Organization, Designs, and Quality of Work in Relation to Individual and Social Development." *Contemporary Justice Review* 3(1):73-88.

Gilligan, J. (2001). *Preventing Violence.* New York: Thames & Hudson.

Lederach, J.P. (1998). *Building Peace: Sustainable Reconciliation in Divided Societies.* Washington DC: U.S. Institute of Peace Press.

Minnesota Department of Corrections (2001). "Caseload/Workload Reduction, 2001 Report to the Legislature." Saint Paul, MN.

Montgomery, D. (2002). "Inspiration Investor." *The Washington Post,* April 9, p.C01.

Reiman, J. (1998). *The Rich Get Richer and the Poor Get Prison.* Boston, MA: Allyn & Bacon.

Sider, R.J. (1997). *Rich Christians in an Age of Hunger.* Dallas, TX: Word Publishing.

"Universal Declaration of Human Rights" (1948). (www.un.org/Overview/rights.html.)

Zehr, H. (1990). *Changing Lenses: A New Focus for Crime and Justice.* Scottdale, PA: Herald Press.

Chapter 31.
What Are The Implications Of Restorative Justice For Society And Our Lives?

by

Dennis Sullivan and Larry Tifft

Although differences might exist over where restorative justice had its beginnings and which restorative processes best foster healing when people are faced with the pain and suffering of harm, all of us who embrace the spirit of restorative justice agree that, at its core, restorative justice is a process that is concerned about meeting human needs.[1] We also agree that this process of personal healing and human growth is indiscriminate in its aims for it seeks to meet the needs, not of some, but of all those who find themselves in a situation of harm (Sullivan and Tifft, 2001). In this sense, restorative justice does not emerge out of a storehouse of correctional practices but out of a political philosophy of relationship that says people develop, interact, and live fully when their needs are voiced and taken seriously by others (Gil, 1999). That is, we develop our potentialities as human beings and enhance our collective well-being when our needs are mutually respected and ultimately met (Kropotkin, 1968).

Restorative justice is indeed a process of "talking things out," of increasing an awareness of self and others, as the Navajo say when describing their ancient peacemaking process (Zion, 1998, 1999; Yazzie, 1997, 1998; Sullivan, 2002). But it also has to do with taking action, first, in meeting the needs of those engaged in the immediate conversation and, second, in designing and living in social arrangements that prevent both interpersonal and structural violence from occurring. That is, restorative justice involves preventing violence that derives from needs denied, potential thwarted, and personhood dismissed (Dyck, 2000; Mika, 1992). In other words, restorative justice must concern itself as well with creating social arrangements that foster human dignity, mutual respect, and equal well-being from the outset (Miller, 1976).

When we say that meeting the needs of everyone and expanding our collective potential is central to the principles and practices of restorative justice, we immediately come face to face with issues of power because an ethic of power justifies satisfying the needs and creating the well-being of some at the expense of others. Power reflects an ideology of differential human worth whereby one person or group regards itself as having greater value than others. Hence, actions taken for reasons of power — even those that might be said to heal, make things right, foster voice or meet emergent needs — perpetuate violence. They defy the spirit of restorative justice for they support cultures of privilege and institutionalize patterns of inequality. Clearly, as proponents of restorative justice we are all called upon, therefore, to examine and understand the workings of power in all aspects of our lives.

Voice And Participation

Because the process of uncovering, expressing, and meeting human needs resides at the core of restorative justice and restorative social arrangements (Zehr and Mika, 1998), it is essential that we know in any given situation what each person's or group's needs are. Hence, the cultivation of each person's voice and participation is critical to the restorative process. This means creating a social climate in which people take themselves seriously and know they are taken seriously. It means creating social processes wherein people believe that their story is worth telling and worth being heard. It means creating social environments in which each of us is listened to as we would like to be listened to. It means interacting with others in ways that they desire to be interacted with. It means neither exercising power nor allowing others to exercise power. In short, it means getting out of power (Wieck, 1975; Goodman, 1961, 1963).

Clearly, then, in all social situations our narratives are an essential aspect of living restoratively because, by telling our story, we not only develop a deeper sense of self but also expand and deepen our connectedness to each other. As we uncover and begin to tell our stories, we discover what our true feelings and needs are (Rogers, 1961). And this is true not solely in some conference or circle after someone has been harmed, but in everyday life — in our families, schools, and places of work.

In her poignant book, *Aftermath: Violence and the Remaking of a Self*, Susan Brison (2002), who had been sexually assaulted, reflects on the importance of narrative creation and expression as a process for reconnecting one's self with others as a more whole person. She (Brison, 2002:54) says that, although it is not possible to control the entire story that unfolds in and around one's life, "one can control certain aspects of the narrative and that control, repeatedly exercised, leads to greater control over the memories themselves, making them less intrusive and giving them the kind of meaning that enables them to be integrated into the rest of life." And yet, for this kind of emotional integration or restoration to occur, one must find a community, a support group, in which one's story is taken seriously and listened to and in which the needs that unfold from its telling are met.

However, as Susan Hirsch (2002), whose husband, Abdurahman Abdulla, was killed in the 1998 U.S. embassy bombings in Dar es Salaam, Tanzania, tells us, this was not her experience. The officials who orchestrated the response to her husband's death were interested in only those parts of her story that would enable them to have those standing trial for the bombings executed. The nature of the victim impact statements allowed gave only lip service to the importance of her story and the feelings of others harmed by the violence. Who she was and the nature of her needs were treated as incidentals. As she struggled to heal amidst her devastating loss, state officials became perpetrators of further harm and suffering. She felt betrayed; her emotional well-being and human dignity were not restored, only the legitimated power of the state and existing world distributions.

The late 20th-century composer, John Cage (1967), social designer, R. Buckminster Fuller (1987), and ecologist, Murray Bookchin (1971) all noted years ago that as a world community we had the means available to meet everyone's essential needs. But, they also recognized that these means are unlikely to be adopted in a world in which nations clash over state sovereignty, resource extractions and allocations, and future world order configurations. They are even less likely to materialize as our current oil wars become water wars (Barlow and Clarke, 2002; Glennon, 2002) and global corporations convert the world's environment into

property and human beings into market-value resources for the privatized well-being of a privileged few (Chomsky, 2002).

As these institutions of power and privilege designate us as either
"obstructions to development" or as "consumer units" whose manu-
factured needs their packaged goods are designed to satisfy, meeting the
needs of all — including those needs required to sustain our natural environment — is a sabotaged possibility from the outset (Illich, 1977).
Power-based political-economic arrangements require structural violence
and injustice to thrive (Sullivan and Boehrer, 1999). So when we talk
about human needs and the restoration of people to their everyday lives
through the agency of narrative, we must ask ourselves in the same
breath what kind of world to which people are being restored (Christie,
1993)? To social arrangements designed to meet the needs of some at
the expense of others? To arrangements of power, violence, exploitation, and inequality, rather than those that support life, human dignity,
and equal well-being (Chomsky, 2002)? To arrangements that limit the
stories of people to only those utterances that bolster retributive, scar-
city-enforcing acts? This is a non-restorative world, one that refuses to
understand and accept a reality based in "the true cost of things" (Sullivan, 1986-87; Sullivan and Tifft, 1998).

Restoration Of Life

As contemporary writer, Arundhati Roy, pointed out in her Noam
Chomsky Award address at the 2003 Justice Studies Association Conference, if we wish to restore life to those who have been trampled upon,
we must engage in restorative interventions but, at the same time, we
need to dismantle those social arrangements responsible for the tram-
pling: the violent political-economies of the nation-state and the global,
transnational market. Their interest is not in creating a matrix of civil
societies or interdependent, global civil societies in which the needs and
well-being of all are taken into account and equitably met (Strang and
Braithwaite, 2001; Chomsky, 1994a, 1994b). Rather, it is in shaping a
populace of warriors of empire who must witness (or share in) exhibi-
tions of mass death-dealing, systemic mal-distribution and intentional
neglect, and, in pockets of survival, the dashed dreams of those con-
signed to become consumers of goods and services that are compatible

with the packaged self they purchase — probably on credit and at a discount price (Tifft, 1993).

If we wish to embrace the spirit of restorative justice, each of us must begin to examine the ways in which we contribute to and fit into the existing arrangements of social and distributive injustice as well as into their corollary punishment and disciplining structures. Do we, in our daily lives, share in the docilization and disciplining of others rather than in promoting/restoring their growth, dignity, and enjoyment of life? To what extent do we deny others the freedom to direct the social construction of their true selves? To what extent do we dismiss the importance of their needs, failing to see the connections between self-development and living healthfully with others (Schumacher, 1998; Gil, 1986, 1996)? And to what extent do we realize one of life's great ironies, that in every instance where we deny voice to others, it is because we have been denied our own voice; when we treat the needs of others as inconsequential, it is because our own needs have been treated as inconsequential (Foucault, 1977; Tifft, 1979). Our dismissals and denials of the needs of others become a way to secure relief from our own suffering and to purchase an insurance policy against a present riddled with anxiety, conflict, and fear, however illusory such insurance is (Tifft, 2002). To submit to this way of life is to become like the person who denies the enjoyment of present reality by saving for a rainy day only to find out that, by failing to meet one's present needs, each and every day becomes a storm-filled encounter with self and others. Hardly a restorative ethic.

Living Justice

What we are saying is that to understand and fully appreciate restorative justice as a way to respond to the needs of those who have been harmed, we must first imagine and experience just and restorative relationships in our own lives — in our families, schools, and places of work. We must see a connection between the work we do and the lives we live, between the lives we live and political-economies of being that denigrate or enhance human worth.

In a just and restorative daily life the boundaries between self and others begin to more fully overlap. We are moved to incorporate the insights, sensitivities, and concerns of others into our lives and to work toward their happiness as we do our own because we see their well-being as inextricably connected to ours. As psychoanalyst Melanie Klein (1964:66) says, "In the depths of the mind, the urge to make people happy is linked with a strong feeling of responsibility and concern for them, which manifests itself in genuine sympathy with other people and in the ability to understand them, as they are and as they feel." This is, for Klein and for all who embrace the spirit of restorative justice, the foundation of love and compassion, the way we make a home for each other in the world.

But we cannot emphasize enough the value of the imagination for creating the foundations of such a home. The imagination is, as the poet William Carlos Williams (1970:120) recognized, "an actual force comparable to electricity or steam, it is not a plaything but a power that has been used from the first to raise understanding." Hence the more enlivened our imagination is, the better able we are to experience what another feels and the more intense and delicate our moral sense becomes (Sullivan, 1982). Peter Kropotkin (1968:95) saw this as incontrovertible. He said that, "The more you are drawn to put yourself in the place of the other person, the more you feel the pain inflicted upon him, the insult offered him, the injustice of which he is a victim, the more will you be urged to act so that you may prevent the pain, insult, or injustice."

Through the active imagination we open ourselves up to the living narrative of others. We become keenly aware of our responsibility for their needs. Co-founder of the Catholic Worker movement, Dorothy Day (1970:9), experienced this kind of transformation during her first days of solitary confinement.

> I suffered not only my own sorrow but the sorrows of those about me. I was no longer myself. I was man [sic]. I was no longer young girl, part of a radical movement seeking justice for those oppressed. I was the oppressed. I was that drug addict, screaming and tossing in her cell, beating her head against the wall. I was that shoplifter who for rebellion was sentenced to solitary. I was that woman who killed her children, who had murdered her lover.

Collaborative community and moral development begin here. We live justly and act restoratively, not as professionals or experts donning an institutional mask of love, but as members of a community dedicated to meeting the needs of all who come our way (Sullivan, 1980; Tifft and Sullivan, 1980).

Demonstration Projects

In order to live a just and restorative life, demonstration projects become critical because they show us how it is possible to transform both ourselves and existing social arrangements (Drumble, 2002; D. Sullivan, 1998). As we have indicated, such a transformation begins when our imaginations connect us to others in such a way that we can no longer interact with or react to them through power, violence, and retribution (Tifft, 1993). Yet, these non-power relations do not arise *sua sponte*; they require the development of new skills that demonstrate our commitment to restorative values.

For most of us, family interaction patterns provide the most familiar and understandable demonstration project of needs-based social interaction and therefore serve as a core model for the practice of restorative justice (Sullivan and Tifft, 2001). We see people with children develop "restorative intelligence" and extend these experiences to others when they relinquish the "good provider" and "good caretaker" roles that commonly lead many couples to live parallel lives, in separate spheres (Tifft et al., 1998; Bernard, 1986; Schwartz, 1994). These couples choose to base their relationship on love/companionship, equality, and needs-meeting, creating what sociologist Pepper Schwartz (1994) calls "peer marriages." In such partnerships they experience a deep, rich, intimate friendship through their mutual commitment to generating real conversation, collaboration, and warmth. In these relationships, each person's life plan is given equal consideration as the partners collaborate in the undertaking of family work ("household tasks"), making family decisions, and creating arrangements that attempt to ensure equal access to family resources (i.e., family discretionary funds; family TV).

These partners also share in what many in our society refer to as "the task of childcare," "the chore of taking care of the children," or, for some men, "babysitting the children." They see this task not as a self-sacrificing, unfamiliar, burdening activity, but simply as "being with" the children. In such families the children do not feel they are objects of a dynamic that reflects the exercise of power and inequality. Rather, like their peer parents, they experience needs-based access to family resources and participate in family work, fun, and decision making. Their stories are cherished. There are many such family demonstration projects in existence today that reconfirm our beliefs and hopes that we can successfully extend such need-meeting arrangements to other spheres of life such as the school, the workplace, and of course our practice of justice (Tifft, 2000).

In examining schools for restorative learning experiences, we find an increasing number which have incorporated conferences and similar restorative processes in which children and their teachers can participate after some harm has occurred. But we give our attention here to those schools that have incorporated restorative practices into their very design. When John Sullivan (1998) arrived as principal of Spruce Run elementary school several decades ago, he observed that certain features of the school's physical environment were not designed to meet the needs of the children and would have to be changed immediately. The counter in the main office was far too high for the children to communicate their concerns to their elders autonomously; the automatic-eye toilets flushed with such a startling sound that the youngest children became frightened. Sullivan also saw that the learning environment would have to be transformed from one of comparing, differentiating, homogenizing, and excluding students, to one that was fully inclusive and appreciative of each learner's gifts and needs (St. John, 2003).

Learning at Spruce Run became a collaborative process, one organized to give children a chance to select the modes of learning through which they learned best and to have voice in what they explored. The children were also encouraged to learn from one another so as to better appreciate what they learned and to determine what else there was to understand. As they created portfolios to demonstrate their accomplishments, each child increasingly grasped how to take responsibility for his or her own learning within a community of learners. In such a collaborative environment, as J. Sullivan (1998:184) suggests, "the expert teacher, like the collaborative principal, will understand the basic needs of people such as the need to control one's destiny, and involve students in making decisions affecting their existence in their workplace."[2]

In other places of work we can see the effect that restorative structures and processes can have on the overall quality of life of those who work there (Gil, 1989, 1990). In such work environments the distribution of desirable/undesirable tasks is not a major problem (Kinkade,

1994) for the workers have a great amount of personal choice in deciding what they will do. Workgroups can select, design, direct, and make policy decisions about their work, even about what they will produce or provide (Marshall, 1995). They flourish because their ideas are respected from the outset and for their commitment to quality work they receive a fair and stable income (Krimerman and Lindenfeld, 1992).

When this level of well-being exists in a workplace, feelings of envy and resentment toward co-workers and coordinators are significantly reduced. People feel restored. And the more restorative the work becomes, the more each person accumulates positive experiences to share with his or her family members and others they meet (Kimbrell, 1992; Hart, 1992). We witness an integration of one's work life with other aspects of life, especially the family (Shifley, 2003; Lindenfeld, 2003). Clearly a restorative ethic.

CONCLUSION

We have only hinted at some of the many possibilities that exist for creating restorative relations in our daily lives, the ways in which we can positively affect who we become, how we organize our work and families, and how we can create a meaningful future for ourselves and others. But we leave with the caveat that, unless advocates and practitioners of restorative justice embrace its needs-based spirit within the larger structural contexts we have discussed, the work we do will likely become indistinguishable from the work of those who execute retributive measures of justice. We will not have become in our own lives a personal demonstration project through which we can remain attuned to the essence of restorative justice, of life itself. If we wish to move toward a more civil society, one in which the needs of all are met in our primary social institutions and one in which we respond restoratively to the harms and injustices we face, at every level of life we need to create social arrangements that will transform our present world into a federation of democratic, needs-based societies — one relationship at a time.[3]

Address correspondence to: Authors Dennis Sullivan and Larry Tifft may be contacted by e-mail, respectively, at <gezellig@global2000.net> and <tifft1ll@cmich.edu>.

REFERENCES AND SUGGESTED READING

Barlow, M. and T. Clarke (2002). *Blue Gold: The Fight to Stop the Corporate Theft of the World's Water.* New York: W. W. Norton.

Bernard, J. (1986). "The Good Provider Role: Its Rise and Fall." In: A.S. Skolnick and J.H. Skolnick (eds.), *Family In Transition* (5th ed.). Boston, MA: Little, Brown.

Bookchin, M. (1971). *Post-Scarcity Anarchism.* San Francisco, CA: Ramparts Books.

Brison, S. (2002). *Aftermath: Violence and the Remaking of Self.* Princeton, NJ: Princeton University Press.

Cage, J. (1967). *A Year From Monday: New Lectures and Writings.* Middletown, CT: Wesleyan University Press.

Chomsky, N. (2002). "Restoring Rights; The Assault on Freedom and Democracy." *Contemporary Justice Review* 5(2):103-119.

—— (1994a). *Keeping the Rabble in Line: Interviews with David Barsamian.* Monroe, ME: Common Courage Press.

—— (1994b). *World Orders Old and New.* New York, NY: Columbia University Press.

Christie, N. (1993). *Crime Control as Industry: Towards Gulags Western Style?* New York: Routledge.

Day, D. (1970). *Meditations: Selected and Arranged by Stanley Vishnewski.* New York: Paulist Press.

Drumble, M.A. (2002). "Restorative Justice and Collective Responsibility: Lessons for and from the Rwandan Genocide." *Contemporary Justice Review* 5(1):5-22.

Dyke, D. (2000). "Reaching Toward a Structurally Responsive Training and Practice of Restorative Justice." *Contemporary Justice Review* 3(3):239-265.

Fuller, R.B. (1981). *Critical Path.* New York, NY: St. Martin's.

Foucault, M. (1977). *Discipline and Punish: The Birth of the Prison.* New York: Pantheon.

Gil, D.G. (1999). "Understanding and Overcoming Social-Structural Violence." *Contemporary Justice Review* 2(1):23-35.

—— (1996). "Preventing Violence in a Structurally Violent Society: Mission Impossible." *American Journal of Orthopsychiatry* 66:77-84.

—— (1990). *Unraveling Social Policy* (4th ed.). Rochester, VT: Schenkman Books.

—— (1989). "Work, Violence, Injustice, and War." *Journal of Sociology and Social Welfare* 16:39-53.

—— (1986). "Sociocultural Aspects of Domestic Violence." In: M. Lystad (ed.), *Violence in the Home.* New York: Brunner/Mazel.

Glennon, R. (2002). *Water Follies: Ground Water and the Fate of America's Fresh Waters.* Washington, DC: Island Press.

Goodman, P. (1963). *People or Personnel: Decentralizing and the Mixed System.* New York, NY: Random House.

—— (1961). *Growing Up Absurd: Problems of Youth in the Organized System.* New York, NY: Random House.

Hart, E. (1992). "Salsedo Press: Community Roots, Quality Printing." In: L. Krimerman and F. Lindenfeld (eds.), *When Workers Decide: Workplace Democracy Takes Root in North America.* Philadelphia, PA: New Society Publications.

Hirsch, S. (2002). "Victims for the Prosecution: A Survivor of the Embassy Bombings on the Limits of Victim Impact Testimony." *Boston Review* 27(5):21-25.

Illich, I. (1977). *Toward a History of Needs.* New York: Pantheon.

Kimbrell, A. (1992). "Time For Men to Pull Together." *Utne Reader* May/June:66-74.

Kinkade, K. (1994). *Is it Utopia Yet?: An Insider's View of Twin Oaks Community in its 26th Year.* Louisa, VA: Twin Oaks Publishing.

Klein, M. and J. Riviere (1964). *Love, Hate and Reparation.* New York: W.W. Norton & Company.

Krimerman, L.F. and F. Lindenfeld (1992). "Drawing in and Reaching Out: Strategies to Strengthen the Workplace Democracy Movement." In: L. Krimerman and F. Lindenfeld (eds.), *When Workers Decide: Workplace Democracy takes Root in America.* Philadelphia, PA: New Society Publications.

Kropotkin, P. (1968). *The Conquest of Bread.* New York: Benjamin Blom.

Lindenfeld, F. (2003). "Commentary on 'The Organization of Work as a Factor of Social Well-Being.'" *Contemporary Justice Review* 6(2):127-132.

Marshall, E.M. (1995). *Transforming the Way we Work: The Power of the Collaborative Workplace.* New York: AMACOM.

Mika, H. (1992). "Mediation Interventions and Restorative Justice: Responding to the Astructural Bias." In: H. Messmer and H-U. Otto. (eds.), *Restorative Justice on Trial: Pitfalls and Potentials of Victim-Offender Mediation International Research Perspectives.* Dordrecht, NETH: Kluwer.

Miller, D. (1976). *Social Justice.* Oxford, UK: Oxford University Press.

Rogers, C.R. (1961). *On Becoming a Person.* Boston, MA: Houghton Mifflin.

Schumacher, J. (1998). "Questions for Students of Justice." *Contemporary Justice Review* 1(2- 3):213-241.

Schwartz, P. (1994). "Modernizing Marriage." *Psychology Today* September/October:54, 56, 58-59, 86.

Shifley, R. (2003). "The Organization of Work as a Factor of Social Well-Being." *Contemporary Justice Review* 6(2):105-126.

St. John, P.A. (2003). "The Songs Teachers Teach are Not Necessarily the Songs Children Sing: The Boy Who Would Be An Airplane." *Contemporary Justice Review* 6(1):47-53.

Strang, H. and J. Braithwaite (eds.), (2001). *Restorative Justice and Civil Society.* Cambridge, UK: Cambridge University Press.

Sullivan, D. (2002). "Navajo Peacemaking History, Development, and Possibilities for Adjudication-Based Systems of Justice: An Interview with James Zion." *Contemporary Justice Review* 5(2):167-188.

—— (1998). "Living Restorative Justice as a Lifestyle: An Interview with Fred Boehrer." *Contemporary Justice Review* 1(1):149-146.

—— (1986-87). "The True Cost of Things, the Loss of the Commons and Radical Change." *Social Anarchism: A Journal of Practice and Theory* 6(2):20-26.

—— (1982). "Mutual Aid: The Social Basis of Justice and Moral Community." *Humanity and Society* 6:294-302.

—— (1980). *The Mask of Love: Corrections in America, Toward a Mutual Aid Alternative.* Port Washington, NY: Kennikat.

—— and L. Tifft (2001). *Restorative Justice: Healing the Foundations of Our Everyday Lives.* Monsey, NY: Willow Tree Press.

—— and F. Boehrer (1999). "The 'Celling' of America, the Political Economy of Force, and the Violence of Economic Sanctions in International Relations: An Interview with Ramsey Clark." *Contemporary Justice Review* 2(1):5-21.

—— and L. Tifft (1998). "The Transformative and Economic Dimensions of Restorative Justice." *Humanity and Society* 22(1):38-54.

Sullivan, J. (1998). "Meeting the Individual Needs of All Learners in the Inclusion Classroom." *The Justice Professional* 11(1-2):175-187.

Tifft, L. (2002). "Crime and Peace: A Walk with Richard Quinney." *Crime & Delinquency* 48(2):243-262.

—— (2000). "Social Justice and Criminologies: A Commentary." *Contemporary Justice Review* 3(1):45-54.

—— (1993). *Battering of Women: The Failure of Intervention and the Case for Prevention.* Boulder, CO: Westview Press.

—— (1979). "The Coming Redefinitions of Crime: An Anarchist Perspective." *Social Problems* 26:392-402.

—— and D. Sullivan (1980). *The Struggle to be Human: Crime, Criminology, and Anarchism.* Over-the-Water, Sanday, Orkney, SCOT: Cienfuegos Press.

—— J. Sullivan and D. Sullivan (1998). "Discipline as Enthusiasm: An Entry into the Recent Discussion on the Moral Development of Children." Paper presented at the annual meeting of the Association for Humanist Sociology, Pittsburgh, PA.

Wieck, D. (1975). "The Negativity of Anarchism." *Interrogations: Revue Internationale de Recherche Anarchiste* 5, December:25-55.

Williams, W.C. (1970). *Imaginations.* New York: New Directions.

Yazzie, R. (1998). "Navajo Peacemaking: Implications for Adjudication-Based Systems of Justice." *Contemporary Justice Review* 1(1):123-131.

—— (1997). "The Navajo Response to Crime." Paper presented at the meeting of the American Judicature Society on A National Symposium on Sentencing: The Judicial Response to Crime, San Diego, CA.

Zehr, H. and H. Mika (1998). "Fundamental Concepts of Restorative Justice." *Contemporary Justice Review* 1(1):47-55.

Zion, J.W. (1999). "Monster Slayer and Born for Water: The Intersection of Restorative and Indigenous Justice." *Contemporary Justice Review* 2(4):359-382.

—— (1998). "The Use of Custom and Legal Tradition in the Modern Justice Setting." *Contemporary Justice Review* 1(1):133-48.

NOTES

1. In a past issue of *Contemporary Justice Review* (3:4, December, 2000), Paul McCold, Lode Walgrave, John Braithwaite, Carolyn Boyes-Watson, Virginia Mackey, Gordon Bazemore, and Hal Pepinsky openly debated the boundaries and founda-

tions of restorative justice. The 7:1 (March, 2004) issue of the journal presents a similar symposium, this one focusing on the differences among four modes of claimed non-retributive justice: restorative justice; community justice; transformative justice; and just community.

2. In the Carondelet music school that she had established and in her research on classroom social climates that foster the growth and development, Patricia St. John (2003) saw how a needs-based approach to learning radically changed the life of Thomas, a young boy who was reticent to become part of the music community. Through her attentiveness to his unique needs, figuring out what he was trying to say by his actions, and learning what was going on within him, rather than forcing him to conform to a set of pre-ordained behaviors, Thomas became not only a giving member of the community, but a person who sought to re-create for others what he himself had experienced.

3. Here, as elsewhere, we write out of our own life experiences, on the one hand having refused to accept the marginalization and dismissal we felt early on from those within the scholarly traditions we embraced and, on the other, having created (in line with the counsel of Allen Ginsberg and Noam Chomsky to take action) social arrangements that reflect the restorative social ethic we espouse and strive to live by. The international journal, *Contemporary Justice Review* (www.tandf. co.uk/journals) and the international association, Justice Studies Association (www.justicestudies.org), are two such arrangements, inclusive forums, in which we, with the support of our friends and colleagues, have sought to create a home for everyone one room at a time. Hopefully, this is a home where no one feels forced to save for a rainy day and where the sun always shines brightly on individual uniqueness.

CLOSING REFLECTIONS

The contributions in this book have addressed profound issues, some of which get at the very core of restorative justice theory and practice. While the authors have proposed some answers to the questions raised, over all we are left with more questions than answers. Moreover, many more issues and questions could be raised than space has allowed.

While some may find this multiplicity of questions and problems overwhelming, we — the compilers and editors of this book — believe this ongoing state of uncertainty to be both normal and healthy. In fact, we find this dialogue much more energizing and hopeful than discouraging. Many of these issues are inevitable in any kind of social movement. As a friend once observed during an extended and agonizing dialogue in another arena, the only thing worse than talking through such issues out is not talking them through.

How we experience these dilemmas and uncertainties depends in part on our approach to knowledge and to life. The Western way of knowing has been deeply influenced by the philosopher René Descartes. Descartes' primary epistemological approach was doubt. Doubt everything, he said, until you can find something that is certain; for him, the one thing that couldn't be doubted was the axiom, "I think, therefore I am." This stance of doubt has strengths but it can lead to a great deal of cynicism and skepticism.

While our approach to this field of restorative justice — and to this book — certainly includes doubt, more important is a stance of wonder — an appreciation of mystery, of ambiguity, of paradox, even of contradictions. An ability to live with the unknown, with surprises and with the seemingly irreconcilable, is essential to good restorative justice practice.

David James Duncan, in his book *My Story as Told by Water* (2001), defines wonder like this: "...wondering is unknowing, experienced as pleasure." In that case, reading this book should have been a pleasurable experience!

Throughout this book you have been encouraged to listen to yourself, to examine yourself and to apply principles and practices to your own situation. We believe this is important both to integrity and to learning. In Part VI, Bonnie Lofton rightfully reminds us that individual change is not enough. Nevertheless, Dennis Sullivan and Larry Tifft, also in Part VI, argue that we must start there.

Over the years we have heard many testimonials about restorative justice. Statements such as these have always mystified us, however: "Restorative justice has changed my life"; and "Restorative justice is a way of life."

How can a conceptual framework — a very simple concept, actually — designed to respond to crime be seen as life-changing or even a way of life? (Certainly we've never heard that — at least positively — about the legal process!) It is understandable, perhaps, when a victim and offender talk about having experienced healing on their journeys through a restorative process. But restorative justice as a way of life?

We have come to believe that restorative justice as a "way of life" has to do with the ethical system that restorative justice embodies. Some argue that restorative justice reflects, and taps into, some universal values, and that is why it connects with so many indigenous and religious traditions. Whether this is accurate or not, it does seem that restorative justice embodies a coherent, internally-consistent value system in a way that "criminal justice" does not. We want to end by exploring this further, thus returning to some extent to the issues raised in Part I.

The Western criminal justice system is intended to promote some important positive values: the rights inherent to each person, the delineation of acceptable behavior, the importance of fairness and consistency. However, it does so in a way that is largely negative. It says, "Do this, or else." We will do to you what you have done to others; suffering requires suffering, a mirror image of the offense. One reason for the vast literature rationalizing the principle of punishment is that the state is empowered to do what, for individuals, is usually seen as morally questionable.

To keep the system humane and to mitigate the suffering we cause, we are therefore forced to bring to bear important values from outside the ethical system of justice. Moreover, in itself, this approach to justice does not offer us a vision of the good or of how we want to live together.

Restorative justice, we believe, offers an inherently positive and relatively coherent value system. Moreover, it suggests this vision of the good and how to live together.

Restorative justice, like so many indigenous and religious traditions, is premised on the assumption that we as individuals are interconnected and that what we do matters to others and vice-versa. Thus, the basic principles of restorative justice, however they are articulated, suggest guidelines by which most of us want to live in everyday life. Restorative justice reminds us of the importance of relationships. It calls us to consider the impact of our behavior on others and the obligations that our actions entail. It respects the dignity that we and others deserve. So, perhaps restorative justice does suggest a way of life.

This brings us back to our introduction to the book and the emphasis upon two key underlying values of restorative justice: humility and respect.

By humility we include its common usage, the idea of not taking undo credit. Indeed, this is an important value for restorative justice practitioners. When justice is practiced well, participants often overlook the role of the facilitator, and it is important for practitioners to be able to live with that lack of recognition.

But by humility we also mean something more basic and more difficult: a profound recognition of the limits of what we "know." A core principle of restorative justice is that it must be contextual, shaped from the ground up in a particular context. As a result, humility requires a real caution about generalizing what we think we know to others' situations.

Humility also requires a deep awareness of how our biographies shape our knowledge and biases. Our gender, culture, ethnicity and personal and collective histories all profoundly shape how we know and what we know, and in ways that are often difficult to bring to consciousness. Humility calls us, then, to a deep appreciation for and openness to others' realities.

It is when we are humble that we can prevent a form of justice that may seem liberating to us from becoming a burden on others or a weapon that is used against others, as has happened in so many previous "reforms."

The other value that must guide us in this dialogue is respect. Our experiences lead us to believe that issues of respect are fundamental to much offending and to the negative ways in which offenders so often experience justice. Likewise, we have come to believe that issues of re-spect and disrespect play important roles in victims' trauma and recov-ery as well as the way they so often experience justice.

Restorative justice, in a word, is about respect. Only if we seek justice with respect and humility about what we know — only then can we do justice restoratively. And only with a stance grounded in respect, humil-ity and wonder will we find a way through the issues that have been raised in this book.

REFERENCE

Duncan, D.J. (2001). *My Story as Told by Water.* San Francisco, CA: Sierra Club Books.

Appendix.
Critical Issues In Restorative Justice

AN INADEQUATE AND OVERLAPPING OUTLINE...

The following is an outline of the critical issues questions that guided the design of this book. The following definition of "critical issues" was used:

> *Critical issues are those that affect the integrity or overall direction of the field — including gaps in theory or practice and ways that restorative justice is in danger of going astray or failing to live up to its promise. The term "critical" suggests that these issues are crucial to the field, but also implies a critical stance toward the field.*

Principles And Concept:

- To what extent is real-world restorative justice straying or being co-opted from the principles?

- Is it a problem that there is no agreed-upon definition or set of principles? Should there be? Could there be? How restrictive should such a definition be?

- Should restorative justice be envisioned in terms of processes? Goals? Principles? Values?

- Can we articulate more clearly the values underlying the principles? What type of discussion is necessary to clarify and advance these values?

- To what extent is the concept biased by culture, gender or class?

- Who should be involved in defining principles, values and benchmarks? Is the present circle of dialogue and leadership sufficiently diverse and representative to do this work?

- Has restorative justice been developed into an adequately comprehensive theory?

- Has restorative justice adequately addressed and/or incorporated the diverse meanings of retribution?

- Have clear and appropriate benchmarks of restorative practice been established?

Victim Issues:

- Is restorative justice living up to its promise to victims?

- To what extent is the victim focus of restorative justice theory being co-opted by offender or community concerns?

- What are the impressions and perceptions of restorative justice among the victim services community? What can be done to increase understanding and collaboration between this community and the restorative justice community?

- What is the relevance and meaning of "putting right" and reparation in cases such as homicide?

- Can and should efforts to promote healing and to provide symbolic reparation fully take the place of punishment or retribution for victims?

- If justice is to be victim-oriented, how do we respond to victims who demand vengeance or retribution? Is there a tendency for practitioners to distinguish between "good" and "bad" victims based on their orientation?

- Can restorative justice be adequately done without the existence of, and collaboration with, an independently-established victim services community?

- Can there be true restorative justice without a process for developing and funding plans for victims as well as offenders?

Offender Issues:

- What are offenders' perceptions and impressions of restorative justice? Has the philosophy listened to, and been formulated to speak to, offender perspectives, concerns and worldviews?

- Is restorative justice adequately addressing the needs of offenders?

- What are offender advocates' understandings of restorative justice, and what are the implications of this?

- Is treatment or rehabilitation part of restorative justice? If so, what does this treatment look like within a restorative justice framework?

- To what extent is the risk-assessment movement distorting the practice of restorative justice? Does the "needs" language of restorative justice get confused with criminogenic needs and thus with risk factors?

- Is restorative justice adequately addressing prevention issues?

- What, if any, place does punishment have in restorative justice?

- Is restorative justice adequately (or too) concerned about the overuse of prisons? To what extent is restorative justice an alternative to prison? Should it be? To what extent could and should it provide a vision for transforming prisons?

- What forms can restorative justice take within prison? For offenders who do not have access to restorative justice programs? Could and should there be a restorative approach to imprisonment?

- What are the possibilities and dangers of shame theory as applied to offenders?

Community Issues:

- How should community be defined in theory and practice?

- What is the place and role of community in theory and in practice?

- When should community needs take precedence over individual needs (e.g., those of the victim and offender)? How is this to be decided and safeguarded? What are the dangers?

- Can we trust the community to use authority appropriately? What dangers does community involvement pose in general? What safeguards are needed?

- How can we find an appropriate division between state, societal, community and individual concerns and interests?

- When the community is involved, does this in practice mean primarily women? If so, what are the implications?

- Is community involvement being used as an excuse to reduce services or funding?

Government And System Issues:

- What should be the relationship between restorative justice and the existing system?

- What should be the state's role?

- What should be the relationship between community-operated and state-operated programs?

  - To what extent can and should indigenous and community-based justice processes operate independently of the system? How can adequate safeguards be provided?

  - To what extent should restorative justice be developed within the existing criminal system and the state bureaucracy as opposed to a separate system or "track"? In the latter case, how can appropriate interfaces and safeguards be provided?

  - What are the implications of a bifurcated track system? For example, if there is a "soft" and "hard" track, does the soft track receive less critical scrutiny? Is it hard track more likely to go unchallenged?

- Is restorative justice relying too heavily on the state-based, "retributive," system? Is it providing an adequate challenge? To what extent should restorative justice aim to change the system? What are the possibilities and dangers of this? Will a gradualist strategy be successful?

- To what extent has restorative justice been co-opted and diluted (by the state as well as other forces) and to what extent is this problematic? Can we do more to identify and counteract those co-opting forces?

- What are the actual and potential unintended consequences of the growing spread of restorative justice? How should they be evaluated and responded to?

- What kind of legislation, if any, is needed or desirable? Should model legislation be developed?

- Is restorative justice adequately addressing human rights and due process issues? Is it too predicated on an assumption of social order and a functioning legal system?

- Is the low-level of funding for restorative justice giving it a reputation as "cheap justice," similar to what happened with mental health?

- To what extent can and should restorative justice be institutionalized? For instance, Ivan Illich asks, Can you institutionalize "liberating practice" at all? Can there be real-world restorative justice without some form of institutionalization?

- To what extent does and could restorative justice represent the "commodification" of care masquerading under the "mask of love?"

Some Specific Co-optation And Dilution Issues:

- Are conferences becoming too settlement and/or restitution-driven as compared to the transformative model of mediation? Not restitution-driven enough?

- Is restorative justice practice too offender-oriented and, as a result, not victim-oriented enough?

- Is restorative justice practice assuming an overall punitive framework?

- Is restorative justice becoming too inflexible and bureaucratic?

- Is the community co-opting the place of victims in some forms of practice?

- To what extent is restorative justice leading to net-widening? To what extent is that problematic?

- To what extent, and how, is restorative justice being shaped by the self-interests of those promoting it, e.g., practitioners who use it as a source of income?

- To what extent is restorative justice becoming diverted by discrepancies in the goals and visions between those who lead movements and the actual practitioners?

- Is it possible to realize a needs-oriented approach to justice within a culture characterized by a desserts-based ideology?

Practitioner Issues:

- To what extent should practice be, and has been, professionalized? What are the implications of this?

- How is restorative justice impacted by the growing trend toward practice as income-generation?

- Is there adequate accountability and oversight for practitioners? How can it be provided?

- What impact is restorative justice having on the personal lives of practitioners?

- Is current training adequate for practitioners, especially in such areas as severe violence?

- Are practitioners practicing what they preach, i.e., dealing with internal conflicts restoratively?

- Are practitioners adequately sensitive to cultural dimensions of communication and conflict-resolution and concepts such as victimization, offending, shame and trauma?

- Are there hidden cultural biases not only in practices and also in the recruitment and selection of facilitators?

Some Specific Practice Issues:

- Is restorative justice practice too wedded to certain (and rigid) models? Are some models "better" than others?

- To what extent are gatekeepers and gatekeeping processes distorting the practice and potential of restorative justice?

- Are the dominant forms of facilitation adequately transformative? How can practice be encouraged to be more transformative?

- Is restorative justice practice being adequately evaluated? Are practitioners open to and heeding evaluation?

- Is restorative justice as a field offering adequate programming for victims where offenders are unidentified or uncooperative?

- Are processes adequate for genuine victim involvement?

- What are the implications of those models where authority figures serve as facilitators?

- Is restorative justice focusing too much on "lesser" offenses? Is it becoming overly cautious and avoiding risks? Conversely, is it naively taking on severe or problematic cases?

- Are there adequate guidelines of good practice? Who sets these? How prescriptive should they be? How do we ensure adaptive, practice-informed policies?

- What is the appropriate role of professionals?

- Are conferences providing adequately for the safety of victims and/or offenders?

- Is there a tendency to associate restorative justice with specific models or practices?

- In conferencing, is there a drive to get to the "table" at the expense of preparation and follow-up?

- Are practitioners alert to other issues and needs that arise in conferences? Do they have sufficient resources to address these?

- Should offenders be required to participate? If they are not, are victims disempowered as a result? Are offenders being inappropriately coerced into agreements due to, for instance, power imbalances?

- Should victims and offenders be required to have support people present? What distortions then happen when victim or offender do not? When offenders decline to involve support people, does this suggest they are not taking full responsibility?

Indigenous And Religious Traditions:

- When indigenous approaches to justice are part of restorative justice, to what extent has the philosophy stayed true to those traditions? Co-opted them? Been used to maintain separate-but-unequal and/or neo-colonial forms of justice?

- What is the appropriate relationship between state justice and indigenous justice?

- What are indigenous perceptions of and concerns about restorative justice?

- What roots or affinities does restorative justice have in various world religions?

- To what extent is it fair for restorative justice to claim indigenous traditions? To what extent can the latter be fairly characterized as restorative?

- Is the spiritual dimension of restorative justice getting enough attention? Can and should it when the state sponsors it?

Social Justice:

- Does restorative justice adequately address causation and prevention issues in specific cases?

- Should restorative justice be speaking to larger issues of social justice? If so, what does restorative justice have to say — theoretically and practically — to the social structural conditions that create harm?

- Is restorative justice helping to perpetuate the individualization of harm, wrongdoing and responsibility? Is repairing harm being seen primarily as a micro event, an interpersonal problem? Are there ways it could go beyond this?

- To what extent does restorative justice practice reinforce the split between "haves" and "have-nots"?

- Is there, for example, a "restorative economics?"